T0244397

THE
PRICE OF POWER

HOW MITCH McCONNELL

MASTERED THE SENATE,

CHANGED AMERICA, *and* LOST HIS PARTY

MICHAEL TACKETT

SIMON & SCHUSTER

NEW YORK   LONDON   TORONTO   SYDNEY   NEW DELHI

Simon & Schuster
1230 Avenue of the Americas
New York, NY 10020

First Simon & Schuster hardcover edition October 2024

SIMON & SCHUSTER and colophon are registered trademarks of Simon & Schuster, LLC

Simon & Schuster: Celebrating 100 Years of Publishing in 2024

For information about special discounts for bulk purchases,
please contact Simon & Schuster Special Sales
at 1-866-506-1949 or business@simonandschuster.com.

The Simon & Schuster Speakers Bureau can bring authors to your live event.
For more information or to book an event, contact the
Simon & Schuster Speakers Bureau at 1-866-248-3049
or visit our website at www.simonspeakers.com.

Interior design by Ruth Lee-Mui

Manufactured in the United States of America

1 3 5 7 9 10 8 6 4 2

Library of Congress Cataloging-in-Publication Data has been applied for.

ISBN 978-1-6680-0584-2
ISBN 978-1-6680-0586-6 (ebook)

Image Credits: US Senator Mitch McConnell Archives: 1, 2,
3, 4, 5, 6; Associated Press: 7, 8, 9, 10, 11, 12, 13

CONTENTS

Foreword   vii

1. Polio   1
2. Dean and Mac   15
3. A Changed Man   24
4. Jim Crow South   33
5. Becoming Yankeefied   41
6. The Exercise of Power   53
7. "Antsy as Hell"   67
8. The "Lost Decade"   82
9. "Role Playing"   96
10. "Win or Die Trying"   108
11. Land of Giants   121
12. Research and Destroy   136
13. Mastery of Process   149
14. "First-Class Ass-Kicking"   162
15. "No Substitute for Winning"   175
16. Dream Deferred, Achieved   189
17. The Power of No   201
18. "Anybody . . . Know How to Make a Deal?"   216
19. "Scalia's Seat"   233

20. Power Base   250
21. "Not Very Smart, Irascible . . . Despicable . . .
     Beyond Erratic"   259
22. "The McConnell Court"   280
23. January 6   293
24. The Fall   310
25. Power   320

     Epilogue: "The Last Thing You Do"   345
     Acknowledgments   357
     Notes   359
     Bibliography   375
     Index   377

FOREWORD

Mitch McConnell walked along the vaulted Brumidi Corridors of the Senate wing of the Capitol, offering commentary like a well-versed docent. "This is a working museum," he told me as he held forth on the life-size marble busts of the vice presidents and the portraits of nine senators on the walls of the Reception Room, men informally considered members of the chamber's "Hall of Fame." McConnell added his assessment of the worthiness of each selection—he knew something about each of them—heartily endorsing fellow Kentuckian Henry Clay.

He remarked on the Mansfield Room, the Johnson Room, and the Old Senate Chamber, where he had won several of his elections as the Republican Senate Leader. Then he walked slowly onto the Senate floor, turning to the right, to the farthest corner of the chamber, where he first took his seat at his nineteenth-century wooden desk as the lowest-ranking Republican member after his upset election victory in 1984.

He talked about the many stories the chamber holds—the desk of Senator Roger Wicker of Mississippi was once used by Jefferson Davis, the president of the Confederate States. He looked to the one occupied by Clay, Kentucky's most famous politician, who was known in his era as "the Great Compromiser," and said it was now the seat of fellow Kentucky senator Rand Paul, often a lonely voice of libertarian-leaning dissent. "Henry Clay would be appalled by Rand Paul," McConnell said. He opened his own desk to show me where he had carved his name alongside those of the Republican leaders who had preceded him. A leather-bound Senate Manual bore his name in gold embossed print. He knows the rules so well, the book's spine had not been cracked.

McConnell, an avid student of American history and of the Senate, has a prodigious library, almost all of it works of biography and history. He can speak fluently about almost any period. From the day he took control of Republicans in the Senate, he knew which senator had held the position of party leader the longest: Mike Mansfield of Montana, a Democrat.

The Senate has been McConnell's workplace since 1985; it also has been his life. His journey to this place was highly improbable. He was a child of the middle class, not born into wealth or privilege. He had no famous name, nor did he ever make one for himself through military valor, success in business, or dominance in sports. He had not been a governor, held statewide office, or served as a member of the House.

In almost every respect, he earned his place through a combination of relentless drive and ambition, fueled by the hypercompetitive instincts of an elite athlete, something he hoped to be but never could. When he was stricken by polio at the age of two, his mother followed doctors' orders and forbade him from walking for two years so as not to impede his recovery. She also taught him how to stand on his own two feet when he was well, and instilled in him a belief that there was nothing that he could not do, even as it was evident that his polio still left him with physical limitations.

In those years, he was powerless. But he was also forging what would become his essential strengths: discipline, focus, and tenacity. That combination drove him in his pursuit of power. When his body failed him in sports, he channeled that competitiveness and striving into politics. Even in the Senate, a body of class presidents, McConnell's ambition stood out.

In high school, unlike his classmates, he plotted his first campaign for student council president two years in advance, and succeeded. He would do the same thing in college in Louisville, where he told his classmates he wanted to be a senator one day. They did not laugh. Even then, he had a serious air about him, like a forty-year-old in a college man's body. Sure enough, he clawed his way to local office. Then, in 1984, he pulled off the biggest upset of the year in his long-shot race against a popular Democratic incumbent. He had one eye on the short game, and the other, always, on the long one.

In the Senate, he accrued power by taking jobs others did not want, by winning positions that made him a partner in his colleagues' electoral success, and by waiting until the opportunity to lead finally came to him. He understood the value and virtue of patience.

Most senators cannot stop talking. McConnell is known for his inexhaustible capacity to listen. Lyndon Johnson was renowned for his ability to cajole or browbeat his colleagues into submission. McConnell's approach is more supple and subtle. He finds out everything he can about a colleague and offers almost nothing about himself. He cedes the stage at times, he applies pressure privately, and he lives a hermetic life devoted almost entirely to winning a Republican Senate majority. He made his colleagues' goals his goals. He mastered arcane rules and exploited them expertly. Few other senators have had his inside game.

As Scott Jennings, a CNN pundit and McConnell protégé, told me, "I think people have never been able to understand his ability to divorce political decision-making from emotional overreaction. . . . He does not get bogged down in grudges, tweets, insults, haymakers. He just has this uncanny ability to remove negative emotions from strategic decision-making."

He is a master of talent scouting and opportunism, of planning and execution, in the business of politics, where winning is the measure of success. He was the prime mover for raising and spending almost $1 billion to help Republican Senate candidates, mostly incumbents, since 2016, building a financial-political ecosystem that brought him no small measure of loyalty. While other Republican leaders in the House were toppled, McConnell endured as he delivered on issues that mattered most to the party's social conservative core and to its wealthiest benefactors when he engineered the construction of a conservative supermajority on the U.S. Supreme Court. These maneuvers, and the raw use of power that enabled them, changed the course of the nation on issues like abortion, affirmative action, and federal regulation.

Unlike other senators, he had no desire to be president. Instead, self-aware as he was, he wanted to be the party leader, the partisan fighter who sits in the center of the chamber and argues the cause, day after day. He was determined to leave a mark. And he did. By almost any measure, McConnell is the most impactful Senate leader since Lyndon Johnson. He has inarguably transformed American politics and American life, and he has achieved a place in history, even if it's not necessarily the one he envisioned.

His colleagues think he has another superpower: he does not care what people think about him. As a result, even while he is one of the most powerful senators, one poll showed he also had the lowest approval rating. He is not weakened by temporary needs like getting applause.

It is partly for this reason, perhaps, that a recurring portrayal of McConnell—one likely to persist—holds that he only ever wanted power for power's sake, casting aside principle and constitutional norms in its pursuit. One Democratic senator was so intrigued, and often vexed, by how McConnell wielded power that he, too, at one point considered writing a book about him.

"Mitch McConnell is tough and strategic," he told me. "I think he's the most strategic politician alive. He has a preternatural sense of when an issue has arrived and capitalizes on that. He also doesn't care what anybody thinks about him. I'm not saying that the guy is perfect in his job or to be admired. I don't admire him. I think he's a terribly cynical human being. I would never want to be like Mitch McConnell. But he's incredibly effective."

While it is true that McConnell had a thirst for power and a sharply honed instinct for wielding it, this popular portrait of McConnell is decidedly incomplete. There is a more nuanced story of how he became one of the most consequential political figures of his era.

McConnell's career paralleled fundamental changes in a party that lurched rightward, became more populist and nationalistic, less discernibly "conservative," and less ideologically coherent. When he started in the Senate, the GOP had room for moderates like Lowell Weicker and Bob Packwood. But the Reagan era begat the Gingrich era, and the party since then has consistently marched in one direction.

The economic dislocation of the financial crisis that began in 2008 gave rise to the Tea Party, and then its progeny, the Freedom Caucus. At the same time, the country's population was rapidly changing, becoming more racially diverse and more economically stratified, creating a deep well of grievance among voters of the white working class, who turned to Donald Trump and his acolytes as vessels for their discontent.

In the age of the Republican Party under Trump, McConnell had to fight not only Democrats but also Trump himself, a man for whom he has much disdain and little respect. Because of Trump's influence, McConnell also had to fight intramural battles among Senate Republicans, whose restive, anti-government, and isolationist leanings signaled the direction of the party. Three Republican House speakers were ousted, while McConnell, never seen as a purely ideological figure, managed to keep his perch the way he always had: dispassionately assessing strengths and weaknesses and fashioning a path to retain his position. In his view, he tried to stop the GOP from heeding the darkest impulses of Trump, but it must be noted that he never put himself or his job in jeopardy to do so.

Was McConnell an enabler of Trump, who tried repeatedly to undermine democracy to serve his ends? Or did Trump enable him when it came to the courts? Did he exceed and abuse his authority by denying Merrick Garland, President Barack Obama's choice for the Supreme Court in 2016, and if so, at what cost to the Senate, the courts, and the country? Was he the last line of defense between the continuation of a vital political party and its disintegration under Trump's autocratic ways? These questions, when considered carefully and fairly, resist simple answers.

For much of his time as one of the most powerful politicians in America, Senator Mitch McConnell has been a sphinx, saying little, revealing less, all the while making strategic and tactical calculations to outwit and outlast his opponents.

I knew this when I approached Senator McConnell in March 2021 about writing this biography, and my expectations, accordingly, were modest. We had never spoken before. Perhaps he would say he would consider it, I thought. Instead, halfway through our first hour-long meeting, he surprised me by agreeing to cooperate and give me access to his vast personal archive: thousands of pages of personal letters, official correspondence, family photos, medical records, and a richly detailed oral history covering each year of his life and career, which he began recording in 1995. It was as if, even as a young man, he knew— or rather hoped—that one day his life would be examined. As I began my research, it became clear to me that this was true.

He also said he would ask his famously tight circle of former aides and advisers to talk to me. He did, and they obliged. I told him that the book would only be seen as credible if my work were independent, not subject to restriction or review by him. McConnell, who has read scores of political biographies, agreed, and he honored that commitment throughout a process of more than three years. "I know you won't have any trouble finding my enemies," he told me.

To many, including those who applaud his work, McConnell is a monochromatic caricature, a dour, humorless figure seen speaking behind a microphone. I found him to be far more complex and complicated than that. He has a strong, dry sense of humor, and his eyes well with tears when he speaks about certain times in his life. His staff is fiercely loyal, out of affection, not of fear.

But make no mistake. He plays the power game, and has done so longer and more effectively—at times nobly, at times destructively—than any American political actor in this century.

THE
PRICE OF POWER

ONE

POLIO

On July 20, 1944, a ninety-degree day in the town of Five Points, Alabama, two-year-old Mitchie McConnell was in tears. His mother, Dean, tried to comfort her only child, but the unexplained burning pain and redness in a finger on Mitchie's left hand did not subside.

They were living with her oldest sister, Edrie Mae, and her husband, Julius Smartt, in a modest wood-frame home set along the curve in the road of a place so small it didn't need a stoplight. Her husband, Mac, was with his Army unit at Fort Bliss in El Paso, Texas, preparing to deploy to fight in World War II.

When the pain and redness in Mitchie's finger did not resolve, Dean took him to the nearby town of LaFayette to see Dr. Aaron Wheeler, who concluded the boy had an infection and enlarged lymph nodes, but nothing serious. Up to that point, Mitchie had been a healthy child and a source of great pride for Dean and Mac.

Until that July day, Dean had meticulously recorded the normal milestones of her son's infancy in his "Baby Book." Mitchie stood at eight and half months, took a step at ten months, and was walking consistently at about eleven months. He began saying words at about the same time: "Daddy," "Mamie" for his grandmother, and "birdie" for an airplane. She also observed that her infant son had a "habit which has lasted some time, his sucking index and middle finger on his left hand and feeling his eyelashes with his finger on his right hand." On his first Christmas the family had a tree, but no lights due to a war-related shortage. Dean recorded that Santa brought her son a teddy bear, rag doll, a hobbyhorse, toys with bells that ring, Mickey Mouse rattles, and a washable Democratic donkey.

Seven months later, that sense of normalcy was swept away when twenty-five-year-old Dean realized she was dealing with something far more serious than a common infection. By the end of the week, her son complained of pain in his legs and back. She noticed that his legs were "cold and clammy." She kept him in bed until the second week in August. Then she noticed he "limped badly" when he walked. She decided to get another opinion and took him to see Dr. W. Park Phillips, in LaGrange, Georgia, a much larger town about twenty-five miles east, with a thriving commercial sector and a local college. Dr. Phillips's diagnosis was far more profound: "acute anterior poliomyelitis"—polio.

It was a terrifying moment for Dean. The word "polio" had been striking fear in American parents for years, and now the disease had infected her young son. At the time, the world was a decade away from an effective vaccine, and parents struggled to find treatments for their children as doctors tried to assess the damage that the virus caused to the body. One prominent clinician likened polio to a "guided missile that does one thing: seek out, damage, and destroy the neurons that 'activate' you—the ones that activate your brain and muscles. The poliovirus is the perfect human 'OFF switch.'" In its worst form, polio caused serious and sometimes lifelong paralysis, even death. Beyond this, little was known about the disease, and rates were spiking across the United States.

With her husband headed to Europe for a long and dangerous deployment, Dean was left to figure out how to deal with her son's potentially crippling illness largely on her own.

Though the South's polio rates had historically lagged behind other regions of the country, an outbreak in the early 1940s had begun to chip away at the gap. Even so, Alabama was hardly a hot spot for the virus. The day Mitchie first complained to his mother, the Associated Press noted that only eight new cases of polio had been reported to the Alabama Health Department, and just five had been reported the previous week. The more dominant stories were about Democrats nominating Harry Truman to be President Franklin Roosevelt's running mate at their convention in Chicago, and numerous accounts of the war raging in Europe and in the Pacific.

Though polio was in many ways mysterious, Americans were more aware of the disease than other viruses because they knew it had afflicted President Roosevelt. The president, who used a wheelchair or walked with heavy braces because of the ravages of polio, had started a national charity that would become known as the March of Dimes. FDR often sought treatment in Warm Springs, Georgia, a town of just over six hundred people, where he could come for comfort and healing in the warm mineral waters, and where he had established the nation's best-known polio rehabilitation facility. Fortuitously, it was also only an hour's drive from Five Points. Dean arranged to have her son evaluated there.

The two-lane road from Five Points to Warm Springs carves through rural areas, framed by pines and oaks and marked by an occasional farm. But Warm Springs was known well beyond its borders because of Roosevelt. On the winding road leading to the facility, deep purple wisteria curled around the pine trees, and visitors said it had the feel of a park or college campus.

In his memoir, *My Place to Stand,* Bentz Plagemann described how "we came upon a hidden group of buildings, a small principality, like an eighteenth-century manor house. A great pillared building faced a lawn, before which the driveway curved; grouped about this were low outbuildings, set among gardens with a formal air; all of it giving an impression of completeness and self sufficiency."

All of it, Plagemann wrote, came to be seen as a refuge against the backdrop of a world at war and a virulent virus that struck children far more often than adults. Some researchers thought that the virus destroyed muscle, but that was not the case. "Actually it's not the muscles themselves which are struck by the polio virus but the nerves which control them," Plagemann wrote. "The impulse from the brain does not reach them. The knowledge that the muscles are there but useless is particularly distressing."

The care at Warm Springs was geared not only toward physical rehabilitation but also toward the idea that patients could triumph even if polio left them with a disability. Plagemann went on to recount a conversation with Miss Alice Lou Plastridge, the head of physical therapists, who told him, "Only a particular group of people contract polio. It indicates a highly organized central nervous system, which usually means talent, or special ability of some kind." She could have been telling patients that to boost their confidence rather than relying on empirical evidence, but the message had the desired effect.

While the facility had the look of a campus with a grassy quad, there was one major difference: it also had a shop for making braces to help polio patients walk upright. Some patients, like Plagemann, referred to themselves as "a polio," a marker of the stigma the virus carried after rendering so many people fully or partially paralyzed.

Roosevelt's case was acute, the muscles in his legs incapable of holding him in a standing position. As a person of wealth and means, he had access to the best care and treatment, but could never recover full use of his lower limbs. He made his first trip to Warm Springs on October 3, 1924, in what the World War II Museum says was his "last hope for finding a cure for the polio that had left him crippled three years earlier."

The following day, by the museum's account, he swam in the Warm Springs pool and "soon he was able to stand in four feet of water—something he had been unable to do previously."

In a rare interview, he told Cleburne Gregory of the *Atlanta Journal* that he was able to move his right leg for the first time in three years. The headline on the article published October 26, 1924, read "Franklin Roosevelt Will Swim to Health." An accompanying photograph showed his shriveled legs, and that inspired polio patients to travel to Warm Springs in search of healing. The episode also prompted Roosevelt to open the Georgia Warm Springs Foundation in 1927 as a polio therapeutic treatment center.

FDR traveled by train to Warm Springs frequently, and each visit set off a festive, parade-like atmosphere, with locals and tourists alike trying to get a glimpse of the president. His trips received favorable coverage in newspapers, and photographers honored the code of the time to not portray his obvious disability. In that era, the American South was overwhelmingly Democratic, and FDR was a hero.

McConnell was treated at the facility at least twice when the president was staying on the grounds in the Little White House, a cabin-like home Roosevelt consciously built to modest scale so as not to seem ostentatious. When FDR arrived—and patients would know by the sudden arrival and movement of Marines protecting him—he often talked with the patients and tried to bring cheer and optimism. Movie stars of the era also traveled to Warm Springs to be in the president's aura and reinforce his message of hope. McConnell said his mother once held him up when the president's car drove past. Roosevelt died at Warm Springs on April 12, 1945, around the time of one of McConnell's visits.

For Dean and her son, the first visit to doctors in Warm Springs on August 22, 1944, previewed the arduous road ahead. "Patient was extremely uncooperative and muscle test should be considered probably quite inaccurate," his medical records state. "The best idea of his weakness was obtained from watching the child walk." But doctors also determined that his case was not severe enough to require inpatient treatment. Instead, his recovery and progress fell almost entirely on his mother. His doctors wrote that the boy "will return for examination and further instruction each week. Mother was advised to enforce complete bed rest and not to allow the child to stand on his feet at any time. There seems no necessity to apply hot packs but passive motion should be carried out 4 times a day."

Each patient had a general physical, a muscle exam by a trained physiotherapist, and an orthopedic review. The cost was roughly $25, which would equal more than $425 in 2024. More than four decades later, McConnell said his family "almost went broke" paying for his treatment, but Dean persisted, relying on money that her husband sent home from the war, and probably money from "Sister" and McConnell's paternal grandparents. At one point, Dean had to ask doctors to write to the gasoline rationing board in Alabama so she could buy the extra fuel needed to make the trip to Warm Springs.

McConnell's examination revealed "minimal tightness in posterior group with marked weakness in anterior group." His back and abdomen were "apparently good to normal," as were his upper extremities. The impact of polio was most pronounced in his left leg, where doctors noted "diffuse involvement, definitely more severe than on the right, with greatest weakness in quadriceps and gastrocnemius. The left knee is markedly hyperextended when walking."

Doctors and physical therapists gave Dean precise instructions for passive motion exercises to be conducted four times a day at home, about forty-five minutes at a time, how to bend or lift the leg, engaging the other major muscles in the area, turning and stretching to try to regain a full range of motion and to restore strength. McConnell would later refer to his mother as both a "stern disciplinarian" and a benevolent "drill sergeant" when it came to the routine.

Most important, though, was the vexing order to keep her son off his feet to prevent further damage to the muscles. Somehow, she was being asked to force her toddler son to unlearn the ability to walk and essentially spend all of his time lying down.

"They said, 'We don't want him to become a psychological cripple, but you must somehow convey to this child that he *can* walk,'" McConnell said in an oral history. "What they're saying was 'We don't want him to think he can't walk, but at the same time, we don't want him to walk yet, because if he starts walking too soon, his leg is going to be stiff. We won't be able to rehabilitate the muscle.'"

So McConnell and his mother were, for the most part, confined to their small house in a remote town, with an uncertain future and the fear that even the doctors at Warm Springs could not guarantee he would ever recover. There are several photos from that era, most of them showing Mitchie sitting in the grass or on the porch. In one photo that Dean sent to Mac, she wrote a caption on the back: "Five Points Lonely Hearts Club."

There was a grinding tedium to the daily ritual of rehabilitation at home, interrupted by the trips to Warm Springs. After one such journey, Dean called one of her brothers, Arnold Shockley, who lived in Birmingham, to tell him the grim news about Mitchie. "I will never forget this," his daughter Nell said of her father in an interview almost eighty years later. "He cried most of the night." His reaction reflected the panic that the word "polio" could engender, and the next day he packed his family in a car to show support for his sister and her stricken son. "It was almost like if you contracted polio you may not make it," Nell recalled.

Shortly after they arrived, Nell watched as Dean, composed and—to Nell's nine-year-old eyes—looking "like a movie star," showed them how she put Mitch through physical therapy. She laid quilts on a table in a room just off the kitchen, then placed her son on them face up. She would take each straightened leg and bend it toward the abdomen, again and again. "This was a very trying time for his mother," Nell said. "I was struck by how good she was constantly."

Mitchie was confined to a bedroom just off the living room. Dean read to him; they would color and draw, and "create little towns on his bed with his toys." But otherwise, when he wasn't receiving physical therapy from his mother, he spent hours alone, passing time by drawing a train along the walls just above the baseboard. His mother was aghast, but his aunt thought it was charming and at first asked that Dean not clean the walls.

"Sister" had been Dean's surrogate mother. Their mother died when Dean was five months old and Sister was only eleven. Sister and her husband, Julius, did not have children. Their home was across the street from the center of town life, the general store that they owned. Sister, with a stern demeanor, often staffed the cash register, and she kept detailed entries in the ledger book for those who bought on credit, which was most people. She was also a substitute teacher, and students recalled her as kind and patient in the classroom. Julius was well known in the area, and it was common for him—a sturdy five foot ten and 180 pounds—to go door-to-door to demand payment from those too far in arrears. He would go on to become wealthy by the standards of Five Points, owning eleven rental properties, more than 1,400 acres of farmland, and several commercial buildings. He eventually bequeathed one quarter of his estate, $250,000, to McConnell in 1996.

Most people in the area made their living from farming, either crops or timber. The town had a Baptist church and a Methodist one, which Sister attended, along with a bank, post office, and a small drugstore. When McConnell visited in 2021, the general store was a weathered shell of itself, and most other businesses were closed. Officials in Five Points had to fight simply to keep the post office. The population had withered from 780 when McConnell was a boy to 114 by 2020.

By October 1944, McConnell began to show signs of improvement, which doctors described as "very gratifying." He still had significant problems in his "gluteus maximus, hip abductors, internal rotators and quadriceps . . . left knee tends to go into the back knee position."

By January 9, 1945, his progress had advanced such that Dean was asked to bring him in every three or four weeks. His appointment that July, months after his first visit, found him in "excellent condition." By May 1946, he was walking well, but with "noticeable atrophy of the left thigh." At age two, his left thigh was three-quarters of an inch smaller in circumference than his right. That gap would grow to at least two inches in adulthood.

Later inquiry would question the value of some of the treatment McConnell underwent. A British researcher, W. J .W. Sharrard, did a three-year study of polio patients and concluded that there was "little further benefit" from "physical therapy 10 months after the polio attack."

The immobility he was prescribed early on also may have harmed more than helped. Dr. Richard Bruno, director of the International Centre for Polio Education in New Jersey and an authority on the aftereffects of polio—who reviewed McConnell's records at my request—said doctors may have prescribed the strict isolation and lack of movement because McConnell was an outpatient and they were concerned that he would move too much and inhibit his recovery. "It seems like he was kind of shut down for those two years, and it possibly was not necessary, and it may have limited him when he did start to walk," Bruno added.

While Dean tended to her son, her husband was serving on the battlefront in Europe, eventually reaching what was then Czechoslovakia. When the two were apart, either during the war or even when Mac was away for a few days, they were prolific letter writers. Much of their correspondence while he was deployed was lost, but some letters were saved. When Mac was doing his basic training, he would encourage his wife to "rough up the boy for me," and talk of missing them both dearly. But he did not, at least in the letters I reviewed, write specifically about polio. Neither did Dean.

It is possible that Mac did not fully appreciate what his wife and son were going through, particularly given that he had his own literal battles to fight in a unit that had suffered serious casualties. His memories of his son were those of a thriving toddler.

As the war wound down, with victory at hand, one day stood out as joyous. On VE Day, May 8, 1945, McConnell wrote to his wife from the Czech city of Pilsen. "My dearest one," he began. "At last I have time to write and as you can see I can tell you where I am. I have been here several days—of course I can't tell you how many." He spoke of "10,000 things I want to tell you about but it will take several letters. First, I want to tell you that I was in the big middle of everything until the very last but now peace has come here. . . . There is no way of expressing how I feel about peace even to you. I trained to be a soldier and then I fought as well as I knew how but now it's over here and I believe that soon Japan will be whipped." He described women and children lining the streets in celebration, giving the American soldiers cognac, cookies, and kisses.

"For the first time I'm really homesick," he confessed, "but we won't talk about that. You are so very pretty, honey, and Mitch is looking so well. He is really practically 100% recovered, isn't he? He is so fine looking—like his mommie. You are right, he is really all boy now and I long to see him and his mommie."

Mac went on: "I have thought of our dead President [FDR] quite a bit today and we have talked about how happy he would be if he were here. I guess he knows about it tho. I wish he could have lived until this day at least."

For his part, McConnell has no tangible memory of his struggle with polio, other than what the records provide, but he believes his mother's strict regimen saved him from a much more challenging life. "There's not a doubt in my mind that I would have been disabled, at least in the sense that I would have walked with a limp," he said in his oral history.

Instead, he later recalled, polio was in some ways a positive. "I have many faults, but I think one of my strengths is discipline and planning and tenaciousness," McConnell said. "And I think it really must surely have been a lesson imparted at that very early age by this experience."

In McConnell's telling, there is a storybook ending. After he had been released from treatment at Warm Springs at age four, his mother bought him his first pair of shoes: low-top saddle oxfords, most likely at Solomon's, a still-thriving shoe store in LaGrange. After two years of being told not to walk, he could walk again, without a brace or a limp.

The story of polio's effect on McConnell's life, though, is far more layered and consequential than his account, both physically and psychologically. His version tracks with what a leading medical historian, Daniel J. Wilson, called "a mid-century post–World War II stoicism" that has been documented in studies of polio survivors and their families. Many of those survivors became intensely driven high achievers, but ones who were also highly sensitive to criticism and deeply fearful of failure.

Like others who had polio in that era, McConnell and his parents clearly wanted to put the struggle behind them. The fact that McConnell's parents didn't mention polio in the letters I reviewed, and that their son chose not to emphasize it in his own life, is in keeping with how most families who had a child with polio in the 1940s behaved. Those who did not have to use a wheelchair or crutches were seen as "cured" and were expected to move on with life.

But there were little reminders. Those lace-up oxfords that McConnell could finally wear required a 3/16 inch posterior heel wedge on the left shoe, which was designed to compensate for weakness in the calf and other parts of the leg, his medical records show. McConnell's father, after returning from service, also wrote to Warm Springs, inquiring about special shoes.

Wilson, who had polio himself, found that polio patients then were subject to a "try harder" mentality to overcome the disease. "The cultural expectations of the mid-twentieth-century American compounded polio patients' difficulties in coming to terms with their illness and disabilities," he wrote. "Prevailing cultural values held that the only acceptable response to the disabilities caused by polio was to try as hard as possible to overcome any disability."

McConnell's life often followed such a pattern. "The fact that McConnell has become who he has become is consistent with what a polio survivor would do," Bruno said. "Manipulate the circumstances to their benefit, take the focus away from disability-related issues, and then achieve tremendous things."

It is not clear whether McConnell's polio was the reason his parents had only one child. But what is evident is that they focused on Mitchie with a loving but hovering presence, always there to nurture his dreams. "Candidly, I think it was a great advantage," McConnell said of being an only child. "Far from all the comments about being spoiled and all the rest, I think there's something to be said for getting enough attention in terms of how you see yourself and your willingness to compete and all the rest. I think it had an enormous positive impact on me, and I really don't feel badly about not having had brothers and sisters."

In the decades that have passed since the polio vaccine was developed, researchers have studied "the polios" to see how the disease might have affected patients throughout their lives, both physically and psychologically.

Dr. Bruno has studied more than seven thousand survivors. He is one himself. And he focused his life's work on the impact of the virus.

When polio survivors first came to him in 1982, he discovered that polio had a profound effect on earning and learning. He realized that, more than the expected, percentages of polio survivors are corporate executives, members of both houses of Congress, and professionals of all types—teachers, lawyers, doctors, and nurses. This level of achievement was "startling," he wrote. Polio survivors who were told that they would never go to college or even get a job became America's 'best and brightest.'"

Polio survivors also had common personality traits: "hard-driving, time-conscious, competitive, self-denying, perfectionist, overachieving 'Type A' personality." That hard-charging ethos for some also exacted a psychic toll. The more Type A behavior that was exhibited, the more sensitive that person would likely be to criticism. Bruno found in later research that polio survivors were more prone to "thinking of themselves as failures." That is among the reasons why polio survivors "discarded in childhood any evidence of polio." They wanted to "both act and appear 'normal.'" For most polio survivors, Bruno wrote, "it's more important to appear 'normal' and take care of others than it is to physically or emotionally care for themselves."

Among those who recovered from polio was the Supreme Court justice William O. Douglas, who wrote, "I struggle valiantly to be as much like, or better than, especially better than, every other child in every way that I could." Since he couldn't compete physically, he vowed to be smarter. "The idea that I was a weakling festered and grew in my mind. . . . I decided to prove my superiority over my contemporaries in other ways." This was the instinct behind the successful careers of Olympians Wilma Rudolph and Johnny Weissmuller, *Washington Post* editor Ben Bradlee, and the actors Alan Alda and Mia Farrow, all of whom were stricken with polio.

Even so, polio continued to surprise. By the 1970s, two decades after the Salk and Sabin vaccines nearly eradicated polio in the United States, doctors had started hearing from former polio patients complaining about unexplained muscle weakness and fatigue.

In 1984, *Newsweek* magazine published an article called "The Late Effects of Polio," as an increasing number of people who had polio in their youth or young adulthood were now seeing the virus, in effect, manifest in a different but still troubling way. Bruno wrote in his book *The Polio Paradox* that "Polio was thought to be a 'stable disease.' Once polio survivors recovered muscle strength after the polio attack, their physical abilities were supposed to remain for the rest of their lives." Contrary to this common belief, many polio survivors saw their physical strength in affected parts of the body start to waste away.

"Several thousand victims of polio epidemics during the 1940s and 1950s have come down recently with 'recurrent polio'—new symptoms of muscle and joint pain and weakness that in a few cases have been more serious than the original disease," Victor Cohn wrote in the *Washington Post*. Two years later, he wrote that an estimated three hundred thousand Americans had "post polio syndrome," often involving muscle degeneration that "goes beyond mere aging."

By 1991, three special issues of the medical journal *Orthopedics* were devoted to "post-polio sequelae," or sequel. For many people with post-polio syndrome, researchers found that the symptoms prompted them to try to speed up, rather than slow down. They were disinclined to delegate or let others help them, and they exhibited a need for control. Another health risk was also present for many: heart disease.

In McConnell's case, the most he will say is that a comeback of the disease seems to have affected his mobility. In a 1995 interview for the oral history project, he said: "The only way it affects me today is I do have a hard time going down stairs." The difficulty started a decade earlier, he acknowledged, which would fit within the time frame for the onset of post-polio syndrome. But later in life, the physical signs would be even more profound.

Polio would remain his unwanted gift, and his haunting ghost.

TWO

DEAN AND MAC

The bond that formed between Dean and Mitch during those years in Five Points—where they spent so much time in isolation, enduring the arduous monotony of physical therapy—was unshakable. The young woman with the perfectionist streak would spend her life trying to ensure that her son could pursue every opportunity, no matter how seemingly unrealistic. Everything that had been lacking in her life, she tried to fill in his. It was all the more notable because she had no one from whom she could model that behavior.

Long before she was old enough to realize it, Julia Odene Shockley had experienced tragic loss. Her mother, Lala Viola, died on January 4, 1920, when she was just five months old, and she viewed "Sister" as her "mother."

The Shockleys lived in Wadley, Alabama, a town that had 508 people in the 1920 census and has grown little since. They were subsistence farmers who missed out on the prosperity of the Roaring Twenties and then were punished again and more harshly when the Great Depression came a decade later. Julia's father was also from a large family, so big that Shockley lore held that his parents never got around to giving him a name, so they just called him "Babe," an appellation that stuck—along with his lifetime resentment of what he saw as willful neglect. Julia's family insisted on calling her by her middle name, Odene, which inspired its own kind of bitterness, and she eventually discarded it in favor of Dean.

Her parents were not educated beyond grade school. They farmed, scraped by, and lived in a narrow, isolated world deeply segregated by race and economic station. But even from a young age, Julia, bright and inquisitive, fixed a gaze beyond Wadley. At age ten, she started keeping a detailed diary in a deep red, palm-size notebook with a tiny wooden pencil attached with a string.

She made notes about meals, Sunday school, playing games with friends, and music lessons, but she always had her eye on a bigger horizon. She described watching airplanes "come and go," and marveled at the stunts pulled by the pilots. She also wrote of taking a drive to a high ridge, where "we saw all the lights of the city" and saw homes "where the richest people of Birmingham lived. The houses were just like a mansion." In a later entry she played a wishing game and wrote, "I wish I had a million dollars."

Then on September 1, 1935, the final entry, in different handwriting that could have come from Sister, said, "Don't forget to ever be a good girl. Be kind to everyone. Speak evil of no one."

For her sixteenth birthday, Odene received an autograph book and friends complimented her on her looks and good nature. She was also an excellent student, earning all A's both in grade school and in high school, where she wrote thoughtful essays in perfect Palmer Method cursive on *A Tale of Two Cities*, "The Legend of Sleepy Hollow," and *Macbeth*, and participated in class plays.

It was about this time that she was so bothered by her birth name that she started signing letters "Little Iodene," an apparent mocking of the word "iodine."

Though her academic record when she graduated from Wadley High School in 1937 strongly suggested she could have attended college, not many women in a place like Wadley took that path. But she clearly wanted more than her small-town, hardscrabble upbringing. So after high school graduation, she moved to Birmingham to live with one of her brothers, who worked in a factory. She enrolled in Massey Business College, essentially a secretarial school, earning highest marks in penmanship, bookkeeping, commercial law, application, and English, a B in shorthand, a B+ in typing, and a C in "rapid calculation."

Birmingham, Alabama's largest city, known in that period for its steel production, was several worlds away from the rural folkways of Wadley. Its nickname was "the Magic City" for its rapid growth and cultural vibrance, and for the elements in its soil that made it fertile for iron production.

Dean arrived there highly motivated to have a better life. She thrived on order and organization. At age twenty, she typed a list of twenty New Year's resolutions that seemed impossible to keep. Among her goals: "Keep my nails and hair neater," "avoid unnecessary chattering and silliness," "be more courteous and lady-like than I have been," "put more time in to learn about business and business principles," "spend my money more wisely and not let debts accumulate," "attend church more regularly," "never engage in conversations which deal in gossip," "read Bible daily," "avoid the habit of chewing gum," "never use profanity," and "make the most of what I have and try to be content with commodities within my means." Number twenty was: "STRIVE EVERYDAY TO BETTER MYSELF IN EVERY WAY."

Her ambitious goals notwithstanding, Dean struggled to stay out of debt, and at one point even applied for unemployment compensation. She eventually landed a job in the office of the CIT finance company, and was soon attracted to a handsome, muscular, outgoing man from Athens, Alabama, A. M. "Mac" McConnell, who worked in loan repossessions.

Mac was born in Limestone County, Alabama, near the Tennessee line. His grandfather was a "circuit-riding Calvinist preacher" who carried his Bible in saddlebags. The McConnells weren't wealthy, but they were prosperous compared with the Shockleys. Mac's father ran the McConnell Funeral Home on the town square in Athens. During the depths of the Great Depression, he would barter the cost of a funeral for items such as an antique clock. Like many white families in the South, his ancestors were slaveholders.

Like Dean, Mac was an A student through much of elementary school. But his parents, unlike hers, put a premium on education. His older sister, Ethel, known as "Dick," attended Rice University in Houston, and his brother, Robert, attended Furman University in Greenville, South Carolina, after military prep school. Mac's grades were good enough to earn him a spot at Darlington School, a college preparatory boarding school in Rome, Georgia. He excelled in football and went on to Wake Forest University in Winston-Salem, North Carolina, on the promise of playing there. At Wake Forest, he earned A's in French and math, B's in English and religion, and a D in history. There is a photo of Mac in his football uniform, but his career was brief. He left Wake Forest after a year and transferred to Auburn University in Alabama. That only lasted a year as well. He then dropped out for good.

That eventually led him to Birmingham and the job at the finance company. Mac was bored by his work, though he was good at collecting the money. So he set off for the burgeoning oil fields of Texas, like so many who chased the promise of quick, newfound fortune, taking a job with the Humble Oil Company, which would become Exxon. But he could not leave behind his desire for Dean, pretty and petite, who always appeared as though she were about to be photographed—hair coiffed, skirts cinched tightly at the waist, makeup just right.

They exchanged a series of letters—two people in their early twenties trying to navigate love and adulthood—that showed an unusual level of both vulnerability and trust, especially given that Dean was engaged to another man by the time Mac left.

Mac's older brother, Robert, lived in Texas, but otherwise Mac knew almost no one. He spent his lonely nights in a hotel in Baytown run by Mrs. J. D. Tyree, where rooms could be booked by the day or week. On hotel stationery, he wrote Dean with escalating urgency about their relationship. He wanted her to know that he could be a provider, telling her that work was going well and he was expecting a raise.

Still, he lamented that Dean seemed destined to marry someone else. "I realize how impossible it would be," he said. "You weren't ever in love with me while I was there and you were engaged to someone else when I left so as yet I haven't figured out why I had the slightest idea you would consider coming out here.

"Dean, I have a horrible habit of taking the things I enjoy in life and completely ignoring the things I find unpleasant. . . . Happiness with me would be a gamble for you or any other girl. You see I have always tried to forget that you weren't in love with me. Since I got your letter, I have felt farther away from you than ever before. . . . I always thought that when the time came you would find deep in your heart that I was 'the guy.' Now, I'm a thousand miles away and I'm not fool enough that I don't know that distance and time will at best leave us exactly where we were."

After all, he noted, "I didn't get to first base after trying for eight months. . . . I will hardly have the slightest chance of ever making you love me now," and it was time "to say goodbye because, as you know, love can be such a hellish thing if it is one-sided." He figured he'd "just get drunk and eat my heart out over it."

On August 7, 1940, he seemed ready to give up. "Let me know the day of your wedding is to be so I can go out and celebrate it," he wrote. Four days later: "All I want to say is I love you but that would be silly.

"Or would it?"

Then he received a letter that gave him hope. On August 9, Dean wrote to tell Mac that "I'm afraid you won't get to celebrate. Grover has changed his mind. He said he's not ready to get married and he even said he just didn't feel the same way he did about me. . . . I've never been as hurt and unhappy in my whole life." As she often did in a difficult time, Dean headed to Sister's home in Five Points. On August 15, 1940, she wrote to Mac from Sister's house, concerned about her own health. She said Sister was "cramming pills down me this week—4 at a time." She said it felt good to be away from the demands of her office work, but she was clearly also getting over Grover breaking their engagement. "I'm through making a fool of myself. I'm not 'fat and forty' yet." She hadn't heard from Grover "and I've found myself not caring a great deal."

Then she offered the kind of encouragement Mac had craved. "I wish I could see you. There are so many things I want to tell you that I don't want to write."

Mac was sympathetic in his reply. "I was sincerely sorry to hear of your trouble with Grover and hope that it will all 'come out in the wash' if that is what you want," he wrote. "If I can't have you, I want you to be happy with someone else, at least."

Still, he also wanted to persuade Dean, finally, to leave the despair of her breakup behind and come to Texas and marry him. Mac, emboldened by several beers, tried to contact her on August 16, calling Sister's house at 12:30 a.m.

"I can't remember much except that it scared me simply to death," Dean wrote the next day. "Mac, I just couldn't disappoint you last night, but I had to think and I didn't have enough time to do that. . . . There's such an awful lot to be considered. One has to be absolutely sure, and that applies to you too."

Mac was certain. "Dean, I want you here with me. I want to marry you now. I have nothing to offer you but my love and understanding. Someday I may have more but I know that I do have all the love in the world for you now."

For all of Mac's earnestness and persistence, Dean still had reservations.

"Mac, I don't intend to hurt you when I say I'm not quite ready to get married at present and I don't think you are either. Couldn't we just go along for a while and work things out?" She added: "Life is much too short to make a lifelong mistake. I do miss you and would love to see you."

One reason for Dean's reluctance was financial. She still owed payments for her fur coat and what she called not her hope chest, but rather her "Hopeless Chest." "My hands are tied, as the Loan Sharks say. . . . Trusting that you will understand and respect my position. Love, Dean."

In the days that followed, Mac's tone became more intense. In a letter dated August 21, 1940, he spoke of his revelation one week earlier that he could never be happy without her. "I fought against the idea until Friday night. I tried to call you at seven but couldn't get you. Then I decided that maybe I could wash it all out with a bunch of beer—that didn't work either so finally when my call went through it was worse than ever." Then the plaintive pitch: "Dean, if you do love me, let's don't wait around for things that never come. Let's grab things up in our hands and do the best we can. I need you and, crazy as it seems, I think you need me."

She continued to be wary. "You're sensible enough to know that two people in our positions just can't up and get married," she wrote. "There's just more to it than that—if they expect to stay married." She admonished him for turning to beer to wash away his lovelorn angst. "That's not the time to drink."

Dean's practical reasons for resisting—mostly burdening him with her debt—finally gave way, and she agreed to Mac's proposal. She tried to pull her life together and gather the few things she could take before heading off to Texas, a place she had never been, to marry a man she had not seen since he left Birmingham.

He said they would meet on September 20, 1940, in Houston, and marry that evening. He told her he had picked out a furnished apartment. She hesitated one last time, writing again to say her debts were holding her back from committing further, and she itemized them for him: $79 to Massey Business College, $58.50 to two doctors, and $65.62 to the Burger-Phillips department store, along with a balance of $68.70 on her fur coat. She declined his offer to help pay off her bills. "Forget it," she said. "I got myself into this jam and I'll have to be the one to get myself out."

By mid-September, Mac had finally won the day. "I'm ready to come now if you'll come for me," Dean wrote. "Maybe you have changed your mind by now." Then the clincher: "If you think we can work it out, then let's don't wait. . . . I do love you as much as I could ever love anyone."

They decided to tell only a few people. "Nobody knows about this so we'll just 'pull a fast one on them'—I hope," Dean wrote.

In a letter that she headlined "Friday 13th" of September, Dean was now eagerly anticipating the move. "I haven't been able to eat, much less sleep," she wrote. "I'm simply dying to see you." The next day, she wrote another letter, trying to explain her change of heart. "I'm simply trying to say, Mac, that when I said 'yes' to you there was some power much stronger than my fickle self dominating. Not for one moment since that moment has there been the slightest shadow of a doubt." She added: "To avoid mincing a lot of words, I love you more than anything in the world."

At 7:50 a.m. on September 19, Dean boarded a train from Birmingham to Houston, a trip of about twelve hours, with a stop in New Orleans. She told Mac what she could bring to start their household: sheets, pillowcases, seven bath towels, seven bath cloths, a tablecloth, and a luncheon set.

The ceremony was on September 20, 1940, a Friday night at 8 p.m., hastily put together in the home of Mac's aunt. Mac's brother, Robert, was one of only two witnesses.

Dean wore a "costume suit," soldier-blue sheen wool and a fitted princess coat, outlined with red fox lapels, navy pumps, and a bag, along with a single piece of jewelry, a yellow bracelet of Sister's. Mac, deeply tanned from work in the oil fields, wore a light blue double-breasted suit. They were a handsome couple.

The reception was simple: individual angel food wedding cakes with ice cream. After the wedding, they took a brief honeymoon in Galveston, staying at the Jean Lafitte Hotel. Dean kept a matchbook from the hotel for the rest of her life.

Dean took time to write Mac's parents, "Mamie and Dad." "I pray that I may even make you proud of me as another daughter." She was thinking of her own, long-ago loss: "I shall tell you now, Mamie, that in my heart I've taken you as my Mother, too, something you know I've never known through the years of reaching womanhood since I was robbed of that treasure at the age of five months."

The couple's time in Texas was brief. The riches Mac had hoped for did not materialize, and both yearned to be back in Alabama, a place of family and deep familiarity. They eventually settled in Athens, where Mac's family had deep roots.

Dean wrote notes about their anniversary—dinner at Andy's Grill, with Mac ordering pork chops and Dean having shrimp. Mac also had a present for his new wife. "A.M. was sweet in giving me a lovely white satin negligee and blue satin slippers," Dean said. After their improbable courtship, they started to settle into a more conventional married life. They were entering into a familiar milieu in the South, hoping to make it up the rungs of the middle class, to have a family, and enjoy stability after living through a depression.

THREE

A CHANGED MAN

Athens was a somnolent southern town of about 4,300 when Mac and Dean moved there from Texas. It was defined by the Limestone County Courthouse, a formidable neoclassical structure with four two-story columns at its entrance. Small businesses lined the streets of the square, including the McConnell Funeral Home. Mac's parents were prominent enough to warrant frequent mention in the local newspaper, and his uncle was a probate court judge and former alderman.

Mamie and Dad were religious and abstemious, or at least that's what Mamie thought. Dad would frequently retreat to the bathroom to rinse his mouth with "mouthwash" that was actually whiskey, and return to his chair in the living room. Dean and Mac moved into a small apartment around the corner from them.

The post-Depression sense of normalcy for their family and all Americans was altered forever on December 7, 1941, when Japanese forces bombed Pearl Harbor, prompting the United States to formally enter World War II. Men by the tens of thousands were drafted into the service, and both men and women were taking jobs in wartime industries.

Three months after the attack, Dean gave birth to Addison Mitchell McConnell III.

For the first two years of his life, Mitch's childhood was unremarkable. He was healthy and doted on by his parents and grandparents. Dean also stayed close with Sister, including some extended stays with her son in tow, which Sister wished were more frequent because she was so fond of her nephew.

Mac, twenty-six, married with a child and older than most conscripts, took an administrative job at the Redstone Arsenal in nearby Huntsville, Alabama, as the fight in Europe and the Pacific seemed to grow fiercer by the day.

Mac felt conflicted between being a new father—which, along with his age and work in a war-related industry, could have given him a waiver from active duty—and the desire to fight for his country. The latter won out. "I won't accept a deferment under any conditions," he told his wife. He tried to secure a spot in the Navy, but was rejected. Then he enlisted in the Army, taking his preinduction physical on March 21, 1944. He entered the service on May 13, awaiting orders for his deployment.

In June 1944, he left for training at Fort Bliss, and settled in with his unit. In early July, he sent home a photo of himself posing in front of his barracks, smiling and in uniform. Within about two weeks, his son contracted polio.

Mac was granted a nine-day home leave after the diagnosis, but there was little he could do, and after he returned to his unit, Dean threw herself into Mitch's care. Still, it was clear from later letters written during the war that Mac was distressed by his son's malady, yet felt powerless to do anything about it. That year for Christmas, Mac's parents sent their grandson a war bond.

Before Mac set off for Europe, the couple were able to spend some brief time together. "It was, of course, too short but every minute is accounted for with memories and hopes that will mean strength to both of us in the long months ahead," Dean wrote to Mac's parents on February 17, 1945. She assured them that "he knows his job of soldiering well" and has the confidence "to do the job expected of him."

She also updated them on Mitch, who she said was "fine in every way . . . at last I think we've reached about the end of a very long road." After a visit to Warm Springs a few days later, she said the news "was quite good. . . . The nurse said that that might be the last time. She said that functionally Mitch is normal but she wanted him to be 100% all over, even on the muscles he is not supposed to be 100% on." By this, the nurse meant she wanted him to work on building strength in the muscles that were not paralyzed but nonetheless weak. She also made sure he was vaccinated for whooping cough and other viruses and said she did not want to take the "slightest chance" of her son getting another serious infection.

While Dean was overseeing McConnell's treatment and ferrying him back and forth to Warm Springs, Mac was more than four thousand miles away. He was part of Company A, 38th Infantry Regiment, in the Second Infantry Division, which was known as "Indianhead." His unit sailed from the United States on the USS *Monticello*, then landed in Liverpool, England. From there, the troops traveled overland to Southampton before taking another ship to Le Havre, France. They made their way to Belgium, Luxembourg, then into Germany through Durenburg, Nordhausen, Leipzig and, as Mac put it, "a hundred other towns I don't remember." He added: "Then the guns started booming for me."

A marksman with excellent rifle scores, Mac was deployed as a scout, meaning he was on the front line of his unit both for offensive and defensive moves, depending upon the enemy positions. His division endured heavy combat losses in Europe, with deaths in the thousands. Mac's only wound was being struck by shrapnel in the chin, which gave him a small permanent scar, but not a significant injury.

Four months after D-Day, the Second Infantry entered Germany on October 4, 1944, crossing the border ten miles east of St. Vith,

Belgium. For the next sixty-eight days, "the Second waged incessant patrol and artillery warfare with German troops in the deep pine forests and ridges," the U.S. military newspaper *Stars and Stripes* reported in an evocative account of the pitched fighting, published in a booklet.

"By day and night reconnaissance patrols roamed the forests seeking out enemy positions," it relayed. "Ambush scouts pounced on unwary Germans. Combat groups jabbed enemy lines and battled enemy patrols in a mine-strewn no-man's-land. At night, German patrols made raids through gaps in the lines that existed in the wide sector."

Another account, the official one by the Army, said that starting that December and through January 1945, the 38th was in "constant contact with the enemy" in the form of shelling and "buzz bombs." His unit crossed the Rhine River and eventually into Czechoslovakia. The Army said his unit had cleared more than a dozen towns.

Mac's regiment had bored through Germany, at one point progressing 161 miles in six days. On Easter Sunday 1945, German SS troops mounted a furious attack on the unit's anti-tank company in Bonenburg, said the Army report. "In overwhelming numbers that night they [the Germans] fought into the town—and into the houses with the Antitankers, who grimly fought them from room to room and called artillery down on their own positions. The company had cleared most of the SS from the town next morning."

Under relentless fire, Mac's company moved on four successive nights, "enveloping the enemy," then swung to the outskirts of Leipzig. "Here the opposition crumbled and the 38th moved into the city with little difficulty." Casualties on both sides were heavy.

In a letter from Germany on April 11, 1945, to his sister "Dick," Mac wrote, "As you have read in the papers they are really keeping us on the go these days." He described the European countryside as beautiful, yet added, "I wouldn't trade it all for one acre of good old Alabama red dirt."

He saw the horrors of war up close, as his letters make clear, even as he was guarded about the details.

"You will notice that I haven't mentioned war and I don't want you of all people to misunderstand," he told his sister. "It's this way—I understand why men don't discuss their war experiences now that I have had some and I find that I try to avoid even thinking about it any more than possible. I hope you understand.

"I will say let's all hope it will be a good lasting peace that will continue for the lives of our children."

The letters swung wildly from the gravity of battle to the simple desires, like asking his sister to send a box of candy and food, which she promptly did. A month later, Mac replied, "We ate everything in about 30 minutes. Thanks a million." She also enclosed a book of poems, and he said he adopted one as his own:

Since what we choose is who we are
And what we love we yet shall be
The goal may ever shine afar
The will to win it makes us free

He told his sister that Dean had sent him five pictures of herself "and the boy which I enjoyed very much." He asked Dick to send a family picture that he could keep in his billfold. "I want to tell you that this soldier's morale has been a heap higher since I started getting mail."

By May 1945, Mac's unit was in Czechoslovakia and the war in Europe was rapidly coming to an end, even if many of the troops did not realize it. Finally, on the morning of May 8, Mac's commanding officer told the men that the fighting was over and VE Day had arrived. The fierce fighting with Japan in the Pacific continued.

He told Dean: "On this day I'm feeling so very close to you and I'm so deeply thankful for peace."

Stars and Stripes said the welcome given to the U.S. troops in Pilsen "made a tremendous climax for the war in Europe. In the Czech border towns, with heavy German populations, there had been little cheering. But on the approaches to Pilsen and in the city itself, the

Czechs lined the roads and streets in a demonstration of gratitude that correspondents said was even greater than that of Paris."

The carnival spirit that seized the Czechs and Americans alike continued for days, *Stars and Stripes* said. "Pilsen's mayor, just released from a concentration camp and given his job back, brought the traditional Czechoslovakian welcome of bread and salt to General Robertson and some of the country's finest musicians, allowed to play only certain compositions under the Nazi Regime, held a concert for the American commander. The official V-E announcement the next day brought further celebration and entertainment by the Czechs in honor of their Liberators. Dances and parties also were held by the Division."

The next week, Mac wrote to Dick and again struggled with how to be specific about his duties, yet also conveyed his relief at having the war end.

"I know you are wondering how I felt," he wrote on May 14, 1945. "I can't tell you how I felt because there are no words to express my feelings. First it was a feeling of 'well, I made it—they won't get another chance at me here.' Then I had a quiet feeling of thankfulness way down deep inside me and a feeling that 'the lights have come on again.'" With "God's help and a little luck," he added, victory would come soon in the Pacific and "then all the boys left will come marching home."

Mac's relief, though, was tempered by concern that he'd be sent to fight the Japanese next. "I'm not afraid—just weary," he told his sister. "Don't mention that please. I can't explain my feeling about it. I never felt that way about the Germans." *Stars and Stripes* said that concern was widespread among the troops in Pilsen. "The question in most of the doughboys' minds was whether this marked the war's end for them or whether they would have to begin another campaign in the Pacific," its account said. "For the civilians of Pilsen, the war was over, but for the Americans it was a different story."

The troops had encountered horrors even beyond the brutal fighting in their thrust to Czechoslovakia—concentration camp survivors, en-slaved laborers who were newly freed, and emaciated American soldiers they rescued from prison camps. Without going into such details, Mac told his sister that he and his fellows would sit around "and talk about what happened. I think it helps us all to bring all those thoughts out in the open and let them air a little. That way we can laugh about a lot of it, and then too it keeps us normal—we don't want to be 'different' when we get home." And to make that possible, he advised the men like him who had been in combat: "When they come home give them a break and let them tell you about things they want to talk about."

For the last weeks he was in Europe, Mac and several other soldiers lived with a local Czech family and were even able to see a couple movies. He enjoyed the musical comedy *Hollywood Canteen* and took in a USO show. A Polish boy gave him German currency and a Czech man gave him souvenir photographs.

Even after months of duty in Europe, Mac was concerned that he would be sent to help fight the Japanese in the Pacific. "I think he knows he will go," Dean wrote to Dick. "In letters he keeps referring to 'not sending your birthday present this year' 'you do understand, don't you?'"

She continued. "I suppose this is another one of those things but it is a bitter pill to take, isn't it?"

In less than two months, President Harry Truman would give the order to drop the atomic bomb on Japan, and Japanese troops surren-dered unconditionally only a week later. For his valor in combat, Mac was awarded the European–African–Middle Eastern Campaign Medal with two Bronze Stars. He was also awarded the Distinguished Service Medal, which honored units for exceptional performance in battle. But the war would inflict a deep cost for his family. His brother, Robert, the one who'd helped him settle in Texas, had also joined the Army and was killed in a noncombat gun accident in 1942. And Mac's sear-ing combat experience never left him entirely. Even months later, when Mac returned to Alabama and was stationed at Camp Swift, near Austin, Texas, he wrote his sister about the memories of war that "still thundered in my ears."

He also told Dean of his deep "distrust" of the Russians and his belief that by weakening Allied forces in Europe, the United States was emboldening the Soviet Union. He did not elaborate on the source of his geopolitical views, but he would pass on his skepticism about the Russians to his son. "It's a hell of a mess now and frankly I'm getting where I just don't give a damn. Oh I know that's the wrong attitude but I'm getting sick of the stupid way our foreign policy is being handled. Why won't the people listen to the men who were over there fighting the war?" He said he thought that the U.S. should continue the military draft so that troop levels were not too badly depleted.

He also allowed himself to think of returning to family life in Athens in a letter to Dick. "I have been well pleased with the news I've had from home about the way things are working out both as to Mitch and Dean and Mamie and Dad. I love those four a lot more than anyone would ever guess.

"With Mitch—well do you remember singing 'Don't be a sissy' to me? It's sort of like that. I wanted him to be a regular fellow and then this trouble came and I find myself literally tearing my innards out hoping he will still be in spite of this. . . . I find myself saying to myself 'I'll make him a regular guy' but I know I can't make anybody anything nor can anyone else.

"I've kept going when I had no strength to go with, kept going simply because I willed it so, but this is another human being and not my legs. He's a swell little fellow and I'm counting on him so terribly much—too much.

"I think if someone asked me what my postwar plans are, my only truthful answer would be 'Mitch.'"

In December 1945, there were finally signs that his family would be reunited. Mac was home for a sixteen-day furlough to celebrate Christmas with his family. "So here I am at home by the fire where I should be," he wrote to Dick.

"We have had a wonderful Christmas here. . . . We all got a big kick out of Mitch—honest he was really beside himself. Last year wasn't much for him as he didn't understand all about it and then too I know he couldn't really be happy without the use of his legs. We tried to make it all up to him this time and I believe we succeeded."

His sister sent him another book of poetry, and he typed out the verse he thought most meaningful.

> *I like the man who faces what he must*
> *With step triumphant and heart of cheer*
> *Who fights the daily battle without fear*
> *Sees his hopes fail, yet keeps unfaltering trust*
> *That God is God, that somehow, true and just*
> *His plans work out for mortals.*

On the eve of his departure from Fort Meade in Maryland, where he had traveled from New York to return to Alabama, Mac authored another of his love letters to Dean, a handwritten, three-page poem. It included what seemed like oblique references to the war, "guns and loneliness and of ships and trains and unhappiness," but was overall tender and loving. "I'll tell you of my wife, the finest girl I've seen in all my life," he wrote. "And of our little boy who to me has brought great joy . . . our boy is a towhead lad. He has eyes that are never sad."

He met up with Dean at the Redmont Hotel in Birmingham on July 25 for a three-day reunion. They settled back into their lives, with Mac making occasional trips to Warm Springs and following up on an order of special shoes for Mitch.

Gone was the swashbuckling notion of striking it rich in the Texas oil fields. Instead he was looking for stability, a job that offered a path to the middle class that so many Americans were chasing, and one that would allow him to provide for his family. Finally, the three could restart their family. Like so many American soldiers, Mac returned home from war a changed man.

FOUR

JIM CROW SOUTH

Not long after the war, the McConnells moved from their apartment to a modest, whiteboard rental home on North Houston Street, to a life deeply enmeshed in the Jim Crow South. Mitch McConnell knew only a world of segregation, in schools, movie theaters, and the public swimming pool. There were separate drinking fountains and entrances to local businesses. Racial epithets rolled casually off the tongues of whites in a town where about one in three residents was Black. His family didn't question things because they had always been that way.

"As a young boy that's just the way it was," McConnell said in an oral history interview discussing his childhood. "I mean African Americans in those days were the people who helped with the chores around the house and did the cooking, and from my earliest recollection there was always Black help at my grandmother's."

Schoolchildren celebrated Confederate commander Robert E. Lee's birthday with a day off. They also had a half day off to honor the birthdays of Jefferson Davis, president of the Confederacy, and General Stonewall Jackson.

His family employed a Black woman named Texie, and her husband, Archie. Texie did domestic chores for the family and Mitch was quite fond of her. An enduring memory is the cake she baked for him on his fourth birthday.

"Archie would come over and help in the yard with my granddad, and Texie was always in the house with my grandmother," he said. "Your impression, obviously, was that they were in a certain place in life that was clearly and distinctly different from white people and on a much lower scale. When I was six or seven years old, I really hadn't begun to focus on the injustice."

He had no Black friends and only saw where the Black population lived when his family drove the maid home. "It was a completely segregated society," he said. For Black townspeople, "an entirely separate world and clearly inferior in every way."

Texie made a lasting impression on the family. She was strong, resourceful, and resilient. McConnell's cousin, Ann Fox, recalled playing with Mitch, when Texie came out, grabbed a chicken out of the coop in their grandparents' backyard, chopped off its head with her hatchet, watched it run headless for a few moments, then gathered it up and prepared fried chicken for dinner. She also raised a girl as her daughter, who went on to earn her college degree at Berea College in Kentucky. Decades later, McConnell sought her out and reconnected with her, including a visit to her home in 2022. During that visit, several relatives of the woman met with McConnell and challenged him on the issue of voting rights. While he was calm in the moment and tried to assure them that Republicans were not trying to suppress the vote, when he returned to the car, he was angry.

McConnell's parents at the time were strict Southern Baptists, often attending the First Baptist Church on Wednesday nights and twice on Sundays. They went through a fundamentalist period, "adhering to a pretty rigid brand of Southern Baptist theology" that limited activities on the Sabbath. McConnell later recalled, "I remember not liking that, frankly, not liking not being able to play on Sunday." At the age of eight, he was baptized, with the minister fully submerging his body. Even as a child, McConnell found the atmosphere oppressive.

He had a number of playmates in his neighborhood, including one who was both a friend and foe. In one photo from his boyhood, McConnell and two friends are seen lying on the ground dressed as cowboys, aiming their toy pistols. One of them is Dicky McGrew, the son of the local newspaper publisher, who lived across the street. McGrew was larger than Mitch and often picked on him. At some point, Mac had seen enough and demanded that his son cross the street and confront his bully. McConnell told his father that McGrew was bigger and stronger, but Mac made it clear what he was demanding of his son. So Mitch went across the street, fists flying, flailing punches on McGrew. That was the end of the bullying.

It was such a moment of triumph that even when McConnell, nearing the age of eighty, returned to Athens to visit his boyhood home and the cemetery where relatives are buried, he recounted it to the locals gathered to see the famous senator. He told the story with great relish, adding emphasis on the detail "I bent his glasses" as he let out a laugh. McConnell said the two became friends before parting in adulthood—only to run into each other once in Washington when McGrew was working as an Alabama congressman's press aide.

The family didn't have a car or a television when they moved to Athens. Mitch and his parents listened to *The Shadow* and *Amos 'n' Andy*, *The Thin Man* and *The Lone Ranger* on the radio. It was typically just the three of them. The "little sisters and others" that Dean referred to earlier were not to be. They did have two Boston bulldogs, Button and Cookie.

When he needed a car, Mac borrowed his father's. Then, in 1949, they bought a Plymouth, the largest purchase his family had made to date and a great source of pride for them.

Mac served as a scoutmaster in the Boy Scouts, but his son never made it past Cub Scouts, and didn't even like that. "The thought of spending the night outside never appealed to me," McConnell said. Mitch entered first grade in Athens and found himself seeking the title of "king" in a school pageant. He got the part and later said it "may have been an early, early indication that I was going to be somebody who wanted to lead and who wanted to be recognized."

Though both Mac and Dean were close to Mac's parents, Mac had little interest in the family funeral business and he accepted a transfer from the Redstone Arsenal, where he had returned to work, to Camp Gordon, near Augusta, Georgia. The city, with a population of about seventy thousand, dwarfed Athens in size, and while Dean did not balk at moving, she also did not feel comfortable in what she viewed as such a big city.

She wrote to Mac's parents about being homesick for Alabama and trying to adjust to her new town. They set out early so they would see the city during daylight. "We wanted Mitch to see it. He had never seen a city so big. He has been such a darling." She also wrote about cleaning and unpacking their possessions, with help that she found wanting. "The Negroes were so slow, we told them to go on out of the way."

While she was uneasy, her son seemed to take quickly to his new surroundings, riding his bicycle and honking the bike horn that his grandfather had given him.

McConnell made new friends and they often played Civil War, though it was difficult to find a boy who wanted to be a Union soldier, unless he was the son of a current soldier who had been transferred from the North. "You couldn't get a single kid of a native to be a Yankee, even for kid games," McConnell said. "They simply wouldn't do it—another way in which the residue of the Civil War was still very much present in Augusta, Georgia, in the early fifties."

He also started taking piano lessons from Miss Maxine Day in the fourth grade and learned to play "The Marines' Hymn" and Sousa's "The Thunderer." "I loved it, absolutely loved it, but I was the only little boy in the class who took piano and it was sort of viewed as a sissy thing to do, and I let it get to me and I said I wanted to quit. The only mistake my mother made raising me was letting me quit. I shouldn't have quit." She also made him take ballroom dancing, which he detested at the time, but appreciated when he was older.

He kept in close touch with his grandparents, writing them letters about his life in a new place. "Dear Mamie and Rube, I love you. My ears are well. Thanks a lot for sending my gun and billfolder. Everything doing fine. . . . Hope you are doing O.K. daddy and momie doing fine so are button and cookie. I miss you very much but I enjoy being home. You grandson, Mitch."

Mac was also gaining new opportunities. The DuPont Company was building a massive facility for refining materials for nuclear weapons at the Savannah River plant twenty-five miles away in South Carolina. In 1952, Mac was offered a job in the personnel department, one that made him so proud that he wrote his parents with all the details, enclosing a check for $75 that he owed them as the last installment of a loan. "They're paying me $7200 per year plus 2 weeks vacation, hospital and life insurance and many other benefits. It's all so big and so much that I feel very small but I am very happy with it all." He also wrote that he and Dean had given ten-year-old Mitch a radio for his birthday "and I don't believe he has turned it off." Mitch also displayed an interest in politics, wearing an "I Like Ike" pin on his shirt for his school photo.

In October 1954, Mac wrote his sister a letter that opened with a portrait of happiness. Mitch, he said, played a football game that day and then babysat a neighbor's two small sons. "He's 5-4½ tall now, is a Junior Deputy Sheriff (which allowed him to get into the movies for free), is making mostly 'E's (for excellent) in school and is a 4-H Clubber." He had to be at school early to raise the school flag.

But all was not well with Mac, who was diagnosed with a heart condition that frightened him, and, he said, gave him purpose. "I feel swell that my life will have new depth and meaning now. . . . Mitch took it hard at first but understands better now and seems to accept it okay."

His health seemed to improve, and within months he was back teaching Sunday school and other activities, including golf.

Mitch wanted to be an athlete like his father, but his initial efforts were not promising. He tried football, but quit, saying he didn't like getting hit. He tried basketball, then gave that up because he couldn't keep up with the running. His favorite sport was baseball, but his skills were pitiable.

He was undeterred. Fortunately for him, a neighbor—Bernie Ward, a school principal—was a former college baseball player at Mississippi State. Ward was a patient teacher and McConnell was an eager student. He spent hours practicing the techniques that Ward taught him, and little by little his confidence, and his skill, grew. He largely limited himself to the positions that involved the least running, so he mostly played first or third base and pitched.

His parents dutifully clipped articles from the small community newspaper, which devoted outsize attention to Little League baseball. There were no fancy uniforms, and the infield was dirt, but the stories were endearing. Mitch was on the Fleming Bulls, and the paper carefully tracked his highs and lows both as a pitcher and hitter. "McConnell pitched excellent ball for the Bulls allowing only two hits," it reported. Then, in "the 4th inning, he allowed 3 runs to cross the plate." In one game he walked seven and struck out seven. His coach also had him pitch when the league championship was at stake—and the Bulls won, on a performance that included a one-hitter by McConnell on the mound and a triple at the plate.

By McConnell's account, he ended the year with a batting average of .675 and two home runs.

The league was composed of kids living outside the city of Augusta, and McConnell was named to the all-star team. When it came time to face the city kids and their best players, McConnell encountered a different level of competition. Entering the game to pitch, he walked the first three batters he faced, then a fourth to walk in a run. The next hitter crushed a grand-slam home run, and McConnell and his father rode home in silence.

But McConnell had proven, to himself at least, that he had a future in baseball, and he was eager to keep his career going. Who knew where it might lead?

Baseball became a source of bonding with his father as well. Mac and his son attended dozens of the Augusta Tigers games in the Class A Sally League. McConnell also started to follow Major League Baseball and landed on the Brooklyn Dodgers as his favorite team, listening to games on the radio when he could find a station that carried them.

One memory that stuck with McConnell was when the Augusta Tigers finally had a Black player, nearly a decade after Jackie Robinson had broken baseball's color barrier with the Dodgers. The player was cheered, but also seen as "quite a curiosity."

Augusta, like Athens, remained highly segregated, with no Black students in McConnell's schools, even after the Supreme Court's decision in *Brown v. Board of Education* in 1954 found segregation in schools unconstitutional. "Obviously the southern society did not respond to that quickly and there were some politicians calling for, quote, 'massive resistance' and other things," McConnell recalled years later. He said his parents were "very sympathetic" to the *Brown* decision. "It's not that they really were happy about the prospect of having the local school become majority Black students, which really would change in every way the school, but in terms of the injustice of it, both of them, when confronted with segregation through the *Brown* decision, were sympathetic to making change.

"I remember my parents being all along very sympathetic with the civil rights movement as we understood it in the fifties and sixties. This was way before preferential treatment, when civil rights meant striving for a colorblind society. And consequently, I was as well."

At the same time, Mac's political leanings were changing. An ancestral Democrat, with party allegiance tied to the Civil War, he was gravitating for the first time to a Republican, General Dwight Eisenhower, who had commanded U.S. forces in World War II. Dean's leanings moved along with her husband's.

Mac was also making his way in the corporate culture of DuPont. Gone was the feisty man his son referred to as "a rounder," and in its place was someone more in the mold of the 1950s Organization

Man, conforming to the white-collar cultural homogeneity that had emerged since World War II.

By 1956, Mac had made a favorable impression on a manager, who asked him to join him in a transfer to Louisville. So with his family and their two dogs, he headed to Kentucky. To them, that meant moving to the North, which came as a bit of a shock to Mac's family.

Mac's father was quite concerned that Kentucky had not seceded from the Union and that their family was moving to live among the Yankees. Mitch knew the answer, then told him, "They didn't, but, Big Dad, I think they were mostly sympathetic to us." McConnell recalled the lesson his grandfather had imparted on his father at an early age: "I want to explain politics to you. . . . The Republican Party is the party of the North. The Democratic Party is the party of the South."

They drove several hours and stayed in Asheville, North Carolina. "On to Louisville tomorrow," Mac wrote his sister. After making it through the war and a depression and struggling in the oil fields, Mac was looking for security, and he found it with DuPont. He took it as a measure of success that his wife did not have to work outside the home.

That did not mean Dean was content. Once again, she was moving to a place much larger than she was accustomed to; Louisville was five times the size of Augusta. "My mother never got over it," McConnell said. "I don't think my mother ever was comfortable here."

FIVE

BECOMING YANKEEFIED

The McConnells arrived in Louisville in January 1956 to find a rare sight for southerners: snow. The family settled into their new home at a time the old city along the Ohio River founded by George Rogers Clark was undergoing a rapid and uneasy transition, with an extraordinary economic boom fueled by more than half a billion dollars in postwar industrial development, an awakening in the arts, and a surge in population. "Here is the only American city which has ever used culture as an industrial asset," the biographer and historian William Manchester wrote in *Harper's Magazine* a year earlier. "Louisville has succeeded where other Southern cities have failed, because it has deliberately made itself a pleasant, stimulating place to live."

Manchester's flattering portrait of a river town with modern cultural sensibilities and enlightened business and civic leadership took little note, however, of something fundamentally at odds with both the notion of being culturally advanced and economically prosperous. Louisville's schools and hospitals were segregated. Public accommodations, including parks, were separate, as were most neighborhoods. But through the prism of white commentators, Louisville was "exceptional among southern cities in its community efforts to solve racial problems."

Beneath the platitudes bestowed on the city there was roiling discontent, with obvious inequality between Blacks and whites. Before the Civil War, Louisville had one of the nation's largest slave trades, its location along the Ohio River making it a ready transit point for reaching the Mississippi River and ultimately the slave markets in New Orleans. Though Kentucky remained with the Union during the Civil War, as young McConnell noted to his grandfather, its allegiances to the South and the Confederate cause were enduring. Indeed the veneration of Confederate heroes with monuments can still be seen in Kentucky.

Between the end of World War II and 1950, however, most of Louisville's population growth came from an influx of Black residents, and they concentrated in the city's West End, triggering white flight to the suburbs. This had one political benefit: Blacks were able to elect aldermen and state representatives. Black voters were historically Republican until the New Deal, but by the 1950s, the political registration in Louisville among Blacks was split equally between Republicans and Democrats. At times that made Blacks a key swing voting bloc, though it was a tenuous form of political power. But for all of its growth, the city was being held back by those who could not abide this demographic change.

The influential Louisville *Courier-Journal* editorial page, and publisher Barry Bingham, began to take up the cause of civil rights in the late 1950s, in a moderate, center-left way. There was also a budding civil rights movement, led by Blacks who were unsatisfied with both the pace and scope of change that others had praised.

Change was coming, and Louisville schools were officially desegregated in the fall of 1956, when McConnell was entering high school at duPont Manual. While other cities had angry, vile demonstrations by whites protesting Black schoolchildren, Louisville, as the *New York Times* reported, was a notable exception. Even so, Louisville did not have its own version of a civil rights law until 1963.

As the family was settling in, a young amateur boxer named

Cassius Clay Jr., born one month before Mitch, was starting to make a name for himself in Louisville, his hometown, winning bouts on the way to the 1960 U.S. Olympic team. He became the state's most famous resident, known the world over as Muhammad Ali.

"The large city of Louisville, with its strong Southern traditions, has shown that integration of the public schools need not bring on another era of ill-will between the states," Benjamin Fine wrote in the *Times*. "Without fuss or bother, almost nonchalantly, this community of 400,000 and its suburban area of 150,000 slipped out of the past into a troubled but confident future." He continued: "On last Monday, thousands of white and Negro boys and girls for the first time went to school together. They did not go with reluctant step, they went quietly, without any show of blustering or arrogance."

Even in the South, the *Times* said, "integration can be made to work without violence."

McConnell, too, recalled that those first days of integration were uneventful. He said integration was somewhat easier in Louisville than in the Deep South because it had a smaller Black population. "It was a much more radical change for them," he said of states like Alabama, "and you can understand why it might have gone a little smoother further north where the numbers were quite different." He also said that the legacy of segregation meant that the "educational level, the social skills, and all the rest were so dramatically different and, looking at it from our society's point of view, inferior, and we all know why that was the case, but nevertheless that was the case."

Only small steps had been taken toward integrating Louisville's public recreational facilities before a Supreme Court decision in 1955 forced city leaders to desegregate the parks. Nevertheless, white Louisvillians maintained that this slow but continuous pattern of progress reflected well on the city and should be a model.

Mac McConnell started his new job at DuPont, enthused about his promotion as the number two man in the personnel department. Meanwhile, Dean and Mitch were more resigned than happy. Mitch enrolled at duPont Manual High School, the state's largest, in the middle of the academic year, stuck in a new, unfamiliar place with no friends. Dean's friends were still back in Alabama. Each day Mitch would take the bus to school, then come home and spend time with his mother and their dogs. It was a lonely start.

"I was lost, I mean just lost," McConnell said of this period. His early recollections of Louisville were "deepened by ties with my mother, because I didn't make friends very quickly, and so she was the one to talk to every afternoon when I came home."

After renting a small house, the family was able to buy a larger one, and the McConnells enjoyed the kind of middle-class comfort that provided "as normal and healthy a family situation as you could possibly have. . . . I think a lot of who I am and what I became may well be related to having a full-time mom and a lot of interest in what I was doing, a lot of encouragement." He credited both his parents with giving him the strength to take risks and "kind of lay it on the line."

By late spring, baseball offered young Mitch an opportunity to make friends—and make a mark—in a way that school had not. "Baseball was sort of the way I measured my worth in those days," McConnell later said. He attended the Beechmont Pony League tryouts at the baseball field at the Naval Ordnance Plant on the south side of town. McConnell said he was the number one draft choice, selected by the Giants. McConnell, by the account of his teammate Billy Reed, who went on to become one of the nation's best-known sportswriters of his era, was the best player on the worst team.

"I remember him as being a bit aloof and more mature than the rest of us," Reed wrote. Reed acknowledged his own mediocrity as a player and recalled a game when he was put in right field. Mitch was pitching, and Reed let a ball drift over his head, leading to another Giants loss. "Mitch didn't say anything at the time, but years later he would never fail to bring it up. His standard introduction was, 'This is my friend Billy Reed, the worst baseball player I ever saw.'"

By the ninth grade McConnell had made some friends and felt

THE PRICE OF POWER

more confident, emboldened enough to enter his first political race, for class vice president. He won, he said, unopposed. By chance, the boy elected president, Terry McCoy, could not be at school the day of the final assembly to address the convocation. Instead it fell to McConnell, who with his father, wrote a speech titled "Great Expectations," after the Dickens novel. The speech does not read like it was written solely by a ninth grader.

"The days and weeks and months that lie ahead hold for each of us great expectations. At this period of our lives, we have laid the foundation of our future. Like a good novel, our lives must have no loose ends. Our activities must be closely knit and well organized. Like the characters in *Great Expectations*, we shall have people to help or to hinder the shaping of our lives. We, too, shall have joys, fears, disappointments, and turmoils in our relations with others. This will make our life interesting and worthwhile." In 1995, McConnell pronounced those words "rather prophetic."

Manual High School was a facility with collegiate Gothic architecture so formidable that it drew the notice of *Architectural Digest* for its design. With its U-shaped structure and courtyards, it has the feel of a small college campus. Its central entry "is marked by a five-story tower framed by three double doors between gothic pilasters with huge stone arched transoms." It was originally conceived as a school to prepare young men for a trade. When he entered the school for an opening convocation, he stood at the rear of the imposing auditorium and saw the student council president address those assembled. At that moment, he had no idea what he wanted to do, but he knew what he wanted to be: the center of that kind of attention.

He went home and told Dean of his ambition, and, as always, she encouraged him and told him he could be anything, including student council president. His interest in politics was growing. In the summer of 1956, at age fourteen, McConnell watched both the Republican and Democratic National Conventions, gavel to gavel.

In an essay titled "New Beginnings," McConnell, now a sophomore, wrote with optimism about high school: "We have much to look forward to at Manual because it has much to offer." His teacher gave him an A on the paper and added, "You seem to have high ideals as well as good ideas."

McConnell was searching for a way to fit in and make the forbiddingly large school seem smaller. He naturally thought he could find a spot on the baseball team. To his disappointment, he was simply not good enough and he was cut.

He channeled his desire for competition into politics, and as early as his tenth-grade year he was devising a strategy that could lead to him being student council president as a senior. He shared few qualities with successful student leaders at Manual. He wasn't an athlete, and he later described his grades as "mediocre." But he could make political calculations that were years ahead of his peers. This knack paid off: he won a seat on the student executive board, a prerequisite for seeking the higher office. He also had a classic disappointment for a high school student, flunking his driver's exam on the first try.

His parents started treating him more like an adult. His father wrote him a letter on Christmas Eve in 1958, saying, "There are two presents we did not put under the tree because we did not buy them. We want you to go downtown or to the shopping center and buy yourself a pair of slacks and a new pair of shoes, whatever you want within reasonable price limits." He signed it, "Just the same old, Pop."

He was also more attuned to politics, especially John Sherman Cooper, who was dashing with a backwoods charm and broad worldview. McConnell would describe Cooper to others as the "first great man" he ever met, and he held him up as a role model. Cooper's success also helped deepen McConnell's alignment with the Republican Party. "It's a lot easier in forming your party affiliation to be in the vicinity of success than surrounded by failure," he said. "Mostly I was thinking about school politics, but to the extent I thought about real politics, my Republican leanings were already taking hold."

In his student council race, his opponent was McCoy, an excellent student and one who was more popular than Mitch. So McConnell devised a strategy. Typically, the students elected athletes, but no athletes were running this time. McConnell saw his opening in a way that McCoy did not.

With Mac's help, he made a twenty-five-foot banner that said "McConnell for President," and he placed it so that any students descending the stairs would have to see it. Then, knowing he was not particularly popular, he recruited athletes and cheerleaders to endorse him; the first time he understood the value of such validation. "I figured since I wasn't particularly well known, I would find people who were well known." He built a coalition by using the endorsements to win over younger students. He made pamphlets to show off all the jocks and cheerleaders who were backing him, and he put them in students' lockers. He handed out flyers headlined "We Want McConnell for President" that featured endorsements from supporters like Janet Boyd, homecoming queen and cheerleader; Bobby Marr, named the best high school pitcher in the state; and Pete Dudgeon, an All-City football player. He then persuaded those popular kids to be in a skit that laid out the case for his candidacy. "I had thought about it a lot, worked on it a lot, worked every angle, and really put forth a major, major effort and it worked. . . . If I hadn't worked every angle I would have lost." He added, "I don't believe I've ever gotten anything as a result of luck." McCoy didn't take the race as seriously, and McConnell won, with 921 votes to McCoy's 819.

McConnell took his duties seriously, though "there wasn't much to do." In block capital letters, he wrote out his address to the student association on the morning of September 14. "The purpose of this organization is to foster such a loyal, cooperative spirit among the student body that the students will assume all responsibility outside of the classroom, thereby practicing citizenship in preparation for participation in city, state, and national affairs," he said.

He was already contemplating a career in politics. His student council election led to a trip to Pittsburgh for a national convention, one of the few times he left the city. But he wasn't certain. He also considered trying to become a doctor, and listed that as his career ambition in the school yearbook, saying he wanted to attend Vanderbilt. He quickly realized he had no interest in science, but the yearbook reference lived on. He said he liked the music of Percy Faith, Julie London, and Frank Sinatra, and that he patterned his hairstyle with a neat part on the side after the TV character Peter Gunn. *Wagon Train* was his favorite TV show. He noted the artists more for effect, and said he actually preferred Elvis and Little Richard. He held a job as a soda jerk at a drugstore.

He went through a phase where he tried to build muscle, calling his workout "the making of Mitch's Mighty Muscles." He ordered barbells and free weights and recorded his workouts and his body development. August 1959, he said he had twelve-inch biceps and a thirty-four-inch chest, and that his waist had gone from 28 to 35. The numbers are almost certainly inflated.

In September of his senior year, he wrote an essay titled "Now I Am a Senior," which had a melancholy tone. "Being a senior is very sad," it began. "Now that I am in my last year in high school I suddenly realize that by next fall I must grow up and give up being a kid. This thought grieves me deeply because I have always enjoyed being irresponsible and getting a bang out of life. I know that I must change my attitude and improve my study habits by the time I enter college because my future depends on it.

"Money has always appealed to me and doing something for humanity has also. My goal in life will be to arrive at a happy medium and satisfy both ambitions. When I die I want to be able to say to myself, 'I made a contribution to this old world and tried to make it a better place to live in.'"

In another essay, titled "You and Time," he began to express himself in more mature terms and offered a preview of how he would calibrate his expanding aspirations. "Each of us has an unlimited amount of opportunity but a limited amount of time. Success depends on the ability to convert opportunities into accomplishments, but remember, our time is limited!"

By his youthful rendering, one's most productive years would be from age forty to fifty in some lines of work. "It is safe to assume that we have 10 to 20 years to accomplish our goals in life." He then cited Dwight Eisenhower as one who had made the march from "mediocrity to greatness" in a "remarkably short period of time." He extolled Babe Ruth for his impact on baseball. Then he wrote, "There was another man, who lived only 33 years. He never traveled more than 100 miles from his birthplace; he went about his life's work for only 3 years and died the death of a common criminal. Yet, in so short a time, he changed the world. The man? Jesus the Christ." It was a curious framing given that McConnell has never been overtly religious.

He said it was better to be great at one thing than average in many things. "We must have that relentless, never ceasing desire to obtain our goal. We should try to be the best in our selected field. As Emerson said, 'hitch your wagon to a star.'

"A man whose life has been a success," he said, "should be able to answer 'yes' to these questions: Have I lived well, laughed often and loved much? Have I gained the respect of intelligent men, the love of little children? Have I filled my niche and accomplished my task? Have I left the world better than I found it, whether by an improved poppy, a perfect poem or a rescued soul? Have I never lacked appreciation of earth's beauty or failed to express it? Have I looked for the best in others and given the best I had? If you have answered all these 'yes,' then your life has been an inspiration and your memory will be a benediction."

McConnell did not give anyone credit for his phrasing, but it tracks in many respects word for word with the poem "Success" by Bessie Anderson Stanley, written in 1904.

The school newspaper, the *Crimson Record*, highlighted the outgoing McConnell as "the epitome of a Southern gentleman but he claims he has become 'Yankeefied' since he moved to Louisville four years ago and lost his Southern accent."

His commencement ceremony was held at the massive Freedom Hall on the Kentucky State Fair grounds, and McConnell was the recipient of the Kiwanis Efficiency Award for the student who "proved his efficiency as a student and as a leader and who has shown broad interest through school activities."

After graduation, McConnell and a friend, Mike Butler, who was a year older and had just finished his freshman year at the University of Louisville, went on a coming-of-age adventure. They traveled to California on Route 66, then home on a northern route that took them to San Francisco and back through Yellowstone National Park. It was the first time McConnell had been west of the Mississippi River.

The trip was an exercise in independence, and his mother needed some persuading before giving her permission. He stayed in near daily contact with his parents, through postcards that he found along the way, most of them featuring 1960s-era humor. One showed an oversize Texas rattlesnake who said, "I'm so big, I can't find a pit to hiss in."

"Man, it's hot in Texas," McConnell wrote. From Oklahoma, he reported seeing in a service station window "a rattlesnake skin about 5 or 6 ft. long and it had 22 rattlers. It was one of the biggest snakes ever killed in Oklahoma. So said the Indian that worked there." So far, he wrote, the trip had been "truly wonderful." "Believe it or not, I miss you all already," he wrote. "Howdy from Winslow, Arizona." They saw the "fabulous" Grand Canyon and the bright lights of Las Vegas.

Their time in Las Vegas was an awakening. They stayed at the Dunes Hotel, which had opened on the Strip just five years earlier. "Went to La Parisen," McConnell wrote, "starring Diana Dors and many other gorgeous gals." What he did not detail to his parents was that they had managed to get into a burlesque show. "It's not an overstatement to say we [were] impressed by the lack of clothes from the waist up by a bunch of beautiful women," McConnell said. "That is nothing I had seen at that particular juncture."

"Las Vegas sounds like quite a spot," Dean replied.

Then, on June 30, after arriving in California, he wrote, "I have some sad news. I lost 2 pairs of bermudas and my jewel case in Las Vegas. . . . You remember my Honor Society pin, my Student Council pin and my Key Club pin were in it. You were right. I should have left it at home. I never took the stuff out of my bag so it must have been taken by the maid.

"On a happier note, we went to Disneyland today. It was absolutely fabulous. . . . We've been lined up with a couple of dates for next Monday night. However, they will probably look like a mud fence."

McConnell wrote the hotel asking that they try to find his bermudas and jewel case, and added that the only other person who had been in the room was "the maid." A few days later, he wrote to his parents, "Good news! I found my jewel box in one of my dresser drawers and my bermudas in the suitcase. Boy, am I a goof!"

In California, the young men stayed with Butler's parents and went deep-sea fishing ("Wham. I threw in the reel and the fight was on") and saw Disneyland, but a highlight was seeing the Dodgers play in Los Angeles. He kept the ticket stub from the game, July 5, 1960, at Los Angeles Coliseum.

His correspondence with his parents underscored how close they were, with Dean and Mac involved in the most minute details of his life, and their son writing to them with remarkable candor for a young high school graduate. Dean signed some of the letters "Little Iodine," just as she had as a young woman. "Goadmorning," she wrote. "Mudder loves ya. . . . Found any interesting females of age?"

On July 12, Butler's father had arranged dates for McConnell and his friend. "They lined up a couple of 'PIGS' uh I mean girls as companions for us. I utterly detest those arrangements (and that makes the 2nd such thing since we've been here)." He added he was also hearing from a girl back home. "I've been getting a letter from Carlene every day. What do you think about that? Just call me Joe Lover."

He was taken by Butler's father, who he described as a "swell easy going type" who "smokes cigars constantly." McConnell was also taken by his financial success as a physician. "His office of five doctors took in over half a million dollars last year." But he lamented that he had to babysit while the Butlers went golfing at the country club. In another letter, he added, "After five weeks I'll be plenty ready to get back home."

Three days later, they crossed the border into Tijuana, Mexico. "Those Mexicans are real cards. I had a blast bargaining with them," McConnell wrote.

His mother wrote him back frequently. "Thought you'd like to know that I am not worrying about you. Of course I'll be anxious about your safety, but I'm sure you know that we never question your behavior. Thanks for being such a fine son, and it's no joke that you're our pride and joy."

He stayed up late to watch the Democratic National Convention in Los Angeles nominate John F. Kennedy for president. McConnell was unmoved as Kennedy summoned Americans to become pioneers at the edge of a "New Frontier."

As it turned out, his friend's father lived in Whittier, the hometown of Kennedy's Republican opponent, Richard Nixon, whom McConnell enthusiastically supported. "I voted for Richard Nixon, proudly, and remember being deeply disappointed in the outcome."

McConnell was concerned because he had not yet heard about his admission at the University of Louisville. Mac checked with the testing office and assured his son that everything was on track. He added that his son might want to take advantage of U of L's strong "testing and counseling program." His acceptance letter soon arrived.

SIX

THE EXERCISE
OF POWER

When McConnell began his journey to college, he did not have far to go. The University of Louisville was only a few miles away from his home, and he lived with his parents through all four years. He liked the idea that his mother would still do his laundry, cook meals, and that his parents granted him a lot of independence. Yet he later reflected that it would have been better "to have gone away and had a more normal kind of college experience."

In his freshman year, he drove a Corvair back and forth to campus, then traded that for a 1961 MG, a car that looked better than it performed, with plastic windows that froze in the winter. The university was known as a commuter school, as most students lived off campus. The turmoil of the later 1960s over Vietnam, civil rights, and political assassinations had not yet arrived. Students at U of L leaned conservative, though there were liberals, too. McConnell identified with the former.

He joined the Phi Kappa Tau fraternity his first semester and immediately started assessing political opportunities on campus. The fraternity was a mix of young self-serious men thinking of their future, like McConnell, and others who cared more about beer and bourbon than books. Much of campus life revolved around two major factions of allied fraternities and sororities, known as combines. They formed coalitions and worked to persuade independent students to vote for them. The spoils for the winner were the power to oversee student government and select the editors of the school newspaper and year-book. McConnell studied the system carefully and plotted a strategy for winning. "It was really quite a learning experience in the exercise of power," he said.

The fraternity factions were not divided by ideology. "It was strictly just a question of control," McConnell said. "Power. It was a pure Machiavellian exercise. It was part of the competition."

And McConnell was driven by competition and winning, but his first two runs for campus political office resulted in defeat. He was convinced that one of his fraternity brothers voted against him in one of the elections, and he never forgot it. Many years later he exacted a quiet revenge.

McConnell began taking his studies more seriously than he had in high school, especially when he took his first political science courses. "As soon as I figured out what political science was, I knew that was for me." He was influenced by one professor in particular, Grant Hicks, who stood out for his conservative views. McConnell said Hicks some-times had to eat by himself because other professors did not want to associate with him.

"He was treated like an unpleasant relative showing up," McCon-nell said. Hicks lived on a farm in southern Indiana, was married to a woman from China, and held strong anti-communist views. He was also influential in a budding organization called the United Associa-tion of Constitutional Conservatives, which was closely aligned with the views of Senator Barry Goldwater of Arizona, an emerging force on the political right whose conservatism had a libertarian strain. In a statement of principles, the association asserted its "belief in the primacy of individual freedom, the subordinate and service role of government, and the original purposes and binding force of our constitutional agreement."

The key theme of one of McConnell's courses taught by Hicks was "Freedom vs. Authority: The Eternal Dilemma of Man in Society." One of his lectures was on Friedrich Hayek's *The Road to Serfdom*, which Hicks described as "an analysis of the classic contention that economic freedom and personal liberties are inseparable—that economic planning inevitably leads to a regimented, coercive and totalitarian political and social structure." McConnell told one of his biographers, John David Dyche, that Hicks had an "enormous influence" on him.

A serial joiner, McConnell hoped to expand his political network by padding his campus résumé. He dated prolifically, his companions ranging from a woman nicknamed "Miss Thoroughbred" to a bright, attractive history major, Sherrill Redmon, who seemed intrigued by McConnell's idea of a career in politics one day. While McConnell focused on political science and history, Redmon suggested that he branch out. So he tried an art appreciation class and received a D, even though he studied hard. "I thought to myself, somebody's telling me something here," McConnell said. "I am not going to be a Renaissance Man."

The campus was its own isolated bubble. In downtown Louisville nearby, local high school students engaged in nonviolent demonstrations demanding laws to end racial discrimination. Several of the activists were arrested on Fourth Street, the epicenter of many of the protests. It did not cause much of a ripple at the university.

In 1962, as McConnell became increasingly involved in campus Republican politics, he helped persuade Goldwater to come to speak to students. They knew Goldwater was likely to run for president and considered it a coup to attract him to Kentucky. McConnell escorted Goldwater and gave a brief introduction, looking every bit the part of the president of the College Republicans in his suit and tie, his short hair parted neatly on the left side. A photo of McConnell, Goldwater, and the university president, Philip Davidson, appeared in the next morning's edition of the *Courier-Journal*. (McConnell secured a print of the photo, and after his first election to the Senate, he asked his fellow senator, Goldwater, to autograph it for him.)

Goldwater was already honing a hard-right, values-laden campaign message, and his speech at U of L railed against materialism. "In a speech of almost evangelistic fervor," Bill Woolsey wrote in the *Courier-Journal*, "Goldwater declared that 'it's better to be poor and free' than to 'lie down (before Communism) like a satisfied animal.'" In that moment, Goldwater seemed to embody the kind of conservatism McConnell could embrace.

Goldwater's message, however, did not include advocacy for civil rights. In a question-and-answer session with students, Goldwater said he was "totally opposed to segregation of any sort," but that he did not believe the Supreme Court's ruling in *Brown v. Board of Education* was the "supreme law of the land." He went on to say that while he disagreed with Mississippi governor Ross Barnett's refusal to integrate the University of Mississippi, "I think he has the constitutional right to do it." In what would prove to be an enormous miscalculation, he also said that Medicare was a "dead fish" and that "there is no interest in it around the country."

At the end of his junior year, McConnell ran for a second time to be president of the College of Arts and Sciences Student Council, one of the major elective offices on campus and one he had unsuccessfully pursued the year before. This time, he worked hard, secured commitments, and won.

In the summer of 1963, before his final year of college, McConnell worked as an intern for Kentucky congressman Gene Snyder, a right-wing conservative who also opposed civil rights legislation and would be among the few Republicans to vote against it. The first U of L student in the school's inaugural congressional internship program, McConnell was drawn more by the opportunity to work in Washington than any admiration for Snyder. "Young Republican Mitch McConnell is opening up a new frontier here for the University of Louisville's political science department," the *Courier-Journal* wrote.

Other than his long trip to California, a summer in Washington represented a rare break from living with his parents. He drove to Washington and found an apartment to share for $19.50 a week. "It's a pretty shabby place," he wrote to his parents. "There are many Puerto Ricans and displaced Cubans around. But there are also college kids and many sports cars."

He focused more on his office in the Capitol complex and his first-hand observations of political figures that he had only read about. In his first week, he almost "ran into Sec. of Defense [Robert] McNamara." He saw Teamsters boss Jimmy Hoffa speak, describing him as "sharp as a tack, which should be expected since he's managed to stay out of jail." He also attended speeches by former New York governor Averell Harriman, who was the best-known diplomat of his era, and the economist John Kenneth Galbraith.

In what would turn out to be a lifelong pattern, he began to think about his next step, law school. He made Yale his top choice, along with Harvard, and, for a time, the University of Virginia. "I have become convinced that I must go to one of these schools for superior education and increased post graduate opportunity," he said in a letter to his parents.

In the meantime, his work as an intern consisted of responding to constituent mail and other low-level tasks. McConnell was struck by the racist tone of some of the letters, so much so that he made copies of them and sent them home. "President Kennedy wants the Niggers to have more freedom than the white people," said one.

He took full advantage of intern gatherings to meet with senators and mingle with Supreme Court justices. He noted that most of the interns seemed to come from Ivy League schools. Rather than be intimidated, he said, "I must always size up such people as they are potential competition. . . . I figure there were about two future congressmen and Senators a square foot in that room," he wrote of one such event. The milieu, he said, has "only reinforced my opinion that government and politics is for me." He set his sights for the next summer on either a campaign job or as an intern in Senator Cooper's office. "Our Senators don't have anybody not from the Ivy League but if I'm lucky I'll be a rising freshman law student at Yale this time next year."

He seemed fixated on the allure and prestige of the Ivy League. Cooper had gone to Yale, then Harvard Law School. McConnell told his parents that if he got into Yale or Harvard, he'd probably land a scholarship. "It would be good to get out of the South," he said. He quoted praise from a U of L teacher and declared, "I'm not being cocky but it is going to look good. . . . I've just got to get in Yale. That's really what I want and have wanted for quite some time." Those big dreams came crashing down when McConnell received his less-than-stellar scores on the law school entrance exam, the LSAT.

Social life was active, and McConnell dated a number of women who also were working on Capitol Hill, but he told his parents he tried to be frugal by sticking with "25 cent beer and free Shakespeare plays." "I got rid of that babe from West Virginia I was fooling around with and am making a more concentrated effort in the Selby direction. She came in the top 5 of last year's Miss D.C. contest." He also continued to date Sherrill, and asked his parents to meet her because "they will probably be" her in-laws. McConnell also told Mac and Dean he'd had a bout of optic neuritis—a painful swelling of the optic nerve that can cause temporary vision loss—but that he was feeling better and the inflammation had cleared up.

Goldwater spoke at one session, but McConnell did not get the chance to reintroduce himself. He praised Goldwater's ability to answer questions, but said in a letter home he was more ideologically comfortable with Senator Kenneth Keating, a moderate from New York. "As you know he is a liberal Republican," McConnell wrote. Keating voted for Medicare the previous summer, but McConnell told his father, "Don't get upset Pop, I wasn't and still ain't for the Medicare plan."

As for his own boss, Snyder, McConnell was contemptuous. "Snyder has been in a good mood consistently but he's still an incompetent, pompous ASS!" he wrote. Meanwhile, he had high praise for the Tennessee senator Estes Kefauver, the Democrat who was Adlai Stevenson's running mate in 1956. "Here was a guy who had the guts to be a progressive integrationist from Tennessee and the beautiful part was he got away with it," McConnell said. "Underneath that coonskin cap was a keenly intellectual mind."

As the Kennedy administration was pushing a public accommodations bill, which McConnell favored, he got into an argument with others in Snyder's office. "Sometimes I actually think many conservatives are racial bigots. I think Snyder is. . . . I contend that the American people are more than money hoarding property owners but living breathing individuals demanding full constitutional rights regardless of race or religion."

The broad window onto political strategy and tactics was teaching McConnell lessons that no classroom could, and with it came bravado. "I've picked up many ideas about campaigning, etc. All those other aspiring Republicans better look out—cause Old McConnell is getting ready to swing into action."

It was a momentous time in the nation's capital. On August 28, McConnell stood outside the U.S. Capitol and saw the National Mall teeming with people who had gathered for Martin Luther King Jr.'s March on Washington and King's "I Have a Dream" speech. He did not join the march and could not hear the speech from his vantage point, but he knew he was watching history.

In a letter to his parents the next day, he wrote, "I was so proud of the Negroes and happy that their march went so well. After talking to you all Monday night, I got to thinking about who had brought up the possibility or probability I should say, of violence. None other than the Southern politicians. I was kind of ashamed of myself for being fearful of deprived American citizens exercising their constitutional rights to assemble anytime, anywhere."

Though the moment of the speech became part of the collective national memory of the civil rights movement, McConnell said decades later that the choice then was just a fundamental issue of right versus wrong.

"This was the period when the civil rights movement was in many ways pretty simple," McConnell said. "You were talking about access to public accommodations, you were talking about equal opportunity, and it seems to me the civil rights movement became much more complicated years later when you started talking about preferential treatment.

"But as long as it was knocking down barriers, I think there was widespread sympathy for it," he went on. "I'm not trying to diminish the controversy, but . . . a lot of people believed that this was elementary fairness, that you ought to be able to go into a place and get something to eat or that you ought to be able to vote."

McConnell's views on civil rights caused him to break from Goldwater. He became increasingly "irritated at the conservative Republicans over the civil rights thing" and initially supported the more moderate Pennsylvania governor William Scranton over the Arizonan for the GOP presidential nomination as a result. Conservatives, he said in a letter home, were on the "wrong side of the civil rights issue . . . and I didn't want my party to be on the wrong side of that issue."

That in no way made him a supporter of President John F. Kennedy. He was not moved by the Kennedy aura like so many people his age. He had persuaded his father to put a Nixon bumper sticker on the family Oldsmobile. But McConnell recalled with clarity the early afternoon of November 22, 1963. He had just watched an intramural football game between his fraternity and rival Lambda Chi on the campus quadrangle. He was headed toward the student center for lunch when another student came up and said, "The president's been shot." "Within thirty minutes or so we all knew he was dead, and like a lot of Americans, I was just devastated," McConnell said.

He went to the fraternity house to make sure they had canceled the party scheduled for that night, though he said that some "jack-asses" seemed totally unaffected. His parents were out of town, so McConnell sat at home alone all weekend. "I literally sat there and watched [the television coverage] all weekend long." Then, on Sunday, after making himself a ham and cheese sandwich, with lettuce and tomato on rye, he sat down in the den only to see Jack Ruby shoot Lee Harvey Oswald on live television. "It was the most surreal weekend that anyone could ever have experienced," he said.

Despite his many criticisms of Kennedy, McConnell had agreed with his views on civil rights. In a 1964 essay in the *Cardinal* news-paper, he collaborated with a fellow student, Bonnie Meyer, to argue that civil rights should be above property rights—countering a core segregationist argument—as they worked to rally support for a march on Frankfort, the Kentucky capital, in support of the civil rights move-ment. "As long as basic rights are denied to any group, a strict inter-pretation, which ignores these injustices, is innately evil," they wrote. "In order to realize the ideals of the Constitution, all segments of soci-ety must do their part to insure the BASIC RIGHTS OF ALL citizens, regardless of race, creed, or national origin."

In addition to coauthoring the essay, McConnell was one of four student leaders named on a flyer promoting the "Freedom Now" rally. The purpose of the march was to "demonstrate citizen's support for a state public accommodations law which would give equality of treat-ment to all Kentuckians in all facilities open to the public."

He had planned to attend the rally. Instead, as he walked out the door of his fraternity house, he and two fraternity brothers were con-fronted by pledges who had just endured their "Hell Week" initiation. After evading it for two years, McConnell was finally being "taken for a ride," a ritual in which pledges corralled upperclassmen, then drove them to a remote part of the state, leaving them to fend for themselves to get home. "I never had any desire to be taken for a ride. There were those suffering from prolonged adolescence who really did think it was an honor. And by God they got me."

So, the next morning, instead of marching in Frankfort, McConnell found himself in Golden Pond, Kentucky, a place known for its moonshine, having been dumped there in the middle of the night. Eventually, a Good Samaritan took him and his friends to a bus station. They made it back to Louisville a day or two later.

The experience didn't still his enthusiasm for campus activism. He invited Norman Thomas, at the time one of the nation's best-known socialists, to speak to students. "I thought we ought to have a little balance," McConnell said. He enjoyed Thomas's speech and found him engaging, even though he fundamentally disagreed with him.

As the outgoing student council president, McConnell presided over a final student election. Some students charged that he had improperly allowed an independent candidate to run. A letter to the school newspaper from two other student council members said he showed "blatant disregard" for the campus constitution. McConnell apologized for the "fuzzy provisions" in the constitution and said he hoped it didn't shake faith in student leaders. But later, in an early example of what would become a characteristic defense, McConnell said, "It is easy to smear and difficult to produce leadership and initiative. We have chosen to produce."

Among those offering support for McConnell was Redmon, who conceded in her letter to the editor of the student newspaper that she lacked "complete objectivity" when it came to her boyfriend.

McConnell soon made a break from campus politics. His more passionate interest lay six hundred miles away in Washington, D.C. His internship with Snyder had given him a taste of the life he sought. This time he decided to aim higher, seeking an internship with Senator John Sherman Cooper. He traveled to Washington during spring break and waited around Cooper's office until he had a chance to make his case.

He was selected and found himself in a far more rarefied environment. Cooper was a leading light on a number of issues, popular with Republicans and Democrats, and his progressive views on civil rights strongly reinforced McConnell's. He had served as ambassador to India in the Eisenhower administration and as a delegate in the United Nations General Assembly. He denounced Senator Joe McCarthy's red-baiting anti-communist crusade. Cooper was also outspoken against the Vietnam War, another belief that McConnell held, though after McConnell had left his employ. Ultimately, McConnell voted for Lyndon Johnson in 1964 because of Goldwater's opposition to civil rights legislation.

The work in Cooper's office was similar to the work in Snyder's, but the stakes felt higher. Cooper wielded power and influence in the Senate, and his approach to the job left a lasting impression. "One of the things I learned from Senator Cooper was that while he was sensitive to what his constituents were interested in, he was not controlled by it." Cooper ranks among McConnell's few heroes. He was tall, handsome, and charming, an intimate of President Kennedy, an internationalist, and very much a moderate Republican. Lyndon Johnson appointed him to the Warren Commission to investigate JFK's assassination. "You sort of had the feeling every time you were around him that you were in the presence of greatness," McConnell said.

Looking back, McConnell said that letters flooding into the office were overwhelmingly against the civil rights legislation. "I asked him about the mail, and he said, well his view was that he was doing the right thing and that he hoped that people would ultimately see it the way he did, even though they might not today. And if they didn't, implicit in that was that they would have the opportunity to vote against him." Cooper easily won reelection in 1966.

McConnell's parents, who had only known life in the segregated Deep South, were also resolutely for the civil rights laws. Writing to her son in Washington, Dean lamented that the moderate Scranton would probably lose to Goldwater. "It seems to me that his [Goldwater's] vote against the Civil Rights Bill coupled with the sickening situation in Miss. [the killing of three civil rights workers by white supremacists] will all be to his advantage in the South.

"Let's hope the WORM TURNS,'" she wrote. She said she was

going to purchase the book *Mississippi: The Closed Society* by James Silver, a Mississippi native, that one review said "awakened the nation to the daily horrors of life inside a police state." "Wouldn't you like to have it too?"

On July 5, 1964, McConnell's father made his case for the civil rights bill. "I thought the enactment of the Civil Rights Bill right at July 4th was significant," Mac wrote. "As you know, I sincerely wish we didn't need such a law, but we do and I'm glad it's done. I hope and pray it will all work out with little violence.

"God gave a man certain dignity and rights and I wish we didn't have to fight over it. I hope you never forget the importance of every single one of us. In my view, each man has the right to stand up and be counted where he fits and all this talk about some are immoral, some are weak, some are this or that is for the birds. A lot of us went to battle because people didn't believe in 'one man, one vote.' I would fight over a man's rights quicker now than I did 20 years ago."

McConnell told his parents he was "ecstatic" that Scranton had entered the presidential race, but after Goldwater secured the nomination he referred to the Republican National Convention in San Francisco as a "wake."

Back in the Senate, he read a book by Senator Joe Clark of Pennsylvania, *Congress: The Sapless Branch*, which argued for a stronger executive branch and a weaker legislative one. McConnell strongly disagreed and said he believed in balance among the branches of government. "You don't have to be a Barry Goldwater to offer an alternative to that kind of executive autonomy."

Sherrill was taking the summer off before beginning graduate school. "I don't envy her however," he wrote. "This idea of completely goofing off all summer is as repulsive to me now as it was 2 summers ago." Sherrill was actually traveling, including a long trip to France. "She eats up a culture center like Paris just like I love Washington for its government," he added. He also said that his former boss, Congressman Snyder, was busily running for reelection. McConnell said he was wavering about whether he wanted Snyder to lose, or to win, "until I can get a crack at him in a primary. He is a real first class loser."

He was also taking a measure of fellow interns as possible competitors for full-time staff jobs with Senator Cooper. He thought he would fare well, noting that two of his colleagues were not from Kentucky and "both are Jewish which would kill them politically in Kentucky. There might be a real opportunity here for me."

He remained fascinated by the Senate and the seeming power its members had, and the aura surrounding them. He told his parents he nearly ran into Indiana senator Birch Bayh coming around a corner and had been watching "Teddy" Kennedy on the Senate floor. That night both were injured in a plane crash in Massachusetts. "It almost seems [as] if there is some conspiracy against the Kennedys."

With an Ivy League law school well out of reach, McConnell decided to attend law school at the University of Kentucky, in Lexington, more than an hour away from home, though he still would frequently take his laundry back to his mother. He entered law school not so much with a desire to become a practicing attorney as to gain another credential as an aspiring politician, and to meet people from other parts of the state. Redmon also went to the University of Kentucky, to work toward her doctorate in history.

McConnell didn't like law school and performed poorly. Halfway through his first semester, he considered dropping out to pursue a graduate degree in history instead. The summer after his first year, he returned to Washington, and stopped by to see Senator Cooper on a historic day. Cooper asked McConnell to come with him to the Capitol to see Johnson sign landmark civil rights bills. McConnell was taken by LBJ's size, and by the moment. But it did not change his politics.

Back at law school, he was no fan of torts and contracts, but was attracted to moot court, and by the chance to run for an elective office, secretary of the Student Bar Association. "It appeared to me pretty clear I was not going to be a good student like I had been in college," he said. "At least I had some other outlets." He went on to make the

moot court team and be elected president of the Student Bar Association. His mother was so proud of her son that she started her letter on
March 25, 1966, with a simple exclamation: "Happiness!" She went
on, "Now, from your unbiased, unprejudiced Mom you really have an
outstanding speaking voice, your gestures are good, not too many. . . .
If this all sounds like a few pages of praise, it is just that. . . . We raised
ourselves quite a son."

At a school dance after his election, the tightly wound McConnell
broke into a rendition of "Wabash Cannonball."

His memory fresh with Senator Cooper's stand on civil rights—
going against his constituents to lead—McConnell led a campaign to
change Kentucky's antiquated state constitution and to have the law
school adopt an honor code. Both efforts failed decisively, and he considered it a political defeat and a direct rebuff of his ability to persuade
people to follow him.

"That made a lasting impression on me," McConnell reflected.
"And I think what I learned is that courage is one thing, but you also
have to have a sense of where your constituency is. It's one thing for
John Sherman Cooper, on an issue like the civil rights bill, which is
kind of a broad national issue, to go against the flow. It's quite another
for a president of an organization to try to ram down the throats of a
reluctant student body, a code they didn't want to adhere to.

"So I remember leaving law school a little bit confused about leadership and when you can lead and be applauded for it, even though
you fail, and when you just fail and get condemned for it. So that was
a very, very important leadership lesson, kind of in the opposite direction of the lessons that I had learned in the summer of '64 observing
Senator Cooper."

During law school, McConnell came to realize something about
himself: He had no real desire to be a lawyer. But he still saw a legal
career as a traditional path to elective office. As he sought jobs with
Louisville firms, he was met repeatedly with rejection letters, many of
them softened with praise, but not with offers.

SEVEN

"ANTSY AS HELL"

By the summer of 1967, there were nearly half a million U.S. troops in Vietnam. Mitch McConnell, fresh out of law school, did not want to be among them. Like so many white men of some privilege, he was able to secure a spot in the Army Reserves, military service that made overseas deployment highly unlikely. He had little interest in putting his life at risk in a conflict that he did not support. But he shared an aim with other would-be politicians: enhancing his political viability with the credential of military service while avoiding the peril of the jungles of Southeast Asia.

McConnell was assigned to an Army Reserve unit at Fort Knox, Kentucky, and things went poorly from the start. He had difficulty with the physical drills, especially running, because of his polio-weakened left leg. What's more, he did not like delaying his dream of entering politics, and he was agitating to leave shortly after he had arrived. His efforts to attain a status to exempt him from the draft had been unsuccessful: he had solicited recommendation letters from his law professors to work for firms in Louisville, but had not received an offer; he had sought a position as a lawyer in Senator Cooper's office, but Cooper told him he did not have any openings.

He soon told his military superiors that he had a medical reason that should have prevented him from being inducted in the first place: a history of optic neuritis, an inflammation around the optic nerve that can blur vision. He contacted his doctor in Louisville, Edward C. Shrader, asking him to write a letter outlining episodes of the condition in his right eye that had occurred in 1958, 1963, and 1965. He also produced a record from 1958, in which a consulting physician said that "the possibility of multiple sclerosis could not be ruled out at that time." Dr. Shrader went further and said there was a "high index of suspicion as far as multiple sclerosis is concerned." It's true that McConnell had written to his parents about "eye trouble" during one of his congressional internships, but he also said that it had resolved fairly quickly with steroid medication. Likewise, while optic neuritis can indeed be an early sign of MS, McConnell's service records noted that neither he nor his family had a history of the condition.

His initial eye examination at Ireland Army Hospital at Fort Knox showed he had twenty-twenty vision in both eyes and additional tests "were all essentially within normal limits." Still, his diagnosis from the military doctor said, "History of recurrent optic neuritis in the right eye, possibly secondary to preclinical systemic disease as multiple sclerosis with residual visual field defect manifest." The doctor's report, dated July 25, 1967, concluded that McConnell "fails to meet induction and enlistment standards . . . and it is our recommendation that he be separated from the service." An additional report said McConnell should not use weapons except for "familiarization and qualification" and should not use power tools or work with mechanical equipment like an engine, nor should he drive military vehicles.

In an accompanying document, McConnell's medical evaluation also highlighted that his left thigh was at least three inches smaller in circumference than the right, which explained its weakened state. McConnell had not mentioned either polio—always trying to appear healthy and strong—or optic neuritis in his initial induction physical.

On July 31, McConnell filed his formal request for a discharge on the grounds of "having been erroneously inducted or enlisted" and said that a medical examination ten days earlier revealed that "I have a medical condition which would have permanently disqualified me for entry in the military service had it been detected at the time."

After his discharge was approved, he still had to wait for additional paperwork before he could actually leave, and he grew bored and anxious with his duties as a "barracks supervisor," charged essentially with cleaning. His father contacted a member of Senator Cooper's staff in Kentucky for assistance. He was told that McConnell needed to provide at least some rationale for the expedited dismissal. So McConnell said he was planning to attend New York University for graduate studies in law, even though he was well past any application deadline. On August 10, 1967, Senator Cooper quickly wrote a brief note to the major general at Fort Knox, asking for assistance: "Mitchell anxious to clear post in order to enroll NYU. . . . Please advise when final action can be expected."

About a year earlier, in the fall of 1966, McConnell had indeed asked a professor at the University of Kentucky to write to a colleague at NYU about his prospects for attending its law school. The director of the graduate division, Bert Prunty, sent back an application form, which he said had to be completed by January 2 for spring 1967 admission and by May 15 for summer admission. Considering that McConnell so disliked law school that he had considered quitting after his first semester to become a history professor, it is unlikely that his interests in NYU were scholarly.

To help him try to facilitate a belated application, McConnell enlisted his girlfriend, Sherrill Redmon. His handwritten notes to her indicate that he missed the deadline but still wanted to try to apply. "Must enclose letter from someone explaining the late application. . . . Tell Oberst [his UK law professor] not trying for money—all I want is in. . . . Make up a letter explaining late application—because of medical discharge—had planned to apply for spring.

"Type it and forge my signature."

In a letter dated August 6, 1967, to Prunty, McConnell explained his late application and his desire for an additional degree in labor law. "Although my law school grades are only average, I did graduate with honors in college. I hope this will be taken into account in considering my admissibility."

On August 15, five days after Cooper's letter, McConnell received a certificate attesting to his honorable discharge from the Army. There is at least one photo of him in his Army uniform from his five weeks of service time. He said that he never sent the application to NYU.

He had passed the Kentucky bar, and he was now free to pursue his legal career and to try to lay the foundation for a political one. For a time, he moved back in with his parents while he looked for a job. He responded to an ad in the *Courier-Journal* for a position at the firm Segal, Isenberg, Sales, and Stewart and soon accepted an offer.

The grind of first-year associate work bored him. As one measure of how inconsequential his legal work was, McConnell could not recall what service he rendered to earn his first legal fee, on October 23, 1967: $15 from Jerry and Colleen Skaggs. Years later, he joked that his clients had probably overpaid.

His personal life was not faring any better. He and Sherrill broke off their engagement in the fall of 1967. On September 21, Sherrill wrote a long, gracious letter to Mac and Dean.

"It looks as if an era has ended and I didn't want to let it end without a note to you both. It very much resembles a kind of five year thank you note, I guess." She told them she was grateful for their friendship and "many generosities" and thanked them for their patience "with our antics." "I'm sure our vacillations were perplexing and put you in some awkward situations. . . . Perhaps there will come a time when we can renew our friendship without undue awkwardness."

In politics, though, he had his first significant opportunity when Marlow Cook, the county judge for the area that includes Louisville, announced that he would seek the U.S. Senate seat of the retiring Thruston Morton. McConnell secured a meeting with Cook, who was impressed and named him the campaign's youth chairman, a position of some importance in a state where eighteen-year-olds could vote. More important, it was work McConnell actually wanted to do.

In what would be a signature of his approach to his own campaigns, McConnell was relentless, working more hours than almost anyone on the staff. "We traveled the state that summer organizing college campus organizations," said John Yarmuth, then a Republican who would go on to become a Democrat in Congress representing the district that includes Louisville. "I had not met him before then. But what was incredibly interesting to me was that he really didn't have any interests other than politics. That was all he talked about, and it seemed to me it was all he thought about.

"He was extremely knowledgeable. He was very politically savvy. He thought about things that I would have never thought about. He was much more familiar with Kentucky outside of Louisville than I was."

They put thousands of miles on the road visiting colleges. There was not much levity. McConnell was all business, and that's the way he seemed to like it. "I had a ball working in the campaign, loved every minute of it," McConnell said. "I would get there earlier than anybody else and stay later than anybody else and we won."

Only a few years older than Yarmuth, McConnell carried himself as a wise political hand. He could back it up, too, with detailed knowledge about the politics of Kentucky, and he was capturing contacts and context about the state's power brokers and politics to save for another day.

His personal life took another twist when he and Redmon reconciled—and decided to wed. In a letter to McConnell's parents, Sherrill wrote, "I don't guess I need to say how pleased I am to rejoin the McConnell family. I love you and A.M. like second parents. I haven't the remotest thought that you will be a 'mother-in-law' in the stereotyped sense. You must be my uvver muvver. I know I'll depend on your advice when I begin to set up our little household. (My knees are quaking at the very words.)"

They were married on March 15, 1968, at 4:30 p.m. in a small ceremony at the Duncan Memorial Chapel, a nondenominational facility. McConnell's best man was Daniel White, a high school friend. Redmon's maid of honor was her sister, Lee Ann.

The two started their married life together, soon acquiring a pet kitten they named Rocky, for Nelson Rockefeller, governor of New York, a member of one of the nation's wealthiest families, and the personification of moderate Republicanism. McConnell continued trying to climb the rungs in politics, while Redmon worked toward her doctorate in history from the University of Kentucky.

Though socially liberal, Redmon adopted McConnell's politics, at least outwardly. She wore a "Nixon for President" button, and she supported her husband's fervent desire to find a place for himself in politics. When Cook won the race in November, he offered McConnell a job as a legislative assistant. So the young couple moved to Washington and rented an apartment at 3025 Dumbarton Street in the capital's Georgetown neighborhood.

McConnell continued his habit of writing frequently to his parents, with a blend of humor and substance. When his parents were traveling to his boyhood home in Athens, Alabama, McConnell said, "I hope you haven't forgotten to tell everyone about Dicky McGrew," referring to his boyhood triumph over a bully.

He also discussed Senator Cook's committee assignments, which included the Judiciary Committee and a select committee on nutrition. McConnell noted that the nutrition committee was chaired by Senator George McGovern of South Dakota, and also included Senator Edward Kennedy of Massachusetts, both Democrats, and Senator Charles Percy, a moderate Republican from Illinois. "Three grandstanders if you ever saw them," McConnell said.

While working for Cook, he had his own political future in mind, expressing interest in the "agriculture program especially tobacco, for obvious reasons," namely that it was then Kentucky's vital cash crop. He was totally comfortable in the setting.

"I couldn't think of anything I didn't love about being involved in politics," he said.

He was attracted to the power; when his good friend Joe Schiff was drafted, McConnell wrote his parents, "He has really turned out to be a great friend. We are going to do what we can to keep him out of the infantry and maybe even get him assigned up here although that is hard to pull." Schiff indeed managed to secure an assignment in the Washington area, but not through McConnell.

At the same time, McConnell was building a new network of contemporaries in Washington, who, like him, yearned for high office and were getting their initial taste of power. One of them was a young man from Tennessee who exhibited the gentlemanly bearing of an older man: Lamar Alexander.

Alexander was a twenty-nine-year-old White House staffer when he met McConnell, then a Senate aide. Howard Baker, the Tennessee senator, told Alexander, "You might want to get to know that smart young legislative assistant."

Alexander was impressed with McConnell, and the two saw themselves as part of an emerging group of aspirational Republican leaders. Asked much later if he ever envisioned McConnell's political career playing out the way it did, Alexander replied, "I'm sure I wasn't thinking that. He may have been thinking that. Probably was." McConnell's drive and ambition were that apparent.

Additional evidence came in a six-page memo that McConnell wrote to Cook six months after the senator's swearing in, titled "Where do we go from here?" Its tone in part was strategically solicitous, suggesting that Cook might even be of presidential timber. But its broader message was an early example of McConnell's desire to accumulate power.

He acknowledged that as the legislative director he was not the top aide in the office; nonetheless, he proposed a reorganization that would give him authority over both legislative and press operations. "I have observed that the legislative and press activities are interrelated and should be part of one overall entity which we could call anything but in fact is our 'think tank.' The legislative area should create and the press area should provide the delivery system to the public."

He said he would like to elevate the press secretary and marginalize another staff member to do the "crap." To help cement his position, he promoted the idea of giving more authority to Dave Huber, a low-level aide at the time who had been McConnell's fraternity brother at the University of Louisville. "In short, he is our kind of Cook man." McConnell proposed that Huber deal with committees that were less appealing to him, and that McConnell keep the judiciary and nutrition committees and "move further into foreign affairs with the hope of building up a real speciality in this area."

The think tank should meet weekly, McConnell said, and serve as a clearinghouse for smaller meetings with Senator Cook. His aspiration was to build "the hard core of the 'tough, smart, loyal, ruthless, efficient, dedicated and professional'" Cook team. He noted that he had taken those traits from a *Washingtonian* magazine article describing the staff of Senator Edward Kennedy. "We can develop a comparable staff," he said.

Then his memo larded on the praise. "Sherrill and I were discussing recently how very proud we are of you. I know so many staff people who are dissatisfied with their bosses. . . . The positions you have taken and the courage with which you have spoken out could only be described as statesmanlike. . . . If all this seems idealistic maybe it is. Idealism is one of the traits of our generation about which I am quite proud.

"Maybe I am overstating the case but I feel a man of your ability who makes it to the Senate at such an early age owes it to his party and his country and, yes, indeed, to himself to go just as far as possible. . . . You have already been recognized by the politically astute staff people as the one new Republican who is of Presidential caliber."

He sized up the competition, dismissing Percy of Illinois, Charles "Mac" Mathias of Maryland, and Edward Brooke of Massachusetts as "too liberal," and Bob Dole of Kansas as too conservative. He pronounced Senator William Saxbe of Ohio—only fifty-two—too old and Richard Schweiker of Pennsylvania too bland. Bob Packwood of Oregon is "not tied together too tight," he wrote. So he saw an opening for Cook.

"I . . . hereby dedicate myself to helping you build the best goddamn team this town has ever seen. Just say when, boss, and I am ready to begin."

Cook did not adopt his plan. Years later, McConnell acknowledged that he "was sucking up to him by acting like he had a lot more potential than I thought he had."

Meanwhile, Cook immersed himself in a number of issues, including a proposed Equal Rights Amendment for women, working with a lead sponsor of the measure, Bayh, a Democrat with his own presidential dreams.

It was natural for McConnell to follow Cook's lead, as he felt personally committed to the ERA. Redmon, in an oral history related to a feminism study, said of her husband in that period: "I think he would have thought of himself not exactly as a feminist at that time, but he had helped a junior Senator from Kentucky work through the judiciary committee in '69 and '70 to get the ERA passed."

"We think this issue probably will be the No. 1 civil rights issue of the 1970s," McConnell told *Courier-Journal* reporter Ward Sinclair in a front-page story after an effort to pass the ERA in the Senate failed. "Women's inequality is the last big vestige of discrimination. We feel that if people begin thinking of it as a civil rights issue that will help some senators view it in the same light." It is notable that the story quoted McConnell by name, rather than Cook, given that most Senate aides were mindful of the unwritten rule that the elected official's name belonged in the newspaper, not the staff. McConnell would ultimately change his position on the ERA, deciding that it was not necessary, and that it would create a new swath of legal challenges and market impediments.

McConnell's most substantive work for Cook was on the Judiciary Committee, and it unfolded at a consequential time because there were two openings on the Supreme Court, and the committee would be the first stop for the nominees. In 1969, President Richard Nixon had nominated Clement Haynsworth of South Carolina to the U.S. Supreme Court. Cook backed Haynsworth, who *Time* magazine reported was "reviled by labor and civil rights groups for rulings related to union representation and school desegregation." Haynsworth also was accused of a conflict of interest over a possible financial stake in a case he decided while serving as a federal appeals court judge. McConnell thought the real motivation behind the attacks on Haynsworth was that Democrats saw his nomination as part of Nixon's "southern strategy" to win over white Democrats who opposed civil rights and were concerned about crime. McConnell judged the strategy as astute tactical politics because it could help Nixon win in the South, another early signal that he prioritized winning.

McConnell wrote the remarks regarding Haynsworth's nomination that Cook delivered on the Senate floor on November 14, 1969. "We must not allow a new standard to be created to stop an appointment some find objectionable for political reasons," the remarks said. "New standards, if they are needed, and I happen to think they are, must be established by legislation, not accusation." Cook tried to make the case that a judge's ideology was a matter for the president to consider, and the Senate should make its judgment solely on a nominee's qualifications. It was during this process that McConnell also worked with the Justice Department official tasked with coordinating Haynsworth's nomination, the head of the Office of Legal Counsel, William Rehnquist. But the nomination ultimately failed on a Senate vote of 45–55.

McConnell thought it unlikely that any second choice by Nixon would be rejected, unless that nominee had glaring issues. Harrold Carswell, a federal judge and Nixon's next choice, did. He, too, was criticized for his previous support for segregation, among many other shortcomings.

During an unsuccessful campaign for a state legislative seat in Georgia in 1948, Carswell gave a speech to the American Legion chapter in Gordon, Georgia, in which he said, "I am a Southerner by ancestry, birth, training, inclination, belief, and practice. And I believe that segregation of the races is proper and the only practical and correct way of life in our states. . . . I yield to no man . . . in the firm, vigorous belief in the principles of white supremacy. . . ."

Even Carswell's defenders had trouble making a case for him. Senator Roman Hruska, a conservative Republican from Nebraska, was asked if mediocrity should disqualify a judicial candidate. "Even if he were mediocre, there are a lot of mediocre judges and people and lawyers," Hruska said. "They are entitled to a little representation, aren't they, and a little chance? We can't have all Brandeises, Frankfurters and Cardozos." Cook, Hruska's fellow Republican, disagreed strongly and voted against Carswell.

McConnell recognized that Carswell was an abysmal choice and wrote Cook a memo outlining the pros and cons of opposing him. A vote against Carswell, he said, was a "vote against mediocrity," and it would help Cook with civil rights and labor groups and "make an immeasurable contribution to your developing national image for independence and integrity." He strongly urged Cook to vote no.

That led to Nixon's third choice, Judge Harry Blackmun of Minnesota. McConnell was not ready to let go of the treatment that Haynsworth received. In a memo to Cook he argued it was almost impossible to square Blackmun's ownership of stock with Haynsworth's and not conclude that Blackmun should also be stopped from joining the court. McConnell wrote that the fact Blackmun was a northerner—"from Minnesota and not from South Carolina"—might be the real reason he could be confirmed.

Blackmun was unanimously confirmed on May 12, 1970; Cook ended up supporting him.

Less than three years later, Justice Blackmun would write the majority opinion in *Roe v. Wade*, the 7–2 landmark decision that found women had a constitutional right to seek an abortion, a ruling that stood for nearly fifty years. Abortion had not been an issue during the confirmation process. McConnell said that he really did not pay much attention to the ruling, other than to recognize its obvious importance, and he did not offer any public comment on it.

The experience with failed Supreme Court nominees, and a changing atmosphere around confirmations and how nominees were evaluated, proved formative for McConnell. In the floor speech he wrote for Cook, he analyzed the historical precedents for doomed nominations. Then he went a step further and published an article in the *Kentucky Law Journal*, his only scholarly article, which gave him a rare foundation of knowledge about how members of the Supreme Court are confirmed.

McConnell argued that Haynsworth's rejection—only the second in the century at that point—was unfair on the merits, that he did not have a serious conflict of interest, and rather his opponents—who included a number of Republicans—were punishing him for being a southerner. "There could not have been a worse time for an attack upon the men who administer justice in our country than in the past year, when tensions and frustrations about our foreign and domestic policies literally threatened to tear us apart." He called the process the start of a period of "senatorial assertion." Going on to acknowledge the highly political nature of the confirmation process, McConnell said senators "sought to hide their political objections beneath a veil of charges about fitness, ethics and other qualifications."

Another such attack, he said, was leveled against Justice Roger Taney of Maryland back in the 1830s. Though Taney is reviled for his infamous decision in the *Dred Scott* case, his record before that made him an outstanding jurist at the time of his confirmation hearing, McConnell wrote.

McConnell's overall assessment of the role that politics played in judicial nominations proved prescient. "The inconsistent and sometimes unfair behavior of the Senate in the past and in the recent examples . . . do not lead one to be overly optimistic about its prospects for rendering equitable judgments about Supreme Court nominees in the future." Later in his career, it would be he who would in effect rewrite the rules about Senate confirmations.

Though McConnell's grasp of history was sophisticated for a man in his mid-twenties, his complaints about politics interfering with sober deliberation of the credentials of nominees betrayed a youthful idealism that would melt in the fire of partisanship. It's a flame McConnell learned to stoke masterfully. Looking back on his years of machinations in judicial selections as well as in legislative affairs, his wish in those days for a process unsullied by political calculation seems quaint.

Bayh, the Indiana senator who led the opposition to Haynsworth, came in for particular scorn from McConnell, who argued that his evidence was thin and sloppily assembled. McConnell dissected the strategy behind the opposition with a litigator's zeal, foreshadowing the approach he would take to politics in general: exploit any weakness.

The Carswell matter was entirely different. His record, particularly compared with Haynsworth, was abysmal. He had been reversed more than twice as often as the average federal district judge. "A federal district judge's duty in most instances is to follow the law as laid down by higher authority. Carswell appeared to have a chronic inability to do this." McConnell found Carswell's rejection entirely justified.

But he also noted that "anti-southern prejudice is still very much alive in the land and particularly in the Senate." Defeating Haynsworth while elevating Blackmun, when both men had similar potential conflicts of interest, he argued, "can only be considered to demonstrate sectional prejudice."

Even as he was critical of how the Senate exerted its prerogatives, he wrote that some good had come out of the confirmation fights. "Such assertions help restore the constitutional checks and balances between our branches of government, thereby helping to preserve our institutions and maximize our freedom."

His conclusion was triumphal, not in keeping with the tougher tone of much of the article. "It is suggested that the true measure of a statesman may well be the ability to rise above partisan considerations to objectively pass upon another human being."

Reflecting later on such sentiments, McConnell said that he had been hopelessly credulous in thinking that the confirmation process should be based on a candidate's credentials divorced from politics. "It was clear after Clarence Thomas that there's a political calculation in appointing him and a political calculation in opposing him, and suggesting that you take the politics out of politics was naive, shall I say, when I was twenty-six."

His regard for Cook continued to diminish, and the two had a serious falling-out. McConnell was far more ambitious than the senator, who, McConnell said, would not even go back to Kentucky on weekends, which in McConnell's eyes indicated a lack of passion and commitment. "He was lazy," McConnell later said. "Not particularly interested in issues." After two years in Cook's office, McConnell concluded his boss would have a hard time being reelected; indeed, Cook was crushed in the 1974 election by Democrat Wendell Ford, part of a vast roster of Republicans ousted in a post-Watergate Democratic romp.

McConnell and Redmon tried to establish themselves in Washington, with Sherrill still working to complete her dissertation, an analysis of the author W.E. Woodward, who coined the term "debunk." They attended dinners, visited galleries, and started to build a social circle. They rented a canoe and paddled around the Tidal Basin and the Jefferson Memorial and attended the Maryland Crab Festival. They went to French restaurants and tried to learn more about wine. They attended a Washington Senators baseball game. They ate on the porch some nights, by candlelight. Sherrill kept McConnell's parents abreast of their activities with frequent letters and postcards. "Served the last of the ham at our cocktail party last Sat.," she wrote on February 4, 1970. "It was a good party, M and I conclude immodestly."

She also said that most of the congressional staffers and families were "sympathetic" to Senator Ted Kennedy after his car careened off a bridge in Chappaquiddick, killing his passenger, Mary Jo Kopechne. But she was suspicious about other news from that family.

"We don't know what to make of the announcement that Joan is 4 months p.g. [pregnant]. Nancy [Senator Cook's wife] talked to her just 2 weeks ago and she at least implied was not p.g. by saying that she hoped to have some more children but not yet. If they announce a miscarriage in a couple months, I am going to be awfully disappointed. That is too crafty for my tastes. A blatant bid for sympathy; a strictly political move. They will be betraying people who have given them a lot of sympathy since 1963 if this is, indeed, a ruse. . . . I will suspend my judgment."

In fact, Joan Kennedy was pregnant and did have a miscarriage— her third—weeks after she attended Kopechne's funeral and, publicly at least, stood up for her husband.

Sherrill often started her postcards with "Dear Pares" or "Dear Folks" as she worked to develop a close relationship with them. She referred to herself as their "daughter."

McConnell was trying to prove his bona fides as a public thinker and build his résumé with impressive stints in Washington. He was offered a job in the Nixon White House in 1971, and, fortuitously for him, he turned it down. His preoccupation with building a political career in Kentucky spared him any taint from Watergate and Nixon's resignation. Before Nixon's downfall, the president had nominated Rehnquist to the Supreme Court, and McConnell, at his own expense, went to Washington to help him prepare for his confirmation hearings. The *Courier-Journal* took note of McConnell's presence at the hearing. McConnell said that when he called Rehnquist to congratulate him on the nomination, Rehnquist invited him to come help during the confirmation. "I thought it was a good opportunity to help somebody I happen to think is extremely brilliant."

He was ready to launch his own political career. It would prove far more difficult than he envisioned. As Sherrill wrote to his parents: "You know Mitch is antsy as all hell to get on with it all!"

EIGHT

THE "LOST DECADE"

McConnell returned to Kentucky long on ambition and short on any clear path to elective office. John Sherman Cooper had left the Senate and was serving as ambassador to East Germany. There were ill feelings between McConnell and Cook. He was hardly a household name and had almost no connection to political donors.

He was strapped financially, and his obligations were growing with the expectations of a house and family. For all of his outward confidence and ego, he was flailing. "I was going from one thing to another, figuring out how to survive and pay the bills," he told me. He had seven jobs in ten years, a period he came to refer to as the "Lost Decade."

He leveraged the University of Kentucky law review article into speaking engagements, like Kiwanis lunches around the state, as a way to gain recognition among civic-minded Kentuckians. It enabled him to practice both his public speaking and his ease in meeting strangers. At one point, he even offered to write book reviews for the *Courier-Journal* just to get his name in front of readers.

The first office he sought was at his alma mater, where he ran to be an alumni trustee. The University of Louisville had transitioned from a municipally funded school to a public state university, and as part of that move, one alumni was to serve on its board of trustees, chosen by the governor, Louie Nunn, from the three top vote-getters. McConnell campaigned hard for the position and was the runaway leader. "I was trying to move ahead and build my résumé in every way I could," McConnell said. But Nunn snubbed him. McConnell believes this was because Nunn had run against Cook in a Republican primary for governor in 1967 and still held a grudge "because I was a Cook guy."

One of McConnell's defenders was Jerry Abramson, a Democrat with his own political ambitions who would go on to serve for two decades as Louisville's "mayor for life." Abramson had attended the same high school as Sherrill and played in the orchestra with her, and they had a mutual friend in Joe Schiff. In a letter to the editor in the *Courier-Journal*, Abramson complained about Nunn's decision. "I want to register my complete dismay," he said. "Mitch McConnell would have been responsible to no one but the graduates of the university who overwhelmingly supported him, and at age 28, he would have provided an important bridge across the generation gap."

So instead of another résumé item, McConnell was left to confront other realities. He had to borrow money from his parents to buy a house. Sherrill wrote a lengthy thank-you note to Mac and Dean. On top of that, Sherrill was pregnant. She and McConnell referred to the coming child as "Quimsey." "How can Quimsey and I thank you for all your help in making ready for him-her. . . . Mitch and I are very grateful to you and A.M. for your generosity," Sherrill wrote. "Do you think it possible for little Q to live up to our expectations? . . . Thanks for everything. Love, Sherrill."

During this period, McConnell also worked on the failed campaign of another Republican gubernatorial hopeful, Tom Emberton, in 1971. He lost that race badly to the Democrat, Wendell Ford, who would go on to be a long-serving senator and a persistent McConnell critic.

In the period after the Emberton defeat, McConnell said, "I sat around for three weeks, literally not knowing what I was going to do next and it was a miserable experience. I don't know how people who are unemployed deal with it psychologically."

Soon there was an opening for a seat in the Kentucky legislature, and McConnell quickly leaped into the race. Too quickly, in fact. The newly drawn district included Louisville, where McConnell had moved, but his Republican opponents seized on the fact that the state constitution required a candidate to live in the "county, town or city for which he may be chosen" for at least a year. He had only been there a few months.

His opponents filed suit, and McConnell responded with a novel legal argument, namely that since the district boundaries were new, he could not have lived within them for a year. He represented himself in court and lost. "It was really dumb," McConnell told me. The man who always saw the value of meticulous planning had blundered terribly in this case, recognizing later that he had let his ambition get in the way of his judgment. He also realized that he had not used the same strategy that he had employed to become student council president in high school, when he learned "that having a plan, an early plan, and spending a lot of time on it over a long period of time makes a difference."

So he eventually joined a firm with a politically connected lawyer and successful businessperson, Barney Barnett, but he did no significant legal work. The new firm was called Barnett & McConnell, and McConnell acknowledged it was a stretch to say he was a name partner. McConnell did not flourish, but he had a job, and needed it, especially when he and Sherrill's first child, Eleanor Hayes McConnell, was born on July 15, 1972.

There was a Senate race, with former governor Nunn running on the Republican ticket. McConnell did not play a role in Nunn's race, and the Republican ended up losing by 33,895 votes to the Democrat, "an obscure forty-six-year-old Elizabethtown radio station operator and state senator" named Walter "Dee" Huddleston, a name McConnell would come to know well.

McConnell tried to learn from the defeats. He came to see that leaders who won and were effective were those "who took their time, understanding the issues, learning the system, paying attention to what voters were asking for, and making sure they were superbly prepared. I vowed that this would be my approach going forward."

Whatever lessons he drew from his losses, he was also dealing with personal obligations: he had a wife and child to support, and no clear path to earning a living in politics, leaving him to once again return to practicing law, an occupation he detested.

He tried to immerse himself in Jefferson County Republican politics, and was named its chairman. "I'm a strong believer in the art of the possible," McConnell said in an April 18, 1973, story in the *Louisville Times*. "To be effective you have to superimpose over your idealism the realities of political life. . . . I have a very strong conviction that the best kind of change is gradual change. . . . You have to deal with what's possible and discourage those who advocate radical change."

But the Republican brand in Kentucky was hardly robust, and the burgeoning Watergate scandal in Washington wasn't helping. McConnell called the behavior "totally repugnant" and said Nixon should "rid the administration and the party of the stench of Watergate by cleaning house from top to bottom." He did not, notably, call on Nixon himself to resign. But he realized that Republicans in general and Nixon in particular were badly damaged, and he decided to step down as county chairman to try to avoid any taint.

Instead, McConnell tried to cloak himself with the mantle of reformer on an unlikely issue: campaign finance.

The *Courier-Journal* published an op-ed by McConnell on December 10, 1973, in which he argued that underfinanced candidates—like McConnell—couldn't compete and were priced out of the market, leaving voters to choose only among the wealthy or well-funded, regardless of their ideas or qualifications. "Many qualified and ethical persons . . . will not subject themself to questionable, downright illicit practices that may accompany the current electoral process."

He advocated strict limits on campaign contributions—as low as $300 for some races—and full disclosure of all political donors. He also supported a trust fund for contributions to be "maintained and operated by the city controller" that candidates might use, and he backed a full and transparent accounting of campaign spending. To make the strictures stick, he promoted an "Enforcement Commission" made up of civic leaders, along with a "Special Investigative Force" to ferret out "both honest mistakes and intentional violations." Perhaps most audacious was his call for a limit on overall spending.

Any ordinance that "maintains the private contribution system to finance public elections," he said, "is but a Band-Aid on a cancer. . . . Clearly public financing at least for presidential elections is an idea whose time has come."

McConnell later told biographer John David Dyche that he had been "playing for headlines" with his proposals rather than speaking with conviction. Against the backdrop of Watergate, sounding like a reformer to get money out of politics showed McConnell being an opportunist. He knew well the premium that candidates placed on having money to fund a race.

In that period Democrats still dominated Kentucky politics, an allegiance based more on ancestry—a legacy of Civil War–era southern fealty—than on policy positions. McConnell wanted to change that, but under the cloud of the Watergate scandal, it was a decidedly uphill effort. Nevertheless, for the annual Lincoln Club Dinner, he lured a star-caliber guest in former Texas governor John Connally, a one-time Democrat turned Republican who many thought would make a strong presidential candidate.

In a thank-you letter dated March 13, 1974, McConnell told Connally that the crowd of 1,100 was the largest since Nixon had addressed the dinner in 1966. (The dinner still operated at a deficit of $960.80.) He went further, casting himself as an old hand in politics, even though he was in his early thirties. "Having been in politics as long as I have, I am generally reluctant to make early commitments, but in your case if you decide to run for President please let me know as I fully intend to be on your side." Other party leaders, he noted, were leaning to Ronald Reagan before the dinner. "The leadership as well as the rank and file were extremely impressed by your speaking ability, your obvious intelligence and your political sagacity."

The next day, Sherrill weighed in with her own letter to Connally's wife, Nellie: "Everyone was wowed by the governor's speech. Mitch was high as a kite all week—a rarity in itself. . . . Your husband's remarks provided new ammunition with which to defend the party, the Administration, and the nation itself." She continued, expressing sentiments that contrast sharply with her later feminist work. "But beyond that I was delighted to make the acquaintance of such an exceptional political wife. It is a calling which appeals to very few women—and for good reason. Public life demands more sacrifices of your husband's time and attention the higher he rises. . . . Most women do not have the generosity, candor and warmth you displayed here. I found you an inspiration."

Among some Republicans in Kentucky, McConnell's ambitions were a source of friction. Cook supporters accused McConnell of somehow trying to keep Cook off the ballot in the 1974 campaign because he wanted to run himself. "Some of his cronies always thought I was too ambitious or something," McConnell said. "They concluded that I had something to do with his screwing up his filing papers. I remember a couple of his buddies trashing the hell out of me."

Part of the problem was a column in the *Courier-Journal* speculating about who might be next if Cook did not run. It mentioned McConnell's name. Not even McConnell took that seriously. "It would have been absurd for me to run," he said.

So it was back to his law practice, and more self-doubt and reflection. His firm had several labor-related clients and a partner sent him to monitor a union election near Shreveport, Louisiana. "So there I am, miserable as hell practicing law, in a hospital monitoring a union election in Shreveport, Louisiana, and I said to myself, 'This is not going to

work.'" After tossing and turning all night, he got up at 4:30 a.m., having decided once and for all that he simply couldn't go on doing legal
work. He had his sights on an office that would be open in about three
years, county judge executive in Jefferson County, the same position
that had propelled Cook to the Senate. It was a bold, and likely unat-
tainable plan, but he was taking a long view.

At 9 a.m. he called a friend, Vince Rakestraw, who headed the Justice Department's Office of Legislative Affairs in the Ford administration, looking for work. For validation, he noted that he had the backing
of the deputy attorney general, Laurence Silberman, whose sister, Jan,
was a college friend. "I've got to get out of here," McConnell recalled
telling him. "I said, 'Vince, got any jobs?' Vince said, 'Actually I do.'"

McConnell flew from Louisiana to Washington. "I thought this
was my ticket out," he told me. "This is right after Nixon has resigned, so Ford is president now. That's a sensitive issue, because at
whatever point I ran for office I sure didn't want to have the extra baggage of having worked for Richard Nixon. So Ford is president. That
problem is solved."

He was offered the job of deputy assistant attorney general for legislative affairs, and soon set off for Washington, leaving Sherrill and
their daughter, Eleanor, back in Louisville, where he commuted on
weekends. Because of the federal Hatch Act, which is designed to prevent government officials from being directly involved in politics, Mc-
Connell was limited in what he could do to advance his own efforts to
run for office. "It was not a terribly productive period," he said. But "I
could make a house payment."

Shortly after McConnell arrived, President Ford named Edward
Levi, the president of the University of Chicago and former dean of its
law school, to replace William Saxbe as attorney general. Saxbe went
on to an ambassadorial appointment and took McConnell's patron,
Rakestraw, with him. McConnell was self-aware enough to know
that he wasn't particularly qualified for the job he held, but Levi in-
dulged him.

"Levi was very tolerant of my hanging on even though it was pretty clear I didn't have the swat to get the job. But I got to go to the staff meetings," McConnell said. That staff included budding conservative legal luminaries Robert Bork, Antonin Scalia, and Laurence Silberman. "I had never been in the presence of so much brilliance and so much humor in my entire life. I never opened my mouth, for fear of saying something stupid. Talk about an intimidating bunch."

He stayed in the job for fifteen months, always with one eye plotting his return to run for county judge executive. "I finally just made a decision that I am going home at the end of '75 and I'm going to spend two years running for county judge and I've got to figure out how to put bread on the table."

He favored Ford over Reagan for the Republican presidential nomination in 1976, which helped inform the perception that McConnell was a moderate, a portrait he told me later had been overdrawn.

He went home with a loose arrangement in his law firm and—with Barnett's connections—managed to persuade a couple of local companies to put him on boards of directors, with modest fees and little work, meaning he had even less concern about billable hours. But there were some internal disputes, so he went off on his own to practice. It was not a thriving picture.

What he lacked in resources he made up in what he called a "seething" ambition, and he set about raising the money he needed to take on an incumbent, always a difficult proposition. He had no real mentor or political network, only the lessons he had drawn from previous campaigns, both winning and losing ones.

"The stresses were enormous, but fear of failure will drive you sometimes, too," McConnell said. "During that whole ten years I said to myself I will get an opportunity at some point and I am going to get myself in a position where I could spend almost full-time on it."

He worked the first six months of his campaign doing everything he could to build a potential pool of donors, going to lunches often three times a week where he would do his best to make the case that he could beat the incumbent county judge, Todd Hollenbach, a Democrat. As more and more money started coming in, he was careful to keep his efforts quiet so Hollenbach would not know how well he was doing.

He made the announcement of his candidacy for county judge executive in his home alongside Sherrill and their two older daughters, Eleanor, age four, and Claire, one, with a fire roaring in the fireplace behind them, a classic political appeal of the era: the upstanding family man.

Sherrill, he said, was totally supportive of his campaign, putting in long hours herself. His parents were skeptical, but backed him unconditionally. "What I had chosen was a highly-likely-to-fail path and I think they were always a little bit astonished that I was such a risk-taker given the fact that's not how they looked at life," McConnell told me. "Honestly, I think both were probably surprised I succeeded."

Day-to-day campaigning was another matter. He suffered frustrations, hosting neighborhood coffees only to have no one show up. He felt shooting pains in his stomach from stress when he went to Catholic picnics on Saturdays and African American churches on Sundays. He staked out a position on the median of Dixie Highway and shook hands through car windows at stoplights. He went to the GE Appliance Park factories to hand out flyers as the morning and evening shifts arrived; then he'd stick around to pick up the ones that workers had quickly discarded. It took him a week to cover the sprawling complex.

Early on, he didn't have a finance chairman, choosing to talk to donors himself, a process that he took to quite easily. He often did so over lunch at the Pendennis Club in Louisville, a fusty gathering spot for the city's elite that at the time excluded Blacks, women, and Jews from membership.

He leaned on his old friends Dave Huber and Joe Schiff to run the campaign, but McConnell was always his own chief strategist. He knew that he needed to raise an enormous amount of money if he were to have any chance of winning. Another friend, John Heyburn, whom McConnell would later help become a federal judge, introduced him to a young woman who could work on the campaign and open doors to raise money. Her name was Meme Sweets.

Sweets, who had recently attended Swarthmore, was smart, energetic, and willing to work the long hours a campaign required. She also brought something more: She was the great granddaughter of the founder of Brown-Forman, the famous Louisville distillery often credited with being the first to sell whiskey in a sealed glass bottle. Hers was an old-money family with a lot of connections, which she readily used to make introductions for McConnell. "It was natural for me to introduce him to my family," Sweets said, and to open doors for him to meet "people who could make a financial difference."

With McConnell's relentless focus augmented by Sweets's connections, the fundraising flourished. He brought in enough money to hire political consultants from New York and spend freely on television ads, most of them negative. Sweets said McConnell was also a teacher and mentor, showing her how to build a power base and develop her political skills. She said he saw in her "gifts she never" thought she had, including the ability to connect with people, and connect those people to a cause. "And that was very empowering for me," she said. "I was a cog in the wheel, and Mitch always made me feel important, not important for female reasons, important for professional reasons. And he made me feel like I could do things."

As a campaigner, though, McConnell did not talk about the well-heeled and connected. He began his campaign aligned with working-class Democrats, saying he was one of them. "We came up the hard way, the right way," he said. There was some truth in his assertion. He listed his assets at $96,724 and liabilities at $32,358. The previous year, he and Sherrill had only earned a combined $30,798.

"I really felt like I was rolling the dice. This was my one opportunity to finally get elected to something I wanted to get elected to." He chose the office carefully, trying to craft an eventual path to the U.S.

Senate like Cook had done. "It took a helluva lot of discipline to keep going when things looked bleak as hell," he said. "I thought it was highly likely that I was going to lose." But like Lyndon Johnson before him, McConnell said, "I wanted to be able to say to myself, 'You didn't fail to do anything you could to try to put this in the win column.'"

By August 1977, he had cut Hollenbach's lead by half, but still trailed by twenty points. His ads almost always attacked his opponent. One featured him walking in Washington with John Sherman Cooper, one of the few Kentucky political figures whose endorsement was actually valuable. Cooper said of Hollenbach, "Two terms for county judge is enough."

Todd Hollenbach, thirty-seven, was a boy wonder seeking a third term. Though he knew the odds were long, McConnell had a clear theory of the case for a victory. "The way you beat an incumbent is people have to decide they want to fire the incumbent." He compiled a list of what he thought were Hollenbach's many shortcomings and made sure voters knew them all: "What you are talking about here is a race between Mitch McConnell and Todd Hollenbach—two personalities, both of whom by election day will be well known quantities."

He also made sure that his candidacy was not seen as a threat to the Democratic establishment in Louisville. Abramson said that, at the time, he and many others saw McConnell as pro-woman, pro-consumer, and pro-abortion rights. "I know that he was, and I know people who know he was," said Keith Runyon, a former editorial writer at the *Courier-Journal*. "It was a critical issue for the newspaper back in the late seventies. We were a very pro-choice newspaper and we got the message from Mitch, and we didn't tape interviews in those days, but I think anyone who was in that meeting with him in the fall of '77 would agree that he gave us every reason to believe he was pro-choice." McConnell denies that he supported abortion rights and told me no one has offered concrete proof otherwise.

McConnell began to draw support from unlikely places for Republicans. The union representing county police endorsed him, as did the tobacco workers, who, notably, endorsed no candidates in other races. Hollenbach tried to argue that the police should not be involved in politics. McConnell shot back that Hollenbach was merely angry that the police had not endorsed him. The Greater Louisville Central Labor Council endorsed McConnell as well, which the *Courier-Journal* said had to be a "stunning revelation" for Hollenbach.

Years after the campaign, McConnell conceded that, on one issue, collective bargaining for public employees, he had been utterly disingenuous. He campaigned on a state law that he knew had no chance of passing. "It was one of the few things I've done in my political career I'm kind of ashamed of. It was an open pandering for labor support." It worked.

He also tried to exploit the fact that Hollenbach was divorced and, as the *Courier-Journal* noted, "isn't inclined to let the burdens of public office keep him from having a few drinks with his friends at night spots," while McConnell was married with two young daughters.

The campaign was tough. Some polling had McConnell trailing badly, and he continued to believe that the only way to close that gap was by hammering Hollenbach mercilessly. He was also creating what he called the "perception of credibility."

"The reality is that he's blowing me away," McConnell said. Even so, Hollenbach was nervous as he saw his lead slipping away and challenged McConnell to a debate; McConnell readily agreed and put his moot court skills on display, besting his opponent with a strong command of facts. He shaped perception in another way, by brazenly announcing a transition team two months before the election, when his victory was in no way assured.

Both candidates sought the coveted endorsement of the *Courier-Journal*, which in that time was one of the state's most powerful cultural forces. Its prize-winning investigative stories changed industries and rooted out government corruption. Its columnists held rarified civic status. An endorsement by its editorial page could be a ticket to an election victory.

McConnell worked on the publisher, Barry Bingham Jr., and editorial board members like Runyon, a tall scholarly journalist who was also a University of Louisville alum. He persuaded them that he was a reform-minded moderate Republican who would bring integrity to the office.

The newspaper's endorsement editorial noted the obvious aspiration of both McConnell and Hollenbach, describing them as "two unmistakably ambitious young men" who "are battling for what has become the community's most important political office: county judge. . . . Both, one suspects, will eventually seek higher, statewide office." McConnell, the paper said, was easily the most politically skilled challenger Hollenbach had faced. It went on to say that McConnell had offered voters a "plausible" and "more attractive" alternative than Hollenbach. He had both the "intelligence" and "commitment" to respond to community needs. The editorial also said it hoped that McConnell could work effectively in bipartisan cooperation with Democrats who controlled other county and city offices. "We strongly recommend that Mitch McConnell be given a chance to show what he can do as county judge."

As McConnell's career progressed, and his conservatism became more apparent, Bingham would tell Runyon and others that the endorsement was the paper's worst mistake during his tenure as publisher.

In the local press, McConnell was described as the "peripatetic" candidate, and he conceded he did not even know the definition of the word. His campaign adopted it as its call to action and the headquarters had a large banner across the wall: "Peripatetic." One ad in particular captured the imagination of voters, especially those working-class men McConnell worked so hard to court. It featured a farmer mucking out a horse's stall, claiming that Hollenbach had raised taxes while serving as county judge, then lied about it. "When Judge Hollenbach says he's cut my taxes four times he doesn't give me credit for as much sense as ol' Nell here. . . . Maybe Hollenbach ought to have my job, because in my job I deal with that sort of stuff every day."

The farmer then threw a shovel of manure directly at the camera. McConnell approved buying time during the 1977 World Series for the ad. The next morning, McConnell's campaign received a call from former senator Thruston Morton, a Republican, who was livid about the tenor of the ad. "Tell Mitch to get that goddamn ad off the air," McConnell recalled him saying. "He's going to blow the campaign."

But McConnell wanted to see how the ad was playing among working-class voters and dispatched Schiff to a bar to find out. The patrons loved it. After it started to air, his campaign saw the numbers move their way. McConnell later told Dyche, "If you can make 'em laugh at the other guy, he's gone."

McConnell worked nights, weekends, twelve to fourteen hours a day, to try to persuade voters to fire Hollenbach. On election night, November 8, 1977, he prevailed, finally, and won his first public office. The young man in a hurry had caught up. He found the victory thrilling, in no small part because the prospects of losing were so frightening. "Most people don't risk everything," he said.

"I found out pretty early on that setbacks, which are different from failures, are usually not fatal unless you allow them to defeat yourself," McConnell said. "I had plenty of setbacks along the way, particularly in the lost decade, one setback after another, but by not giving up and keeping on pushing, I discovered you can work your way through these things." Among the first to call to congratulate him: Senator Bob Dole of Kansas. National Republicans were taking at least modest interest.

The next morning, on the *Courier-Journal*'s front page, a large photo showed McConnell and Sherrill beaming. Finally, the plan was working. There would be no more decades lost.

NINE

"ROLE PLAYING"

The moment he was sworn in as county judge executive, January 2, 1978, 12:01 a.m., McConnell fixed his gaze on his real goal: the United States Senate. From a travel schedule that took him around the state, often with little purpose beyond raising his profile, to the Brooks Brothers oxfords that he bought to emulate Senator John Sherman Cooper, McConnell had already started his next campaign.

In his inaugural address, he pledged to be a pragmatist who would put partisanship aside. "I see my role in this effort as a builder of bridges spanning the gaps which have in the past impeded our progress and threatened the partnership that is so vital to our growth and development." He vowed to be an environmentalist, warning of highways choked with cars and exhaust "polluting our fragile environment." He said he would work to reduce urban sprawl that "makes us prisoners of our automobiles" and to make public transportation more appealing. Polluters would be punished. He pledged to restore "the county's beauty through an emphasis on planting and nurturing trees."

He would be a champion for the inner city. "We desert the central city in a leapfrog manner, leaving decay in our wake." He savored the moment and the receptions that followed. There was a sense of his ascent. "I see a rising star over Kentucky," Reverend Isaac Shoulders, a well known Black pastor, said of McConnell at the time.

He again gave many the impression that he was a moderate Republican. Sweets, for one, was struck by his progressive views. "It felt like the battle of good and evil. He cared a lot about the libraries, arts, and preservation."

Years later, McConnell told me that he was merely adapting to the situation. As the only Republican elected to a top county post, he said, he had to at least give the appearance of accommodation and moderation. He did not want to concede that he had evolved and changed.

"There were plenty of ways, if you were in local government, to not get yourself labeled in a way that made it impossible to win," he said. "As I look back on those years, all these stupid comments about how I was a liberal who reinvented myself. This is county government. I was surrounded by Democrats. I am not going to make it even harder to have a working relationship."

Yet, in an oral history interview in 1997, McConnell framed it much differently. "In fact, I think it would be correct to categorize me prior to that time as certainly a moderate Republican. I was somebody whose sympathies were with Gerald Ford in the race against Ronald Reagan."

The differing postures show how, later in his career, when moderates were all but extinct in the Republican Party, McConnell did not want to allow even the suggestion that he was once a moderate to take hold.

Democrats made it hard on him anyway; when he first took office, they even blocked him from hiring his own staff. Though the title county judge executive sounds lofty, the powers were circumscribed. He was not a judge, rather he was the head of the county government, somewhat like a mayor but with less responsibility. To overcome the Democratic blockade, he had to go to court to even obtain the authority to unilaterally hire or fire anyone.

He found a way around it because he was empowered to give or take away duties of a job. Two Democrats were running departments and McConnell wanted to dismiss them because, he said, they were not doing their jobs. So he took away their responsibilities and put them in a different office and "they had nothing to do. Amazing enough, they decided to leave," he said.

He also used his authority to take care of friends. In his first term he named Chase Forrester, who had been his fraternity brother at the University of Louisville, to run the Community Development Agency. The two men shared something else: Forrester had a crippling case of polio that left him essentially paralyzed from the shoulders down. "Every time I saw him, I thought, 'There, before the grace of God, goes me,'" McConnell said.

He packed his top staff with loyalists. Schiff was deputy county judge, and Huber was his chief of staff. He had a small brain trust of up to half a dozen trusted aides, at times including Sweets.

He also appointed Sweets to be his first press secretary. She initially told him she was not qualified for the job, having no experience dealing with the media or developing communications strategy. McConnell assured her she was up to it, saying he would help her learn what she didn't know. "He looked at me and he said, 'I know you can do it. I've watched you,'" she said. "And he said, 'You do not shrink back from conflict.'

"When you're Mitch's fundraiser and when you're his press secretary, there are pretty much no two people who are more important," she said. "I was his fundraiser and then I was his press secretary." Sweets was an early example of McConnell appointing women to positions of power and authority.

Often brittle about criticism, like many polio survivors, McConnell was highly sensitive about news coverage of him. At times he flashed a fiery temper, particularly if he didn't like a story in the *Courier-Journal*. "He could get really mad about a news article and he would come out and throw the newspaper on the desk and say, 'You're

going to call this reporter and you're going to tell them,'" Sweets recalled. With time, he began to realize there was no way to avoid criticism in public office. "I guess I began to figure out how to take a
punch," he said in his Senate office. "That's certainly been helpful the
last eighteen years."

He told Sweets he wanted to have a press conference on a different subject every week, all part of his strategy to keep his name in the
public eye. She watched as he built his power base, always coming
back from a lunch or meeting with the business card of a potential
supporter.

One of McConnell's first challenges was how to handle a discrimination lawsuit brought by Black applicants to the county police over
the department's hiring practices. "I looked at the record and we were
guilty," McConnell said. They entered into a plea agreement. The police were angered and turned from supporters to loud and angry critics.

At the same time, despite his later claims that he was never an environmentalist, he also cites his use of federal grant money to purchase
parkland in the county as one of his top achievements. "If you are surrounded by a bunch of liberals who would like to see you fail, I was
hoping to cover issues anybody in urban government would be interested in." That forest now includes the Mitch McConnell Loop Trail.

Early reviews of his tenure were positive. Mike Brown wrote in the
Courier-Journal that "even Democrats agree privately that McConnell
in his first year has been smart and energetic and certainly far more
capable than his adversaries in capturing public opinion."

To try to get some political balance on the Fiscal Court, which was
dominated by Democrats—though one of them, Sylvia Watson, often
voted with him—McConnell embraced the campaign of Carl Brown,
a graduate of Vanderbilt Law School, a champion debater, and a man
whose ambition and working-class Louisville background McConnell
could appreciate.

Brown won his race, but soon started behaving erratically, and
McConnell became a target of his ire. Suffering at the time from an

undiagnosed mental illness, Brown even began to threaten McConnell physically, to the point that McConnell had to have police stationed outside his home. At Fiscal Court meetings, where the two would sit within a few feet of each other, McConnell had the front row packed with police officers to deter Brown, who was also a black belt in judo.

Brown eventually was placed under court-ordered psychiatric care at the University of Louisville Hospital in 1983. He was only thirty-one. Police said Brown had threatened McConnell's life and at one point called him "an evil man."

"It's the only experience I ever had in my entire public career where I actually knew somebody who was after me," McConnell said. "And every time we had an election we would get additional security because the feeling was that would have been a perfect time for him to come after me." McConnell realized that Brown had a mental illness and said, "I didn't want to seem insensitive to him. On the other hand, he was threatening to kill me."

Other than the drama around Brown, most of McConnell's duties as county judge were subordinate to his larger objective, which was to make voters see him as a potential senator. He had an opportunity to develop at least rudimentary foreign affairs credentials when he was chosen for the American Council of Young Political Leaders and toured Israel, Egypt, Saudi Arabia, and Sudan. His roommate was another young man with an eye on higher office, John Ashcroft, the Republican attorney general of Missouri, who would go on to serve as governor, senator, and attorney general of the United States.

On one highly sensitive and politically fraught issue—abortion—McConnell demonstrated an adroitness in the legislative process that foretold one of his signature skills in the Senate: stopping legislation. After the *Roe v. Wade* decision legalized abortion, its opponents presented a measure to the Fiscal Court that would have added significant local restrictions to abortion.

Jessica Loving, another U of L alum who had known McConnell

for a decade and had voted for him, was the executive director of the local chapter of the ACLU and strongly opposed the measure. After McConnell was elected county judge, she contacted Chuck Simpson, a well-regarded lawyer and longtime friend of McConnell whom McConnell eventually helped become a federal judge. She said Simpson told her the right-to-life proposal clearly ran counter to *Roe*. With Simpson's connection, they quickly got a meeting with McConnell. After reviewing the proposed legislation, McConnell agreed the legislation was at odds with *Roe*, and he said he would "absolutely" help them, according to Loving. "He was the best elected official that I worked with during that time period dealing with anti-abortion, anti-choice legislation," she said.

McConnell used a procedural technique to bottle up the proposed legislation in a committee, and it never came to the Fiscal Court for a vote. "Mitch was just brilliant in being able to deal with it without causing a big fuss," Loving told me. "He understood the legal and constitutional issues just brilliantly. And he understood that the legislation was unconstitutional."

McConnell did not want abortion in headlines that mentioned him. He wanted to make news that was politically positive. He was thinking of how he would seek reelection in 1981. But he was also thinking ahead to the election after that, a U.S. Senate race in 1984, and he continued to try to raise his profile in the Republican Party. Dole had written him after his victory in 1977, and he was seeking the Republican presidential nomination in 1980.

He attended the Republican National Convention and was described by a local reporter as being "rather quiet and subdued." But there was a good reason. He knew that shortly after he would return to Louisville, he and Sherrill would announce they were getting divorced, and there would be a story in the *Courier-Journal*.

"We had essentially negotiated this divorce between the two of us with counsel, and really the only thing we did publicly by mutual agreement was to issue a statement, which I had written and she thought was appropriate, and that was all we gave to the press and said nothing else." The statement read:

"With regret, we jointly announce that by mutual agreement our marriage of twelve years has ended. Neither of our careers was in any way a factor in our decision. We have wrestled with some fundamental differences for a long time, but our parting is amicable. Our children will be cared for in joint custody. A settlement has already been agreed to and signed by both of us."

The *Courier-Journal* ran a short story on page three (August 9, 1980), noting that McConnell was living with his parents. "The petition states that the McConnells' marriage is 'irretrievably broken,' the standard claim under Kentucky's no fault divorce law."

Sherrill made no public comment.

One evening, relatively soon after the divorce, Sweets and her husband, Keith Runyon, invited McConnell to their home for dinner. Runyon recalls vividly one thing McConnell told the couple. "Over dinner he said, you know, Keith and Meme, I've got to do like John Sherman Cooper," Runyon told me. "I've got to find myself a rich wife." After divorcing his first wife, Cooper married Lorraine Rowan Shevlin, a wealthy Washington socialite who spoke four languages and was at ease in any circle of power.

After Reagan won the Republican Party's nomination, McConnell was fully supportive, despite the fact that George H. W. Bush, seen at the time as among the more moderate Republicans in the race, had been his preferred candidate. Reagan, McConnell said, was "probably my fourth choice in those days." During a campaign stop in Louisville, McConnell draped a garland of roses around Reagan's neck, an homage to the folkways of the Kentucky Derby. The photo was so memorable it was included in *Life* magazine's annual collection of the year's best photos, though McConnell was not mentioned in the caption.

McConnell also had developed a partnership of sorts with Democrat Harvey Sloane, who had been elected mayor of Louisville a few years before McConnell won his first race. Sloane, an Ivy League–educated doctor, was many things that McConnell was not. McConnell feared that Sloane would challenge him for county judge in 1981, and he tried to persuade him to not enter the race. Privately, he said, he was almost certain Sloane would have beaten him, which would have seriously diminished his chances of running for the Senate. One morning, over breakfast at Sloane's home, McConnell made the case that they both had statewide political aspirations and "if we fight each other, we won't make it." Sloane did not realize it, but McConnell was bluffing. He was deeply relieved when Sloane said he would run for another term as mayor.

"He was a really reasonable guy to work with," Sloane said. "He was relatively constructive. But also he was always looking for that '84 race," and how to win it. "If you've got money he's going to engage you. If you are going to advance his power, he will be with you. But he's not a guy who's warm." Sloane is also among many in Louisville who said of McConnell at the time, "He was pro choice and pro labor," but also could not deliver proof.

While he was trying to maintain his footing politically, on the personal front he was struggling, especially financially. The county judge's salary was paltry and now he had to also pay additional expenses related to the divorce. So he gave paid lectures at U of L. The donors who funded the talks were kept private. McConnell also began serving on corporate boards for a fee, something public officials today in most cases can not do.

McConnell's plan was to win reelection by such a wide margin that he would not face much of a challenge in the Republican Senate primary in 1984. He did things to cultivate his reputation, like cooperating with a piece in the *Courier-Journal*'s Sunday magazine that carried the headline "A Mellowed Fellow?" "Once known as 'Mean Mitch McConnell,' the Jefferson County judge is trying to polish up his image. . . . And he's getting a brighter outlook on his public and private lives."

The cover photo shows him with his hand steadying his daughter

Eleanor on a horse. Another shows him with his arm around Claudia
Starr, a former jockey, smiling with their eyes locked on each other. The
article described Starr as having "flawless complexion, tawny hair and
eyes the color of $18 sherry." McConnell said Starr made him happy.

"For a long time, Louisville and Jefferson County's highest ranking Republican office-holder, Mitch McConnell, gave the impression
of being a man old for his years and dignified beyond his decades," the
story said. "The county judge executive didn't smile. In fact, to some
people he looked the way Alice Roosevelt Longworth described Calvin
Coolidge: 'As if he had been weaned on a pickle.'"

The article also highlighted McConnell's pattern of hiring women
and reinforced the idea that he did not see himself as a Reagan conservative. "Women in policy-making positions are highly visible in
his administration. Six women are in top level jobs—a fact, he said,
that is overlooked by many of those who call him a conservative. He
rejects the label." The article went on to say that as Reagan was pushing for cuts in welfare, "McConnell seems eager to put some distance
between himself and certain aspects of the Reagan Administration."

He spent countless hours raising money, hoping that he could
overwhelm his opponent. But he also tapped two friends at the time,
John Heyburn, the man who brought Meme Sweets into the campaign,
and John Yarmuth, whom he had worked with on Cook's campaign.
The idea was to run as a candidate slate to give a sense of Republican
strength. There was another motive: both Heyburn and Yarmuth had
connections to wealthy donors that McConnell also hoped to tap.

"We finally figured out the reason Mitch wanted us on there was
basically so we could raise money that went into the joint campaign
because we were both from relatively affluent families," Yarmuth said.

"All the money we raised went into the central campaign. Mitch
made all the spending decisions, and he made all the tactical decisions.
So we would always be sent out to the International Harvester plant at
five in the morning for a shift change and we would do this day after
day after day, and Mitch was never there. It was always just the two of

us. Plus, at plants like that, two-thirds [of the workers] were not from Jefferson County. The last week, we went to a big office building in suburban Louisville in a Republican area, and we were there at eight thirty, and everybody who came by was interested in talking with us. Why haven't we been here the whole time? Because Mitch wanted to get us out of the way."

The ticket proved to be a mistake. There was no appetite for a Republican slate in what was still largely a Democratic area. Heyburn and Yarmuth lost. McConnell won narrowly over the Democrat, Jim "Pop" Malone, a nice man but a weak candidate, and McConnell's reputation as a political force was badly diminished.

"It was the worst race ever," McConnell said. "I was lucky to survive." His victory was so slender and the race so poorly run that Senators Wendell Ford and Dee Huddleston, both Democrats, said his career was probably over. "They were probably right," McConnell said. "That's how bad I came out of the '81 reelection. About the only thing you could say about it is I survived." Others in Kentucky recalled that Ford also said that Democrats might rue the day that they hadn't defeated McConnell at this point in his career.

Looking back, McConnell saw the campaign as a "classic example of letting your government goals get in the way of your political goals. And in the end I didn't achieve any of my government goals because none of the people I was trying to help won."

Sloane, on the other hand, won reelection for mayor in a landslide. The Democrat appeared to have an abundant political future.

Once reelected, McConnell focused almost exclusively on the Senate race three years away. His duties were few—the Fiscal Court only met once every two weeks—and Huber, his loyal aide and friend, could call him if he had to make a decision. McConnell spent most of his time traveling the state, shaking hands, and spoiling for the opportunity he had craved since he was a teenager.

He knew he had to win the Republican primary in 1984, so he established a political committee in 1982 and tried to rack up a list of endorsements to scare off potential challengers. "I never start late," McConnell said.

He had been studying the Kentucky electorate for more than a decade, and one thing he knew with certainty: Republican voters were almost universally opposed to gun control measures. So when his friend on the Fiscal Court, Sylvia Watson, proposed a form of a waiting period, McConnell voted against it. The vote prompted the political cartoonist Hugh Haynie to draw a blistering condemnation of McConnell. McConnell has that drawing framed on a wall in his office in Washington, part of a collection of criticism that he likes to showcase. McConnell was right about the politics, though, and the voters rewarded him.

He spent far more time on a less contentious issue. McConnell was quick to embrace the cause of missing and exploited children. He created a fingerprinting program and held hearings around the state, another dual-purpose use of his office to advance a worthy cause and his political future. The *Courier-Journal* noted, "McConnell is obviously doing this in part because of his impending statewide election." McConnell readily admits the political motivation: "It was clear I was doing that." He tried to visit every county in the state.

He named a chairman for every county fingerprinting effort. It generated dozens of positive newspaper articles around the state, and McConnell's photo often accompanied the stories, the kind of earned media any politician craves. He named himself chairman of the Kentucky Task Force of Missing and Exploited Children. He invited John Walsh, whose son, Adam, had been abducted and killed, to Kentucky. Walsh was emerging as a national figure on the issue—this was several years before he created and hosted *America's Most Wanted*—and he posed for pictures with McConnell and local chairmen, which McConnell's staff sent to weekly newspapers.

Walsh eventually agreed to do an ad for McConnell's Senate campaign.

As he eyed his potential Republican rivals for the nomination,

McConnell focused on Jim Bunning, a Hall of Fame pitcher who wanted to run for public office. McConnell essentially forced Bunning into a pledge to not run for the Senate; in return, McConnell would support him in his run for governor. To be certain, McConnell made sure the pledge was in writing, and when Bunning tried to renege, McConnell was ready to remind him. Bunning eventually honored the deal.

Democrats knew McConnell was the strongest Republican candidate, though they thought he was eminently beatable. Early on, they quoted Republicans praising the incumbent senator, Dee Huddleston, the man who had defeated Marlow Cook. Huddleston was seen as a senator of moderate bearing, likable and nonthreatening.

Even the Senate majority leader, Republican Howard Baker of Tennessee, was among those seeming to back Huddleston, saying, "If I were going to pick 10 senators who contribute the most or provide a stabilizing influence in the Senate, I'd put Dee in that category." McConnell was furious, and he wrote to Baker to complain about the "problems" Baker's remarks were causing among McConnell's supporters. "Our problem is: how do we blunt this effort?"

He had his staff compose a letter to the editor for Baker to sign that would be sent to newspapers throughout Kentucky. The episode with Baker was one of many instances in which national Republicans seemed to discount McConnell's chances. The Reagan White House and the National Republican Senatorial Committee also questioned how much financial aid to pump into McConnell's long-shot effort initially.

McConnell, who was not among Reagan's most enthusiastic supporters, never forgot that slight. He also was not deterred. He had raised money, worked to assemble a staff, and set about trying to find reasons that voters should fire Huddleston. McConnell was also helped by a brief primary challenge to Huddleston from John Y. Brown, which suggested a sense of vulnerability.

But as Mitch McConnell embarked on his decades-long plan to run for the Senate, there was near universal agreement on one thing: he had no chance.

TEN

"WIN OR DIE TRYING"

For his long-planned Senate campaign, McConnell again surrounded himself with familiar faces, like his friend Joe Schiff, to lead his campaign team, but its beating heart was a woman named Janet Mullins. Taut and tough, Mullins had been working a boring job in the state capital of Frankfort, but before that, she'd held a much more high-profile and powerful job in Washington as the chief of staff to Republican senator Bob Packwood of Oregon.

Mullins, a single mother who could swear like a drill sergeant and hold her own in any political argument, had returned to Kentucky to give her daughter more stability. She came from a line of Catholic Democrats who revered John F. Kennedy and the pope. Her father drove a beer truck and her mother did not work outside the home. Theirs was not a family where politics was discussed at the dinner table, but Mullins became interested in it at a young age. One of her early experiences was going door-to-door for the Democrat, Sloane, in his campaign for mayor. In college, she majored in political science, then she went to Washington to earn a master's degree at American University.

She wanted to work on Capitol Hill, so she submitted her name to the Senate Placement Office and was offered a secretarial position on Packwood's legislative staff. Within three years, she was administrative assistant, a job that now is called chief of staff—a rare achievement for a woman at the time.

She had spurned the advances of Packwood, who was known to be predatory toward women, earned his respect, and spent a lot of time protecting other young women on the staff. She quit a couple of times along the way. "I didn't have any problem telling people to fuck off," she said.

She loved the excitement on Capitol Hill, though felt a strong pull to come back home. She worked her connections to get a job in the Kentucky Commerce Cabinet, the state agency for job creation and investment. It was low-voltage work compared to what she had been accustomed to in Washington, and the culture seemed drawn from another time. "Everybody in the elevator was smoking, and I was like 'holy shit.'"

McConnell and Schiff came to Washington a couple times to pitch his potential race in 1984 to national Republicans, and Mullins knew McConnell was from Louisville. When his plans became more concrete, she agreed to meet him for dinner. He laid out the reasons he thought he had a chance at winning and offered her the chance to manage his campaign, something unheard of for a Kentucky Republican.

"He intuitively knew that women worked a lot harder to prove themselves," Mullins said. "He was woke before woke, I guess." She attributed McConnell's attitude toward women to his admiration for his mother's strength, both in persuading the doctors at Warm Springs to let her son get treatment and in living almost alone while McConnell struggled with polio.

Their discussion was almost exclusively about politics. McConnell struck Mullins as someone who was not ideological. "It was about pursuing his dream of national politics more than it was 'I am going to change the world.'" She agreed to join his campaign.

Mullins's daughter, Shannon, was concerned about her mother's new job bringing them back to Washington, but Mullins assured her she would not be returning to the capital because there was no way McConnell would win.

Because he had begun fundraising years earlier, McConnell had enough money to start a credible campaign, an amount sufficient to air his first ads the day after his announcement, followed by an expensive two-minute ad that featured his biography. (McConnell would later say he had wasted money because voters had yet to engage in the race.) Even so, his initial efforts were not enough to impress Indiana senator Richard Lugar, chairman of the Senate Republicans' campaign committee, or Mitch Daniels, the group's executive director. They thought time and money were better spent on protecting incumbents. The Reagan White House, likewise, was not particularly hopeful.

McConnell did not take the snub well, but he pressed on. He had Schiff and Mullins as a foundation for leadership on his campaign staff. They were his professionals. He also needed the kind of young, hungry staffer who would work long hours for little pay, never complain, and yet somehow be grateful.

He found one in Terry Carmack, who grew up on a farm in western Kentucky, twenty miles from Paducah. He worked at a gas station as a teenager, earning enough money to buy a white Pontiac Firebird and cover tuition at Murray State University. During his junior year in 1983, a high school friend at the college suggested he get to know Mitch McConnell, who was running for the Senate.

Carmack's response was a single word: "Who?"

He had long been interested in politics, and though his parents were both longtime Democrats, he wasn't particularly ideological. So he wrote McConnell a letter expressing a desire to work on the campaign. For McConnell, Carmack had obvious appeal. He was a Democrat from a part of the state where McConnell was not well known but would definitely need votes. After meeting McConnell, he was hired as an "advance man." Carmack dropped out of college and moved to Louisville.

Campaign officials gave him the "advance man binder," which provided instructions on how to handle the media, the crowds, and VIPs who attended campaign events. But in the campaign's early months, there were no media, crowds, or very important people to be found. Carmack ended up being reassigned as one of McConnell's drivers.

His friends thought he was crazy, that McConnell had no chance, in large part because Kentucky rarely elected Republicans. But Carmack did it, and as he later said, "it changed my life," starting what would become a forty-year association with McConnell.

He also had a driver's-side seat to how McConnell approached campaigns, an intense amalgam of preparation, focus, discipline, and tirelessness. The "Mellowed Fellow" of the *Courier-Journal* magazine piece was a well-concocted confection. McConnell radiated intensity. "From a twenty-one-year-old's perspective, he was kind of scary," Carmack said. "You could see this drive to win and you wanted to do everything just right."

Everything meant everything. At events, Carmack recalled, McConnell would ask how many people wanted a bumper sticker, then wryly say to the crowd that he wanted to make sure the sticker was put on the car, telling them that Carmack "is going to come around with his legal pad and take down a description of your car, so when you leave tonight, the bumper sticker will be on your car already." Carmack also came armed with Windex and paper towels to make sure the bumper sticker adhered to a clear rear window on the driver's side. Carmack had other instructions: how to hand out campaign literature, how to attach a paper clip to a business card for a note, and how to get from one town to another using only a paper map.

Each campaign stop initially was geared toward raising money. Carmack carried a shoe box filled with 3x5 cards bearing people's names, addresses, and donor history, all organized by county. Carmack would schedule as many meetings as they could jam into a day, with McConnell soliciting campaign contributions from doctors, lawyers, and local business owners. If a reporter showed up, Carmack had a press kit ready. After each meeting with a donor or a prospect, Carmack would hand McConnell a piece of paper so he could write a follow-up note in the moment, which they would send along with an envelope for a donation. Carmack made a copy of every letter back at the office so they could track success.

There was no deviation from the schedule, no stops for food or drinks or ice cream, not even bottled water. McConnell made little small talk, instead spending any quiet moments thinking ahead to the next day. To save money, they used a classic pay phone scam to call campaign headquarters from the field. Carmack would say he was calling collect for Jane Smith, then leave the pay phone number. The office had a WATS line, enabling it to make calls on the cheap, and they'd use it to dial them back. McConnell's campaign saved another dime.

It was slow going. In March, former Republican senator Marlow Cook, for whom McConnell had worked, came out and endorsed the Democratic incumbent, Walter Huddleston, the clearest indication of the enmity between the two men. Cook called Huddleston a "very good friend and extremely damn fine Senator." McConnell's rejoinder was printed in the *Courier-Journal:* "You have to understand, Marlow Cook is a lobbyist."

Huddleston anticipated a harshly negative campaign from his opponent, but vowed early on not to engage. "My intention is to run a very positive campaign," he told the *Lexington Herald-Leader.* "We are going to let him do whatever he has to do. And of course we know he is going to run a negative campaign . . . that's going to be a major part of his strategy."

Huddleston was right. To fund that effort, McConnell was in a constant, fevered pursuit of campaign money. He was able to persuade major Republican donors such as W. Clement Stone, the Chicago insurance executive, and Nelson Bunker Hunt, the Texas oil tycoon, to host a fundraiser for him at Hunt's Circle T Ranch near Dallas.

In the summer, according to his account in his memoir, *The Long Game,* McConnell thought he should make some positive ads to help introduce him to voters. He took that idea to Roger Ailes, a high-powered media consultant who was emerging as an important force in Republican politics.

"Sure we could do that," Ailes said. "I'll do positive ads that make you look nice so people like you. You'll lose but you could always run next time."

McConnell asked, "What do you suggest?"

"Do you want to look nice, or do you want to take out your opponent and win this thing?"

"I want to do what it takes," McConnell said. "I want to win this thing."

"Then leave the ads to me," Ailes said.

McConnell, fearing failure, asked Ailes if the campaign was already lost.

"No," Ailes said. "But I have to be honest, Mitch. I've never seen any candidate come from this far behind this late and win."

Rather than take this news as a defeat, he took it as a call to work even harder. The fact that no one, not even Carmack, thought that he would win, meant that he had to try to change the race. He got better as a campaigner, more at ease with crowds and strangers. Still, in July, the Huddleston campaign released a poll that found him leading McConnell, 67–23.

Near the end of summer, in early August, McConnell prepared for a quirky but vital Kentucky political event that dates to 1880 called Fancy Farm. It was held in the western part of Kentucky, a region known at the time as the "Gibraltar of Kentucky Democratic politics." Candidates used the gathering as an opportunity to demonstrate a show of strength in terms of supporters, to deliver stem-winder, highly partisan speeches, and try to create energy and momentum for the fall campaign ahead.

Huddleston attacked McConnell for lacking experience and for not being a native of Kentucky. The incumbent added that he would be the better protector of the tobacco program and price supports, deriding his opponent as an "urban freshman." The state's other senator, Wendell Ford, was far more harsh and personal, raising the issue of McConnell's divorce and saying senators needed a "strong family life" to be effective.

McConnell spent the night before at a Holiday Inn. He was not satisfied with the speech his campaign staff had written for him and instructed Carmack to get him a stack of plain white envelopes. He wrote the speech himself in his hotel room.

As Carmack drove him to the event, they passed a handful of campaign signs that said "Switch to Mitch," but Democrats had an overwhelming advantage in numbers. They took one side of the stage at Fancy Farm, and it was packed with elected officials. McConnell sat with only a couple of county chairmen on the Republican side. The image embodied what everyone saw as a mismatch in the Senate race: a comparatively unknown politician from Louisville trying to defeat an incumbent Democratic senator. McConnell thought his own speech went well, but the press coverage of the event focused on something entirely different, Ford's argument with a heckler, and the gathering was another lost opportunity for McConnell.

Huddleston was an eminently likable sort, not flashy, but a go-down-easy Kentucky politician, and a tough guy to make voters hate. In August of 1983, he ran a poll that showed him fifty-two points ahead of McConnell, and McConnell did not dispute the findings. As a result, Huddleston did not take McConnell's challenge as much of a threat. Despite his tireless efforts, McConnell had done little to undermine voter confidence in his opponent.

He was certain that he and his staff weren't working hard enough on the problem. "Mitch would constantly say, 'Where's the silver bullet?'" Mullins recalled. How could he pierce the incumbent's armor? Ailes kept emphasizing that nothing the campaign had unearthed so far would stick in an attack against Huddleston. So McConnell told Mullins there must be something in Huddleston's record they were missing.

Mullins buried herself in Huddleston's Senate record, looking at financial disclosure statements, campaign finance records, votes, speeches, and newspaper articles.

"It was really late at night, and I had a 'holy shit' moment," she remembered. "I realized Huddleston prepared his own disclosure statements, which included honoraria that he made from paid speeches." Then she compared those dates with important Senate votes and found that he had missed votes two dozen times while making money. Normally politicians would cover their tracks in such cases; it was easy enough to record an honorarium payment late. Huddleston had recorded the honoraria on the day he made the speeches, and that act of honesty would cost him dearly.

She called McConnell at 3 a.m. "Holy shit, this is it," she said. "I called him and said, 'You're never going to believe it.'" They quickly convened a meeting of top staff. Ailes, a rotund man fond of food and drink, puffed on a pipe and said, "I see dogs. I see hound dogs."

Ailes could envision how the ad would unfold: a tracker, with wild eyes and a weathered face, would send a pack of bloodhounds in a search for the absent senator. He arranged for the first commercial to start on the lawn of the Capitol, with the bloodhounds ready to chase. They weren't supposed to be there, and Ailes told the crew to try to get it in one take because otherwise the Capitol Police might catch and arrest them.

In one of the initial ads, McConnell said of Huddleston, "He's told the people of Kentucky the best reason to reelect him is that he's been there twelve years. I say, that's the best reason to bring him home."

Mullins also leaked campaign research to Mike Brown of the *Courier-Journal*. "Enclosed please find information on Huddleston's voting and attendance record. . . . These are Huddleston's missed votes since 1974. As you will see, they are significant votes on important subjects. Our position is that missing votes to make money giving speeches is never acceptable."

The ads were an instant hit, a humorous attack that underscored a legitimate criticism. The race started to turn. McConnell finally had an opening. The bloodhound ads fundamentally altered the race, putting Huddleston on the defensive and undercutting his appeal as a humble, shoulder-to-the-wheel politician. McConnell continued, with Ailes's counsel, to pound Huddleston mercilessly, on television and radio, with a torrent of negative attack ads.

"Without Janet and Roger Ailes I wouldn't have come even close," McConnell said.

On September 26 the campaign finally got some encouraging polling, but it only released the results that showed President Reagan leading Walter Mondale by twenty-five points in Kentucky. The campaign held back the fact that McConnell was now down twenty points, a yawning margin, but one that also showed he had cut Huddleston's lead by half in a matter of weeks. He continued to run ads that criticized his opponent over the Panama Canal, federal spending, and school prayer, among other things. Each ad also had a line about Huddleston's attendance, reinforcing the theme of the bloodhounds.

National Republicans started to see some potential in McConnell's race, including former president Gerald Ford, who campaigned in Kentucky for him. Still, by October, one month before the election, a Senate Republican poll showed McConnell trailing badly.

Fortunately for McConnell, Reagan, near the peak of his popularity en route to a forty-nine-state landslide win over Mondale, was coming to Louisville for a presidential debate. At a post-debate rally, the kind of moment McConnell thought might help to ignite a home-stretch push, he had a film crew ready to record the moment for an ad. Reagan had performed poorly in the debate, and Nancy Reagan, who McConnell later noted could be a "shrew," was not happy. McConnell asked if he could walk over to the president, and Mrs. Reagan gave him an icy stare. He did so anyway, so the scene could be used in a commercial. In his remarks, Reagan then referred to his good friend "Mitch O'Donnell."

Soon, Vice President Bush came to campaign for McConnell,

another opportunity for him to burnish his credentials with the support of a popular national figure. Bush referred to him as "Mayor McConnell of Louisville." It wasn't quite the endorsement he'd hoped for.

After a long day of campaigning in October, McConnell came home to his condominium in Louisville and saw that a tree he had watched grow for four years in his front yard had been struck by lightning and ruined. When he went inside, the last fish in his aquarium was dead, belly-up, a victim of McConnell's neglect. "It was just a sort of metaphor for the whole year," he said.

But McConnell had another eleventh-hour chance to revive his candidacy in a debate with Huddleston, and his skilled performance gave voters a reason to see him as a credible alternative to the incumbent, in a year when Reagan was exceptionally strong.

McConnell took another poll October 5 and 6, and it showed him trailing Huddleston now by twelve points. "I don't take polls to kid myself. You take them to find out what the situation is."

Senator Lugar and the Senate campaign committee said a win was possible, promising additional financial support, and McConnell, who had been spending heavily on television, needed the help. He stretched every dollar, and even exploited his position as county judge to help his effort, sending out $20,000 worth of direct mail in Jefferson County boasting of his accomplishments, but framing them as simple announcements of good things happening for county residents. One postcard showed trees in a forest from a land preservation, and the card from McConnell said, "I wanted to drop you a note to give you some happy news for the children of Jefferson County." Any moment he was not out campaigning, he was on the phone trying to raise more money.

The numbers started to look better. With less than a week to go, Huddleston's lead was in single digits. Finally, outside money from Lugar's committee and national donors started to pour into the Republican's campaign. Further evidence of McConnell's momentum came in the form of a campaign visit from Senator Dole, who was running to be majority leader, and his wife, Elizabeth.

To try to seal a clear chance of winning, McConnell returned to the theme that had started his rise, the bloodhounds. Ailes said it would cost $20,000 to produce another ad. McConnell said "go for it."

He found an out-of-work actor, Marvin Silbersher, to play the tracker. Silbersher set about buying the costume he would wear, a red plaid shirt, one pair of heavy rubber boots, leather gloves, a Sherlock Holmes pipe, a pouch of tobacco, a magnifying glass, and a hunter's billed cap. He also rented Sherlock Holmes and Inspector Clouseau costumes. For all that, and a few cab fares, he billed the campaign $538.01, and it may have been the best political investment McConnell ever made. Ailes also enlisted a dog trainer and four dogs for the shoot. In it, the hounds finally caught up with another actor playing the senator, chasing him up a tree. "Dee Huddleston, we've got you now," the ad closed.

On election night, NBC projected that McConnell would win at 9:30. Huddleston conceded defeat. McConnell went to the ballroom of the Henry Clay Hotel for his victory celebration. The man who considered himself perpetually prepared had not written a victory speech.

But McConnell noticed that Mullins and Schiff were not in the room. He soon found them sitting quietly and asked Mullins if there was a problem with the count. She told him his margin had shrunk to a few thousand votes. Even as he made the rounds of network morning shows to talk about his victory, he was plagued by a fear that it would slip away.

After a canvass of the votes was completed two weeks later, McConnell's victory was officially confirmed. He had won by just 5,100 votes—a .3 percent margin. Huddleston was the only Democratic incumbent senator in the country who lost.

Many, if not most, political professionals thought Reagan's coattails propelled McConnell's narrow win. "Jefferson County Judge Mitch McConnell, swept along by a strong Reagan tide, apparently defeated Democratic U.S. Senator Walter 'Dee' Huddleston yesterday by a narrow margin in one of the major upsets of the 1984 campaign," said the *Courier-Journal*. A dejected Huddleston said, "It appears that we just ran into one too many landslides, the other way." Huddleston would later say that his campaign was wildly overconfident and had underestimated McConnell's tenacity. He also said McConnell was an early adopter of a harshly negative approach, which proved brutally effective.

McConnell did not agree that he won because of coattails. Rather, he thought it was the focus and intensity of his campaign, and the remarkable impact of his attacks on Huddleston. McConnell's campaign aides had persuaded Reagan to do an ad for him in the closing days, but their surveys indicated it had little effect.

"We'd lost seats in the Senate while Reagan was carrying forty-nine out of fifty states, and why there were no coattails anywhere else and there were in Kentucky was nonsense. So I was kind of resentful of that," McConnell said. "Obviously thrilled to have achieved my lifetime goal, but resentful at the way it was sort of denigrated as being somehow less attributable to my skills."

About a month after the election, McConnell's father wrote him a two-page letter saying he was "delighted" with how his son had handled success. "On Election Night, you showed real class in your comments about Huddleston. I wasn't sure that you were sincere. As I have read your comments in the newspapers, heard you on TV and talked with you, I have seen the real Mitch—the one I know—emerge and I must tell you that I have liked what I have seen and heard. . . . Now I believe very strongly that you will be a truly great leader and senator."

In that period, Mullins saw in McConnell all the traits a politician needed to prevail, but in no way did she foresee the heights he would reach. "His ambition was not an accident and his rise was not predictable, but it was certainly planned and worked for," Mullins told me in interviews before her death from pancreatic cancer in 2023. "I would have scoffed and laughed on election night in 1984 if you would have told me someday Mitch McConnell would be majority leader or even win a second term."

"Where do you channel your energy when you are not a natural athlete or a homecoming king?" Mullins asked. "Politics was a great leveler for people who didn't have the Harvard education or the wealth. He was just good at it and loves the game."

Like a dog with a bone, she said, "McConnell basically willed himself to win in 1984. He was either going to win or he was going to die trying."

ELEVEN

LAND OF GIANTS

When McConnell walked onto the Senate floor for the first time as a member in January 1985, he headed to the far right corner of the back row, befitting his status as the lowest-ranking Republican in seniority. It was not long until he focused on the middle of the chamber and saw Senate Majority Leader Bob Dole of Kansas, a Republican, and the Democratic leader, Senator Robert Byrd Jr., of West Virginia. From that day he had his next goal: to one day sit behind Dole's desk, with its ceremonial gold spittoon on the floor underneath, and to follow the tradition of carving his name on the inside.

McConnell invited his idol, former senator John Sherman Cooper, to walk with him, along with his parents and daughters, for his swearing-in. He took the oath before Vice President George Bush, placing his hand on a four-inch-thick, heavy family Bible that had been used by his grandfather. In photos that captured the moment, Mac is beaming, Dean is more stoic, and McConnell is almost giddy, at least for him.

He had finally joined the club to which he had so long coveted membership. But like most new senators, particularly those who had not served in the House, he was hit by a sobering realization: he was not sure how to do his job.

The Senate in that era was populated by giants: Senator John Glenn of Ohio, the famed astronaut; Senator Bill Bradley of New Jersey, the Princeton basketball star who paused his professional career with the New York Knicks to be a Rhodes scholar; Senator Daniel Patrick Moynihan of New York, the towering intellect of the body; and Senator Edward Kennedy of Massachusetts, the brother of JFK. On the Republican side was Dole, the wounded World War II hero, along with Senator Barry Goldwater of Arizona, the 1964 GOP presidential candidate McConnell had embraced and then spurned, and Senator Richard Lugar of Indiana, the erudite foreign policy mandarin. Among the freshman senators who drew most notice was Jay Rockefeller, a Democrat of West Virginia, bearing one of the most famous American names of the twentieth century. There were also conservative Democrats like John Stennis of Mississippi and liberal Republicans like Lowell Weicker of Connecticut; the parties were more ideologically diverse than the monoliths they would become.

Two dozen of the senators in the chamber that day would run for either president or vice president, including then-senator Joe Biden of Delaware, who would do both. On that score McConnell stood apart. He had no designs on the White House, and it would serve later to be a core strength of his among Senate Republicans. Instead, he watched the leaders, how they interacted with members, how they carried themselves, and how they conformed to the esoteric folkways of the Senate.

One such norm was the often faux sense of gentility, when a senator would address another as "my dear friend" or "my dear colleague," then proceed to tear an argument apart. Another was when they spoke of themselves in the third person, with McConnell referring to himself as the "senator from Kentucky" in a colloquy. The members at that time still thought of themselves as part of one of the nation's most exclusive clubs, and there was an air of collegiality. That sense would steadily erode during McConnell's tenure, but for the time being, the Senate was a serious place for policy. People like Lugar were trying to determine what to make of the new leader of the Soviet Union, Mikhail Gorbachev. There were acts of terrorism to reckon with, like the seizing of the *Achille Lauro* and the hijacking of TWA Flight 847. Cocaine trafficking was emerging as a crisis. Reagan was reshuffling his top White House team and unveiling a tax bill.

As a freshman, Senator McConnell was in the middle of none of it.

He knew his place in the rank order and consciously decided that it would be a mistake to come in, talk a lot, and try to be assertive. "This is a club; it's a club that takes a while to get into," he told the Associated Press.

To the extent McConnell had any profile at all, it was thanks to the fact that he was the only Republican to defeat a Democratic incumbent. The bloodhound ads had given him a measure of fame, but there was an air of mystery around his policy positions. *The Almanac of American Politics* referred to McConnell as "Kentucky's new, and surprise, Senator," noting his generally moderate views and predicting that "he is likely to be much more Bob Dole's than Jesse Helms's kind of Republican." Sure enough, when it came time to choose the Republican Senate leader, McConnell voted for Dole, who had shown foresight in courting McConnell when he was county judge executive. Dole won, but McConnell also followed Reagan's brand of conservatism.

Before he was sworn in, Senator Cooper invited McConnell to stay with him at his Georgetown home. "It was a thrill. Exactly twenty years before that, I had been an intern in his office, and that was a time when I had basically said, 'This is what I want to try to do.'" McConnell's views were already more conservative than Cooper's, so he did not see Cooper as a mentor on policy positions, but he deeply admired how Cooper had gone about his job, and in that sense, McConnell still saw him as a role model.

"He was a highly independent decision-maker, who, on big issues, frequently went against the flow, and I liked that, admired that, and have done that frequently myself," he said in an oral history interview in 1998. "People are willing to cut you some slack if they think you are operating on the basis of conviction."

At the same time, he did not feel beholden to Reagan, rejecting assertions that he had drafted on Reagan's coattails and otherwise would have lost his race to Huddleston. Reagan didn't help things by proposing to abolish the federal tobacco program in January 1985, putting McConnell in a rare alliance with his Democratic counterpart, Wendell Ford, and at odds with the president, who had just won in a landslide. Eventually the administration relented.

He also began his reelection strategy, vowing to visit all 120 counties in Kentucky in the next two years, a goal he later said was foolish, and a stunt he did not repeat. In the process, he learned to loathe town meetings because they generated "bad headlines" and tended to draw out a community's "malcontents." More productively, he made allies at two major Kentucky military bases—Fort Campbell and Fort Knox—worked to keep both bases active, and continued to solidify his support in the western part of the state.

In the Senate, his first piece of legislation was a farm bill largely written by the Farm Bureau. ("That is not to say that I knew a thing about the subject," McConnell later said.) He worked to get a spot on the Agriculture Committee, recognizing that as a man from Louisville he needed to have a strong connection in rural Kentucky, where voters often provided the margin of victory for Republican candidates in statewide elections. Moreover, the committee had jurisdiction over tobacco policy, vitally important in Kentucky. He found working to pass the farm bill "boring" and "arcane and difficult to understand."

He took greater risk in foreign policy, introducing a bill that would level sanctions on South Africa for its apartheid practices. Robin Cleveland, McConnell's top adviser on the issue and another woman he had selected for a position of power, said he returned from a trip to Kentucky in March of 1985 full of sympathy for South Africans who were protesting apartheid. He had read a *Time* magazine article about children being shot while protesting on the anniversary of the

Sharpeville Massacre of 1960. He also noted that African Americans in the United States were driving domestic interest in the issue and said, "They are an important constituency in this country." To draft the legislation, McConnell joined with liberal senators Christopher Dodd of Connecticut and Ted Kennedy. "This was a hard call for him," Cleveland said. "He is the most junior of bankbenchers."

The bill, which eventually passed over Reagan's veto, was McConnell's first step in trying to fashion himself as an "internationalist and an interventionist." The *Courier-Journal* praised his work on the issue and Kentucky's state NAACP asked him to speak to a gathering in Frankfort.

McConnell said in an oral history that when considering whether to go against the popular Republican president, his mind went back to the 1960s when Cooper went against Goldwater and other Republicans to vote for the Civil Rights Act of 1964. "I felt we needed to do everything we could to change the apartheid regime and my vote on this would be the first time I'd show my colleagues, and myself, that while I was a great admirer of Reagan, I wasn't afraid to go against the prevailing party view if I thought it was wrong."

To have power in the Senate, he realized, he needed to immerse himself deeply in some issues. "The person who knows the most about a subject is most likely to achieve a result," he said. "And if you're just a total dilettante and sort of skip from one thing to another, and never really learn much about a single subject, you're not likely to make that much of a difference."

He also began learning where real senatorial power could be wielded. Introducing legislation, he said, was ceremonial, like a trophy. The real impact was in offering amendments to bills, and that's how he chose to operate. Though he and Ford, the Democrat, were never friends and often actively criticized each other, they did find common cause in trying to protect Big Tobacco. They were able to pass significant legislation that benefited the industry by persuading Packwood, chairman of the Finance Committee, to use a procedural maneuver called budget reconciliation, meaning the bill would not have to overcome a filibuster. It passed, then Byrd pushed through new Senate rules so they could not do it again.

He also got his first taste for influencing the federal judiciary. Ford and Huddleston had worked out an arrangement so each senator would get three choices for federal district court nominees, and another three would be selected by the Kentucky Bar Association. McConnell used one of his slots to push his friend Chuck Simpson, who ultimately was narrowly confirmed. McConnell did not like the system (he later single-handedly abolished it to consolidate his authority over the process), and as a Republican with a Republican president he could have pushed all of his own nominees, but he was also thinking about his political standing. "I had to appear to be pretty bipartisan," he said. "I announced publicly that defeating Ford was not a priority. Obviously that was something I didn't have to do. But I wasn't going to spend any time trying to do the undoable and thereby weaken myself any further, knowing full well I wasn't all that strong anyway."

Indeed, he was not. He ordered a poll in Kentucky and found that despite his recent election, he was not at all well known. The 1984 race had been a referendum on Huddleston. Knowing his position was precarious, he "had to work like hell for the full six years" to prove he deserved a second term. He worked hard for home state interests, traveling to Japan and Korea to push the sale of American tobacco, making no mention of the health consequences of smoking.

He worked to build up his campaign account, relying on contributors from Big Tobacco among others, and to shore up his personal finances, given that he was maintaining homes in Louisville and Washington. So he eagerly engaged in the practice of giving paid speeches, earning $29,000 in honoraria—with tobacco and distillery companies happy to cut the checks. Unlike Huddleston, McConnell took great pains to never miss a vote.

Mike Brown, the *Courier-Journal* reporter who covered McConnell in Washington, was unsparing in his assessment of his first year, writing that McConnell was not catching on very fast. "It was a pretty tough article," McConnell said. "In retrospect, I don't think it was entirely inaccurate."

He found one way to make a headline in early December of 1985, when he got ahead of other officials and announced that Toyota would be opening a major automaking plant in Georgetown, Kentucky, a coup for the state that McConnell had little to do with; credit instead belonged to the Democratic governor, Martha Layne Collins. McConnell had seen two Democratic senators in Tennessee, Al Gore and Jim Sasser, do the same to upstage his friend Lamar Alexander, now Tennessee governor.

"It was a stupid mistake," McConnell said. "It made me look opportunistic and overreaching. It was embarrassing and I should have been embarrassed by it. . . . I ended up getting creamed by the press, which I richly deserved, and learned an important lesson about not taking credit for things I don't deserve, including getting really sort of ridiculed from one end of the state to the other."

His other mistakes were personal. He had become engaged to a woman named Pam Schultz, a blond, thirty-two-year-old assistant principal from Bardstown, Kentucky. On May 14, 1985, their engagement was announced on the Channel 11 noon news in Louisville. The *Courier-Journal* wrote a story about the couple and how Schultz was looking forward to moving to Washington. She often was seen accompanying McConnell to political events. He took Schultz to a state dinner for Canadian president Brian Mulroney in early 1986.

Janet Mullins, for one, did not think the relationship was good for McConnell, an assessment he came to share. But breaking off the engagement wasn't an easy choice. In talks with Mullins in the Senate Dining Room, he agonized over the decision. "He is so deliberate in everything that he does, so this was out of character, and he didn't want to hurt her. He was embarrassed, but he knew he had to do it."

McConnell entered the Senate with starry-eyed hopes of what he might become, and ended the first year with a string of embarrassing personal failures, and in the chamber, "not feeling like I knew what I was doing."

In one area, however, he'd had a clear impact: the lethal effectiveness of the bloodhound ads led to what *Congressional Quarterly* said was the highest Senate attendance in thirty-three years.

His next year started at least as badly when the *Wall Street Journal*, assessing seven freshman senators, wrote, "Even fellow Republicans say McConnell seems 'all but invisible.'" Mullins recalled similar concerns of her own, noting that when McConnell was elected, the Senate was "still very much the good old boy system and the hail fellow well met. And as he aspired to leadership roles, all I could think of is that he's out of his league here. He just doesn't have the personality for it."

He still managed to get a seat on the Judiciary Committee, and in 1986 was among those questioning Rehnquist, whom Reagan nominated to be chief justice of the Supreme Court, and Scalia, whom Reagan had nominated to fill Rehnquist's spot as an associate justice. McConnell felt a personal connection, since he had known both men for a decade.

He still put a premium on raising money, as he had since the day he was elected, and had nearly $500,000 in his campaign account—a considerable sum at the time—four years before his next race. In 1986, McConnell also participated in his first Senate debate on campaign finance legislation, laying the early foundation for what would become an enduring part of his impact on American politics. In his own races, McConnell had seen what ample resources could do, and how a financial advantage often led to an electoral one. So he set out to try to remove barriers to contributions.

Democratic senator David Boren of Oklahoma and Goldwater, the venerable conservative whose views on a number of issues had moderated, were proposing legislation that, among other things, would eliminate political action committees. McConnell spoke out against the bill and voted against it. Lacking his own personal wealth, he knew he needed as many streams of donor money as he could get. It was also the start of him trying to become a true expert on the subject, both of the law and the politics.

Republicans in general didn't fare particularly well in the fall of 1986. They lost the Senate, and McConnell, now consigned to the minority, had to shed staff and adapt to not merely being seen as a newcomer, but now one with less power. That downgrade for Senate Republicans set off internal fighting; in one memorable case, Senator Jesse Helms of North Carolina used party rules to muscle his way into Lugar's seat as the ranking member of the Foreign Relations Committee. Seniority won out over competence. At the time McConnell thought it was wrong, but the longer he served in the Senate, the more he came to value the prerogatives of seniority.

In 1987, the Republican presidential race for the following year was forming, and McConnell had to choose between Dole, who had been helpful to him and could directly affect his future in the Senate, and Bush, whom McConnell admired and thought was the stronger candidate. He went with Bush. Dole did not punish McConnell, but he also did little to help him from that point on, and one McConnell aide described Dole as "ice cold" for a long time.

Meanwhile, Reagan, burdened by the Iran-Contra scandal and increasingly seen by McConnell and others as a diminished figure, wanted to reassert his authority. He said he would oppose a popular highway bill—one McConnell wanted to see pass—because of its price tag. The White House summoned him for a meeting with the president on March 30. "It certainly gets my attention," McConnell said at the time. But Reagan did not persuade him. "To be perfectly candid, it didn't bother me to have an example of independence," McConnell added.

He focused instead on his opposition to a campaign finance proposal offered by Senator Robert Byrd, now the majority leader. McConnell said that taxpayer-funded campaigns rewarded "lazy" candidates. His was not a majority view. Campaign finance reform had clear voter appeal, as McConnell had realized before running for county judge executive. Demonstrating his newly honed tactical skills, he came up with a counterproposal he did not believe in, but one he thought would attract enough Republican support to allow the GOP to appear to have an alternative plan.

His tactic was to create a proposal that sounded good, but stood little or no chance of passing. He worked with Packwood to come up with a proposal to ban political action committees, which McConnell said he knew was "blatantly unconstitutional and something I really wasn't even for." He called the maneuver a ploy, and the media called him on it. "I was, of course, called on the carpet for my hypocrisy, and the only answer I could give, I gave to the *Washington Post*, 'As long as PACs existed, we like them to help us.'"

His contrarian position on campaign finance served to elevate his visibility in Washington. The *Courier-Journal* noted he was "vigilant and often the lone Republican on the floor. He's argued with all comers and displayed a self-confidence intimates say would not have been possible a year ago. Even rival Democrats credited McConnell with being well prepared and articulate."

Not all his attention was positive. He continued to make paid speeches, some of which caused him great embarrassment. ("I needed the extra money to survive.") He said his secretary prepared a list of paid speeches, mostly on the West Coast, bunched together, so McConnell could efficiently make the extra money. On an eleven-day trip to California and Nevada, he made seven speeches and earned $10,500. He disclosed the honoraria.

But *Washington Post* reporter Thomas Edsall was working on a story that examined politicians taking honoraria that highlighted McConnell's travels and noted that he had taken "a friend" along with him. That friend was his former fiancée, Pam Schultz. McConnell found out that her expenses could not be paid for out of his official account, and he ended up repaying thousands of dollars. He came to find that he had done nothing improper, according to the Federal Election Commission, "but I ended up coughing up all the expenses for this lady that I took on the trip with me."

As always, his focus was never far from his next Senate race, and he had a very clear idea of who his opponent would be, Harvey Sloane, the former Louisville mayor and current county judge executive. He spent hours plotting to make it more difficult for him. Sloane had been elected county judge in 1985 and would be up again in 1989. If he won, Sloane's office would give him an opportunity to get a lot of free publicity and make him a more formidable challenger to McConnell in 1990.

"I wanted to make it difficult for Harvey, if not impossible for Harvey, to run for county judge again and turn around and run for the Senate," McConnell said. "In other words I wanted Harvey Sloane out of office, I wanted him with diminished incumbency power in 1990, and I knew that if Sloane had a cakewalk, he would just file again for county judge, get reelected with no effort, and just move right on through into the Senate race."

So McConnell worked to persuade his friend, John Heyburn, who had designs on a political career, to say that he was running for county judge, and perhaps prompt Sloane to not seek a second term. He told Heyburn that "if for some reason he didn't get elected county judge, I would support him for the first federal judgeship that might come open after that. So we had a deal, which we kept to ourselves because it wouldn't sound too good, but we had a deal."

The gambit worked. Heyburn took public shots at Sloane and Sloane did not seek reelection, focusing instead on running against McConnell. Heyburn lost his race, but McConnell honored his commitment and secured him a federal judgeship. It is notable that McConnell deployed the strategy three years prior to his reelection campaign. As McConnell put it, "My experience has been that you make your own luck."

He went further, floating the name of Wallace Wilkinson, the Democratic governor, as a possible candidate for the Senate in 1990, to put additional pressure on Sloane. "I knew if I could get that in print, which I did, even if Wilkinson tried to deny it, it would make it even harder. I was trying to put two pianos on Harvey's back. One was to make it impossible for him to run for county judge, which was through John Heyburn, and the other was to surface another credible candidate for the Senate, which would make it harder for him to raise money. So the Wilkinson thing was entirely a creation of mine."

Meanwhile, McConnell's view on how a Supreme Court justice should be chosen began to change during the nomination fight over Robert Bork in 1987 when Democrats waged an all-out political fight to deny the conservative intellectual a seat on the high court. The tension led to a debate on the Senate floor between McConnell and Joe Biden, with McConnell trying to again assert his naive idea that Bork's qualifications rather than his philosophy should be the principal consideration for his confirmation. McConnell and Biden engaged in an extended colloquy, the Senate's rarefied name for a debate. The language was formal, including the odd folkway of McConnell referring to himself as the "Kentucky senator" and Biden to himself as the "Delaware senator."

McConnell had his law journal article on Supreme Court nominations entered into the record and stood by its central thesis, that the Senate should judge nominees by their qualifications more than their philosophies, which he argued was the province of the president.

"It was pretty clear to this Senator back in those days, and it is still clear to him today, that if we decide that the Senate and the President are on coequal footing on these nominations—in other words, any inquiry that is relevant to the Senate—we have a formula for gridlock in the future.

"What disturbs me is that if a majority of the Senators in this body today decided for whatever reason that the test is no longer competence or qualifications or a variety of other questions of fitness, but that we instead should look at all of the criteria that a President, any President, might take into account, we have a formula for gridlock. If the Senate happens to be conservative at a given moment and the President is a liberal, he might never be able to get a nominee approved."

His words were prescient, even if, later in his career, it would be McConnell himself playing a key role in cementing the gridlock he once decried.

"It seems to me that the appropriate role for us in this body is to look at the character, the professional qualifications, the fitness, if you will, of the nominee and to leave to the one person who is elected by all the people of the United States the philosophical judgment. If a majority of this body follows that standard it will be well served when a President of the United States may be of a different philosophical persuasion.

"We ought to think very long and hard about what our appropriate inquiry ought to be. Otherwise, the Senator from Kentucky feels that we will have continued gridlock over Presidential nominations to the Supreme Court."

Biden countered, "To avoid gridlock, both sides should be reasonable—a President should seek the advice of the Senate, and the Senate should not insist that there be a liberal or a moderate. . . . It is my view that the Framers envisioned the possibility of gridlock when you have a President of one philosophical disposition and when the Senate is controlled by the party of another. That is why they put in the words 'with the advice of.'" It is this view that ultimately prevailed, and not to positive effect.

McConnell then added that if he were to abide by the standard that he was advocating, "I put myself in a position maybe a couple of years from now, of having to choke it down and support a well-qualified nominee whose views I find completely inappropriate." McConnell also warned, though, that if the Senate were to judge Bork based on his philosophy, then he, too, was willing to "adopt that new view if that is going to become the majority view around here." Still, he said, he thought the best approach would be to allow the president to be the one comfortable with a nominee's philosophy.

Bork's nomination was defeated, and the consequences would echo through history. The fraught deliberations signaled the beginning

of partisan wars over judicial nominees, and McConnell forever abandoned his early idealistic beliefs about how the process should work.

He learned to flex his authority in other ways by blocking appointments and putting people like his friend Joe Schiff in mid- or high-level
jobs in the Reagan administration. He said that 1987 was the year that
"I finally began to get some courage and began to use the leverage
and power that you have in the Senate." One way he did that was by
blocking appointees to the Agriculture Department when the administration wasn't giving him what he wanted. Administration officials
pleaded with him to release his hold because families had to make decisions about moving to Washington. McConnell, unrelenting as ever,
"kept them in the cooler for a couple of months."

That decision received little attention, and McConnell was crav-
ing to get noticed by the national media. He described a brief mention
by the conservative columnist James K. Kilpatrick, calling it a "to-die-
for experience." That small victory was reduced by distressing news.
His father was diagnosed with colon cancer, and his prognosis was
uncertain.

Though he wasn't getting the attention he desired from the media,
he was steadily making friends in high places, even receiving an invitation from Bush to come to his family compound in Kennebunkport for
the Fourth of July in 1988. McConnell had been dating Susan Eisenhower, President Eisenhower's granddaughter, and she accompanied
him for the weekend, giving him some additional gravitas. He took
a ride on Bush's cigarette boat, speeding around Walker's Point. He
watched Bush play tennis. McConnell was dazzled by the Bush family
dynamic, the setting, and Bush's seemingly endless energy.

McConnell suddenly found himself in a milieu that was unthink-
able only a few years prior. He worked to ingratiate himself with Bush
in any way that he could, presciently anticipating that there was an
excellent chance Bush would be the next president. Bush called Mc-
Connell and asked him to help with the vice presidential selection
process by talking to other senators about their opinions. McConnell

offered to talk to each Republican, and tell them their advice would be kept confidential, to get their candid assessment. Bush agreed.

He talked to each one, taking detailed notes, then went to the White House to brief the president, who, to McConnell's surprise, did not seem all that interested. After McConnell finished briefing him, Bush said, "What about Quayle?"

McConnell replied, "What about Quayle?"

Bush said, "Well, did anyone mention Quayle?"

"No, no one did," McConnell replied.

"It was clear to me that I was going through a sort of charade for him so that he could say he'd consulted, but that he'd already pretty well made up his mind. . . . It ended up being a controversial selection because Dan was not quite ready for prime time, and it showed."

McConnell's own political calculations were faring better. He had ended up with nearly $2 million in his campaign account, four times the amount that Sloane had raised. In August 1989, in his appearance at Fancy Farm, he gave a preview of how he would attack Sloane in the coming campaign. He ridiculed Sloane's East Coast birth, his Ivy League education, and his second home in Canada—all to undermine Sloane's pitch that he was the candidate of the working class. "Every time Harvey or anyone lays a hand on me, I'm going to hit them back, whether it's early or late," McConnell said in an oral history. His attacks were just getting started.

TWELVE

RESEARCH AND
DESTROY

McConnell entered his reelection campaign confronting a bit of imposter syndrome. He had started to establish himself in the Senate, in a modest way, but one that at least had an upward trajectory. At the same time, there was doubt. If he did not win a second term, then his victory in 1984 would be dismissed as a fluke and his political future would dim dramatically—and possibly end.

He started by making an appeal to voters that he deserved a second term because of the "clout" he had in the Senate, a statement he later conceded was clearly not the truth. "You're going to face a campaign in which people are saying you haven't made much of a difference, and the truth of the matter is you haven't made much of a difference," McConnell said. "So how do you get around that?"

McConnell talked up his closeness to President Bush, whom he had persuaded to do his first fundraiser as president for him at a horse farm in Kentucky. The event was a disaster, with too much mud, too little food and drink, and guests so disgruntled that McConnell had to write them notes of apology. McConnell ordered a detailed after-action report from his staff and poured over the financials like a green eye-shade auditor. The campaign said it grossed $1.3 million from the event. McConnell noted the real net number was $860,879 and at the top of the page wrote, "Long way from netting $1M."

Still, the president reinforced McConnell's message to voters when he said, "In a very short time in the U.S. Senate, he's gained the kind of clout that Kentucky needs in Washington."

McConnell started his campaign talking up his visits to every county and doing a conventional fly-around of the state to "spoon-feed" the television stations and set the rough parameters of the race. More than anything, though, he knew the formula for winning: de-stroy his opponent.

He sought to build on his campaign experiences and run an even more aggressive, professional race. For that he turned to a young law-yer from his Senate staff, a man with the pleasant bearing of a Presby-terian minister named Steven Law. Unlike many of McConnell's aides, who had Kentucky roots, Law had an unusual background: his father was a dentist for an oil company, and he attended high school in Saudi Arabia, then college in California, before graduating from Columbia Law School.

Law had joined McConnell's staff in 1987 for a simple reason: he needed a job, and McConnell was looking for a lawyer to handle ju-diciary issues. The job was not appealing to most young Capitol Hill staffers who were lawyers because McConnell had left the Judiciary Committee. "I was very interested in the paycheck at the time, and I didn't know much about him," Law said. When he told his boss in the office of New York Republican senator Alfonse D'Amato that he was leaving for McConnell, the boss was incredulous, saying D'Amato's fu-ture was bright and McConnell looked like a "one-termer." "My basic argument was 'Well, he's going to pay me a salary,'" Law said, mark-ing the beginning of a relationship that would last more than three decades.

McConnell was becoming increasingly associated with campaign finance issues, and it fell to Law to find precedents that would support the senator's arguments. Law filled Pendaflex binders with his research, which was remarkable for its thoroughness. McConnell saw campaign finance as a path to some prominence, even though he was not on any relevant Senate committee, and it was Law's job to find the grist to make that happen.

McConnell put his strategic cunning on display when he produced a bill designed to fail, but one that would have about two-thirds of Republicans supporting it, securing enough votes to ensure that a competing bill sponsored by Democrats would not survive a filibuster. McConnell became associated with the issue mostly in a pejorative way. He was criticized by the *New York Times*, and his colleagues wondered why he would take on an issue like this when facing reelection. Ultimately, McConnell's Republican colleagues saw his work on the issue as the first tangible example of him mastering Senate rules for strategic advantage, and some of them started to seek his advice.

"And, truth of the matter is, unless you're stupid, there's no way to lose an election over a subject like campaign finance reform," McConnell said. "It's too arcane, too difficult to understand. I counseled my fellow Republicans over the years not to be afraid of it, that they really do have the freedom to do the right thing." McConnell's view of the right thing, though, had flipped.

The tenacity of Law's research on campaign finance led McConnell to think his skill could also be put to use on political opponents, and Law, who said he "had no social life," willingly took on the task. In his free time, Law culled microfiche files, looking for newspaper articles, financial information, and other details of a potential opponent's life. He filled more binders. For the research to be effective, Law wrote, it could "not be controlled by preconceived notions about the opponent or any issues." Equally important, he said, was to explore McConnell's own vulnerabilities, including asking the National Republican Senatorial Committee for its opposition research on him.

McConnell directed Law to plumb Sloane's background. McConnell had a knack for looking not only at his opponents' weaknesses but also their strengths, and Sloane, Yale educated, a physician, a marathon runner, and a public servant who had devoted countless hours to the cause of public health, had many. He was also the favored candidate of the *Courier-Journal* and attractive to Washington's donor class. It was Law's job to round out that picture and turn those strengths into weaknesses.

One could be forgiven for thinking that the mild-mannered, even-keeled Law was not the political killer McConnell needed. But throughout his career, McConnell—who was known to size up potential staff with as little as an elevator conversation—has had a keen eye for political talent, and he saw it in Law. He named him his campaign manager, even though Law had no experience in such an important position.

Law approached the campaign the way a litigator would a high-stakes case. But the room of the McConnell high command was crowded. Ailes, who took up a lot of space, was back, as was Robert Teeter, one of the foremost Republican pollsters and consultants, both of them fresh from their work in Bush's 1988 victory. Armed with Law's voluminous research, McConnell's campaign had a ready rejoinder to almost any attack that Sloane would level. (Somehow, the campaign even managed to make sure that a flattering autobiography of Sloane was not published. Niels Holch, McConnell's top Senate aide at the time, wrote to Ailes, Teeter, and others, "Last year, Harvey Sloane asked one of his county employees, Doug Stern, to help him draft his autobiography. We obtained a copy of the first draft and stopped the project from going ahead.")

With oil prices surging in the United States, Sloane hammered McConnell for taking contributions from oil companies. But Law knew that Sloane also had substantial holdings of Exxon stock, a fact McConnell leveraged into an effective counterattack. The goal, Law said, was not so much to undermine Sloane with voters as it was to erode the confidence that influencers like the *Courier-Journal* had in him to make a larger case that Sloane "just wasn't ready for prime time. . . . It was tactical rather than strategic, but it did have an impact," Law said. His binders full of research were paying off.

The increasing prominence of health care as an issue in the campaign likewise posed a potential problem for McConnell, as Sloane had a long record of trying to expand coverage for people, particularly the working class. To try to cut into that strength, McConnell offered his own health-care bill, in April, to counter the appeal of Sloane's proposal of a form of national health insurance. McConnell's bill wasn't really serious legislation, but the substance was irrelevant because it was a campaign tactic. It worked because voters were not interested in the fine-grain details. By the end of the campaign, voters split evenly on which candidate would help more on the issue. Going a step further, McConnell strongly courted the Kentucky Hospital Association and secured its endorsement, too. "It was a total fraud," Sloane told me. "But it cut into my support."

McConnell wanted to win over about a quarter of Democrats in a state still dominated by them, and in an effort to do so appealed to the Fraternal Order of Police for its endorsement. "I never will forget the night I was out there trying to make the sale," McConnell said. "Some old drunk, retired police officer was sitting down in the front. He interrupted me and he said, 'I don't like you.' And he said, 'And I don't like Sloane.'"

McConnell made a nimble pivot: "Well, you ought to be happy, because in this election you're going to get rid of one of those sons-of-bitches." The crowd loved it, and he eventually got the endorsement.

Law showed his own instincts for attack when he called into a Louisville radio station that had Sloane on as a guest. Without identifying himself as a McConnell staffer, he thanked Sloane for making Louisville a nuclear-free zone. The issue mattered because in western Kentucky, critical to McConnell's chances, several thousand people were employed in the uranium industry, which is tied to nuclear energy.

Unwittingly, Sloane started railing against the nuclear industry. McConnell's campaign had the tape rolling and used it against Sloane. Many in the industry in western Kentucky endorsed McConnell after hearing the tape.

McConnell was also concerned that Ailes, with his growing reputation for brutal negative campaigning, might become an issue, so he had Law preemptively attack Frank Greer, a top Sloane consultant, by showing a reel of negative ads the Democratic consultant had produced.

The mission: Work every angle, leave nothing undone. Do it like LBJ. Law and McConnell were completely in sync.

What they could not control was the national climate, which was becoming increasingly pessimistic, even after the fall of the Berlin Wall. Washington was locked in a budget fight, and Bush, who had gone back on his pledge to not raise taxes, was increasingly becoming a liability. On top of that, the first midterm for a president's party almost always resulted in heavy losses. Incumbency was becoming a minus, not a plus. "Every asset that we were counting on suddenly became not just worthless but counterproductive," McConnell said.

McConnell made an ad positioning himself as a scold of Washington and its hidebound ways. "He made it sound like he was the Prairie Populist who was fighting against the in-crowd in DC," Law said.

As he thought over his campaign strategy, McConnell talked to Law about challenging Sloane to a Lincoln-Douglas-style debate rather than a standard forum where journalists ask questions. Law filled more Pendaflex binders with research, and they studied the Lincoln-Douglas format. McConnell had great confidence in his debating skills going back to his moot court performances in law school. He also thought Sloane would not be as good on his feet and that he could put him on the defensive by asking about things like the agriculture bill, with its hundreds of provisions, including those that affected Kentucky. Law had been prepping McConnell for weeks, writing single-page briefing papers on every subject he could envision coming up, then going through practice sessions with McConnell at the end of campaign days.

Sloane quickly took the bait. McConnell went first and hewed strictly to his strategy. "I'm a member of the Senate Agriculture Committee," McConnell said. "We just recently passed the 1990 farm bill. I would like to ask Harvey to describe the philosophy and some of the principal provisions of the 1990 farm bill."

The challenger's answer showed he had little grasp of the details. "The basic philosophy of the farm bill is to provide for the income of farmers and also to provide for the family farm," Sloane said. Later, Sloane acknowledged, "I didn't exactly have that on the top of my head."

The tone for the debate was set. "Obviously, they don't teach agriculture at Yale," McConnell said. McConnell's performance in the debate was flawless. Facts rolled easily off his tongue, no attack by Sloane went unrebutted, and McConnell knew when to look directly into the camera. There was a youthful energy to his performance and an obvious sense of confidence. He didn't stumble over so much as a word.

The campaign didn't think debates mattered nearly as much to voters as they did to donors and the media coverage. Among that latter audience, though, his aides felt the debate achieved the objective: to sow doubt about Sloane's readiness.

Sloane leveled a variety of attacks against McConnell, including one over the senator's opposition to a ban on assault weapons, an issue made more immediate and relevant after a shooting rampage at the Standard Gravure printing plant in Louisville that left eight people dead. The issue had resonance in Kentucky's cities, but not among rural residents, who saw any effort to restrict guns as a gateway to even greater restrictions.

McConnell, though never a hunter, aligned himself with gun rights groups. But he was concerned enough about appearances that he stopped taking campaign contributions from the National Rifle Association.

"I don't own a gun," McConnell said. "So it's not an issue I feel passionately about one way or the other, but it's been one of the groups that have been sympathetic to Republicans, and, frankly, I just decided I would be allied with them. I have the same enthusiasm for that issue [as] I do with the abortion issue, where I have been allied with Right to Life, but never been a zealot, never made a speech, never offered an amendment."

McConnell continued his feverish pursuit of campaign donations as the summer wore on, but there was one he chose to return. In a letter dated July 10, 1990, he wrote to the New York businessman Donald Trump, 725 Fifth Avenue, New York.

Dear Mr. Trump:

You and I have never met or spoken but you responded in October 1989 to a general fundraising invitation sent out by my campaign.

While I thank you for your contribution, I have noticed several stories in the last few weeks about your financial difficulties. Having been through difficult financial times myself, I know how hard it can be on a person.

Although I am certain you will recover, I have decided to return my contribution of $1,000 because it appears you may need the money more than I do right now.

Thank you for your interest.

Trump's casino in Atlantic City was failing, and he would eventually file for bankruptcy, and McConnell did not want even a modest association.

He had enough money, and he used it to focus on Sloane. He reserved perhaps his sharpest personal attack on Sloane for the Fancy Farm gathering that August 1989. He called Sloane a "wimp from the East," an establishment liberal who had inherited his wealth. Sloane, he said, has come "down here to save us from ourselves." He ridiculed Sloane's ownership of a home in a foreign country, without mentioning that it was in Canada. All of it was designed to position McConnell as the candidate of the working person, a Reagan Democrat aligned with western Kentucky and other rural parts of the state, even though Mc-Connell had lived in Louisville since junior high school. He mocked the fact that one of Sloane's daughters attended a private school in the East, even though his own daughter Eleanor was starting her freshman year at Smith College in Massachusetts a month later.

The next August, Reagan came to Kentucky to campaign for Mc-Connell, making fun of the time he had bungled McConnell's name in 1984. "I'm glad we have leaders like Mitch McConnell, who fight what they believe in and have the respect in Washington to get things done," the former president said.

One issue McConnell had not really fought for, however, was abortion. He pointedly had not made abortion a core part of any campaign and received only a tepid endorsement from Northern Kentucky Right to Life in August. McConnell had refused to respond to the group's questionnaire, which represented the extreme in the anti-abortion position. "McConnell is indeed lackluster and obviously untrustworthy, but Sloane is predictably deadly," their endorsement said. In Washington in January, on the anniversary of *Roe v. Wade*, McConnell had told a group of anti-abortion activists from Kentucky that the election would be a "referendum on abortion." "You're going to have an opportunity to flex your muscles," he added.

He did not mention that mere months prior he had voted for a bill that would have permitted Medicaid-funded abortions for poor women who are victims of rape and incest, a provision he had previously opposed. "Upon serious reflection, I believe an exception should be allowed for those extreme cases," he said on the Senate floor in 1989. "I remain strongly committed to the pro-life position that I have always supported as a U.S. senator. The 20 million lives lost to abortion since *Roe v. Wade* are a national disgrace."

By November he had secured the clear support of the larger, statewide Kentucky Right to Life association. "Senator McConnell's deep pro-life commitment is not new," the group's "Life Alert" flyer said.

McConnell contracted polio at age two when he and his mother lived with his aunt and uncle in Five Points, Alabama.

McConnell's father, known as "Mac," was soon to deploy for combat in Europe.

McConnell's parents married in Texas after Dean came to join Mac, who had a job in the oil fields.

McConnell was an only child and his parents showered him with attention.

As a boy, McConnell fantasized about playing Major League baseball.
Through constant practice, he willed himself to be a better player.

McConnell stunned the political world by defeating an incumbent Democrat in his 1984 Senate race.

McConnell married Elaine Chao in Washington, and another DC power couple was born.

McConnell had a frosty relationship with President Barack Obama but worked closely with House Speaker John Boehner.

McConnell outlasted the other congressional leaders of his era, including Boehner, Speaker Nancy Pelosi, and Democratic Majority Leader Harry Reid.

McConnell tried to with work President Trump on judicial nominations and a tax bill. Their relationship fractured.

McConnell and Biden, old Senate hands, had a productive working relationship on numerous issues.

McConnell argued against isolationism in his party and was an essential proponent of military aid to Ukraine. President Zelenskyy personally thanked him.

SEN. MITCH MCCONNELL
(R) KENTUCKY - REPUBLICAN LEADER

On February 28, 2024, McConnell announced he would step down as party leader, acknowledging the shifting politics of the Republican Party.

On another major issue of the time, family and medical leave, McConnell concedes that he flip-flopped for expedience by endorsing stronger protections. "Frankly, I just chickened out. I just chickened out. I decided to deny Sloane that issue, and in subsequent years I went back to my original position, which the newspapers duly noted, as they should have, that I had sort of done a foxhole conversion in the 1990 campaign, something I'm not particularly proud of."

The source of perhaps McConnell's most damaging research on Sloane remains largely unknown. Though Sloane had been a licensed physician, he did not practice medicine for much of his career, focusing instead on public health and his political career. In 1987, he started to feel the effects of his marathon running, with a disk disease and arthritis in his hips, and he prescribed himself medicine to deal with the pain and sleep issues.

An anonymous source provided information to the *Courier-Journal* that showed Sloane was writing himself prescriptions after his license had lapsed, a possible violation of federal law.

The McConnell campaign claimed it had nothing to do with the leak, though Greer told me he assumed they were lying. It is possible that an outside group working on behalf of the Republican obtained the information and passed it along to a *Courier-Journal* reporter. Either way, McConnell was quick to exploit Sloane's embarrassment. His campaign produced an ad showing a cascade of falling prescription pills.

Another group sent out postcards to Kentucky voters pretending to offer them "a year's supply of Sloane's pills—your choice, uppers or downers." Sloane accused McConnell's campaign of being behind the mailings. Law, with a straight face, said, "Our campaign is proud of the fact that we don't engage in dirty tricks." Later, Law conceded that "McConnell believes very strongly in the potency of negative advertising."

Local columnists wrote admiringly of McConnell's skillful campaign as he went into 1990 with a clear—if shrinking—lead. "The

McConnell campaign apparatus is nationally renowned," wrote Robert T. Garrett in the *Courier-Journal*. "A marvel. A high-tech marriage of big bucks and political cunning. Its voter targeting is so sophisticated that, and I kid you not, it probably can tell you who in McLean County uses Crest and who uses Colgate. The vast gap between the two campaigns in sophistication, discipline and ruthlessness was obvious from the beginning. McConnell is ready for almost any desperate move Sloane may make."

Looking back with grudging admiration, Greer agreed that McConnell was a "very skillful politician," though he noted that he came to think that McConnell ultimately damaged the country later in his career.

It was McConnell's yawning financial advantage that helped him withstand the rapid decline in Bush's popularity and the anti-incumbent mood that was taking hold in the country, Greer said. McConnell's incessant pounding, day after day, took its toll on Sloane, who had entered the race with a good reputation and a long résumé of accomplishments. "It was negative almost from the beginning," Greer said. "I thought they were pretty vicious and stretched truthfulness to a certain degree, but at that point it was the negative advertising of the era. You could get away with almost anything negative."

Amid the frenzy of his political campaign, however, McConnell had to confront a deep personal loss. The pressure of the campaign and dealing with his father's failing health led McConnell to seek counseling from his pastor. Five weeks before the election, his father, Mac, who had been battling cancer, died on September 28 at 11:14 p.m., eleven days after entering the hospital. Mac had been undergoing intensive chemotherapy treatments for colon cancer for more than two years. With his father's passing, McConnell lost the second most important person in his life.

McConnell stopped events for a few days, canceled plans for a second debate with Sloane, and tried to get himself in a frame of mind to finish his campaign. Aides held an emotional meeting. Mac had added a life-of-the-party dimension to all of McConnell's campaigns. Like his son, he had no trouble asking donors for money and took the responsibility of doing so upon himself.

It was a crushing loss, but McConnell had no choice but to get back to campaigning. Even with all the skill and focus on his campaign, McConnell found himself watching his lead shrink by the day in the final weeks. Bush's popularity continued to decline nationally, dragging Republicans' electoral prospects down with it. With a week to go, one night of the McConnell campaign's tracking polling showed he actually trailed Sloane.

Then McConnell went against type. He decided to run a positive ad. Ailes loudly and strongly disagreed, but the candidate prevailed. He used words from the newspaper endorsements around the state— not including the *Courier-Journal* or the *Herald-Leader*, both of which backed Sloane—to set a more upbeat tone. He even showed some humor, donning a karate robe at his last rally, at the Louisville Airport, a riposte to the combat of the campaign.

He ended up winning by five percentage points. Never one to sit on satisfaction, he immediately started thinking about gaining power in the Senate and securing a legacy in Kentucky.

Law wrote a remarkably detailed after-action report from the campaign, notable for its candor about the failings as well as the successes. Which is what McConnell wanted—no romanticizing about the effort, just finding ways to improve for the next time. Law said the campaign needed to impose internal deadlines for research and have one person responsible. Voting analysis needed plenty of details for easy access if it were needed immediately. Finally, Law said, "despite lengthy discussions in consultant meetings, we never adequately pounded out the core themes we would use to attack our opponent and promote the Senator. Even our opponent did a better job at this than we did."

"I don't remember him running on anything he wanted to do," Greer said. "He always had a lot of power and accumulated power because he was a skilled politician. Even in that campaign, I never understood what he wanted to do, what he wanted to accomplish. It was like he was the master of manipulating the political process, but to what end?"

With his victory over Sloane, McConnell finally saw himself as someone who could have a long future in the Senate. He also thought he might have a career one day worth studying. So he decided to create the McConnell Center at the University of Louisville. It had many laudable long-range goals, such as providing full scholarships to ten members of each undergraduate class who were Kentucky residents. He was trying to stop the flight of talented young adults from the state, and to instill in those students a belief that they, too, could find a career in public life.

The center had another purpose, and that was to build toward the study of McConnell himself and serve as a reminder of the impact that he has had on American life. It was an audacious vision at the time, since he had only won a second term. He raised money in the millions for the center from private donors, and both he and the public university declined to disclose who was funding it.

THIRTEEN

MASTERY OF PROCESS

After winning a second term, McConnell felt far more confident that he could have a long future in the Senate, so he set out to increase his power. He thought the best path was to run to be chairman of the National Republican Senatorial Committee, which would draw him closer to the party's most influential donors, build loyalty among fellow Republicans, and play to his core strength as a political strategist and tactician.

It was part of his plan for a long, steady climb in an institution still driven by seniority and waiting in line. But for the first time since he was in college, he lost an election. Phil Gramm, a fellow freshman senator who intimidated McConnell with his intellect and his swagger, defeated him, 26–17, in 1990 to take control of the committee. Neither man was known for his endearing personality, though Gramm, with his doctorate in economics and his name attached to famous budget legislation, had the bigger reputation. Far more important, he came from Texas, and that meant he would be a formidable fundraiser for other Republicans. Gramm beat McConnell again in 1992, by a single vote, but by then Gramm had designs of running for president four years later.

After the first loss, McConnell decided to treat Gramm like he was a political opponent. His staff prepared the equivalent of an opposition research file on Gramm, and found his efforts as chairman of the campaign arm wanting. "Gramm treats all NRSC resources as if they are his, not as if they belong to Republican Senators and he has watch over them," a McConnell staff analysis said. McConnell had the backing of Dole, who was more interested in wounding Gramm as a potential rival for the Republican presidential nomination in 1996 than he was in elevating McConnell.

McConnell never took losing well, but he and Gramm remained good friends even with the competition. "Our careers were on a very different trajectory but I always knew that he was going to be somebody and do something," Gramm told me. McConnell also knew Gramm would be out of his way soon enough.

Gramm was not his only, or even his most important, rival. In the competition for attention in Kentucky, he was also losing out to his Democratic counterpart, Wendell Ford, who had unanimously won a leadership position in his party. He chafed at the idea of being in Ford's shadow.

The first Gulf War broke out in January 1991, and McConnell, almost reflexively supportive of the military, voted for the Senate resolution authorizing the use of force. The swift U.S.-led victory in that conflict led to stratospheric popularity for President Bush, and McConnell assumed he was a cinch for a second term. But the economy started to take a downturn, and so did Bush's standing.

On the domestic front, controversy erupted when Bush nominated Clarence Thomas to serve on the Supreme Court in July 1991. Thomas had been accused of sexual harassment by the law professor Anita Hill, and the confirmation hearings were a televised spectacle. The hearing, like Bork's, was a preview of the kind of hand-to-hand combat that the confirmation process would become. After a remarkably contentious and, at times, riveting process, Thomas was narrowly confirmed, 52–48, with McConnell voting for him. Democrats agreed to an up-or-down vote, and did not try to filibuster the nomination.

"It was very close," McConnell said. "And while there's no question that he was picked because he was Black, in spite of President Bush's protestations to the contrary, he has been the liberals' worst nightmare. . . . In my judgment he will go down in history as one of the better Supreme Court justices."

McConnell watched as several Democrats he thought might challenge Bush in 1992, including Bill Bradley and Jay Rockefeller, stood down, presuming that Bush was going to be very difficult to beat and creating an opening for the lesser known Arkansas governor Bill Clinton.

Bush was wounded during the primary campaign by the insurgent challenge from Pat Buchanan, a bombastic conservative who railed against immigrants coming over the southern border and stoked an economic populism that Bush did not effectively counter even with the decisive military success in the Middle East. Buchanan had spent years on television and was a skilled communicator. Within a few months, Bush did not look so formidable.

Buchanan tapped into a rising working-class resentment. He told Americans the government was inefficient and ineffective and Bush was out of touch with their everyday concerns. That led to the third-party challenge by Ross Perot, who ended up winning 19 percent of the vote, though no votes in the Electoral College. But Perot's campaign was a warning to both parties that a healthy segment of the electorate was fed up with the status quo. McConnell assessed the race like a well-traveled political consultant. "The conventional wisdom after the elections was that Ross Perot had cost him [Bush] the election. That's not true," McConnell said. "Had Perot not been on the ballot, Clinton would have won. . . . But Perot did symbolize, I think, the anger at things." Most later academic research supported McConnell's conclusion.

Mindful of his next election—even though it was four years away—McConnell started eyeing Jerry Abramson, the popular Democratic mayor of Louisville, who decades earlier had praised him in a letter to the *Courier-Journal*, as a potential future opponent. McConnell saw that Abramson was claiming credit for bringing another presidential debate to Louisville. Behind the scenes, McConnell worked with Robert Teeter, Bush's pollster, to make sure the debate did not happen in his hometown. "We always denied it publicly," McConnell said. But the "truth of the matter is we did take it away and Abramson accused me of doing it, and we all kind of vaguely denied it, but it was accurate."

On top of the debate stunt, McConnell instructed Terry Carmack, the man who started as McConnell's driver in 1984 and was now the Kentucky Republican chairman, to "take shots" at Abramson.

McConnell noted with some pleasure that he "helped" Abramson reach the decision not to run for the Senate. "He went down pretty easily, he caved pretty quickly," McConnell said with a laugh. "It's not a game for the fainthearted, and you're going to get beat up, and if you take controversial positions like I have . . . you're going to get beat up even worse." Better to stop potentially strong opponents before they even have a chance to start. Abramson did not challenge McConnell in 1996. As the *Courier-Journal*'s longtime political writer Al Cross liked to say, running against McConnell was like a trip to the proctologist.

McConnell was aware of his reputation, and he wanted to soften some of those harsher edges for the benefit of his legacy. So he enlisted Steven Law to craft the narrative. In 1992, Law wrote a twenty-three-page homage titled "Against the Tide: The McConnell Ascendancy in an Historical Context." It was a fawning work. "In the same way that the Berlin Wall's collapse marked the dawning of democracy in Eastern Europe, McConnell's succession of electoral victories—first in Jefferson County and then statewide—are the first ripples of two-party democracy in Kentucky, after two decades of Democratic hegemony and Republican drought." In fact, Law wrote, McConnell's achievement was even more remarkable.

McConnell, he argued, was not given sufficient credit for his achievements. He was not lifted by other forces as much as he was lifted by his own determination and strong will. He argued against the prevailing wisdom that McConnell was carried to victory in 1984 on Reagan's coattails. "From his first election victory in 1977 to his solid reelection in 1990, Mitch McConnell has made his own history, sculpting it out of the rock of Kentucky's unyielding Senate landscape."

Though obsessed with politics, McConnell tried to have a semblance of a personal life. He had been dating Karen Caldwell, a lawyer, and he recommended her to be an assistant United States attorney. "I decided to recommend her, not because I was going out with her, but I wanted a Republican and I wanted, obviously, a woman lawyer to put in that job, and there were so darn few."

Both McConnell and Caldwell faced criticism, but she was confirmed. "She's a good lawyer, and it was time, in my view, to have a woman in a position of prominence in this state," McConnell said. "You should not refuse to advance a qualified woman because of her personal life." He would eventually recommend her to President George W. Bush for an opening as a federal district court judge, a position she held until taking senior status in 2022, meaning she could take a steep reduction in her caseload and still maintain staff and salary.

While his ties to Caldwell were personal, he also had an abiding fealty to the few people he thought of as heroes. One of them, Senator John Sherman Cooper, died after a long illness in February 1991, and McConnell spoke at a memorial service for him in Somerset, Kentucky. He referred to Cooper's stand for civil rights legislation in the summer of 1964, lauding it as an exemplary lesson on how to make a difficult decision—and a reminder that even when constituents were opposed to one's view, principle should guide an important vote. It was a lesson that McConnell, at several critical moments, would not follow. He would later try to explain the difference. Cooper had lost a race to become the Republican leader in the late 1950s to Senator Everett Dirksen of Illinois. Had he won, McConnell speculated, it would have been harder to him to take those stands and fulfill his more partisan role.

Campaign finance legislation continued to percolate through

Congress, mostly with Democrats pushing for limits on the role that money would play in politics, and Republicans like McConnell trying to stop them. Dole named McConnell to be floor manager of the opposition.

While his tactics to stop the legislation were stultifyingly arcane—he tested the limits of using the filibuster to block the appointment of members of a conference committee, and with it Senate rules and precedent—he also prevailed. In doing so, he set himself apart among his colleagues for his fluency in the rules as one who was willing to take on a thankless role that would benefit his colleagues.

"It was a time for me to really refine my floor skills," he said. "This is the first time I'd been sort of solely out there as the party's principal strategist."

McConnell often fixated on the power of money, and it went beyond campaigns. He had made sure that the McConnell Center at the University of Louisville was amply funded. The center's principal program is to fund forty full scholarships, ten in each class, for students from Kentucky, and to offer study abroad in places like China. The recipients also benefit from speakers that McConnell brings to campus and a private area to study. McConnell wanted the center to offer a conservative perspective, though a student's politics is not part of the selection process.

From the start, McConnell was defensive about the center's funding. He bristled when Kentucky's larger newspapers wrote articles criticizing him. "No good deed goes unpunished," he griped. He said that he had checked the Senate rules and there was no prohibition against a senator raising money for a charity and no obligation to disclose the donors. "I've never realized a penny out of this," he said. "And I very much did not want to disclose, because I didn't want to deal with all those allegations that would come with it." McConnell argued that universities allow anonymous gifts for the benefit of donors who don't want their contribution, if disclosed, to set off a chase by other schools for their money.

McConnell has not, however, addressed the fact that donors could be trying to create goodwill with a powerful politician whose work could affect their businesses in the tens of millions of dollars with a single line in an appropriations bill or amendment to a tax bill.

One of his original million-dollar donors was David Jones, who founded the Humana health care company. For decades, Jones was a strong supporter of McConnell's career, but he would sour on him in the years before his death in 2019. Jones provided something else for McConnell: one of his signature lines. McConnell is fond of saying that " 'focus' is the most important word in the English language." He had heard Jones say that frequently and appropriated it.

Despite his success in raising money for others, however, he was struggling financially, with the oldest of his daughters now in college and her younger sisters not far behind. He ended up teaching on American elections on Saturdays at Bellarmine University, a small Catholic college in Louisville. It helped to pay the bills, but he still had to also take out a second mortgage. He desperately wanted to raise his political profile.

In order to do so, he was constantly looking for issues that would get more attention. One of those efforts proved an embarrassment. His proposed Pornography Victims Compensation Act said that if a victim of a criminal assault could prove the attacker had been inspired by pornography, the victim could sue the filmmaker. Here was a politician who had long thought the country needed fewer lawsuits pushing legislation that would mean more of them. "So it was a bad idea that I decided to shelve and haven't had anything to do with for quite some while," he said years later. "Hopefully it won't come up when my biography is written, if it ever is."

In 1993, McConnell and Elaine Chao, the woman he'd been dating, decided to marry. Chao was from a wealthy family whose fortune came from an international shipping business, a classic story of immigrant achievement. They had met on a blind date arranged by McConnell's friend Julia Chang Bloch. Chao at the time was head of the Federal

Maritime Commission, and McConnell clearly wanted to impress her. The "date" was a party for then–vice president George H. W. Bush in the McLean, Virginia, home of Saudi Arabia's ambassador to the United States, Prince Bandar bin Sultan. Roberta Flack gave a private performance to cap the night's festivities. McConnell and Chao found they had much in common, like, for the most part, keeping emotions to themselves. McConnell said he was "proud to have her on my arm that evening."

But for weeks on end, McConnell did not call Chao again, and she presumed he wasn't interested. About three months later, he finally called, and their relationship deepened. Chao, who had never been married, said she did not want to reach her fortieth birthday still single. McConnell, however, never popped the question. Chao instead proposed to him, and he said yes. But he still needed her family's blessing. So McConnell had to travel to New York to ask her father's permission in front of the whole family. At dinner, McConnell seemed to be avoiding the subject, and Chao wondered if he would ever get around to it. Finally, he did. They wed on Reagan's birthday, February 6, 1993, and another Washington power couple was born.

Back in the Senate, a scandal was starting to unfurl. In November of 1992, the *Washington Post* reported that ten women said they had been harassed by Senator Packwood. Pressure mounted on Congress to investigate, and the timing put McConnell near the center of the fray. Dole, who was going to run for president for a third time, had sounded McConnell out about becoming chairman of the Republican National Committee, but McConnell decided against it. Instead he took on an assignment many members of Congress tried to avoid, a seat on the Ethics Committee in 1993. McConnell said he sometimes made his mark early in his career by taking on the jobs nobody else wanted. In this case, the job in question involved investigating a colleague.

The Packwood revelations were stunning to the public, but less of a surprise to those who knew the Oregon senator well. In his initial response, Packwood issued a broad-based apology and later checked himself in for treatment for alcoholism, efforts that did not stop an inquiry into his conduct by the Ethics Committee.

The scandal surrounding Packwood and the allegations of serial sexual harassment were like a slow-moving, multi-vehicle car crash. The Senate's clubbiness had delayed action for years, but the scale and gravity of his conduct made a reckoning impossible to avoid. McConnell had known Packwood since McConnell's time as a Senate staff member in the late 1960s, so there was a personal connection as well.

The Senate Ethics Committee was often known more for absolving members than finding wrongdoing. McConnell was the ranking Republican member of the committee. He said that other Republican senators, including Alan Simpson of Wyoming and Dole, his party leader, had little appetite for undoing Packwood's career and they made that clear to McConnell.

Initially, he did not see much advantage for himself in leading any effort to get rid of Packwood, and his role in ultimately forcing him from the Senate is a matter of some dispute.

In McConnell's version of events, it was he who made the hard call to stand against his party and its leadership to address serious misconduct. Senator Barbara Boxer, a Democrat from California, has a distinctly different memory of how things played out.

Boxer said that when she found out that Packwood had harassed more than twenty women, she tried to get the Ethics Committee to act, but was blocked by McConnell. She then threatened to try to force the committee to make its hearings public if it did nothing. "Basically McConnell tried to shut me down and shut me up and stop me," Boxer told me. "He actually came up to me on the floor and he said if you continue going after Bob Packwood then I am going after Ted Kennedy and Tom Daschle's wife for being a lobbyist.

"I said, is that a threat or a promise? He said that's a promise. I was livid," Boxer said.

McConnell said Boxer thought that "flouting procedure was good politics in the service of justice. But I found it highly regrettable, especially since I had no intention of sweeping this matter under the rug." The committee typically acted in secret.

"Now, when Mitch wrote his own memoir, he had a completely different story," Boxer countered. "He saw the handwriting on the wall and pushed Packwood out." She said, "It was so bad that I did not talk to Mitch McConnell for twenty years except to say good morning." Boxer's attempt to force public hearings ultimately failed.

Two things can be true. McConnell could have been slow at the start of the inquiry, then central to Packwood's undoing.

His pursuit of the Packwood case also came at a time of great personal pain. Following Mac's death, McConnell had made it a practice to call his mother, Dean, every evening at 5:30. It was a ritual that could only be interrupted for the most important matters, and his staff always cleared his schedule, even if the conversation only lasted a few minutes some days. Dean's health had been declining since Mac's passing. She had fallen and broken her leg, and McConnell had arranged for a home health-care nurse to look after her.

In late October 1993, McConnell received the phone call he had been dreading. The nurse had found Dean unresponsive; she had suffered a serious stroke. McConnell rushed to Reagan National Airport to get on the next direct flight to Louisville. He then made it quickly to a hospital in nearby Shelbyville, where his parents had moved to accommodate Dean's desire for a small-town atmosphere. The doctors did not have good news. Dean had suffered significant brain damage and would not recover.

"I asked the doctor and nurses to leave the room, and I climbed onto the bed, sitting close beside her," he recounted in his memoir. "I stayed with her until night fell, thinking of all the days five decades earlier that she and I lay together on a different bed, this one in Five Points, Alabama. Then, as she fought for my future, helping me to recover from polio, she had transformed that small bed into a nearly limitless world, helping me to erect towns made of toys on my blankets, and reminding me of my own unlimited possibility, despite the odds that were fairly stacked against me. Those days, and all of the days that had followed—in the way she made me feel as if I belonged when I clearly didn't, in her belief in me when my own faltered, in her deep devotion to me—she taught me that if nothing else, I was very deeply loved. Now, as she prepared to die, sitting in bed beside her, holding her hand, I told her again and again that the same was true for her."

Dean died the next day.

McConnell had been preparing mentally and emotionally for his loss, but it still was crushing. She was buried the day after she passed, and McConnell threw himself back into work. By Monday, he was back in Washington for the debate over Packwood's fate.

The investigation played out in long form, with the committee interviewing 264 witnesses, taking 111 depositions and reviewing 16,000 pages of documents. McConnell and the committee were clearly convinced that Packwood "had systematically abused his power and privilege." Then the committee found out that Packwood had kept a diary. When the panel tried to subpoena the diary, Packwood refused to turn it over and the committee took his case to the Supreme Court. The committee eventually got the diary and determined that Packwood had doctored entries to try to mislead investigators.

McConnell knew how serious this offense was and recommended to the committee that Packwood be expelled from the Senate, an extraordinary step. On September 6, 1995, the committee unanimously recommended Packwood be expelled. He resigned instead.

McConnell had weighed the politics of the situation, including the fact that other Republicans might not feel inclined to elevate him to the party's leadership after seeing him move to expel one of their own. He again cited Cooper's admonition to elected officials to "stand firm in what I believed, even when it meant making tough choices like these, and it was the voters' job to decide if these decisions should allow me to stay in office."

The Packwood scandal helped McConnell achieve another objective: his national profile was rising. After Packwood resigned, the *New*

York Times's Michael Wines described McConnell as "a sober-sided legislator with a subterranean profile from a not-very-influential state [who] landed with a thump on the national political scene today." His understated manner, the article said, "belies both real ambition and an almost unerring political instinct." It noted that, overall, many Democrats praised McConnell for his even-handed approach in investigating a member of his own party. "Happily for him, his willingness to shoulder unpopular causes also has won him considerable regard among fellow Republicans," Wines wrote.

There was criticism from some Republicans, but McConnell laid the blame for the scandal solely at Packwood's feet. "As happens with increasing frequency these days the victimizer is now claiming the mantle of the victim. The one who deliberately abused the process now wants to manipulate it to his advantage. That won't wash."

He also started to establish himself on another front, namely stopping things from happening. The House and Senate had passed campaign finance bills, and he was waiting for the legislation to be ironed out in a conference committee. He was even prepared to challenge the law in court if it passed and Clinton signed it, about two months before the 1994 midterm elections. He wouldn't need to.

After several sessions with the Senate parliamentarian, he'd figured out his strategy. There are three motions that have to be made before a member of a conference committee can be appointed. Each is subject to a filibuster. McConnell calculated how to delay each motion to maximum effect, using the entire thirty hours allowed for debate, including seven by McConnell himself. He persuaded his Republican colleagues to join in this all-night road to nowhere, all because he wanted to stop the legislation. He had even talked to the Ashland Oil Company about getting some work for a senator who was soon to be retiring, as a potential incentive for a vote. His staff prepared their speeches, and they set the plan in motion. McConnell had a cot placed just off the Senate floor so he had somewhere to go to get some rest. They beat the second motion to end debate. The legislation was defeated.

Senate Majority Leader George Mitchell, a Democrat from Maine, was furious, and he told McConnell that his party would pound Republicans on the issue in the final weeks of the 1994 campaign. Mitchell was further frustrated when Republicans won a sweeping victory in November, retaking the House for the first time since the Eisenhower era and regaining control of the Senate.

McConnell called it "one of the most exhilarating experiences I've ever had, because nobody in the history of the Senate had ever filibustered motions to appoint conferees, ever." It is the kind of victory only the most inside players could appreciate, but for McConnell that was in some ways the point. He had shown to his colleagues that he could master the process of the Senate. "I was royally skewered, of course, as usual, all across the country," McConnell said. "They were beginning to know who I was, however."

Thinking of his place in history, McConnell also got a resolution passed that the senator from Kentucky could select the Henry Clay desk.

FOURTEEN

"FIRST-CLASS ASS-KICKING"

The Senate in the 1990s was the spawning pool of presidential ambition. Few had more desire, or higher self-regard, than Phil Gramm of Texas. With campaign donations in the millions, and a conservative record that appealed to the party base, Gramm was considered a formidable candidate. At one event, he boasted that he had the "most reliable friend" in American politics: "ready money."

His run for the Republican presidential nomination in 1996 failed spectacularly, and he had no interest in the campaign committee again. That created an opening for his friend McConnell. Finally he could start a climb on the Senate Republican leadership ladder by winning the race to become chairman of the Republican Senate campaign committee.

But first, he'd have to win his own reelection in 1996. He was faring much better politically at home. Having worked to push Abramson out of the race, McConnell focused on his eventual opponent, Steve Beshear, who had served as lieutenant governor and was considered a strong candidate. As was typical, he started planning for the race the day after his second victory years earlier. This campaign was to begin with the usual fly-around of the state, but fortunately for McConnell, the flight never took off. An attendant at the airfield had mistakenly put jet fuel in a prop plane, and had the plane gotten aloft, it probably would have burst into flames.

The national political climate at the beginning of 1996 saw Republicans emboldened by their historic 1994 victories, and the new House speaker, Newt Gingrich, who talked of a Republican revolution, acting in McConnell's words "like he was president of the United States." McConnell thought Gingrich received far too much credit for the '94 victories, saying that the House Republicans' "Contract with America," a set of ten specific conservative bills, played virtually no role in the landslide win. Instead, he believed voters at the time were upset with Bill Clinton and seeking to punish Democrats. But Gingrich, as would be proven over the next several years, was no match for Clinton's political skills. Clinton reframed the '96 race as a future-oriented "bridge to the twenty-first century" and won easily.

McConnell said, "I chose not to run as a revolutionary in 1996," branding the so-called revolution offered by Gingrich and his allies a "phony package." Instead, he chose to emphasize to voters his "common sense" and "clout." Rather than focusing on plans to cut federal spending, he talked up federal money that had helped Kentucky, like the creation of the state's first federal wildlife preserve. The Kentucky Democratic chairman at the time, Bob Babbage, thought McConnell was being disingenuous and called him on it: "McConnell has read the tea leaves and is now trying to run back to the political middle and away from the Republican extremists." Babbage had it right, McConnell thought. "That's exactly what I was doing."

The *Courier-Journal* did not buy McConnell's posture, either. In an editorial that called McConnell a "Houdini of campaign strategy," the paper warned that "Senator McConnell is going to try to squeeze himself out of the cinched straitjacket and heavy chains of the Republican

Revolution in which he wrapped himself so tightly." But in reality, the editorial argued, "McConnell was the godfather of the Republican Revolution here—the rear-area commander of the 1994 blitzkrieg that overran Democrats in Kentucky's 1st and 2nd congressional districts."

McConnell said later, "I love that editorial. I thought they had it about right, and it drove them crazy. It's always driven them crazy, I think, that I have been able to escape their wrath."

One way McConnell had changed stripes was his reversal on flag burning; he once supported a constitutional amendment to ban it, but now embraced it as part of the right to free speech. He prepared for an attack from those who wanted to prohibit flag burning in part by getting a Vietnam veteran, Jim Warner, to appear in an ad for him. Warner was not just any veteran. He had served as a prisoner of war in the infamous Hanoi Hilton next to John McCain. Warner believed he was fighting for free speech, even in the form of flag burning.

Unlike McConnell's previous campaigns for the Senate, this one featured his spouse, Elaine Chao, who was an energetic and effective advocate. Already a polished public speaker who had served as head of the United Way and director of the Peace Corps, Chao was at ease with the small talk and glad-handing. She also had a warmth and suppleness that her husband often lacked. It didn't hurt that Chao's family represented the embodiment of an immigrant success story; she had arrived in the United States in third grade from Taiwan not knowing a word of English, and her father went on to lead a global shipping company.

The race was never really close. McConnell hewed to his strategy that neither he nor his campaign staff should talk to the media any more than necessary. "It's an enticing thing for some of these people to talk to reporters," McConnell said. "They feel like they've got to tell them what they know. I've always thought that was extraordinarily stupid." He divided issues into two buckets, the "walking around" issues that were banal and obvious and "the real issues, the ones you're going to use." He also deployed his tactics for responding to attacks by opponents, namely if your opponent "flips a pebble at you, hurl a boulder back."

"There was simply no way to explain this in any other way than it was a first-class ass-kicking and against a guy that was a credible person," McConnell said. He was better prepared, he raised more money, and he did not allow Beshear to make the contest a referendum on the incumbent. McConnell also had significant financial advantage and the benefits of incumbency at a time when most Americans cast ballots for the status quo instead of change. (Beshear would go on to be elected governor, and to see his son, Andy, win two terms in the same office.)

The notion of setting a record, of making history, was a constant driver of McConnell's ambition. On this front, his third-term election held special meaning, as it made him the first Kentucky Republican in history to win three full terms in the Senate, a fact duly noted by the *Courier-Journal*: "McConnell routed Democrat Steve Beshear yesterday to become the only Kentucky Republican in history to win three full terms in the Senate."

It was also a time to make another run at leadership in his party, so McConnell campaigned for a third time to lead the National Republican Senatorial Committee. The job has one real mission and that is to win a majority in the Senate, because the party in power controls what the Senate does and when it does it. There are also few ways to better ensure the loyalty of a colleague than helping them win elections by raising money and providing wise political counsel.

The new role led to more media coverage, including a piece in the *Washington Post* by George Lardner Jr. that opened with this paragraph: "Sen. Mitch McConnell (R-Ky.) lives modestly. He picks up his own dry cleaning and often does the shopping and cooking for himself and his wife. But he loves money, perhaps more than any other politician on Capitol Hill. He likes to raise it and he likes to spend it. It's what made him the father of the modern-day Republican Party in Kentucky, and it's what he sees as the key to expanding influence for the GOP in Washington."

McConnell had been so taken by the subject of campaign finance law that he and Steven Law crafted a book proposal with the tentative title *What's So Bad about Money in Politics?* The book, the pitch said, would be a "timely and iconoclastic view" that reinforced McConnell's central argument that money was not only speech but the necessary lubricant of electoral politics. So long as there were limits on contributions and disclosure requirements, the authors argued, no additional regulation was needed. But the proposal stood out because it did call for a far more detailed accounting of the "underground sea of soft money that influences elections." "We should at least require complete disclosure of all spending to influence an election and then consider whether some limits may be appropriate as well." It was a view that did not age well for either man.

McConnell and Law were not able to attract a publisher.

After the 1996 election, which had some fundraising scandals, Congress again started investigating campaign finance issues, and the attention brought with it another movement for legislation to impose limits on campaign spending. "That will not happen," McConnell told the *Post*. McConnell, relying on the Supreme Court decision *Buckley v. Valeo*, made an argument that would become the heart of his political identity: campaign spending is an act of free speech. One of McConnell's most persistent and powerful opponents on this matter was Arizona senator John McCain, who had partnered with Democratic senator Russ Feingold of Wisconsin to push for a dramatic overhaul of the campaign finance system, marking the beginning of a yearslong odyssey.

McConnell strove to make money in politics sound virtuous. "I don't think it's a scandal at all. I think it ought to be applauded and encouraged. For Americans to contribute to the party they believe in and the candidate of their choice, bearing in mind those contributions are limited and fully disclosed, I think is something that is healthy for democracy." McConnell had support in unlikely places, like from the American Civil Liberties Union, which also was concerned about limits on free speech.

On the floor of the Senate, McConnell said, "McCain-Feingold is to democracy what I believed the doomed Clinton health care plan was to medicine. I am doing my level best to ensure it meets the same fate." He also put his political skills on display in assembling a coalition that, in addition to the ACLU, included the National Education Association, the National Rifle Association, and the National Association of Broadcasters. These wildly diverse groups backed his fight on behalf of what they saw as free speech.

Asked by a reporter if he were beating a dead horse, since the opposition to McCain-Feingold at the time was already considerable, McConnell replied, "I hope so." In the process, he also started to earn a nickname that he readily embraced: Darth Vader.

"McConnell went nuts trying to stop this," Feingold recalled of the drive toward the landmark McCain-Feingold campaign finance reforms that eventually became law in 2002. "It was the first demonstration of his willingness to fight these sorts of reform things that would undermine something he really believes in, the value of money in politics."

Treating the fight against the campaign finance proposals just as he would a campaign, McConnell probed the weakness in his opponents' arguments, attacked them serially, and clung to the high-ground argument that he was really fighting for the First Amendment. "Opponents of the bill must . . . increase the pain level and demonstrate voter intensity against the bill back home, especially among Republican base voters," a strategy memo said.

It went on to propose a three-pronged approach to "negatively reposition McCain-Feingold": use paid media to criticize the bill to influence Washington's elite; hit editorial boards in the states of targeted senators; and generate direct voter contact with senators. The plan went on to propose a timeline and a budget, with ads paid for by the "Constitutional Coalition," a prototypical nonprofit Washington front group.

Fred Wertheimer, the former president of Common Cause who fought for reducing the role of money in politics for over half a century, has long been a McConnell critic and legislative opponent. McConnell, he said, saw campaign finance as the issue that "made his bones in the Senate over time. And then he tied it together with raising money. I had the impression that this was the only thing he really cared about on a legislative front for years, and it's still the thing he cares most about."

McConnell's effort to stop campaign finance legislation succeeded in 1997, but he wanted to put more resources behind his effort for future fights. He helped create a think tank whose purpose was to protect political spending from government regulation. It was called the James Madison Center for Free Speech, led by the attorney James Bopp, already famous for his legal work for social conservatives on abortion and other issues. As he walked away from reporters discussing the matter, McConnell said he needed to leave to attend "the final funeral service" for McCain-Feingold. He considered the issue the political equivalent of war "about who gets to speak in this country, who's going to have influence, what kind of country we're going to have. And it's a war between two sides that see it totally differently."

The center was to be funded by tax-exempt donations from contributors whom the group was not required to disclose. One of those donors was Helen Elizabeth Krieble, a wealthy benefactor to numerous conservative causes. She told McConnell in a letter that she was so impressed by the work of the Madison Center that she was enclosing a check for $50,000. McConnell also solicited money from other conservatives like Michael Joyce, then the president of the Bradley Foundation; Betsy DeVos, the wealthy conservative donor from Michigan who would one day serve as education secretary; and from the Prince Foundation, a major supporter of conservative causes, asking each to contribute $50,000.

This money represented the early foundation of a financial network McConnell would build over the course of his career, one he returned to years later when he wanted to use undisclosed donor money to help secure a Republican majority in the Senate.

As his national profile grew, McConnell, taken as he was by his version of celebrity, had his staff keep a running tally of his appearances on national television news programs and mentions in newspapers of prominence outside of Kentucky. "People had some interest in me because they wondered who would be dumb enough to stand up against this worthy idea," McConnell said. In February 1997, McConnell made his first appearance on NBC's *Meet the Press*. In June, the *National Journal* named him to the list of the one hundred most powerful people in Washington. The *Wall Street Journal* editorial page started to take notice. The *New York Times* had positive stories. Paul West of the *Baltimore Sun* wrote, "Few outside his home state of Kentucky know the name Mitch McConnell." That was rapidly changing.

"It's a very competitive situation," McConnell told his biographer John David Dyche. "You are in the midst of a hundred of the sharper politicians in America, and it's not easy to break out of the pack. Everybody, no matter what tactic you employ, everybody is trying to have more influence and get noticed more." He said, "If your name is Kennedy, you're going to sort of have that from the beginning. If you don't come in being a war hero, or from a well-known family, you've got to make it on wit and guile. I must say it took me longer than I thought it was going to."

He pressed to get the attention of Rush Limbaugh, then one of the most important forces in conservative media. Limbaugh eventually embraced his battle against campaign finance reform, and McConnell benefited from the positive reviews beamed to the broadcaster's millions of listeners.

Many Republicans thought they had a winning issue on campaign finance reform that would embarrass President Clinton because Democrats had been caught up in a scandal over their use of so-called soft money to dramatically increase the war chest of the Democratic Party. Though McConnell had warned about soft money earlier, he also saw its allure, and this time did not join much in the criticism. Publicly, McConnell said he wanted Attorney General Janet Reno to appoint an independent counsel to investigate possible violations of campaign finance law. "Privately, I kinda hoped she wouldn't because I figured an independent counsel just wouldn't stick with presidential violations but would go after Congress as well." He said Reno was "incompetent." "She's been one of the worst attorneys general in the country but she's been largely untouchable because she's a woman and because toward the end of her eight years, she's also come down with Parkinson's disease and she's somewhat shaky, and I think just kind of a sympathetic character."

McConnell also looked outward, taking a particular interest in the repressive regime in Burma, championing the plight of Nobel Peace Prize laureate Aung San Suu Kyi, who was under house arrest in her country for more than a decade. His advocacy for her release represented one of the starker examples of his willingness to take a position on an issue that had little if any political benefit. He would eventually team up on an op-ed with Bono to advocate for her, quite the unlikely pair.

He also was outspoken in support for Ukraine, at the time a struggling democracy. He earmarked money to help it make a break from Russia and visited the country for a firsthand assessment. His view on foreign aid was that it should be spent if it advanced American interests. "The Democrats tend to view it more as sort of social welfare overseas."

As the chairman of the Senate campaign committee, McConnell put his strategic political skills to work immediately, shoring up the committee's finances, then making tactical decisions about where its spending could have its greatest impact. But things got off to a rocky start. "In '97 I was just trying to dig out of debt," McConnell said. "It was very frustrating. . . . We had a lot of kind of bullshitters who were spending too much money raising the money."

Fundraising letters were sent out in McConnell's name, florid screeds that used terms like "Red China." "Well, fundraising letters are outrageous," McConnell said. "The truth of the matter is—I could never say this publicly—the truth of the matter is, I won't even read them. I think the best thing to do is kind of wink and nod and say, 'If fundraising letters were food, they'd be hot sauce and not oatmeal.'" He was not embarrassed. This was simply how the game was played.

While many Republicans had been hopeful going into 1998, especially after the *Washington Post* published an explosive story in January about Clinton's possible relationship with a White House intern, Monica Lewinsky, McConnell was not nearly so confident. He surveyed the electoral map with an air of detachment. He would not allocate money for candidates who had no chance, nor was he going to give money to incumbents who were almost certain to cruise to reelection.

McConnell did have one ripe target in his sights: Senator Feingold, McCain's partner in the campaign finance legislation McConnell so vigorously opposed. But the Republican candidate in the race, Mark Neumann, rejecting McConnell's advice, emphasized his opposition to abortion. Neumann had made his opposition to late-term abortions a pillar of his platform, and he insisted to McConnell that 85 percent of people agreed with that position. McConnell told Neumann that if he continued to talk about it, voters would view him "as some kind of zealot on this issue and I think it's going to hurt you." McConnell continued to put money into the race. Neumann, who was ahead with nine days to go, continued to run his anti-abortion ad, and lost by two points.

McConnell advised GOP candidates running against incumbents to always attack the person in office and not make the race about themselves. "The campaign is about firing," he said repeatedly. One of the challengers, Peter Fitzgerald of Illinois, took McConnell's advice and beat Carol Moseley Braun; another, Matt Fong, did not, and he lost to Boxer. Candidate quality, McConnell noted, was fundamentally important, a phrase that would get far more attention when he repeated it more than twenty years later.

McConnell's approach to competition, whether against a Demo-crat or in his own party, was essentially the same. The object was to crush the opponent and ensure that he came out looking stronger. He blamed several of the Republican losses in 1998 on poorly run cam-paigns, bad tactics, and an "idiot" who was running in South Carolina, Representative Bob Inglis.

McConnell was also chairman of the Rules Committee, which has jurisdiction over everything from the carpet in the Senate to impeach-ment, and the latter quickly came before the Senate when the House voted to impeach Clinton. While McConnell believed that Clinton had committed an impeachable offense by lying to a grand jury about the Lewinsky matter, he thought the politics of it were bad for Repub-licans. He knew that Democrats almost certainly had the votes to re-sult in Clinton's acquittal, and he did not want to give them the forum to argue that the case was really about sexual conduct. He moved to try to limit the damage.

One way was to push for no live witnesses at the Senate trial, to limit the television exposure. He also argued for the Senate to deliber-ate in private. He succeeded with both. He also eventually was part of the coalition of senators who voted to kill the independent counsel statute, which allowed for the appointment of a prosecutor with nearly unfettered investigative authority.

His involvement led to even more media attention, and he noted that during that period he had been on weekend news programs almost as much as the media-savvy McCain. "Now, why is that important?" McConnell asked rhetorically. "In politics, perception is reality and perception and power is typically related to weekend shows, because when you're on shows like *Meet the Press* or *Face the Nation* or *This Week* or *Inside Edition*, which is a CNN show, or *Fox News Sunday*, the perception is that you're in the middle of what's happened, so it was really a breakthrough for me."

McConnell bathed in the attention. "Everybody likes to be rel-evant," he said. "I mean, if you're in this business, you obviously have some ego or you wouldn't be in it in the first place. . . . It raises your overall profile and also makes you a player in Washington."

He showed rhetorical dexterity in his appearances, even on shows that were dominated by panels that disagreed with him on the issues. He appeared on CNN's *Capital Gang*, whose panel included Margaret Carlson of *Time*; Al Hunt, the Washington bureau chief of the *Wall Street Journal*; Mark Shields, the redoubtable left-leaning columnist; and Bob Novak, a noted conservative—all of them had been loud McConnell critics at various points. "I began the show by saying, 'I'm just thrilled to be here tonight. Margaret's called me a thug and Al's called me a legislative lightweight. Mark has likened me to Dracula, and Bob has called me a backbencher. . . . I feel like a lamb in a lions' convention. I can't wait for the group hug at the end.'" It was a premeditated opening, but also a disarming moment and the panel members broke into laughter.

Even off-the-cuff, he had moments of rhetorical nimbleness that could put fellow senators on the defensive. McCain had called the campaign finance system corrupt, and McConnell challenged him on the Senate floor to name the senator who was corrupt. McCain responded by saying he was referring to the system, not an individual, and McConnell shot back, "Well, that's like saying the gang is corrupt but none of the gangsters are. Who is corrupt?"

McConnell said that standing up to McCain earned him pats on the back from other Republicans, who thought McCain had engaged in years of "demagoguery and threatening everybody and blowing up right and left—and who don't have much use for McCain." He said he enjoyed debating McCain on campaign finance reform because "he doesn't, candidly, know the subject all that well."

After the debate, McCain told the *New York Times* columnist Maureen Dowd, "The exercise we went through, I didn't enjoy it. It wasn't very pleasant, to say the least. But I've faced a lot tougher things in my life than Mitch McConnell's temper tantrums." She called McConnell the hard-boiled madam of this Capitol Hill bawdy house. "By trying to force Senator McCain to whittle down the problem to individual quid pro quos, Madam Mitch hoped to obscure the fact that the whole joint is for sale," Dowd wrote.

While he was seeking his own headlines, McConnell was also always careful to make sure he used his power to do things for Kentucky. He paid slavish attention to state legislative races and county races, always with an eye for talent to build a Republican bench. When it came to federal money, even in an era when McCain and others would rail against wasteful federal spending, McConnell, as a member of the Appropriations Committee, said dryly that his definition of pork was a "project in Indiana."

"The Appropriations Committee is where you bring home the bacon," McConnell said. And he did, for Fort Knox, to help clean up a toxic waste site near Paducah, a chemical weapons disposal facility in Richmond, other federal dollars for the area of western Kentucky known as the "Land between the Lakes," and $5 million for his alma mater at the University of Louisville. He also helped to steer the phase-out of the federal tobacco program. Over the course of his career, the federal money he designated for Kentucky would total in the billions of dollars.

FIFTEEN

"NO SUBSTITUTE
FOR WINNING"

As the presidential campaign of 2000 started, McConnell was certain of his feelings about two of the candidates. He did not think that fellow senator John McCain had the temperament to be president—describing him to me decades later as "singularly inappropriate for the presidency"—and he was concerned, rightly as it turned out, that McCain could win the New Hampshire primary and get a jump on the path to the nomination. The reservations he had about McCain, however, were tepid when compared with his feelings about the likely Democratic nominee, Vice President Al Gore, whom he derided as "an arrogant ass." McConnell backed Texas governor George W. Bush from the start, as did Elaine Chao, who raised more than $100,000 for his campaign.

Bush ended up winning the nomination, and McConnell set out to do whatever he could to help Bush and hurt Gore, especially in Kentucky, where Clinton had won twice. Gore's environmental policies were wildly unpopular in coal country, and McConnell did his best to paint him as an extremist. The election was the most bitterly contested in more than a century, and on election night, there was no clear winner. McConnell stayed at the National Republican Senatorial Committee building until 4 a.m. The outcome was still uncertain.

For thirty-six days, which McConnell described as the most miserable of his life, Bush and Gore waged fights in the courts. "I felt so deeply about that, that it ended up being more important to me than control of the Senate, or anything else," he said, adding that he had never felt so elated as when the Supreme Court delivered the presidency to Bush, stopping a recount in Florida. As the chairman of the Rules Committee, McConnell was in charge of the inauguration ceremony at the Capitol. "The thought of introducing Albert Gore as president of the United States was enough to make me want to call in sick," he said.

With Bush now the president-elect, McConnell began advocating for the new president to put Chao in his cabinet. She was initially interviewed by Bush to be transportation secretary, but he ended up selecting Congressman Norm Mineta, a Democrat from California, to try to take some of the partisan sting out of the controversy over how he was elected. The next option was labor secretary, with Bush initially favoring Linda Chavez. Her nomination was scuttled after it was learned she had hired an undocumented worker.

"So I get on the phone again, I talk to [Senate Majority Leader] Trent Lott, I talk to [Vice President–elect] Dick Cheney and I said to Cheney, 'Look, unless we've got a quota system under which there can't be more than one Asian in the Cabinet, Elaine is perfect for this job. You get a conservative like Chavez without the rough edges, and she's not going to make anybody mad." Bush eventually agreed. Chao picked Steven Law to be her chief of staff.

Gore, as vice president, had to preside over the ceremonial counting of the electoral votes in January. McConnell was more charitable to Gore on this matter, acknowledging how difficult it must have been for Gore to be on the podium at the inauguration after having come within five hundred or so votes of winning Florida and after carrying the popular vote. "It's always hard to lose, but I'm sure that was doubly difficult. . . . He was completely under control. He didn't show any emotion, went through it like he was on automatic."

Many Gore supporters felt the election had been stolen, and that the Supreme Court issued a partisan ruling that started an erosion of confidence in that institution. "But to the credit of Democrats, Gore conceded, nobody tried to have a coup," McConnell said. "We had an orderly transfer." At that point in American history, an orderly transfer was presumed, even after such a disputed election.

While the presidency was settled, McConnell's fate was not. As Senate Republican campaign committee chairman, he had now overseen two election cycles with mediocre results, and he worried his colleagues might be in the mood for change. He had his eye on the number two position, assistant majority leader, the party whip, its chief vote counter in a race two years away. He used that time to fully prepare to move up in leadership. The term comes from foxhunting in which the "whipper's job" is to "keep the hounds from straying from the pack." It aptly applied to politics. He studied everything he could about the other Republicans, the political makeup of their states, what local issues were important, details about their family life, and what they needed to win another term.

Even with the larger responsibilities, one piece of legislation, the McCain-Feingold bill, was of special interest to McConnell, and he would try to generate votes against it, once again making himself the face of the opposition. He wrote an op-ed in the *New York Times* under the headline "In Defense of Soft Money," in which he predicted the dangerous consequences of the bill, which banned large corporate donations to parties, among other provisions.

"It now appears that among the legacies of the Bill Clinton presidency will be a 'reform' of campaign financing that devastates the national political parties," McConnell wrote, without noting that his fellow Republican McCain was the prime mover of the effort.

He argued that if soft money contributions to political parties were banned, the money would find its way into the political system in ways that were even harder to trace. "If special interests cannot give to parties as they have, they will use their money to influence elections in other ways: placing unlimited, unregulated, and undisclosed issue advertisements, mounting their own get-out-the-vote efforts, forming their own action groups . . . shadowy groups with innocuous-sounding names like the Group in Favor of Republican Majorities or the Citizens for Democrats in 2012 that will hold potentially serious sway in a post–McCain-Feingold world where the parties are diminished for lack of money.

"Do we really want the two-party system, which has served us so well, to be weakened in favor of greater power for wealthy candidates and single-issue groups? McCain-Feingold will not take any money out of politics. It just takes the parties out of politics." He was right about the impact on the parties, which in significant ways have been supplanted by Super PACs, including perhaps the most powerful one, which is aligned with McConnell.

Another matter of crucial import would soon spark McConnell's ire. In a break with precedent, Democrats started filibustering some of Bush's nominees to federal appeals courts rather than giving them simple up or down votes. He implored Democrats to return to the previous practice, adding, "I fear if we don't—if we don't resist this game of victory at any cost—the damage will be greater than those who perpetrate it can imagine." It was another example of McConnell seeing the potential of a dramatic escalation of an issue, even if one day he, too, would take brutish advantage of it.

Ever the perpetual planner when it came to his own political fortunes in Kentucky, McConnell was also plotting his strategy on how to best target Lois Weinberg, the daughter of a former Kentucky governor and a likely Democratic opponent in 2002. At the time, McConnell enjoyed a remarkably high approval rating in the state, in the mid-sixties.

His opposition researchers found that Weinberg and her husband were embroiled in a land dispute with a woman named Rose Baker over a parcel in eastern Kentucky that had potentially valuable mineral rights. They also found that the Weinbergs had at one point driven a bulldozer onto the land, suggesting they would soon start excavation. McConnell's team made an alliance with Baker, and at the Fancy Farm event that year handed out toy bulldozers. His researchers also discovered that Weinberg, who held a master's degree from Harvard, owned a home on St. John in the Virgin Islands, which became the backdrop for a commercial in which McConnell painted her as elitist.

As the race played out, it was clear that Weinberg would not be a strong challenger, to the point that McConnell did something out of character: he ran a heavy dose of positive ads. One of Weinberg's prime attacks, over McConnell's opposition to an amendment to prohibit flag burning, fell flat when McConnell ran a counter ad that featured a D-Day hero supporting him and his position. "As soon as she hit me, we hit back, and we hit back hard," he said.

His polling showed he might have a shot at the largest Republican margin in state history, besting that of John Sherman Cooper. The record probably meant something only to McConnell, but he pursued it and achieved it. "It's amazing what winning big does for your image and for the respect with which you are treated," he said. "There's just no substitute for winning and winning convincingly." He had no kind words for Weinberg. "She was whiny and nasty. She wasn't even gracious on election night."

McConnell savored the praise his victory brought, including the credit he was now earning for building the Republican Party in Kentucky. John David Dyche caught the senator's eye with a column he wrote about a week after the election: "Mitch McConnell bestrides the Commonwealth like a political colossus. Friend and foe alike hail him as the architect of the GOP ascendancy in Kentucky."

Winning in Kentucky was the essential predicate to his real ambition: winning in Washington. He had realized as early as 1996 that the whip position would be open in 2002 because of party-imposed term limits. In ways subtle and overt, he had been working toward this opportunity for six years. Still, things had not gone according to plan: he had a middling record achieving results on the Senate campaign committee and feared he might be "a dead man walking in terms of trying to get elected whip." To help his chances, in 2001 he began meeting with senators one-on-one to ask for their support, urging his colleagues to keep the meetings confidential. He started to keep a tally of his commitments. He said he never counts on someone's vote unless they look him in the eye and say, "'I'm for you.' Not 'I may be for you' or 'I'm leaning for you.'" Of all of McConnell's political skills, his ability to count votes ranks high. He received modest opposition from Senator Larry Craig of Idaho, who obviously had not taken the race as seriously as McConnell. He eventually told McConnell he would support him, and the victory was unanimous.

McConnell thought that meant he could look forward to a long Christmas break in Kentucky, but a shocking development tested his political instincts. On December 5, 2002, a large celebration was held for the one hundredth birthday of Senator Strom Thurmond of South Carolina, during which the majority leader, Trent Lott, said the country might be in a better place if Thurmond, who ran for president as an unapologetic segregationist in 1948, had won. (Lott's remarks doomed his career, though McConnell said he thought it was a case of "selective outrage" by the media since Senator Robert Byrd, who earlier in his life had been a member of the Ku Klux Klan, said the "N-word" on national TV the year before without sparking the same widespread condemnation.)

McConnell's first thought in the wake of the Lott scandal was that it could create an opening for him to become majority leader. Then he did a bloodless cost-benefit analysis. After weighing the politics, he decided instead to defer to someone McConnell liked to refer to as "the most interesting man in the world," Senator Bill Frist of Tennessee. Frist was a heart surgeon, heir to a health-care business fortune, and marathon runner who did charity surgeries in Africa in his spare time. He was also a favorite of the White House, particularly President

George W. Bush's political adviser, Karl Rove. More heavily weighted
in McConnell's calculation, Frist had told him he didn't plan to serve
beyond 2006—he was widely believed to be contemplating a run for
the White House—so McConnell would have another opportunity to
run for leader then.

"Would I like to be majority leader? You bet," McConnell said in
an oral history interview in 2003. "Will I be too old in 2006 and have
been around too long? Who knows?" In public, when asked about becoming majority leader, he refused to answer.

Liberals loudly criticized Lott, but in McConnell's estimation, it
was conservatives who actually did him in. He said conservatives had
always been irritated by the proposition that their governing philosophy had been "equated with racism. And it's been something that I
personally have always found offensive." He nonetheless realized Lott
was doomed. "There's certain mistakes you can't make if you're in a
leadership position."

As 2002 came to a close, McConnell, now sixty, underwent his
annual physical with the Capitol physician. He thought it would be
routine, then the doctor asked if he had ever had a heart stress test, and
McConnell said no. The doctor advised him to get one given his age.
Through the holiday season, McConnell said he had a strange sense
of "foreboding." "I remember telling Elaine, 'You know, I never made
any funeral arrangements in case something happened to me.' And I
remember writing down some instructions and just telling her where
I was going to put them."

He came back to the Senate and was sworn in for his fourth term.
Later in the month he attended the Alfalfa Club dinner, an exclusive
gathering of the political and business elite, on a Saturday night before
Super Bowl Sunday. He got up early the next morning for his stress
test. "I flunked it, which was pretty scary," he said. The doctor ordered
a heart catheterization to get a better look, and she wanted to do it that
day. McConnell put it off until the end of the week because he wanted
to attend Bush's State of the Union address. The heart catheterization

revealed that he needed a triple bypass; McConnell said it was "one of the worst days of my life." Senator Frist came to the hospital later that day, agreed with the diagnosis, and recommended a surgeon, who had done a similar operation on Senator Bob Graham, a Democrat from Florida, earlier that very day.

McConnell asked if he could do the surgery on Monday, then spent a nervous weekend contemplating his fate. On one level, the heart issue made no sense. He felt fine, and over the course of his working life, he had only taken one sick day since law school. On Sunday, he was driven to the hospital, took a sleeping pill, and was up by 5 a.m. The surgery went well, but was highly invasive with a slow recovery. The first call to McConnell's new chief of staff, Billy Piper, came from Senator Edward Kennedy asking what he could do to help McConnell.

After three weeks, doctors said he could return to work, but the five hours he spent at the Senate were too much, and he had to scale things back for several more weeks. During periods with a lot of votes, he would cast his, then retreat to a hideaway office to lie down.

He started feeling depressed, a common occurrence after heart surgery. "You feel like you're not getting better fast enough and you begin to wonder if you're ever going to get better," he said. "It was frightening, and it sort of brings home a sense of your mortality."

He spent time watching movies because he was too tired to read. He had gone from being in the thick of important policy debates to simply picking up the *TV Guide* to scan for movie options. He realized how much his world and self-worth were wrapped up in his work.

"What's stressful for me is not having stress," McConnell said.

Though he and Feingold argued bitterly over campaign finance, they were not personally hostile. Feingold wrote him a note to say, "I hope you are doing okay. I miss my Darth Vader." McConnell wrote back, "Don't worry about old Darth Vader."

Indeed, Darth Vader was back on the job soon enough. McConnell's role was clear, to advance the Bush agenda on the backs of Republican votes that he was tasked with securing. To reporters, though, McConnell said he thought he could help reach bipartisan solutions.

One item high on Bush's agenda, adding a prescription drug benefit to Medicare, would in fact require Democratic votes. After it passed, with considerable debate, McConnell was left wondering if the government could actually afford the program and whether other proposed reforms of Medicare would really work. "We don't really know any of this yet, but we do know the politics of it, and the politics of it is that a Republican president and a Republican Congress enacted the first significant Medicare bill since the system started."

Far more contentious was Bush's pitch for more than $87 billion to fund the war in Iraq and rebuild what American armaments had destroyed. McConnell wanted to be the one who closed the deal for the president. It came down to two Republican senators, Ben Nighthorse Campbell of Colorado, who had once been a Democrat, and Sam Brownback of Kansas. He wore Brownback down over time, but for Campbell, he had to make a special deal. He assured Campbell that he had secured a promise from Rove that Bush would hold a fundraiser for Campbell in Colorado. "We certainly didn't say anything publicly about that being the reason," McConnell said. "I turned them both. And it was one of the big accomplishments of the year and widely discussed in inside circles."

After the vote, McConnell led a delegation to Afghanistan, Iraq, and Pakistan, primarily as a show of support for the Bush policy, but privately as a test of his own health to show he had fully recovered from his heart surgery. He took the Capitol physician along just to be safe. He was impressed by the racial diversity in the U.S. military, including its commanding ranks, and came away thinking the war was winnable—all in line with Bush's view.

With, from his point of view, great progress in Iraq and Afghanistan, McConnell began to focus on Bush's reelection campaign in 2004 and the prospect for Republican gains in the Senate. Near the end of 2003, McConnell thought Bush's most likely Democratic opponent would be Governor Howard Dean of Vermont. Dean had rocketed to the top of opinion polls, but his campaign ultimately collapsed after a dismal showing in Iowa, the first contest for the nomination. Even McConnell, with his formidable political instincts, badly misread that one.

He also was on the wrong side of an issue of far greater significance to him, the Supreme Court lawsuit he brought to challenge the constitutionality of the McCain-Feingold campaign finance law: *McConnell v. the Federal Election Commission*. McConnell fought hard to be the named plaintiff in the suit, and to assemble a diverse coalition of advocates, led by the conservative lawyer Kenneth Starr and the famed First Amendment lawyer Floyd Abrams. They were up against two other lawyers with lofty reputations, Ted Olson, who had argued *Bush v. Gore* on behalf of Bush, and Seth Waxman, who had served as solicitor general in the Clinton administration.

McConnell sat in for the four hours allotted for what he said were "very, very animated" arguments from both sides. With Justice Sandra Day O'Connor casting the swing vote, the court upheld the law. "The Supreme Court is the last word," McConnell said, "so we lost." He called McCain to congratulate him on his victory.

Otherwise, he wasn't so charitable. "This law will not remove one dime for politics," he said, "and these stupid restrictions on outside groups are not going to be effective." He called the ruling "the worst Supreme Court decision since the *Dred Scott* case," which upheld the separate but equal doctrine. Money, McConnell knew, would find a way into the system, and in a few years he'd be proven correct, as would his assessment that the ruling would lead to even less transparency about who was trying to influence the political process.

Still, the defeat did not seem to diminish his standing among his colleagues. Carl Hulse wrote in the *New York Times* that McConnell's work on the issue "could pay dividends because Mr. McConnell is viewed as a probable candidate to try to succeed Senator Bill Frist of Tennessee as Republican leader." McConnell was seen as a "tough inside player in Congress . . . who is smart and not shy about letting it show" and is "considered by many colleagues to be among the savvi-est tacticians in the Senate and a relentless opponent, a trait that may have sprung from his battle with polio as a youngster."

McConnell's political skills and his increasing interest in the com-position of the courts was also playing out in the Senate. Democrats continued to block many of Bush's judicial nominees to federal appeals courts, the highly influential panels that sit just below the Supreme Court in the judicial hierarchy. By using the filibuster, Democrats were forcing Republicans to come up with sixty votes, which they could not for the most part do. "They've never been filibustered before," McCon-nell said of federal judicial nominees. He could see around the corner to realize what the next steps in the escalation of the war over judicial nominations would be.

"The sad thing for the Senate as an institution is that the old view that you would never kill a judge on a filibuster is over, and one day there will be a Democratic president and those chickens will come home to roost," McConnell said in December 2003. Democrats, he said, were being "very short-sighted because they're just living in the present and not thinking of the impact of this on them when they get somebody that they like in the White House. Now there will be no barriers against defeating liberal judges in the future. . . . I think it's unfortunate, but I think it's with us forever."

On that point, McConnell was prescient.

Bush recalled his frustration at Democrats blocking his choices for federal appeals courts, particularly Miguel Estrada, a favorite of the conservative movement. When Democrats decided to filibuster the Estrada nomination, "Mitch made it pretty clear" Republicans would not forget, Bush said.

Bush's first brush with a powerful Senate leader came when his grandfather, Senator Prescott Bush, introduced him to Lyndon John-son. By comparison, he said, McConnell was far more understated. "At times he would take me aside and share personal thoughts that he didn't want to air in front of other senators," Bush told me. "He is a quiet man with a lot of experience who was constantly thinking ahead of others."

The 2004 election cycle started with McConnell again focused on helping Republican Senate candidates, with none more important to him than Jim Bunning in Kentucky. He thought Bush got off to a troubling start with an uninspired State of the Union address and many other unforced errors. The fact that Dean was not going to be the nominee also meant Republicans would have a stronger challenger in Senator John Kerry of Massachusetts. Things got worse after the first debate between Bush and Kerry. "Clearly, the president was not ready," McConnell said. "It was a terrible performance. He was smirking and slouching, and the critics were essentially correct, he ran out of things to say."

More discreetly, he was trying to lock down firm commitments for a leadership race two years away, promising fellow senators he would not discuss their position with the media. He began to feel increasingly confident, but noted, "I've got to avoid making a dumb mistake or suffering from hubris or overconfidence."

He held fundraisers for other Republican Senate candidates in his home state of Kentucky, unusual at the time, and he drew $350,000 from his own reelection account to help them. "That's clearly related to leadership aspirations," he said. "We raised half a million dollars for three guys and you know, it probably won't surprise you that two of the three of them are for me for majority leader and the other one I haven't talked to about it yet."

McConnell had studied other Senate leadership races with particular attention to the ascent of Lyndon Johnson. He noted Johnson's astuteness in making fast friends with the powerful Senator Richard Russell from the day Johnson was sworn in. The whip's job opened, and LBJ, with Russell's strong backing, became whip in just his third year in the Senate. The majority leader was ousted a year later, and Johnson took his place. "Everybody remembers how good LBJ was, but in this particular period, he was also damn lucky," McConnell said.

He had read Robert Caro's iconic *Master of the Senate*, and while he agreed with Caro about Johnson's prowess, his view was that the opening that Johnson got had more to do with luck than skill.

Bush slowly started to turn things around, primarily thanks to a Rove-inspired focus on more rural areas in places like Ohio. On Election Day, Bush overperformed in those areas and that delivered him a second term. "I thought the president might lose," McConnell said.

He felt even worse about Bunning's prospects, and he essentially became the campaign's chief strategist for its last two weeks. He persuaded Bunning to reject consultants' advice to run a mix of positive and negative ads and instead do 100 percent attack ads to drive up negative sentiment about his opponent.

Those included ads that noted Dr. Daniel Mongiardo did not support the anti–gay marriage amendment. Still, going into the final weekend, McConnell felt like he had to almost drag Bunning across the finish line. Prone to gaffes, Bunning made one for the ages when he said in front of a camera that he knew little about things happening in Iraq, had not read a newspaper in weeks, and listened only to Fox News. McConnell thought Bunning was in serious danger of losing.

Bunning won, and his victory was just one measure of McConnell's power in the state. Another came earlier in the year when the state GOP had undertaken a dramatic renovation of its state party headquarters. McConnell had raised considerable money for the party, and the party returned the favor by naming the building for McConnell.

He was getting positive national notice, too, including a profile by Howard Fineman in *Newsweek* that called him "the take-no-prisoners ruler of the Bluegrass" and the "master of all of the Kentucky he surveys." Abramson, the Louisville mayor who McConnell had dissuaded from running against him in 1996, told Fineman that the statue of Henry Clay at the Jefferson County courthouse might need to be replaced by one of McConnell.

His station in the Senate had risen. As the party whip, he had a position of power, with a grand office just steps from the Senate floor, a security detail, and the opportunity to build a number of favors among his colleagues. But being a number two, he said, is "a little bit awkward. You're not quite totally in charge. You're always sort of playing second fiddle. I guess I'd rather be second fiddle than playing no fiddle at all, but it's still better to be number one than be number two, which is why someday I would love to have that job."

There was another notable election in 2004, and one that would ultimately help to shape McConnell's reputation in the Senate. A little-known Democratic state legislator from Illinois, Barack Obama, was elected to the Senate.

SIXTEEN

DREAM DEFERRED, ACHIEVED

Given the abundance of towering egos and ample résumés in the Senate, McConnell's climb to leadership was only slightly less likely than that of his Democratic counterpart, Harry Reid. McConnell and Reid had much in common. Both were fiercely partisan, spoke only when it suited them, and were willing to assert the fullest extent of their power to get what they wanted. Neither man was in danger of being named most popular, but either might have been named most effective. Reid lacked McConnell's rhetorical dexterity and some of his social graces, but he could match him in patience and discipline. Neither man was imposing physically, though Reid had been an amateur boxer. From their shared experience as party whips, both knew how to wage a partisan fight and how to count.

Reid and Democrats had blocked ten of Bush's nominees to federal appeals courts by 2008, concerned that Bush was seeding these influential positions with doctrinaire conservatives. Reid's strategy originated during a Democratic weekend retreat in Farmington, Pennsylvania, in late April 2001, when law professors Laurence Tribe and Cass Sunstein counseled Democrats that they were under no obligation to confirm a judicial nominee, and that the filibuster was a tool at their disposal to stop one. Not all Democrats agreed, but Chuck Schumer pressed forward, urging his colleagues in 2003 to use the filibuster to block votes on nominees they opposed.

This caused great frustration among the Republicans, who held the majority in the Senate. They contended Democrats were using a procedural tool never before employed to thwart judicial nominees by denying them a simple up or down vote by the Senate. Even with the controversy over Clarence Thomas's nomination in 1991, Democrats had not resorted to using the filibuster. Thomas was confirmed, 52–48.

Nothing in the Senate rules said a judicial nominee could not be filibustered, but, as McConnell said, "A lot of things you could do but you don't do. The tradition is clear," judicial nominees had not been filibustered if they had majority support. He thought the Democrats' approach was shortsighted. "Because in spite of my best efforts and others, they're going to have a president again one of these days," he said at the time. "And it struck me that this whole thing was motivated by this hatred of Bush, which is so pronounced that they're willing to do anything to either make him look bad or defeat him."

Frist, the courtly surgeon-politician from Tennessee, threatened to use his majority to change the Senate rules and prohibit using the filibuster for judges, which came to be referred to as the "nuclear option." It was a bold move, and one that might have been motivated by Frist's ambitions to run for president.

But a bipartisan group of fourteen senators convened and fashioned a compromise that averted the need for Frist to follow through on his warning, allowing confirmation votes to proceed. For a time, the tradition held, and McConnell noted, "The Senate is very filibuster-averse right now." Even with the filibuster tabled, for the time being, the struggle over judicial appointments raged on.

Senator Edward Kennedy and McConnell were on opposite sides of the confrontation over judicial nominees and much else, but

McConnell invited him to speak at the McConnell Center in the thick of the debate. The Republican came away seeing a measure of greatness in the Democratic Massachusetts senator, a man he had first encountered as a Senate intern in the 1960s. Kennedy delivered what McConnell called a "presidential quality" speech. Kennedy also came bearing a gift, presenting McConnell with a photo of John F. Kennedy and John Sherman Cooper, knowing McConnell's affection for Cooper, with a handwritten note about the relationship.

That sort of comity was an outlier in the clash over the composition of the nation's highest court. The matter had taken on added urgency because there was a widespread belief that there would be an opening on the Supreme Court after its term ended in June 2005. Indeed, on July 1, Justice Sandra Day O'Connor announced that she would retire upon the confirmation of a successor. Less than three weeks later, Bush nominated fifty-year-old federal appeals court judge John Roberts as her replacement. Then, on September 3, Chief Justice William Rehnquist died, and Bush switched Roberts to the court's top job. Roberts was easily confirmed, 78–22, with twenty-two Democrats voting for him. Kennedy voted against him.

That still left the O'Connor opening, and Bush initially announced that his White House counsel, Harriet Miers, would be his nominee. Compared with most Supreme Court nominees of the era, Miers's résumé was thin, raising questions about her suitability for the highest court.

Though McConnell praised Miers publicly, calling her "well qualified" and an "excellent nomination," he privately believed the opposite and thought her nomination was a mistake from the start. In fact, had he not been the party whip, charged with getting Bush's nominations passed in the Senate, he said he would have called the White House and asked how to get the decision reversed. He couldn't do so without jeopardizing his chances of climbing higher in the party ranks, so he counseled Frist, as majority leader, to do so instead. McConnell recalls telling Frist, "This is an unpleasant duty that needs to be carried out, and, unfortunately, I think it's your duty and not mine. But if I were in your job, here's what I would do. I would call the president of the United States myself and I would say, 'Mr. President, this nomination is not going to fly.'" That account, McConnell said in an oral history, has "never appeared in print, and I would like for it not to appear in print again."

To McConnell's relief, the Miers nomination was ultimately withdrawn, with consequences few could have envisioned at the time. Bush instead selected Samuel Alito, a federal appeals court judge from New Jersey, and one with a starkly conservative record.

McConnell and other Republicans left nothing to chance, preparing for Alito's confirmation hearing as though it were high-stakes litigation. Republican staff filled banker's boxes and binders with opposition research, potential questions that Democrats might ask, and sample answers that Alito should strongly be urged to give. They had monitored every utterance from Roberts's confirmation, mining the record for clues as to how Democrats would likely oppose Alito. The goal was clear: No surprises. Say as little as possible, avoid controversy, and let the majority ultimately work its will. The "simple and sound" principles of fairness, McConnell argued, required Alito to get an up or down vote.

"It was one of the least pleasant experiences of my life," Alito told me in an interview in his chambers. "I got a lot of very good advice, a lot of savvy advice about what I should do at the hearings and in getting ready for them. They didn't tell me to say anything that I didn't believe in, but I was the farthest thing from a politician and a Washington insider." If Alito had an answer that staff found problematic, they suggested a more palatable approach.

It worked. On January 31, 2006, Alito was confirmed by a vote of 58–42, with the support of only four Democrats. During the confirmation hearing, McConnell said, "What we guarantee you is a dignified process here, a respectful hearing, and at the end of that process an up or down vote, as has always been the case on Supreme Court nominees throughout the history of the Senate." "There has never been a filibuster of a Supreme Court nomination in the history of the country and I don't think we are going to start to now. . . . We stand today on the brink of a new and reckless effort by a few to deny the rights of many to exercise our constitutional duty to advise and consent, to give this man the simple up or down vote he deserves. . . . If this hyperpolitization of the judicial confirmation process continues, I fear in this moment we will have institutionalized this behavior, and some day we will be hard pressed not to employ political tests and tactics against a Supreme Court nominee of a Democratic president."

Alito would go on to help forge a conservative bulwark on the court, first in his dissents and later in the majority. He benefited greatly from the compromise reached by the bipartisan group of senators over the filibuster. Otherwise, McConnell said, the Alito nomination would not have stood a chance because his record indicated a hard shift to the right from O'Connor. McConnell had another, more personal stake in Alito's elevation: he thought it might give him another opportunity to challenge the McCain-Feingold campaign finance law, as he believed the justice might embrace the argument that money is speech. The broader question of whether a party would filibuster a judicial nominee would wait for another day.

Supreme Court nominations were not nearly so top of mind to Americans as the war in Iraq, and McConnell in that case was quite willing to make the difficult phone call to push through Bush's other priorities. Worried that Republicans could fall short of votes on a deficit reduction bill, McConnell had to contact Vice President Dick Cheney, who was traveling in Afghanistan, to implore him to get back to cast the deciding vote. His return proved essential. The measure passed only by Cheney breaking the tie.

McConnell also had some bipartisan moments. He worked with Representative Jesse Jackson Jr. of Illinois to have a statue of the civil rights icon Rosa Parks placed in the Capitol. "I thought if ever there were an individual who symbolized America's original sin, it was Rosa Parks," McConnell said. He lamented the "complicated" debate of his time over racial quotas and preferences, "none of which I like." But when Parks energized the civil rights movement by refusing to give up her seat in a Montgomery, Alabama, bus to a white man in 1955, "the right and wrong was much more apparent, and I thought she was a worthy subject to be in the Capitol." More worthy than some other people or statues in the place, he added with a laugh.

McConnell rarely goes it alone, but he essentially did with his opposition to an amendment to prohibit flag burning, a case where he was willing to risk his chance to move up in the Republican Senate leadership by standing for what he thought was a matter of principle. A sweeping majority in his party opposed his view, and McConnell's vote ended up being decisive in defeating the amendment.

By early 2006, Bush's favorability numbers had improved from an anemic level in the low to mid-thirties to a more respectable level in the mid-forties. McConnell thought that as long as the president's rating was near fifty, he would not be a drag on Republicans running that year, which would give them the strongest chance to maintain their majority and for McConnell to get the top Senate job.

McConnell was hoping to run for that job unopposed following Frist's retirement, but there were rumblings that Senator Trent Lott might try to regain his old post. McConnell had gotten along well with Lott and had been intensely loyal, a feeling that started to change when it looked like Lott might try to block his path. "I sort of stuck with Lott until the last dog died, when his ass was in a sling back in 2002," McConnell said.

He considered Lott a person who cared about process and not about ideas. "His approach this year has been it seems he has few unexpressed thoughts. In other words, he still walks out in the hall and starts talking to reporters." He added, "Again, since this tape is only for my own use, I think it's been quite childish behavior. It's sort of 'Look at me. Look at me,' you know, and plays for attention. . . . I don't believe a word he's saying right now." McConnell said this in an oral history, which he originally intended to withhold from the public until after he left office.

In the end, Lott did not challenge McConnell for the leadership of Senate Republicans. As he tended his own ambitions to win GOP control in the chamber, McConnell cast his eyes over a troubling landscape for Republicans at large.

McConnell was convinced that Democrats would make the 2006 elections a referendum on Bush and try to nationalize the race to control Congress. For Republicans, the best hope was for each race to be seen as discrete and a judgment on the quality of the candidates. Still, knowing that the sixth year of a presidency was typically a tough one for the incumbent's party in Congress, he thought Democrats had a strong chance to displace Republicans as the majority. There were seven GOP races that concerned him. "I'm very apprehensive about it," he said. Once again, his ability to assess the political winds would prove accurate. He sensed he would not be majority leader just yet. But he was set on leading his party in the chamber nonetheless.

In Kentucky, McConnell's views were much more fixed, his power more certain. Without reservation, he said it was he who controlled the state Republican Party. McConnell worked to recruit candidates for the state legislature and to discourage others, something few other senators did. He raised money for the state party. He gave freely of his strategic and tactical advice. In the process, he built a bedrock of loyalty.

As for his own fortunes, the only real question was whether he would be the leader of the majority or the minority, and the answer would be largely beyond his control, a referendum on Bush more than on Senate Republicans.

In September 2006, two months before midterm elections, McConnell sought a private meeting with Bush, a president he admired and supported, despite his struggles with judicial nominees, his administration's inept response to Hurricane Katrina, and the unpopular war dragging on in Iraq. "Mitch has a sharp political nose, and he smelled trouble," Bush wrote in his memoir, *Decision Points*. Bush quoted McConnell as telling him, "Mr. President . . . your unpopularity is going to cost us control of Congress."

"Well, Mitch," Bush said, "what do you want me to do about it?" In Bush's telling, McConnell replied, "Bring some troops home from Iraq." Bush said he would not withdraw troops unless military conditions warranted doing so. "I made it clear I would set troop levels to achieve victory in Iraq, not victory at the polls," Bush wrote.

McConnell has a distinctly different recollection of that conversation. When Bush's book was published in November 2010, McConnell refused to talk about it publicly. But he was steaming, as his interview with an oral historian a month later made clear. "I found it, frankly, extremely irritating that President Bush made it look like I went to him before the '06 election and suggested that he draw down troops to make us have a better election," McConnell said. "What happened was, it was widely thought around town that he was about to draw down troops, and what I did discuss with him . . . was that if he was going to do that, there was no particular reason not to do it before the election.

"At no time did I suggest he alter his strategy for political purposes," he went on. "I was not suggesting that he do anything he wasn't going to do anyway." McConnell saw no benefit in arguing publicly with Bush over the matter, but he "was very upset about it."

In November, McConnell's fears came true. Democrats crushed Republicans and retook control not only of the House but also the Senate. "We had on our hands an awful lot of angry defeated Republican candidates, frankly with good reason," he said.

His election by the Republican conference was unanimous. He was in the minority, but he was finally on top. "We did a lot early, very quietly," McConnell said. "In spite of my frequent assertions publicly that we were not measuring the drapes, that's exactly what we were doing."

In his first days as leader, he worked to assuage Republicans' dismay and frustration by telling them that the minority party held extraordinary power in the Senate, and that he knew how to wield it. During the 2006 election, McConnell had not been focused so much on regaining the Senate majority, which he knew would be nearly impossible, as he was in making sure he had at least forty-one votes so Republicans would have the leverage to insist on change in legislation or the power to kill it all together. He got that.

When McConnell stood in the well of the Senate on January 4, 2007, his first speech as leader was high-minded in tone, with a reverence for the institution of the Senate and its place in the constitutional order. Because of its rules, mostly the filibuster, he noted that the two parties had little choice but to work together to get anything done. He cited the Civil Rights Act of 1964 as a glorious example.

"Yet the challenges ahead will not be met if we do nothing to overcome the partisanship that has come to characterize this body over the past several years," McConnell said. "A culture of partisanship over principle represents a grave threat to the Senate's best tradition as a place of constructive cooperation. It undermines the spirit and the purpose of this institution, and we must do something to reverse its course."

He called for a commitment to the restoration of civility and common purpose.

He credited Mike Mansfield, a Democrat and the former Senate majority leader, with doing just that by steering civil rights legislation to passage. He noted that Mansfield typically began each day having breakfast with Senator George Aiken, a Republican from Vermont. McConnell was clearly trying to position himself as one who shared Mansfield's bipartisan spirit and reverence for the institution, but, notably, where Mansfield had a clear record of bipartisan work, McConnell did not.

"We used to say that senators were friends after five o'clock," McConnell continued. "We need more of that if we are going to restore this body to its high purpose." The Senate, he said, "has no claim to greatness unless its power is put to great ends."

McConnell singled out judges and judicial nominations for special mention. He called for senators to have a "heightened respect for fairness" and confirm an equal number of judges in the final two years of the Bush administration, as the Senate had done for the previous three presidents. Bush, he said, "has a right to expect that his nominees will receive an up or down vote.

"I will never agree to retreat from our responsibility to confirm qualified judicial nominees."

His admonitions were not heeded in the years that followed, perhaps most starkly by McConnell himself.

He soon met with Reid, who he said had a "deer in the headlights" look on his face. McConnell chalked that up to the fact that despite the Democrats' decisive victory, Reid would still need to pick up nine Republican votes to "do almost everything." McConnell, meanwhile, could lose eight members of his party and still block what Democrats wanted to do. He called the strategy "block and blame"; he'd block what Reid wanted to do, then blame him for not doing anything.

"He's kind of cold," Reid said. "I don't mean that in a negative sense. Just not a warm person. He's all business." The same was often said of Reid.

Initially, Reid made some overtures to have a cooperative relationship. In an interview with me eight months before his death in 2021, Reid said he tried to set up a regular meeting with McConnell. "He didn't want to do that. It's not his style. It wasn't a question of him being rude or embarrassing me, he just didn't want to be meeting with me."

Reid said he tried different approaches to get McConnell to open up to him, but few worked. He proposed that both sides get together for lunch. McConnell said no. It was one thing to give a speech celebrating Mansfield's breakfasts with a Republican, another thing to actually sit down with Reid for lunch.

Reid then proposed that McCain come talk to both parties about his experiences being a prisoner of war in Vietnam. McConnell agreed, and it was one of the few moments when both sides seemed willing to put politics aside. McCain told his harrowing story of pain and resolve under torture, the beatings he endured every few hours for days, and his lifelong embarrassment at being ultimately forced by his captors to denounce America. McCain cried in the telling, Reid said. Republicans and Democrats alike were gripped.

"It was one of the best meetings we ever had," Reid told me. "Wonderful." And in that era and since, rare.

The Senate that McConnell and Reid had joined in the mid-1980s was a more collegial place. As the parties underwent a great ideological sorting in the quarter century that followed, the old mores came to feel quaint, with combat more regularly the order of the day. Both men adapted and were well suited to doing battle. But the consequences were clear. Even major legislation on health care and tax policy, which in another era almost certainly would have required a bipartisan approach, was muscled through by Reid or McConnell on the backs of their own party members.

Years later, Reid placed blame on Bush. "With this president there is not even a pretense of reaching across the aisle," he said. Bush would be out of office at the end of his second term, and Reid had someone in mind to replace him as president. Though he'd been in the Senate for less than two years at that point, and would almost certainly be competing against fellow Senator Hillary Clinton for the Democratic nomination, Reid was privately encouraging Barack Obama to run. McConnell had a good sense of Obama's potential, even then, noting in December 2006 that he thought he would be a candidate, two months before Obama announced his bid for the White House.

McConnell was somewhat indifferent to the fact that McCain was seeking the Republican nomination. "McCain is running a good frontrunner campaign and the Republican Party tends to nominate frontrunners and they tend to nominate people who've been around the track before," McConnell said. McConnell said he would not get involved in the Republican primary. Yet he again privately questioned whether McCain held sufficiently conservative Republican views—especially on issues like the role of money in politics—and he thought Mitt Romney seemed to be seeking the title of "the real Republican" in the race.

His focus was elsewhere.

SEVENTEEN

THE POWER OF NO

Entering 2008, the climate was terrible for Republicans and would only get worse. The fact that McConnell thought Bush seemed to wear his dismal approval ratings as a "badge of honor" did not help. Meanwhile, Democrats were locked in a remarkable struggle between new and old, man and woman, Black and white, with Barack Obama and Hillary Clinton waging an intense, captivating primary battle.

Americans were war-weary and a recession was weighing on the economy, with gasoline prices at $4 a gallon commonplace. After eight years of Bush in the White House, voters were demanding change, and McCain, who'd easily won the nomination after clinching primaries in New Hampshire, South Carolina, and Florida, hardly represented that. Obama, on the other hand, was the personification of change. A gifted campaigner and charismatic speaker, he projected youth and energy in ways not seen since Bill Clinton ran in 1992 or Kennedy in 1960. He had outlasted Hillary Clinton, but he was still seen as untested in a national campaign.

McConnell was on the ballot as well, and he was unusually nervous about his prospects to win a fifth Senate term given the sour national mood. His Democratic opponent, Bruce Lunsford, a wealthy candidate who could pour millions into his own campaign, made the change argument, too. McConnell's twenty-four years in office, he said, were enough. National Democrats were also targeting McConnell, as were outside groups.

Unlike McCain, McConnell had a clear theory of the case to counter Lunsford. He framed the race as one of "change versus clout." He played to a sense of state pride, boasting that he was only the second senator from Kentucky to rise to be party leader, the other being Democrat Alben Barkley in the 1930s and '40s, who later served as vice president under President Harry Truman. With regularity, McConnell reminded voters of the specific spoils of his clout that brought so much federal largesse home.

He had successfully pushed for a generous tobacco buyout program that greatly benefited Kentucky's tobacco farmers, finally removing the incentive to grow a crop that caused disastrous health problems. "It's no accident that Kentucky leads the nation or is close to leading the nation in heart disease and cancer," McConnell said. "We've had a very high incidence of people using tobacco products, and that's been directly the result, in my view, of the tobacco culture. So I think the most important thing about the tobacco buyout will be the positive public health implications for the future, for our state."

McConnell's campaign strategy was not the product of mere instinct; as usual, he looked to the data. His team polled voters to see how much they valued his leadership position and clout versus their desire to make a change. Throughout the year, even as the economy deteriorated, clout held about a twenty percentage point advantage over change. McConnell also benefited greatly from the fact that Obama spent no time campaigning in Kentucky, which was becoming a reliably Republican state. Instead, Obama focused on Indiana to the north, becoming the first Democrat to win that state since Lyndon Johnson in 1964. McConnell ran his race like he was running for governor, trying to avoid national issues like the war and recession, instead emphasizing matters closer to home.

Even that strategy was difficult to execute against the backdrop of a subprime housing crisis that was rapidly spreading to other vital sectors of the U.S. economy, most acutely the banking industry. The calamity escalated quickly, and so did the stakes. On September 18, 2008, Bush summoned congressional leaders for a 7 p.m. briefing with Ben Bernanke, chairman of the Federal Reserve, and Treasury Secretary Henry Paulson. "Let me say it one more time," Bernanke said. "If we don't act now, we won't have an economy by Monday." They implored Congress to appropriate money to buy a staggering sum of hundreds of billions in mortgage-backed securities.

Kyle Simmons, McConnell's chief of staff, noted how unpopular this would be with voters heading to the polls in less than two months. McConnell acknowledged that, but knew that doing nothing would be worse. Consumers would not be able to get loans for cars or tuition or mortgages.

Several days later, Bush convened a meeting attended by McConnell, McCain, House Speaker Nancy Pelosi, Reid, and Obama, among others. Bush called on Pelosi to present the Democrats' position, and she said the party's presidential candidate, Barack Obama, would speak for them.

"Everyone in the room was spellbound," McConnell said. He thought Obama masterfully conveyed his understanding of the complex issues, using no notes, with his party fully behind him. He also recognized that McCain, who said little, was going to be in trouble in November, along with the rest of the party. McConnell himself did not say much, either. In one adroit move, though, he put Senator Judd Gregg of New Hampshire, who was quite versed in financial matters, in charge of negotiations.

The House shocked almost everyone by rejecting the Troubled Assets Relief Program, known as TARP, legislation in late September, sending the stock market into a nosedive. The following morning, it was McConnell, without notes, assuring the country, and more important, a jittery Wall Street, that Congress would pass the measure, which it eventually did. "He helped facilitate the passage of TARP,"

former president George W. Bush told me. "To know Mitch was helping was a comfort. He's very patient and has a way of bringing people
back into the caucus." In his book about the financial crisis, *On the
Brink*, Henry M. Paulson, who was treasury secretary, gives an almost
minute-by-minute account of how the package came together. McConnell gets only a passing mention.

McConnell didn't get credit for his actions at the time, either.
In fact, his standing began to deteriorate. After McConnell voted to
approve TARP, his internal polling found his lead over Lunsford had
dropped from thirteen to just four points. Many voters saw TARP early
on as a bailout for Wall Street.

With two weeks to go before the election, McConnell's campaign
manager, Billy Piper, remembers feeling like nothing seemed to go right
in the race. He organized a multicity bus tour to close out the contest,
emphasizing rural areas. At one of those stops, a supporter took Piper
into a restroom and showed him a roll of toilet paper that had Obama's
face on it. Visceral dislike of Obama was clearly a turnout motivator.

Piper also sent nightly emails to the campaign headquarters in an
effort to lift everyone's spirits. But his campaign cheerleading belied
his true feelings. On the Friday before Election Day, campaign polling
showed that the race was tied. McConnell's pollster told Piper he seriously doubted McConnell could win because undecided voters rarely
break for the incumbent. Piper told him to not mention that finding on
the staff call or to say that to McConnell. Rather, he asked the pollster
to call McConnell and tell him things would be okay. Despite these
reassurances, McConnell was "really worried." The only speech he
proofread for delivery on election night was a concession.

That night, McConnell's campaign staff and supporters were gathered in a room at the Galt House, a downtown Louisville hotel along
the Ohio River. "I know we're looking at a potential loss tonight," he
told them. McConnell went from staffer to staffer, and when he got to
Piper, he started sobbing, a wet, messy, convulsing display of emotion
from a man who almost never showed any.

Lundsford's millions had been augmented by the Democratic Senatorial Campaign Committee and outside groups, and McConnell spent more money by far than ever before. His campaign had built the best field operation in state history, with a get-out-the-vote effort that rural parts of the state had never seen. McConnell oversaw all of it. Finally, when actual returns started to come in, the clouds of doom began to lift. McConnell was running up the numbers in rural areas and small towns even as he was losing the state's two largest counties. It was a measure of rural white voters' continuing march to the right, away from Democrats and into the Republican column—and an early signal of Republicans losing the votes of college-educated voters in cities, while gaining them in rural precincts. By the end, he had won by a comfortable six-point margin. He contacted Piper at 5:30 a.m. and told him to call the *Courier-Journal* political writer Al Cross to emphasize the historic nature of his victory as the first Kentucky senator to win five full terms.

Change was not coming to Kentucky, but McConnell would not forget that national Democrats had targeted him. He suggested Harry Reid would get the same kind of opposition from national Republicans when he was up for reelection in 2010.

McConnell would have to make adjustments. This would be the first time he was party leader with a president of the opposite party, one with whom he had no personal relationship, and not much of a professional one, either. But McConnell saw clearly the historic nature of Obama's victory and the phenomenal popularity he enjoyed.

"Obama captured the imagination of a significant percentage of the American people and demonstrated that in this country all things are possible," McConnell said. "So I think that's a pretty exciting thing for the country." He called the president-elect to congratulate him, and Obama returned the call a few days later, while McConnell was grocery shopping at a Kroger in Louisville. McConnell said Obama was gracious, and he appreciated that the president-elect did not gloat, given the beating his party had just delivered to Republicans. In the

Senate alone, Democrats had gained eight seats. Though diminished with his smaller minority, McConnell was now the most powerful Republican in Washington. "Effectively, I had very little power at all," he said. He understated the case. He still had the power of "No."

McConnell's longtime friend, the federal judge John Heyburn, whom he had recommended to President George H. W. Bush, wrote McConnell a handwritten letter on November 5, 2008, encouraging him to try to have a positive relationship with Obama. "I see the opportunity for you to secure a larger national legacy as one of the great American statesmen and legislative leaders. And, it is the election of Barack Obama that makes this possible for you. I have always thought that you had a unique ability to bridge political and cultural divisions. This is a quality of great men." He added, "As odd as it may seem I see that you and Obama have a similarly methodical approach to politics and problems. I could see you and Obama cooperating on many things for our nation's betterment. Unless Obama badly overreaches or governs in a way that is tone deaf, he will change the flow and tide of American history. It is usually a bad idea to swim against such tides because they cannot be completely stopped."

McConnell did not heed his dear friend's advice. Rather than endeavoring to be seen as Obama's partner, McConnell chose the path of being his political opposition. They were ideological opposites. McConnell thought Obama leaned too far to the left, toward a Western European kind of social welfare state. He was particularly critical of one of Obama's signature proposals, the most far-reaching health-care legislation since the passage of Medicare in the 1960s, which McConnell and his father had opposed. He thought the government should not be involved in private health care, that it would be too costly, and that the private sector could fix flaws in the system. "I'm going to be in the forefront of either trying to slow it down, modify it, or stop it altogether," McConnell said, acknowledging it would be more difficult because of the winnowed ranks of Republican senators.

In Obama's brief time in the Senate, he had few interactions with McConnell, who, unlike a lot of Republican senators, did not get caught up in Obama's aura. He had been impressed with Obama's skills, but not his manner. When asked what Obama was really like, McConnell would respond, "He's like the kid in your class who exerts a hell of a lot of effort making sure everyone thinks he's the smartest one in the room. He talks down to people, whether in a meeting among colleagues in the White House or addressing the nation." His derision verged on contempt.

David Axelrod, Obama's senior adviser, recalled that in Obama's first bipartisan meeting in the Cabinet Room, McConnell said, "A lot of us don't think you should be here, but the people thought differently, so we have to work with that."

"There was this disdain in his voice," Axelrod said. "But he is a very crafty antagonist."

McConnell was far better acquainted with Obama's vice president, Biden, with whom he had served for more than two decades in the Senate. "Joe's a good guy," McConnell said the month after the election. "He's a motor-mouth. He's the kind of guy, my dad used to say, if you ask him what time it is, he'll tell you how to make a watch."

Biden, as opposed to Obama, was also the kind of person McConnell knew he could talk to.

McConnell's professional respect also extended to Rahm Emanuel, Obama's chief of staff, who was McConnell's equal in terms of tenacity, focus, and political acumen. He called a meeting with congressional leadership, including McConnell. Emanuel told them he would be responsive to their needs and attuned to local issues that the others had to deal with. He gave them his cell phone number and said he was available to them twenty-four hours a day.

McConnell then mentioned he wanted the administration to work on entitlement reform of Medicare and Social Security. Emanuel instantly smelled a trap and reminded McConnell how much criticism Bush had come in for after proposing something similar. "So why don't you put out a proposal and we can go from there?" Emanuel recalled

saying. "He looked at me with a wry smile." McConnell could appreciate that Emanuel was not taking the bait.

After Obama's inauguration, as the year played out and the financial crisis worsened, McConnell continued his tactical opposition to
the president's agenda. He voted against releasing the second half of
the $700 billion TARP package. McConnell was even more forceful
in his opposition to Obama's health-care proposal, which was earning the nickname Obamacare. While Democrats thought McConnell
was being obstructionist, conservatives were cheering him. McConnell's supporters saw great virtue in opposing the expansion of the
government's role in health care or its regulatory reach into other
businesses.

Even with some green shoots of recovery starting to show as 2009
came to a close, Americans had soured greatly on institutions and
those who led them. The economic dislocation stoked anger among
the working class in particular. Many people had lost their homes, and
many more were furious over the fact that the Wall Street financiers
who created the crisis seemed to be suffering no consequences. Obama
was trying to prevent the country from plunging into a depression,
hoping to ride the goodwill of the voters and early lofty approval ratings to push through his aggressive agenda. As Emanuel said at the
time, a crisis was a terrible thing to waste.

In public, McConnell said the administration was off to a "good
start." "This is an opportunity to tackle big issues and to do them
in the middle. And it would not be a good idea for the new administration, in my view, to go down a laundry list of left-wing proposals
and try to jam them through the Congress." He then quoted a remark
Obama had made in 2004 about the party in power governing with
"some modesty" and working with "the other side of the aisle."

Internally, McConnell counseled patience to his Republican colleagues. "There's going to be a honeymoon period," he said. "Hopefully it won't last too long." McConnell continued to make little effort
to ingratiate himself with the new president and his administration,

instead thinking ahead to 2010, mindful that the first midterm election for a president's party was often disastrous.

Yet he worried that the honeymoon actually might be a long one, given the "novelty" of Obama's election. "There was a great feeling of kind of pride in the country, well-deserved pride, that we had broken through a major barrier here, none of which had anything to do with issues, but had a lot do to with him personally and how people felt about themselves having participated in a breakthrough."

Some Republicans in the Senate shared that concern. McConnell spent extensive time trying to persuade his members "to keep our fingerprints off" the health-care legislation so in the next election they could highlight the stark difference. Over time, his members, even the moderate ones, "all fell into line."

"Republicans are monolithically against the health care legislation, leaving the president and his party executing parliamentary back flips to get it passed," Carl Hulse and Adam Nagourney wrote in the *New York Times*. McConnell "has come to embody a kind of oppositional politics that critics say has left voters cynical about Washington, the Senate all but dysfunctional and the Republican Party without a positive agenda or message. . . . But in the short run at least, his approach has worked."

Years later, McConnell told me he had to try to do something to revive his party's fortunes in the Senate. Forty votes, he said, was nearly impotent. He saw the health-care plan, and the public's initial resistance to it, as a way to give Republicans cohesion and voters an alternative. In the short run, it worked.

It was essential for McConnell to prevent Democrats from persuading a single Republican; that way, Democrats could not claim Obamacare had bipartisan support. He came to meetings armed with polling data that showed a steep drop in support for the health-care bill. Democrats' best hope was Maine's moderate Republican senator, Olympia Snowe, but Reid told Obama, "When McConnell really puts the screws to her, she'll fold like a cheap suit."

For all of McConnell's hard-line opposition, Obama could count on congressional Democratic leaders, particularly House Speaker Nancy Pelosi and Reid, to push through his programs, though there was no margin of error in the Senate if they were to overcome a filibuster. The Senate passed the Affordable Care Act, 60–39, along party lines on December 24, 2009, and the House passed it, 219–212, on March 21, 2010, with thirty-four House Democrats voting against it.

Snowe had been the only Republican on the Senate Finance Committee to vote to advance Obamacare to the full Senate, upsetting plenty of her colleagues. But as Reid had predicted, she fell into line after that, voting with her party against the bill.

McConnell called Reid's moves to win passage of the bill "unseemly," citing special deals the majority leader struck with Democratic senators from Nebraska, Louisiana, and Florida to get them on board. He and his communications team branded those deals "the Cornhusker Kickback," "the Louisiana Purchase" and "Gator Aid." Yet McConnell had done similar things to push through Bush's agenda, such as getting a commitment from Bush to hold a fundraiser for a Republican whose vote they needed.

The victory represented a triumph for Democrats, who had been pursuing some form of national health care since the Truman administration. But politically, Republicans seized upon the process and the way Democrats had jammed the bill through Congress. They were helped by the fact that in the early blush of the law it was difficult to see its impact. McConnell repeatedly called it the worst piece of legislation he had ever seen. More than a decade later he conceded that the law that had brought health care to 40 million people had become highly popular.

By the end of 2009, Obama's approval rating had dipped more than twenty points from its peak, and polling showed the public did not support the health-care law. Democrats were further stunned when they lost a special election in Massachusetts to fill the seat of Senator Kennedy, who had died from brain cancer. The seat went to a

Republican, Scott Brown, and suddenly McConnell's party had a sense of life. "It's hard to imagine the Senate without Kennedy," McConnell said upon his death. The two had first met in 1964 when McConnell was an intern for John Sherman Cooper. With the election of Republican Scott Brown, McConnell now had enough votes to stop Democrats on almost anything. His edge did not last long, though. In April 2009, Arlen Specter stunned Republicans by announcing he would become a Democrat in the face of a Pennsylvania Republican primary he looked set to lose.

Specter's defection notwithstanding, McConnell saw the pendulum swinging back strongly to Republicans. When Democrats appealed to legislators to "make history" by passing far-reaching programs, McConnell was dismissive. "'Make history' is an argument you use when you don't have the people on your side or you're trying to get people to do something folks don't want to do," McConnell said. The health-care bill also continued to provide Republicans with a wedge issue they could use to draw a stark contrast with Democrats. "Don't muddy it up," McConnell added. "They're for this and we're for this, and let's have a national debate about it."

When Democrats proposed a so-called cap-and-trade energy policy to reduce carbon emissions, McConnell saw another opportunity to argue that they were out of step with public opinion, even while he conceded pollution should be reduced.

"I personally don't know whether the climate issue is real or not, but I think I'm willing to concede it'd be a good idea to have fewer carbon emissions rather than more," he said. "So the way forward, it strikes me, is plug-in hybrid cars and nuclear power."

To build party unity, he met senators one-on-one. He also held a group meeting every Wednesday afternoon at four thirty, all part of a monthslong team-building exercise to encourage Republicans to stick together. In his morning speeches on the Senate floor, McConnell relentlessly railed against the health-care law. "We just keep pounding and pounding and pounding," McConnell said. "Good politics is repetition."

He said Obama had squandered his political capital. McConnell often accused Obama of arrogance, derisively calling him "the professor" because he talked much more than he listened in their meetings. "Almost without exception, President Obama begins serious policy discussions by explaining why everyone else is wrong," he said. He also chafed at Obama's meteoric ascent. After just two years in the Senate, Obama was being talked about as a presidential candidate and two years after that, here he was in the White House. It had taken McConnell two decades to gain power in the Senate.

McConnell sensed a rising anger in the electorate early in 2010 that would probably result in voters punishing Democrats. What he did not see as clearly was the emergence of a faction within the GOP, the Tea Party, that would also present a challenge to his power in his home state.

Rand Paul, an ophthalmologist from Bowling Green, Kentucky, was seeking the Senate nomination against McConnell's handpicked candidate, Kentucky secretary of state Trey Grayson. "I worry that if Paul wins the primary, he won't be able to be elected, because he has some rather bizarre positions, like he would have voted against the Iraq war, which not a single Republican did, and even Hillary Clinton and John Kerry voted for it." Paul also opposed many federal drug laws and the Patriot Act. "Those kinds of things, I think, will make him unelectable in November."

McConnell badly misread that race. Paul won easily, and McConnell tried to work with him, but couldn't shake his skepticism. "He's a smart guy," McConnell said, but he likes to "shock you with what he's going to say, and it'll be interesting to see whether he decides in the Senate that he wants to be kind of an eccentric curiosity or whether he wants to be a player."

McConnell was clearly more comfortable with Republicans who drew their party loyalty more from Reagan's principles than the Tea Party's anger. His relationship with John McCain had actually improved dramatically since their fights over campaign finance legislation. "People always assumed bad blood between McConnell and McCain," said Mark Salter, one of McCain's top aides. "There wasn't. McConnell deferred to John and John respected that. Part of that is shrewdness on McConnell's part."

"We've become buddies," McConnell said. McCain came to the University of Louisville for the opening of McConnell's archives. Mc-Connell initially thought McCain might be an "enabler" for Obama, but instead McCain in many ways was a scold, particularly on national security issues. "This year, he's been marvelous," McConnell said. "He's been a team player . . . we've become close friends."

The fury in the electorate that McConnell sensed early in 2010 only grew, with voters becoming disenchanted with Obama and Democrats in general. Part of that represented a natural snapback from such a decisive election in 2008, but part of it was new and politically powerful. By the fall it was clear that Democrats were likely to take losses in the midterms. The only question was how heavy they would be.

On October 23, with the midterm elections rapidly approaching, McConnell did an interview with the *National Journal* in which he discussed historical patterns for a president's first midterm, and how Republicans should position themselves.

"We need to be honest with the public. This election is about them, not us. And we need to treat this election as the first step in retaking the government. We need to say to everyone on Election Day, 'Those of you who helped make this a good day, you need to go out and help us finish the job.'"

What's the job? he was asked.

"The single most important thing we want to achieve is for President Obama to be a one-term president."

Does that mean endless, or at least frequent, confrontation with the president?

"If President Obama does a Clintonian backflip, if he's willing to meet us halfway on some of the biggest issues, it's not inappropriate for us to do business with him," McConnell said. He added, "I don't want the president to fail; I want him to change. So, we'll see. The next move is going to be up to him."

Some Democrats ridiculed him for the "one-term president" part of the interview, saying he simply wanted the new president to fail, and almost always excluding what he said after that.

At the same time, there was no slip of the tongue.

"No, it was calculated," McConnell said. "In every interview, I try to have something that's pleasing to the base and something that I can say to independents. And your critics on the left will pick up on what you say that's pleasing the base.

"All I thought I was doing was stating the obvious. Of course I don't want a Democratic president in '12. Anything else new?"

The Tea Party wave in 2010 led to significant Republican victories, with the party regaining control of the House, but falling short of a Senate majority. McConnell thought he knew why: several deeply flawed Tea Party–aligned candidates. In Delaware, Christine O'Donnell had acknowledged dabbling in witchcraft, then ran an advertisement that opened with her saying, "I'm not a witch." In Colorado, "Ken Buck spent most of his time with both of his feet in his mouth, including stupidly going on *Meet the Press* to debate his opponent two weeks before the election," McConnell said. In Nevada, Sharron Angle was "clearly the worst candidate we could have run" to defeat Reid.

Supporting Trey Grayson in the Kentucky primary was a rare exception for him when it came to getting involved in races before Republicans had chosen their nominee. But he was starting to wonder if it was a good idea to stand on the sidelines during primary elections. There was another irritant. Senator Jim DeMint of South Carolina had started the Senate Conservatives Fund, which backed the kind of unyielding Republicans who were unlikely to win. McConnell needed to find a countermanding force.

The Obama White House continued to try to work with McConnell, to little avail. On December 14, 2010, McConnell met with Obama and Biden for breakfast—a meeting that was not made public.

That same day, Democrats released a $1.1 trillion spending bill to fund the government through September. McConnell was not persuaded. "I'm actively working to defeat it," he said. But the Senate also passed an extension of Bush-era tax cuts, following negotiations between Biden and McConnell, which the *Times* called "a glimpse of a new power dynamic that is likely to characterize the next two years, as Republicans take control of the House and occupy six more seats in the Senate."

In the two years since Obama's election, McConnell thought Republicans had regained their footing, and their confidence. "This gives McConnell immense clout and doesn't leave Reid with much sway," Julian Zelizer, a Princeton history professor, told the *Times*. "Now that the Democratic majority is even narrower and more Democrats will be worried about supporting Obama, McConnell feels the confidence to be even more aggressive and out front in his opposition."

Blocking and blaming was working.

EIGHTEEN

"ANYBODY . . . KNOW HOW TO MAKE A DEAL?"

The damage from the financial crisis was not the only fiscal disaster facing the country in 2010. There was also an impasse between Congress and the Obama administration over whether to raise the nation's debt limit. The stakes could not have been higher: failure to do so would have resulted in the first default in the nation's history, and likely would have triggered another economic calamity. To try to reach an accord, McConnell dealt not with Obama but with Biden.

They weren't close friends, but they had the shared experience of long tenures in the Senate, and both men understood rhythms of legislative give-and-take. Though he could be windy and was not a giant of the institution, Biden had an "A-plus personality," McConnell thought. They could talk. That did not, however, signal a new era of cooperation.

From McConnell's perch, a divided government actually offered a better chance to do bigger things because it forced compromise. Yet he could never seem to take advantage, with Republicans offering proposals, like raising the age for Medicare, that Democrats found unacceptable, and Democrats talking about raising taxes. Neither side yielded and nothing of significance happened. McConnell, House Speaker John Boehner, and Obama met frequently and accomplished little. It was a period of the federal government grinding its gears awaiting the next election.

That stasis nearly led to the government defaulting on its debt. Partisans offered bills that went nowhere. The financial markets were watching anxiously. Democrats and Republicans talked past each other. "The crisis seemed to demand the involvement of someone with the personal gravitas, political acumen and institutional leverage to move the process toward a final deal," Paul Kane wrote in the *Washington Post* at the end of July 2011. "The moment called out for Mitch McConnell."

"In the category of getting serious, I have spoken to both the president and the vice president within the last hour," McConnell told him. "We are now fully engaged, the speaker and I, with the one person in America out of 307 million people who can sign a bill into law."

Kane went on to write that "McConnell's fingerprints are on every big bipartisan deal and every key spending bill to emerge from Congress in recent years. He secretly negotiated, with Vice President Biden, the deal to extend the George W. Bush–era tax cuts last December. And three years ago, in an environment eerily similar to the current stalemate, it was McConnell who helped rescue a bailout package for the financial services industry from a humiliating defeat on the House floor."

In the debt limit fight, McConnell thought Obama had undermined a deal worked out among congressional leaders, so he then pushed the president to restart negotiations, all the while offering public reassurances that the United States would not default. But the key to the talks was his conversations with Biden. "Whatever deal is reached to raise the debt ceiling, McConnell's prints will be all over it, even if not everyone can see them," Kane wrote.

By early the next week an agreement was reached. The *New York Times* joined in the *Post*'s assessment. "Pivotal to the final deal-making was the Republican minority leader in the Senate, Senator Mitch Mc-Connell, and his back-channel talks with his former Senate colleague, Vice President Joseph R. Biden Jr." McConnell and Biden traded proposals. They had repeated phone calls, and the Sunday before the deal was done, McConnell went on two of the morning news programs to express optimism.

Both McConnell and Boehner came under attack from more hard-line Republican conservatives for making the deal. Those criticisms were early augers of a transformation set in motion by the Tea Party wave that swept through the electorate in 2010. They foretold more serious trouble ahead, particularly for Boehner.

McConnell stuck by Boehner's side, and had kept him informed of his talks with Biden. The two men could hardly be more different, but in these kinds of negotiations, they stayed strategically and tactically close. McConnell calibrates his every word as though he is using a scientific tool. Boehner is free and easy, quick with a quote. McConnell rarely showed emotion; Boehner could seemingly cry on cue. Boehner grew up in a large family, working in a bar. McConnell was an only child, doted on by his parents.

When I interviewed Boehner about McConnell, he sat behind a large desk of dark wood, notable for the plate-size glass ashtray that sat on top, in the office of the lobbying powerhouse firm Squire Patton Boggs, where, in his post-Congress life, he represented the cannabis industry, among other clients. The office, which had a small outdoor balcony so Boehner could smoke, contained a number of mementos, including the wooden Speaker of the House sign that once hung above his Capitol office and a framed photo of Boehner greeting Pope Frances in Washington.

Boehner told me that his partnership with McConnell was close, but strictly professional. McConnell never asked him a personal question or offered anything about himself.

"This guy had his cards locked up against his chest tighter than a bra and nobody got to see those cards," Boehner said. "It took a while to develop this relationship because of this clash of personalities and style, but over time we learned to trust each other, we learned how to work with each other and, frankly, it paid big dividends.

"The only small talk was 'I hope you're not going to light that cigarette,'" Boehner told me. "I wouldn't dare do it in his office, and if I was having a meeting with Mitch, I wouldn't do it in my office, either. Because he would have said, 'Really, are you going to light that thing up?'"

McConnell held his opinions and emotions in a "vault," Boehner said. "It was impossible to get beyond the veil. . . . So there was usually an effort to draw out of him what was behind those eyeballs."

Still, their working relationship was strong, even when they had competing imperatives. "Mitch and I, almost every single time, were in the same place. . . . If Mitch told you something, you could take it to the bank. I never had one reason ever to doubt anything he ever told me because he didn't tell you much. When he did tell you something you knew where he was."

Boehner said he felt that he had a working relationship with Obama, but "Mitch just couldn't do that." The former speaker still shakes his head when recalling McConnell's comment about making Obama a one-term president. "I am thinking to myself, 'Why would he say this?' Maybe that is his goal, but he doesn't have to say it. All it's going to do is get in the way of a relationship. I knew I had to build a relationship with Obama, and I knew that I was the one who was going to have to do all the work."

Perhaps Boehner was right to suggest that McConnell erred in his contempt for Obama, but it was McConnell's work with Biden that solved the debt ceiling standoff, preventing potentially disastrous economic consequences.

A by-product of the debt ceiling deal was the formation of a so-called Super Committee on deficit reduction, a bipartisan effort to cut

spending. When it was established, the committee was seen as a setting wherein both parties could come together and at least approach
a consensus. The committee identified $500 billion in spending cuts,
but despite early optimism, none were carried out. Any significant cuts
would have to come from negotiation between congressional leaders
and the White House, in yet another measure of a congressional committee structure that had grown increasingly weak.

As troubling as the inertia was to both sides, one thing was certain to McConnell. "To win the policy arguments, you have to win
the political arguments. If you don't get the politics right, you don't
have enough people elected to get the policy right." This was one of
McConnell's primary ways of using power. First, he would assess the
politics of the situation, then he would try to fashion a policy to meet
the political imperatives.

There were other reasons for the slothful pace, and McConnell
was responsible for much of it through the use of the filibuster, which
forced the Senate to find sixty votes to proceed with any action. In the
period from 1955 to 1964, the filibuster was used nine times to stop a
measure in the Senate. From 2009 to 2014, when McConnell was minority leader, the filibuster was used 643 times. Democrats have used
it plenty of times since.

Mike Zamore, who cowrote the book *Filibustered!* with Democratic senator Jeff Merkley of Oregon and served as his chief of staff,
said neither party's hands are clean when it comes to mucking up legislative business with the filibuster. But he said the record shows that
it was McConnell who broke the norms, using his delaying tactics to
cement his power and become the "catalyzing actor" for fundamental
changes in the country.

He noted that McConnell aggressively turned his focus to blocking Obama nominees to the influential appeals court in D.C., which
was widely thought to be the court that would hear major challenges
to the regulatory changes in business and environmental practices
that the Obama administration had developed. McConnell also was

the prime mover in stopping appointments to the National Labor Relations Board to the point that it did not have enough members to be able to conduct business. This fit with McConnell's view of the limited role that government should play in business and regulation, and it had the added benefit of aligning almost perfectly with the interests of the major donors to the Republican Party and the ideology of the Federalist Society.

"So much of this stuff is really about norms, not about the rules," Zamore said. "The Senate has been governed for most of its history by a code of conduct as much as rules, and when that code of conduct breaks down you end up with big battles, and a breakdown in the social contract of the Senate. The norms have been sacrificed at the altar of expediency."

This ensured that without larger margins for the Democratic majority, McConnell could engineer the failure of much of Obama's agenda. McConnell used the filibuster so often that it helped fuel a call to eliminate the practice altogether. McConnell and many other senators, including Democrats, saw the filibuster as the essential tool that separates the Senate from the House, forcing compromise on legislation. But McConnell took its use to an extreme.

In a meeting with Obama in April 2010 to discuss a Supreme Court vacancy, McConnell said Republicans want a nominee who will "apply the law, not their feelings," a rebuke of Obama's remark that a nominee's empathy could be an important character trait for a justice. Obama also noted that a nominee should "do right by the poor and by the rich."

McConnell's talking points for the meeting indicated that he would remind the president that in the room only he and Senator Jeff Sessions of Alabama, then chairman of the Judiciary Committee, could say they had never tried to filibuster a Supreme Court nominee. Obama, as a senator, had cast a vote to filibuster the 2005 nomination of Samuel Alito. The position they were discussing that day in 2010 would eventually go to Elena Kagan, Obama's solicitor general.

Whenever he was asked for the rationale behind his actions, McConnell often employed the same argument, one common to schoolyard scraps, barroom brawls, and the halls of Congress alike: the other side started it. He repeatedly returned to Schumer's use of a filibuster to stop Bush nominations to federal appeals courts as justification for doing the same thing to Obama nominees. He also could see the fight escalating, possibly all the way to the nation's highest court. "I don't know if we've reached a point where either side would defeat a Supreme Court nominee with forty-one votes," McConnell said. "I just don't know. I think a lot of that will depend on who the next president is and who they pick."

He called 2011 a "remarkably unaccomplished Senate." Within the Republican conference, though, he took solace in the fact that Senator Roy Blunt of Missouri won a leadership post over the Tea Party–aligned senator Ron Johnson of Wisconsin, a result that McConnell thought also validated his own position as the leader of the Republican establishment.

His seemingly reflexive opposition to Obama gave way to praise when the president ordered the capture or killing of Osama bin Laden and found success in Libya, where Muammar Gaddafi was removed from power. McConnell was also pleased that the president was meeting Aung San Suu Kyi, the political prisoner in Myanmar whose cause he had followed so closely for years. She had finally been released from yearslong detention. "I've never worked on an issue with less result over a longer period of time than this one," he said. He was, though, thrilled to go in front of her house and see her for the first time. "We had a rather emotional embrace."

While results in Washington were limited, McConnell continued to assert dominance in Kentucky Republican politics, building a power base that helped him in his Senate races and a robust party organization that ensured Kentucky's red state status. He gave tough-minded political advice and worked to see who would, and would not, be a GOP nominee for an important race. Todd P'Pool was a Republican candidate for attorney general. When McConnell found out from one of his operatives that P'Pool was running television ads in August, a period when voters were highly unlikely to be paying attention, he called him to challenge the strategy. P'Pool had $150,000 in his campaign account. McConnell told him that was only enough to cover the final two weeks of the campaign, when ads could actually matter. P'Pool balked. Then McConnell said, "Let me put it this way. Why don't you just go down to the bank and withdraw that $150,000 in cash and strike a match to it." P'Pool lost his race.

Among those who did follow his advice was James Comer, who was running to be state agriculture commissioner and would go on to serve in the House of Representatives. McConnell deployed his media consultant to help Comer with commercials. "This is not my first rodeo," McConnell said. Comer won, and often publicly praised the state's senior senator.

McConnell also focused on Senate races for the coming year and the 2012 presidential campaign. He thought Mitt Romney was the only credible candidate who could not only win but also do the job. "They'll demonize Romney as being a Wall Street guy, and it'll be a tough, vigorous campaign, but I think we have a shot."

Romney was the antithesis of the Tea Party–style candidates that McConnell found so irritating. The son of a governor, a former governor himself, and the man credited with saving the Winter Olympics in Salt Lake City in 2002, Romney clearly came from the establishment wing. He seemed to be McConnell's preference, but the senator did not get involved in the presidential primaries.

He also maintained a light touch in the Senate primaries, a decision he came to regret because Republicans seemed to be repeating their mistake of 2010 by nominating candidates well out of the mainstream. Two of them, Todd Akin in Missouri and Richard Mourdock in Indiana, had made outrageous statements that seemed to condone sexual assault. McConnell called the selection of candidates like them "the idiot factor" that cost Republicans dearly.

Both candidates lost, and Democrats retained their Senate majority. McConnell began to seriously doubt whether he would ever have the Senate's top job. But he already had begun to think about ways to avoid the candidate disasters of the last two cycles.

He ended up being right about Romney on both fronts: he was indeed a strong candidate, but the Democrats effectively attacked him as an out-of-touch plutocrat. In the end, Romney was no match for the campaign organization that President Obama had built or the coalition of voters that propelled him to a second term. McConnell may have had little fondness for the president on the personal level, but he appreciated the political masterstrokes of Obama's reelection campaign.

Soon after the election, though, the dysfunction in Washington reached another crisis point. The Bush-era tax cuts were set to expire and a forced reduction in spending, called a sequester, was about to kick in. It set up a potential financial calamity that Federal Reserve chairman Ben Bernanke called a "fiscal cliff," which he warned would have dire economic consequences for a country that was still recovering from a financial crisis.

Obama called McConnell on December 26, 2012, to try to address the problem. Obama and Boehner had been meeting for a month to try to come up with a "grand bargain" that would deal with both taxes and spending. That negotiation collapsed, and Boehner came up with a "plan B," which McConnell embraced. It would have the House pass an extension of tax cuts for those earning less than $1 million and offer changes Republicans sought in the estate tax. "I thought plan B was a really good plan, but the speaker has about thirty of his members who are, frankly, idiots," McConnell said. They took an absolutist stance, viewing a plan that would only raise taxes on people making over a million dollars as a broad-based tax increase. Most of those opposed to the plan were aligned with the Tea Party and not "very smart politically," McConnell added, because they do not understand that "when you only control one part of the government, you can't get one hundred percent of what you want."

McConnell was also clear on another point: if no deal was reached, Republicans would be blamed. "We'll either have to do a deal in the Senate on a bipartisan basis or look stupid, which is exactly where we were" a year ago. He was angry at the far-right members of the House. "Some of the most idiotic members of the far right of our party will probably think I made a bad deal, but in fact, if we don't do anything, everybody's taxes are going up at the end of this very week, and it will look like these crazy Republicans caused it."

Obama told the Senate leaders, "Well, Harry, you and Mitch need to talk about this and see if you all can reach an agreement." Several days went by with the two senators exchanging counterproposals. On Sunday, December 30, with the deadline rapidly approaching, McConnell went to the Senate floor and said, "I can't get a counteroffer from the majority leader. I am looking for a dance partner." Right before he made those remarks, he called Biden and asked, "Is there anybody down there who can make a deal?" The vice president consulted Obama and they came back with a proposal, which served as a starting point for what would be at least thirteen calls between McConnell and Biden. Finally, they reached a tentative accord on December 31. The Senate voted for the deal, ending what the *Washington Post* called a "self-inflicted, nationally televised psychological experiment on Congress."

"An in-depth look at the final four tense days shows that McConnell and Biden resolved the crisis through old-fashioned backroom bargaining," the *Post* wrote. Each side gave a little to get a little, resulting in a smaller bore agreement, but one that prevented a gut punch to the economy.

Avoiding a disaster, even in the chaotic fashion in which it happened, passed for a highlight in 2012, a year McConnell described as "completely and totally dysfunctional" in terms of Senate business.

There was one change coming in the Senate, though, that McConnell thought was quite positive. GOP senator Jim DeMint of South Carolina, who McConnell said was "a pain in the ass," was being replaced in 2013 by Tim Scott, an African American conservative, who

McConnell thought had the potential to bring more minorities to the Republican ranks.

He also decided to be far more assertive in the primaries for the 2014 midterm elections. No more "idiot factor." To do that, he worked with American Crossroads, a group founded by Republican political strategist Karl Rove, who at the time was working with Steven Law, a ubiquitous figure in McConnell's career. McConnell would help to raise money and Crossroads would work to counter the efforts of groups like the Senate Conservatives Fund or the Club for Growth, two more conservative outside groups. "I think the so-called establishment forces both inside and outside the Senate are going to try a lot harder to help us get electable candidates in November," he said.

In March 2014, during an interview with Carl Hulse of the *New York Times*, McConnell made a blunt assertion about Tea Party candidates: "I think we are going to crush them everywhere." The words had such an edge that McConnell said he saw the color drain from his spokesperson's face.

McConnell was about to confront the Tea Party himself in the form of a challenge in the primary from Matt Bevin, a wealthy businessman who cast himself as an outsider and had the backing of ardent conservatives. McConnell applied his admonition about "crushing" Tea Party challengers to his own race, dispatching with Bevin by nearly a two-to-one margin. McConnell's campaign attacked Bevin early, effectively, and relentlessly. The Associated Press called the race for McConnell mere minutes after the polls closed.

In the general election, he faced Alison Lundergan Grimes, the Kentucky secretary of state, a well-funded and credible opponent who raised more money on antipathy for McConnell than support for her. Money from outside Kentucky poured into Grimes's campaign. But she was no match for McConnell's organization, now built and improved over decades. A race that some experts thought would be close turned into another rout for McConnell. His message was simple: "A vote for Alison Grimes is a vote for Barack Obama." A poll in September had

McConnell leading by just four points. He ended up with a fifteen-point margin of victory. "What gets you respect more than anything is victory," McConnell said. "And the bigger the victory, the more respect."

For McConnell, the wider election was a big victory indeed. Republican senators held all their seats, gained nine from the Democrats, and took control of the Senate with a 54–44 margin, along with two independents who caucus with Democrats. McConnell had reached the summit of his ambitions—majority leader—an achievement he had feared might never come.

He sent an initial signal of conciliation in his election night victory speech. "Just because we have a two-party system doesn't mean we have to be in perpetual conflict."

There was little sign, though, of a thaw with Obama. At the White House Correspondents' Dinner early that year, the president joked about critics who said he didn't spend enough time with members of Congress. "Why don't you get a drink with Mitch McConnell, they ask?" Obama deadpanned. "Really, why don't *you* get a drink with Mitch McConnell?"

In November, though, Obama changed his tone, saying, "I would enjoy having some Kentucky bourbon with Mitch McConnell." He said McConnell had always been "very straightforward with me. To his credit, he has never made a promise that he couldn't deliver . . . so I think we can have a productive relationship." There was talk of a "bourbon summit," but it never happened, except for a parody of one on *Saturday Night Live.*

McConnell's first speech on the Senate floor as majority leader was notable in its contrast from the one he gave in 2007 when he was first elected minority leader. Mostly gone were the lofty notions of the Senate's purpose and bipartisan bonhomie.

"We are in a moment of great anxiety as a nation," he said. "The people we represent have lost faith in their government. They no longer trust Washington to do the right thing." He criticized Obamacare for not delivering on the promise that people would not lose their health insurance or be paying less. He spoke to Americans' sense of economic anxiety. "For many, it has never seemed more difficult just to get by." He went on to criticize the president's conduct of foreign policy, talking about "autocrats scoffing at a superpower that doesn't seem to have a real plan.

"The American people didn't ask for government that tries to do everything and fails, and they didn't demand a government that aims to do nothing and succeeds. They simply asked for a government that works."

He vowed also to fix a broken Senate and return the once rote process of committees doing work and offering legislation, of passing budgets, of the Senate doing its job without lurching from crisis to crisis. He called the Senate to a higher purpose. "The promise of the Senate is real. Time and time again it has been an engine for bipartisan achievement."

Still, there was a sharply partisan edge to his words. He challenged Obama, who he said was the only Democrat who "can bring his party on board," saying, "I appreciate that bipartisan compromise may not come easily for the president—not his first inclination. The president's supporters are pressing for militancy, not compromise." As with his "one-term president" comment about Obama, part of McConnell's speech was directed squarely at the party base and the Fox News audience; the other, more sanguine sentiments, to the independent voter. In a moment like this, McConnell is nothing if not intentional.

In January he laid down his partisan arms when he served as the president of the Alfalfa Club, which also highlighted his standing as a leader of the establishment. Rarely one to forgo preparation, McConnell hired a speechwriter, C. Landon Parvin, to craft remarks designed to get a laugh, paying him $20,000 for the effort. Texas senator Ted Cruz was an easy target. "When Ted first came to the Senate, I told him to be himself, which in retrospect was about the worst advice I could have given him," McConnell said, drawing laughter from the grandees in the room.

That environment, at least, had the patina of civility that was becoming increasingly rare in Congress. Every day, McConnell and Reid seemed to trade personal attacks as though they were the required order of the day. McConnell, though, had a personal touch that Reid sometimes lacked. When a member of the Senate was leaving, he prepared remarks that showed real thought, not simply a rote goodbye. He did the same at the Rosa Parks statue unveiling, and in less public moments to members of his staff.

He also did it on June 6, 2015, when his security detail drove him to St. Anthony of Padua Roman Catholic Church in Wilmington, Delaware, for the funeral of Beau Biden, Vice President Biden's son who had died of brain cancer. McConnell was the only Republican in Congress to attend the service, and Joe Biden never forgot the act of kindness.

The Senate seemed a world removed from that somber day. In his hands as minority leader, the filibuster had been, according to McConnell's loftier rhetoric, a legitimate and even honorable way to achieve compromise, the Senate's high calling. As majority leader, he saw things very differently when Harry Reid, now leading the Democratic minority, threw up the same sort of roadblocks McConnell had mastered.

McConnell said that since the November election in 2014 about half the calls he received were from "Democratic senators who now are fully aware that the strategy that Harry pursued of basically shutting down the Senate, not letting people vote, was an abysmal flop." McConnell said he hoped Reid would stay in his job as the Democratic Senate leader because "I think it really helps me, because I want to be different from him in every single way. I want to be as different from him as Mansfield was to LBJ." He was aligning himself once again with Mansfield, who was known for being able to bring sides together rather than Lyndon Johnson who, in lore anyway, was known for using a heavy hand to get results. McConnell's words about Mansfield rarely matched his actions.

It had been nearly thirty years since that thrilling night when he first won election to the Senate and almost immediately set his goal of becoming the majority leader. Nothing about the job intimidated him.

"I've had plenty of time to study how it's been handled by others and to have read about people like Mansfield and Johnson who've had it in the past. So it was one great year. It was hard to believe it finally, finally happened."

McConnell even managed to make amends with Senator Boxer, with whom he had a frosty relationship since they tangled two decades earlier over the fate of Bob Packwood, the Republican senator from Oregon who resigned under threat of expulsion after more than ten women came forward to accuse him of sexual harassment and assault.

The common cause between McConnell and Boxer was a highway bill that both wanted. Boxer said Democrats were initially cool to the idea, so she took it to McConnell. They worked out a deal and passed the bill, which became popular in both parties. The senators took their staff out to dinner, where McConnell gave Boxer a Louisville Slugger baseball bat and she gave him a tie with bridges on it. It was a light moment for a serious man. "Most of the time he's brutal and angry appearing, and I often would say I don't know why Mitch does this stuff," Boxer told me. "He always looks so angry, but he must love the job."

She wasn't wrong, but one aspect of the job that irked him were the continued challenges from his party's right flank, particularly Ted Cruz, who was thinking about running for president and had shown himself to be particularly adept at drawing attention to himself, though not for any legislative accomplishments.

Cruz went so far as to call McConnell a liar on the Senate floor, a serious breach of decorum within the party, but also the kind of attention-grabbing stunt Cruz hoped it would be. At issue was a transportation bill and what Cruz saw as a stealth maneuver to get it passed without provisions important to him.

"What we just saw today was an absolute demonstration that not only what he told every Republican senator, but what he told the press over and over and over again, was a simple lie," Cruz said. "We know

now that when the majority leader looks us in the eyes and makes an explicit commitment, that he is willing to say things that he knows are false. That has consequences for how this body operates."

Many of McConnell's Senate colleagues shared his view of Cruz. But the Texas senator did represent a growing number of Republican members of Congress, and more important, voters, who were disenchanted with establishment leaders. This was particularly true in the House, and Boehner became a prominent casualty of the "idiot factor" when he was forced from the speakership by hard-right members who only seemed satisfied if they got everything they wanted. When he announced his decision to leave Congress on September 25, 2015, he tried to rise above the knife fight he had just lost. "My first job as speaker is to protect the institution. It had become clear to me that this prolonged leadership turmoil would do irreparable harm to the institution." The Republican Party was changing, and quickly, but that change had not yet spread widely in the more tradition-bound Senate.

The weight of those traditions amplified the shock factor of Cruz's frontal rebellion against his leader. But his popular success with his base underscored the growing role of anger as an animating principle of the populist right in the Republican Party.

As important, Cruz was trying to position himself to run for president in 2016, hoping to win the loyalty of the primary voters most likely to align with his hard-line views. He won early praise from conservative groups and Rush Limbaugh, who applauded the "direct hit" on the leadership. Boehner's ouster was just the leading edge of a growing movement, which had taken the Republican orthodoxy of limited government down a fraught path when funding needed to be passed. Its adherents began voting, in essence, for no government. The party was becoming more white, more rural, and less educated—more animated by anger than issues.

Even so, in one important sense, the Republican establishment in the House showed new signs of life when Representative Paul Ryan of Wisconsin was elected speaker in October and promised to try to bridge the divides that had led to Boehner's ouster. Ryan was considered a serious expert on tax and budget policy, and still had some sheen from serving as Mitt Romney's running mate in 2012. McConnell had long seen exceptional potential in Ryan, and he had tried to recruit him to run for the Senate several times.

Boehner had previously asked Ryan to brief McConnell on budget matters, and Ryan said McConnell always asked good, detailed questions and was "temperamentally smooth." They grew close when Ryan became speaker, a job that McConnell had strongly encouraged him to accept. "Mitch was a great mentor to me," Ryan said. "He had very good institutional instincts about what is important to the institution and how to mind the process. He gave me a good worldview on what a real leader in Congress ought to be like."

McConnell had long been thinking ahead to 2016. "Imagine that in 2016 the Democratic contest could be between sixty-nine-year-old Hillary Clinton and seventy-three-year-old Joe Biden, and the Republican contest could be between two guys who aren't even fifty yet, Paul Ryan and Marco Rubio. We'll see who looks like the old shoe and who looks like something new in the very near future."

Not even one with McConnell's political antenna could envision who ultimately would represent "new."

NINETEEN

"SCALIA'S SEAT"

Mitch McConnell was never one for vacations. If the Senate were on a break, he was more likely to be politicking in Kentucky, raising money for Republican Senate candidates, or on a congressional delegation trip abroad than relaxing on the beach somewhere. An exception was the Presidents' Day recess period in February, when he and his wife, Elaine, routinely traveled to the Caribbean for some sun and downtime, more because of her desire to do so than his. When their plane touched down in St. Thomas on February 13, 2016, McConnell looked at his iPhone at 5:10 p.m. and saw a message with stunning news: Supreme Court justice Antonin Scalia had died. One minute later he replied, "Awful. We need to get a statement out."

When McConnell and Chao reached their hotel room, he sat on the bed watching the news reports and checking messages while she unpacked. McConnell's mind raced back to the 1970s when he had sat in meetings at the Justice Department with Scalia, whose muscular legal intellect he found both admirable and intimidating. McConnell was on the Senate Judiciary Committee when Scalia was confirmed unanimously to be on the nation's highest court. He had watched as the justice went on to become the hero of the conservative legal

movement. McConnell viewed Scalia as a friend. They had dinner together occasionally and often spoke at events hosted by the Federalist
Society, the conservative legal organization that Scalia helped to start
at the University of Chicago. McConnell considered him one of the
finest justices in history, in league with John Marshall or Oliver Wendell Holmes. Even many liberals respected Scalia's intellect, no matter
how vigorously they disagreed with his so-called originalist view of
the Constitution.

Then McConnell, who was known to plan years in advance, consider every angle, and execute a meticulously considered strategy,
acted on impulse. Within minutes, he made a decision that would result in what he considers his proudest, most consequential act as a
senator—and one for which he was widely condemned. He told his
staff that President Obama would not fill the seat, no matter whom he
nominated, and they needed to put a statement out quickly, then get
to work on finding a defensible rationale for his decision.

When I first asked him why he did this, McConnell said that he did
not think a president should be able to fill a seat so close to a presidential election if the Senate were controlled by the opposite party, a principal reason he offered at the time of Scalia's death. He defended this
view by citing a nineteenth-century precedent when a seat was not
filled because of the closeness to an election, with the White House
and Senate controlled by different parties. Beyond that, there was no
Senate rule to support his conclusion, but there were some other thin
branches he could cling to. One was a statement by Biden in 1992
that, as Judiciary Committee chairman, he would not fill a seat soon
before an election, which was hypothetical given that there was not an
opening. Another was a suggestion by Chuck Schumer that the filibuster could be used to block a Supreme Court nominee, which had also
never happened. There were other norms and customs of the Senate,
pointing in the opposite direction, which McConnell conspicuously
ignored. The same person who, only years earlier, during the Bush administration, argued strenuously that a judicial nominee deserved an

up or down vote was now doing what no other leader had done to stop one. He was convinced that Democrats would have done the same thing in the same circumstance.

In a subsequent interview, he added another reason. "I had another concern that I did not put in there that's related, I think, to your judgment of how I do this job," and that was a wish "to protect my members" by not allowing a vote. In February 2016, he anticipated a "really bad year for us. We had a lot of exposure. Hillary Clinton looks pretty darn strong, and I had a bunch of guys and gals in competitive races"—referring to Republican-held seats in Pennsylvania, Ohio, North Carolina, and Wisconsin. At that point, he said, "I wasn't too interested in having them have to vote one way or the other. And my job is to try to keep the majority." When McConnell did an interview for an oral history in April 2017, he made no mention of trying to protect his members from taking a difficult vote. McConnell was quick to add in our interview that, in February 2016, it was not at all certain that Donald Trump would be the nominee. "There was no way to anticipate that at the time I made the decision in February."

He had another reason to move swiftly, which was to establish messaging discipline for his own members, many of whom were traveling and no doubt would be asked about the vacancy. On the question of the open seat left by Scalia, he wanted as little distance between himself and the other Republicans as he could manage because he knew that his approach was coarsely against the grain. He made the case to his Senate colleagues that their argument needed to be framed as one about who was entitled to make the appointment, not about the qualifications of the specific nominee. He wanted to completely short-circuit the process so that no drama over confirmation hearings would hang over the election.

"It's the exercise of power in the most vivid possible form," said Martin Gold, a lawyer in Washington considered a leading authority on the practices of the Senate, and an admirer of McConnell and his leadership. "It's the hardball part of it. There is no way that you can establish a perfectly consistent argument." He added, "If I were a Democrat, it would be the thing about Mitch McConnell that would irritate me the most. The precedent McConnell was talking about. There was no rule. . . . The rule that never was."

To try to freeze Senate Republicans in place, McConnell put out a statement saying, "The American people should have a voice in the selection of their next Supreme Court Justice. Therefore, this vacancy should not be filled until we have a new President."

There was an additional imperative: Republican presidential candidates were scheduled to have a debate in South Carolina the night of McConnell's statement, and McConnell didn't want any of them, particularly Cruz, to be seen as setting the terms of filling the vacancy because it could backfire given the antipathy toward the Texas senator. As expected, Scalia's death came up immediately in the debate. Cruz said the seat should not be filled, and Trump said he hoped McConnell could somehow stop an Obama nomination. Trump had called on the right person, for if McConnell had demonstrated anything in his time in the Senate, it was that he knew how to execute a delay.

It was a full circle rejection of McConnell's own view as a younger man, when he wrote that the Senate should only consider a nominee's qualifications and not his or her ideology. He also knew he only had to get forty-one out of fifty-four Republican votes to block a nomination. At that point, a Supreme Court nominee needed to get sixty votes to avoid a filibuster before an up or down vote. McConnell spent much of his vacation pursuing that strategy. One day, he talked to Iowa's senator Chuck Grassley, chairman of the Judiciary Committee. The next day, he had a conference call with his staff, then individual phone calls with Senator Lisa Murkowski, the independent-minded Republican from Alaska, who was probably opposed to his move, and Lindsey Graham of South Carolina, who could be influential in getting other Republicans to back McConnell.

On March 1, 2016, McConnell, Reid, and Grassley, along with Senator Patrick Leahy of Vermont, the ranking Democrat on the Judiciary

Committee, and Vice President Biden met in the Oval Office with Obama to discuss the nomination. McConnell defiantly told the president not to waste his time, that there would be no hearing. He later told supporters in Kentucky that one of his proudest moments was "when I looked at Barack Obama in the eye and I said, 'Mr. President, you will not fill this Supreme Court vacancy.'"

He built a political case, far more than a legal or an institutional one, to defend his decision, repeatedly invoking Biden's remarks in 1992. Biden, speaking less than a year after the divisive Clarence Thomas confirmation, said the Senate "must consider how it would respond to a Supreme Court vacancy that would occur in the full throes of an election year. It is my view that if the president goes the way of Presidents Fillmore or Johnson and presses an election-year nomination, the Senate Judiciary Committee should seriously consider not scheduling confirmation hearings on the nomination until after the political campaign season is over." While it's true that Biden clearly floated a theoretical possibility, he just as clearly stopped short of outright opposing a nomination during a presidential election year.

Biden elaborated on his position in an interview with E. J. Dionne in the *Washington Post*, in which he called for greater consultation between the Senate and the president before a nominee was put forward, "including compromise over the judicial and constitutional predispositions of a nominee." He said he would urge the Senate not to hold hearings, but in his position, of course, he would only offer his opinion because he did not have any greater authority. Biden said his belief was not rooted in stopping a president from making a nomination, so much as it was to protect the nominee from such a volatile process. "I believe there would be no bounds of propriety that would be honored by either side," Biden said. Biden seemed to be trying to have it both ways, and in the process he unwittingly gave Republicans the grist they would need more than two decades later. Sure enough, after McConnell's declaration that the Senate would not fill the Scalia seat,

Republicans branded Biden's 1992 comments as "the Biden Rule," giving it an undeserved gloss of authority.

McConnell also repeatedly cited remarks that Senator Chuck Schumer, Democrat of New York, made in 2007. Schumer said that for the rest of the president's term "we should reverse the presumption of confirmation," later adding that with respect to the Supreme Court, "I will recommend to my colleagues that we should not confirm a Supreme Court nominee except in extraordinary circumstances." So Schumer, too, offered a strong leaning in one direction, but did not categorically say a nomination would not go forward, and like Biden, his words were never tested because an opening did not arise. Schumer, however, more than Biden, might well have followed that course.

There was another flaw in the Republicans' argument. President Reagan had nominated Anthony Kennedy in November of 1987, but he was not confirmed until February of 1988, when Democrats controlled the Senate in a presidential election year.

McConnell, as he had done with most issues, considered the political implications first, which he acknowledged in 2024. "That was a more sustainable position for us politically and a defensible position for us politically, while at the same time having the added benefit of not having my guys in tough states make decisions about whether I should vote yes or no." He conceded "that was very much on my mind at the time."

One thing both sides agreed on: the Scalia vacancy, if filled by an Obama nominee, would change the ideological balance of the Supreme Court in a way the court had not seen since Clarence Thomas replaced Thurgood Marshall in 1991. Some major flashpoint issues, like abortion and gun rights, were at stake. The tension between business and consumer interests would be sharper. A case that fundamentally changed the way that money affected politics, *Citizens United*, might be subject to a new challenge, something that McConnell would have fiercely opposed.

McConnell's chief of staff, Sharon Soderstrom, and his chief legal counsel at the time, John Abegg, started putting together a rationale for not taking up the nomination. Abegg, who was visiting his parents in his hometown of Terre Haute, Indiana, was in a Lowe's hardware store when his Blackberry started pinging with messages. One of those was sent on behalf of McConnell. It read "Barack Obama will not fill Scalia's seat."

Abegg was tasked with exploring whether a president in his final year in office should be able to fill a high court vacancy and to help explain to other Republicans why not. "My reaction when I got the email from Don Stewart [McConnell's spokesperson] as to the boss's decision was—it was bold, it was decisive, and it was correct, but it was not going to be without controversy," Abegg said. He consulted with Leonard Leo of the Federalist Society for strategic advice and to enlist support. Then he and others crafted a statement for McConnell that was quickly sent to all Republican members directly.

With the news so fresh, Obama first put out a sympathetic statement to Justice Scalia's family and complimented his adherence to the law as he saw it. It would be days before names would be floated for his possible replacement.

In the meantime, McConnell "got out there early and just defined the territory," said Senator John Thune of South Dakota, who served as the Republican whip in the Senate when McConnell was leader. "He's always good at playing chess when other people are playing checkers. I think he anticipated this . . . not that Scalia would die . . . but the circumstances. . . . He had developed a template for vacancies on the court." McConnell never mentioned having a template, and it is far more likely that he simply knew he had the power to act as he did and did not flinch about using it.

Obama and his top aides had a number of considerations in selecting a nominee. Part of Obama's calculation was to not offer up a younger candidate, like Judge Ketanji Brown Jackson, who would eventually be nominated by President Biden, but rather to put forth someone who had an established record and perhaps could better withstand the public flogging of Republicans, even if they were ultimately rejected as the nominee. McConnell knew his position was highly controversial, but it also afforded him the chance to show to his members, and perhaps as important to the base voters of the Republican Party, that he was willing to make the call. "I was prepared to take the heat for the process in order to protect my members," McConnell said. He said he sought no outside advice on his decision. And with the Republican Party drifting hard to the right, and anger toward its leaders on the rise, McConnell's own self-interest cannot be dismissed as a reason for his course of action.

On March 17, Obama nominated Merrick Garland, knowing that McConnell had already decided not to put any nomination forward. Garland was a soft-spoken, highly respected federal appeals court judge seen as moderate both in his legal views and his temperament. In his Rose Garden appearance, he was the opposite of a jurist who might inspire an instant dislike, and that was no accident. If Robert Bork had been a portrait in arrogance, Garland was one in humility. If Republicans were going to block a nominee, Obama wanted to make sure it was a person who by any objective measure was qualified for the job.

Soderstrom wanted the team of McConnell aides to portray confidence, but knew that sometimes that pose was more of a facade. Abegg, armed with his research, said it is easier to "defend a principle than it is to fight against a personality"—suggesting they should not take on Garland's character or experience, but rather stand on the argument that the next president should fill the court's vacancy after voters had their say.

Meanwhile, McConnell's team knew they had a fight and not just with Democrats, but also with "handwringer" Republicans—those like Lisa Murkowski of Alaska and Susan Collins of Maine, who were asking why Garland could not get at least a hearing or even an up or down vote. Rather than answer those questions, McConnell's team stuck by the newly created confection that the vacancy in an election year should be filled by the next president. Some members thought it was a very risky strategy. What if Hillary Clinton won the election? Wouldn't she select a more liberal nominee? Some members of Obama's team called Soderstrom later with a proposition: If Hillary Clinton won, would the Senate agree to confirm Garland in a lame-duck session before her swearing in?

Garland had served presidents of both parties and had been confirmed by the Senate nineteen years earlier. Nothing he had done on the bench since compromised him as a nominee. "I hope they're fair," Obama said. "That's all. I hope they're fair." Half a dozen Republican senators expressed a willingness to at least meet with Garland, but McConnell was determined that Garland would not get so much as a Judiciary Committee hearing, let alone a vote.

McConnell immediately dismissed the nomination, and told Garland in a phone call that he would not even meet with him. "It seems clear that President Obama made this nomination, not with the intent of seeing the nominee confirmed, but in order to politicize it for purposes of the election," he said. "The American people are perfectly capable of having their say—their say—on this issue. So let's give them a voice." A *Washington Post* poll at the time found that Americans, by a two-to-one margin, thought Garland deserved to have hearings. Despite his concern for the will of the people, McConnell remained unmoved.

By June, Trump had the Republican nomination in hand. McConnell and others in his party were trying to figure out where he stood on all manner of policies, since he seemed unmoored from any coherent philosophy other than his catchphrase, "Make America Great Again," aping an old slogan of Reagan. "We had this most unusual nominee," McConnell said, "a guy who was giving fundraisers for Chuck Schumer four years ago, and a lot of people were saying, 'Who are we about to nominate here? Is he one of us, or is he somebody else?'"

One Trump adviser was several steps ahead of McConnell and other Republicans. Don McGahn, who served as a lawyer on Trump's campaign, had recommended that Trump be in talks with leaders of the Federalist Society several months before, to reassure them, and to solicit a list of potential Supreme Court nominees. Trump took the advice. "It was a very smart move, because it kind of said, at least to Republican voters, 'Well, we're not totally sure what we're getting here, but on the Supreme Court, he'd be fine," McConnell told me. McConnell urged Trump to make the list public, which he hoped would energize conservative voters but also act implicitly as an insurance policy against a "Judge Judy" kind of nominee. Trump released the list on May 18, and it included several noted conservative judges and no performative Judge Judys.

The list served Trump in a number of ways. Social conservatives became hopeful that he might change the Supreme Court in such profound ways that their long-held dream of overturning the constitutional right to an abortion in *Roe v. Wade* could be realized. It was just the kind of electoral energy Trump needed. McConnell had his own reasons to feel optimistic: those same voters could make the difference in electing Republican Senate candidates.

For McConnell, the commitment of those white religious conservatives, and Republicans at large, would be put to an extreme test a month before the election when the story broke in the *Washington Post* that Trump had made vulgar comments about women when on the set of the television show *Access Hollywood*. A number of Republicans, McCain prominently among them, said they could no longer vote for the nominee. McConnell did not go that far. Other Republicans could disavow him, but McConnell said the moment called for contrition by Trump. "As the father of three daughters, I strongly believe that Trump needs to apologize directly to women and girls everywhere and take full responsibility for the utter lack of respect for women shown in his comments on that tape," he said. It was a blunt statement, and at the same time, one that left McConnell with enough room to have a working relationship with Trump if he were to win.

"What I tried to do, since I had candidates in different states dealing with the Trump factor differently, was to keep my mouth shut,

because I didn't want to become an issue in a given Senate race," Mc-
Connell told his oral historian shortly after the election. McConnell
again spoke up when Trump questioned the importance of NATO,
when he assailed a Latino judge, and after the *Access Hollywood* tape.
"But I never withdrew my support."

Trump went on to emphasize the Supreme Court in his campaign's
closing chapter. In McConnell's view, that helped propel him to a stunning victory that neither McConnell nor Trump thought would happen.

Merrick Garland would keep his seat on the federal appeals court
in D.C., thanks to McConnell's maneuver. "He didn't have any animus about Judge Garland—it wasn't personal," Abegg said of McConnell. "After the election, from a political point of view it worked out
for the Republicans. I think he had the right principle. I don't know
if it's ever going to be vindicated from a philosophical point of view.
Political vindication was borne out by the election and a driving force
in getting President Trump elected."

At the Federalist Society Dinner in November, members gave Mc-
Connell a robust standing ovation. Scalia's widow, Maureen, came up
to McConnell with tears in her eyes and said, "Thank you."

After the election, McConnell was an early visitor to Trump Tower,
where he met with McGahn, who had been designated as White House
counsel. McConnell noted that there was far more at stake for conservatives than the Supreme Court. He had held back so many of Obama's
judicial nominees with parliamentary tactics in the last two years that
there were more vacancies in the federal courts than at any time since
the 1950s. He saw the courts as an instrument to undo legislation and
regulations passed during Obama's time.

Back in 2013, under Reid's Democratic leadership, the Senate
changed its rules so that many Obama nominees—though not ones for
the Supreme Court—could be confirmed by a simple majority. Republicans were infuriated at the time. As the majority, though, they stood
to benefit from the easier path to confirmation that Democrats had
created—especially if they extended it to Supreme Court nominees as

well. Some Republicans encouraged McConnell to change the rules back. He declined, recognizing the potential of exploiting them in the future.

McConnell also met with Trump and emphasized the need for a highly qualified nominee. "I've got members who don't like what was done four years ago," he recalled telling Trump, "and it's not going to be a piece of cake if I have to talk them into doing what we criticized four years ago." He went on: "The single best way to win that argument is for you to send up a nominee who is so conspicuously well qualified that it's really hard not to get him on the court one way or the other."

McConnell had a candidate in mind, Amul Thapar, who McConnell had met at a Federalist Society gathering in northern Kentucky, and eventually backed for a federal district court judgeship in 2007. Trump considered Thapar, and later nominated him for a federal appeals court opening, but for the Supreme Court seat he decided on Neil Gorsuch, a federal appeals court judge from Colorado, whose made-for-TV appearance, mellifluous voice, and scholarly bearing made him a candidate who would be difficult to attack. In his Judiciary Committee hearing, Gorsuch was flawless, McConnell thought. "This guy's a central casting perfect Supreme Court Justice." Every Democrat on the Judiciary Committee voted against him. Then came a filibuster by Democrats.

McConnell knew where he was headed—toward the ultimate step of eliminating the filibuster for Supreme Court nominees. The move would ensure that the court would be seen as more partisan, no matter who the president was, because it would make it so nominees could be confirmed on a simple party-line majority vote. Just as Democrats had done in 2013 with lower court nominees, McConnell lined up his members and changed the rules to require only fifty-one votes instead of sixty to seat Gorsuch. This was the "nuclear option," a stark escalation of the majority's power to shape the high court. The Senate confirmed Gorsuch on a vote of 54–45.

McConnell thought the Democrats had made a strategic miscalculation; because Gorsuch was such an obviously credible nominee, they
should have reserved their efforts to block the next potential opening.
Justice Anthony Kennedy had been sending hints that he might soon
retire.

Though the man who always considered himself an institutionalist had just broken a central norm of the Senate, McConnell said
his engineering of Gorsuch's confirmation "ended up being a kind of
career-making decision for me, because mostly in legislative work, not
too many times can you claim you did something all by yourself.

"But if you look at the consequences of this and the impact the
Supreme Court has on our society, to have a forty-nine-year-old of
this quality on the court could be a real game changer for the country." He was correct in the sense that Gorsuch would become one
of the pillars of the conservative wing of the court, with a particular
interest in scaling back federal regulations and restrictions on business. This wasn't a surprise, as Gorsuch had challenged the power of
federal agencies in one of his decisions on the appeals court, saying
that the Supreme Court had ceded far too much judicial and legislative authority to the executive branch and suggesting that a change
was in order. He was referring to what is known as the *Chevron* decision, in which the high court ruled that when legislation was not
clear on a subject, an agency's view of what a regulation said, based
on the expertise of its staff, should be controlling. Gorsuch would go
on to hear a case in which he and other conservatives seemed highly
skeptical of the precedent.

"Just looking at the politics of this after it was all over, it was a
real image builder for me, because this kind of job is very hard to make
people happy, and with the conservatives, you're never quite conservative enough," McConnell said. He said Democrats who were still pin-
ing for Garland were shedding "crocodile tears."

It was not just Democrats. Murkowski, for one, said that it was just
another accelerant to a deteriorating process, putting such a premium

on politics. "Whenever one side pushes the envelope just a little bit more, we need to be prepared that when the shoe is on the other foot, it's going to get pushed even farther. And each time it gets us a little bit closer to where we're all going to fall off. Sometimes we forget, in the effort to advance our situation and our cause today, it doesn't end there. It just never ends." She knew the decision would have lasting consequences, "far beyond the temporary benefit of getting the individual we wanted." How Republicans treated Garland laid the groundwork "for what I fear to be coming, which is you've got cases coming up, whether it's abortion or who knows what's lying around the corner?" Still, she voted for Gorsuch, but foreshadowed the controversy to come.

Gorsuch was just the start. McGahn had been consulting Leonard Leo at the Federalist Society, and they'd come up with a long list of judicial candidates whose philosophies aligned with theirs. It was a long supply chain to fill the vacancies, and McConnell was more than ready to provide the conveyor belt to see that they were confirmed.

It was a brutish exercise of power. In many ways, he did it simply because he could not be stopped. That didn't mean his colleagues were happy about it. Few people in American politics other than Hillary Clinton saw their fortunes shaped by McConnell's decision more than Senator Tim Kaine, a Democrat from Virginia. Kaine was Clinton's vice presidential running mate, a politician whose résumé seemed almost perfect for someone in his party to one day run for president. He had been the mayor of Richmond, Virginia, the lieutenant governor of Virginia, then governor and senator. He was fluent in Spanish and had done missionary work in Honduras. He is as bright as he is genial.

In many ways, Kaine likes McConnell. They attended Bible study together occasionally, and he was moved by McConnell telling the story of his childhood polio. He gave McConnell the novel *Nemesis* by Philip Roth, which explored the polio epidemic in New Jersey in 1944. They worked on legislation together.

McConnell's treatment of Garland and its impact on the court was another matter entirely, an utter misuse of power in Kaine's view. "What they did on the Garland nomination was an abomination," Kaine said. "I think it has fundamentally warped the court for a very long time. Mitch McConnell could have told the Republicans we're not giving them sixty votes for Merrick Garland. Meet with him. Have a Judiciary Committee hearing. Advise and consent. You can vote no. If he had just done that, he would have gotten what he wanted but none of us could have said that's so unfair. That was a complete perversion of what advise and consent was. That was completely, without precedent, disrespect of a U.S. president to not entertain a Supreme Court nominee.

"But by no meetings, no hearing, no committee vote, no floor debate, no floor vote, they basically convinced every last one of us that's a stolen seat," Kaine added. "Number two, you say this is just going to be the rule in the last year of a president; we one hundred percent believe you are lying about that. We know that as soon as you have an opportunity, you will cast it aside."

Senator Angus King, an even-tempered independent from Maine who caucuses with the Democrats, also has had cordial relations with McConnell, but said the Garland matter "offended my sense of fundamental process and fairness, and it just wasn't right."

Other Republicans, like Susan Collins, and later Mitt Romney, also thought McConnell was wrong on Garland, and their comments added to the public's view that the courts had become politicized.

For some longtime acquaintances, the Garland decision was a breaking point for their relationship with McConnell. To Keith Runyon, who had been an editorial writer for many years for the *Courier-Journal* and had developed a friendship with McConnell going back to the 1970s, denying Garland was unforgivable. "Until Merrick Garland came along, I always had hope that Mitch in the end would do the right thing. I thought he had the internal strength and intelligence. I thought a lot of his positions in the Senate were strictly opportunistic and when a really difficult decision came along, he would come through, and he didn't."

McConnell's decisions about Supreme Court nominees attract the most attention, but he was also largely responsible for getting fifty-four judges confirmed on federal appeals courts. Those appointments arguably have an even greater influence.

"The vast majority of cases never get to the Supreme Court," said Pamela Karlan, a professor of law at Stanford and codirector of its Supreme Court Litigation Clinic. "The courts of appeals are the final place where litigants have a legal *right* to have their case decided and where binding law gets made." The Supreme Court, she said, hears between sixty and seventy cases a year. In 2023, appeals courts had more than forty thousand filings.

The impact has been stark. Karlan noted that "a Sixth Circuit panel upheld the right of a university professor to refuse to call a transgender student by her preferred pronouns; a Fifth Circuit panel blocked the government from requiring Navy SEALS to get vaccinated for COVID; an Eighth Circuit panel held that private parties have no right to sue under Section 2 of the Voting Rights Act of 1965—the main statute protecting the voting rights of racial minorities—even though literally thousands of plaintiffs have used the statute to sue since its passage; and an Eleventh Circuit panel granted qualified immunity for prison officials who blocked an inmate's outgoing emails and gave him no notice or ability to challenge the blockage, on the grounds that a Supreme Court case from 1974 didn't clearly establish that what the prison did was wrong because that case involved snail mail, rather than email."

Overall, Karlan said, McConnell's engineering of appointments from the Supreme Court on down made it "clear to anyone watching that the Court was a political football."

"There's a very real question in my mind whether, after Garland and Barrett, it will be possible for a president to get any nominee for the Supreme Court confirmed if the Senate is held by the other party," she said.

McConnell prided himself on patience and discipline and the ability to see around corners and into the future so much that he titled his memoir *The Long Game*. When it came to Trump and the court, however, his calculation was based on expedience, and over time, the consequences mounted for McConnell, his party, and the country.

TWENTY

POWER BASE

On election night in 2016, McConnell was in his usual perch in the offices of the National Republican Senatorial Committee in Washington. His initial focus was not on the presidential race between Donald Trump and Hillary Clinton, but rather on state legislative contests in Kentucky. By 8:30 p.m., it became clear Republicans had won resounding victories and would control the Kentucky House. It was an affirmation of McConnell's efforts to transform Kentucky into a durably Republican state, and to cement his standing as the state's most powerful political figure.

But he was more concerned about the next set of returns coming in U.S. Senate races, because their outcomes would determine if he would get another term as majority leader. McConnell approached most election nights with a sense of fatalism, often thinking the worst would happen. By midnight, Republican Senate candidates had surprised him, and he realized he again would be majority leader with the power to control the dynamic of the Senate. His time atop the majority would not go down in history as a fluke.

McConnell took special pride in this achievement because this was the first election in which he fully deployed the power of his Super

PAC, the Senate Leadership Fund, a foundational component of his power. In 2010, in *Citizens United v. FEC*, the Supreme Court reversed almost a century of campaign finance restrictions and set off a chain of other cases that led to the legalization of unlimited, unchecked, and at times undisclosed political contributions. Since the Tea Party's ascent, McConnell had wanted an outside political organization answerable to him. In 2014 he had worked with American Crossroads, a group started by three of the best strategists in the Republican Party, Karl Rove, Ed Gillespie, and Steven Law, the McConnell loyalist. But McConnell wanted an organization that was specifically branded for the Senate, and effectively controlled by him. Law convinced Rove that McConnell was determined to have a distinct entity, and came up with the name Senate Leadership Fund.

In McConnell's experience, many donors viewed Super PACs with suspicion, but he knew that most of them gave to the Republican Governors Association, which is itself a Super PAC. Once they had a Senate brand, with McConnell's imprimatur, there was a "treasure trove" of donors ready to write checks, particularly to the majority leader's preferred organization.

Law, with McConnell's approval, also formed a companion group called One Nation, which did not have to disclose its donors. McConnell then set out on a fundraising blitz that raised about five times as much as Crossroads, according to Josh Holmes, McConnell's political adviser. McConnell had the start he needed. "If you open the door a crack, he will stick a foot in, and the next moment he will be on your living room couch," Holmes said of McConnell. "This was not something that was invited."

The fact that McConnell was involved gave him added heft and influence in his caucus, as he made clear that the Super PAC would be there to help them win reelection. Though the Super PAC operated independently, it clearly operated under McConnell's watchful eye, and he and Law talked frequently. The money started to rescue candidates,

and most Senate Republicans were impressed by McConnell's strategic political skills.

Fred Wertheimer, the former president of Common Cause who
had been fighting McConnell and the influence of money and politics
for decades, said that Republicans were initially the ones who benefited most from the *Citizens United* decision, with so-called dark
money flooding to independent conservative groups. But McConnell's
creation of the Senate Leadership Fund dramatically reduced the influence of Crossroads. "They put them out of business is what they did,"
Wertheimer said. "He [Rove] just disappeared. They took his money."
Democrats soon caught up with their own leadership Super PACs, and
an arms race for secret money had started. "They're all tied directly
to the leaders," Wertheimer said. "And there's a fiction that they're
independent."

For McConnell, the Senate Leadership Fund and One Nation were
an essential part of his power base. The Senate Leadership Fund has
taken in millions of dollars from conservatives like Paul Singer, Warren Stephens, Miriam Adelson, Ken Langone, and the Koch Brothers.
Energy companies such as Chevron and Valero also are major donors.
Those disclosures give an image of transparency. But because of the
way the campaign finance laws are written, One Nation can also give
money to the Senate Leadership Fund, identified only by the group
name, not the original donor. Since 2016, One Nation has given more
than $205 million to the Senate Leadership Fund, money that is used
for the kind of brutally effective attack ads that help defeat Democrats
and help McConnell retain his power. One Nation's contributions to
the fund are more than double those of the next largest donor, Miriam
Adelson, widow of the late multibillionaire casino mogul and GOP
donor Sheldon Adelson, who contributed $90 million over the same
period.

In multiple interviews, McConnell insisted that these donors had
not asked for specific legislative action. He also noted that they were
not motivated by social issues such as abortion, but rather business

and regulatory matters that would have a direct impact on their bottom line.

Now that the Senate Leadership Fund provided a structure that he could influence, McConnell spent untold hours and air miles working to raise almost $164 million to seed Senate races in 2016 and to make a difference in their outcomes. He focused on wealthy individuals and corporations, trying to raise as much as he could from as few people as possible. Money, though, was just part of it. McConnell and his team also provided strategic and tactical advice, and if a candidate got in a difficult position, McConnell's team essentially took over the campaign. Not surprisingly, he installed Law to direct both the Senate Leadership Fund and One Nation, which shared an office. McConnell and Law had worked together so closely over so many years that their partnership was seamless. McConnell would make the pitch to donors about what he wanted the Senate Republicans to achieve, all business, no time spent glad-handing or trying to soften up the donor. Instead, he was blunt and direct about what he would do, then he would leave it to one of Law's top fundraisers, David Gershanick, to make the actual request for money, seal the deal, then serve as a "relationship manager" for the donors.

"Basically American Crossroads just kind of went away and we replaced it with this," McConnell said. He had full confidence in Law, and the infrastructure for the organizations was already in place. "They had an office. They had staff. We didn't have to reinvent anything.

"So I set about moving around the country," he added. "I went to twenty-nine cities. I spent endless amounts of time on the phone with high net worth individuals, basically making the argument, 'No matter what other causes you have, whether you like the Koch brothers or whether you give to this group or that group, no matter who you're supporting for president, if the Senate's important, this is the group.'"

McConnell was always a prodigious fundraiser, but he was also an astute judge of political talent—skills that sometimes went hand in hand. In the Indiana Senate race in 2016, he had seen great potential in Todd Young, a former Marine and House member who was seeking the Republican nomination. They had first met some four years earlier at a joint political event to address the need to repair a vital, structurally flawed bridge between Young's district in southern Indiana and Louisville. McConnell was courteous and had carved out a spot for Young to be able to address the media, too. "He didn't leave a backbench member of Congress behind," Young said. "He showed a little humanity. It happened to be good politics as well."

They did not have contact again until Republican senator Dan Coats of Indiana announced he would leave the Senate when his term ended in 2016, creating an opening for Young, who knew whose blessing he would seek to make the move up. Young's political team made entreaties to McConnell's. Young called them "Team McConnell," a cadre of current and former staffers and political operatives.

In March 2015, Young got a meeting with McConnell, and he wanted to make a good impression. McConnell, as usual, said little. Young asked for his support. McConnell gave a positive but noncommittal response. "I'm not one to allow things to be ambiguous," Young said, "so I went back and said, you know I would be grateful for your support. He said 'Okay,'" meaning he understood the request, not that he was ready to satisfy it. "He was going to outstare me," Young said. "Would that be possible, Senator?" he asked. McConnell made it clear to Young that he was going to have to do his own work and prove he could raise enough money, but that McConnell would be watching closely.

"To me that was an interaction that was revealing about McConnell," Young said. "He's very cautious and careful and seemingly always quite clear about how far he is prepared to go in different situations and disciplined in not going further."

Young went out and raised a respectable amount of money, and he was running a good primary campaign, but he faced a challenge from another Republican congressman, Marlin Stutzman, a member of the hard-right Freedom Caucus who had the support of the Club for Growth, another outside group. McConnell thought Young was the far better candidate for a general election, and he sent members of his team to help defeat Stutzman. McConnell's people threatened consultants about doing work for Stutzman. They told vendors not to do business with them. It worked.

"I suspect he looked at the polling and assessed what kind of member I would be and decided to go all in in the primary, and that was helpful to me," Young said.

Young thought his Democratic opponent would be Baron Hill, a former member of Congress and one-time Indiana high school basketball all-star, no small credential in the state. But by the summer, Democrats had another candidate in mind. They persuaded one of the most famous names in Indiana politics, Evan Bayh, to take Hill's place. Bayh, a former two-term governor and two-time finalist for the Democratic candidate for vice president, had served two terms in the Senate before announcing in 2010 that he would not seek a third. Bayh was a surprise late entry into the race, encouraged by polling that found him with an enormous edge in the summer of 2016. He also had $10 million in his campaign account, left over from when he had decided not to seek a third term.

Bayh, whose father, Birch, was also a long-serving senator, had the benefit of being known by almost everyone in the state, while Young was trying to introduce himself to many voters. After Bayh announced his candidacy, Young's polling found the Democrat with a yawning twenty-six-point lead. He had to do something to put himself on Bayh's level. He showed up at the Ham Breakfast at the Indiana State Fair, where Bayh was doing a radio interview, which Young interrupted. He shook his opponent's hand and said, "Evan, Todd Young, very nice to meet you. Did you just fly in this morning?"

It was the kind of in-your-face challenge that McConnell could appreciate. "I had to be aggressive," Young said. "I was running against the great Evan Bayh, so I had to try to make this man who never makes a mistake make a mistake. We had to play a perfect game."

His early attacks did not work. Then his campaign decided the only way to beat Bayh would be to make the argument that he was an outsider who had lost touch with his state while cashing in on a lucrative post-Senate career. McConnell thought that might be effective, but "could use some improvement," Young said. Suddenly, consultants and vendors, all part of the loose McConnell confederation, showed up to deliver that "improvement." Young put them on the campaign payroll and thought the money was well spent.

"But it is a bit of an asymmetric relationship," Young said. "I mean did I have a choice whether or not to put them on? For me there wasn't a choice. He never told me I had to. He just said you need to up your game. My team's telling me this. He trusts his team and we hired them. And they did a very good job. So we certainly got our money's worth and then some."

McConnell's emissaries, notably John Ashbrook, a former staffer and business partner of Josh Holmes, sharpened the attacks on Bayh and dug out more opposition research that proved effective. They questioned whether Bayh even had an address in Indiana. Bayh, under media questioning, gave a residential address, but said it was on a "drive," when it was actually on a circle. "It's peculiar to get your address wrong," Young said. It got worse for Bayh. Brian Slodysko of the Associated Press, based on a confidential source, reported that Bayh's official schedule from his final months in the Senate showed that Bayh stayed at a Marriott instead of the residence he claimed.

Then a reporter for the *Indianapolis Star*, most likely prodded by McConnell's team, set out to further explore the residency issue, knocking on doors near Bayh's claimed residence. The reporter had a video camera and knocked on a woman's door. "Evan Bayh? He lives next door?" the woman asked. "No, he doesn't. That's just not right, that's just not right."

That was all the Senate Leadership Fund needed. Young's campaign and the Super PAC put more than $10 million into advertising to reinforce the message that Bayh had "gone Washington."

Young had been underestimated as a candidate. He was thoughtful and personable and relatively low key. But the former star soccer
player was also fiercely competitive, just the kind of Republican Mc-
Connell worked hard to recruit. There was really only one way to defeat Bayh, and that was to ruthlessly attack him, to portray him as
someone who had lived a cushy post-Senate life in Washington and
had no real connection to the Hoosier state. "Our view was the only
way to get to the finish line was by utterly destroying Evan Bayh's
credibility," Holmes said.

Young started to surge, drafting on Trump's popularity in the state
as well, and Bayh's campaign proved unable to mount an effective
counterattack. Without the hands of Team Mitch, Bayh may well have
won the seat based on his name alone. Instead, Young won easily, by
ten points.

"We played big there, and in the end, we basically fired Evan Bayh,"
McConnell told me. "I mean everything he did after he left the Senate
became fodder for a well-funded campaign against him."

It was a vivid demonstration of how McConnell amassed, then
wielded his power, creating a campaign apparatus to help Republican
candidates and to build loyalty to himself as the party leader. The conservatives on the Supreme Court, in their *Citizens United* decision,
had created a financial pipeline that McConnell built into a vast political ecosystem. It played to all of McConnell's strengths: the politics,
shorn of the weedy details of policy. He helped pick candidates, he
helped fund their campaigns, he delivered strategic advice, his Super
PAC ran millions of dollars in advertisements, and their success was
McConnell's success. It was mutually reinforcing.

Young was just one of the victories the Senate Leadership Fund
and McConnell could claim. There were others. McConnell's imprint
was evident in at least a half a dozen competitive Senate races around
the country, as those additional millions of dollars for negative advertising were put to lethal use. Among them, Senator Richard Burr
held on to win another term in North Carolina, Senator Marco Rubio

won another term in Florida and, in Wisconsin, Ron Johnson defeated Russ Feingold, McConnell's long-time adversary on campaign finance issues.

For the most part, McConnell's efforts engendered loyalty and worked seamlessly. But there was another surprise winner on election night: Donald Trump.

TWENTY-ONE

"NOT VERY SMART, IRASCIBLE . . . DESPICABLE . . . BEYOND ERRATIC"

The assembled powers of the American government, including past presidents and vice presidents, members of Congress, and Supreme Court justices, had gathered in the Capitol on January 20, 2017, a dreary, drizzly, unseasonably warm day in Washington, D.C. They gathered to walk outside to the platform facing the Washington Monument and Lincoln Memorial for Donald John Trump's inaugural address, typically one of democracy's pageants.

Mitch McConnell stood among them. Two weeks earlier, when Congress certified the election, McConnell had told his old friend Biden he thought Trump could be trouble as they walked through the capital together. The new president began his address, which was as sepulchral as the weather, speaking of an "American carnage" that must end. As former president George W. Bush remarked after the speech, "That was some weird shit."

Trump's address merely marked the start of the most chaotic, turbulent, and norm-defying administration in the nation's history. McConnell, like so many Republicans and Democrats, had been wrong about Trump's electoral prospects, first assuming he would never get the nomination, then that there was no way he could be elected.

On election night, the results of the presidential election shifted from Clinton to Trump as votes rolled in, and she eventually conceded.

McConnell, as stunned by the result as anyone, wondered how Trump would govern. Beyond his reality TV, tabloid celebrity persona, there was little to go on—no real sense of his ideology or agenda. But there was one thing about which he was certain: for the first time since he had been leader, his party would control both the executive and legislative branches of government. That meant he could shape the Supreme Court and the broader federal judiciary, and revamp the tax laws in ways that would be more favorable to business, and reduce government regulations.

McConnell thought Trump won because more voters embraced him as the "change" candidate and rejected Clinton as the "status quo." He also saw the returns as validation of a thesis he had been forming for years, that there was an emerging voting bloc of white non-college-educated voters who rapidly were becoming the core of the Republican base. He had seen a growing discontent among the white working class who saw Trump as their champion. It was a group of people brought to life in the popular book *Hillbilly Elegy* by JD Vance, which painted a portrait of an aggrieved group of Americans who felt the system had let them down. He and Vance had exchanged memoirs at an event in Silicon Valley—McConnell's was called *The Long Game*—and he initially was impressed by Vance. They developed a friendly relationship, at least for a time.

Though Trump came to office with no real record on issues, his early cabinet appointments of Rex Tillerson as secretary of state, John

Kelly at the Department of Homeland Security, James Mattis as defense secretary and, of course, McConnell's wife, Elaine Chao, as transportation secretary, gave McConnell a measure of comfort.

Chao had asked her husband for some tips about talking to Trump before her interview for the transportation post. In an oral history McConnell said he told her, "Honey, just get your hair done up and your makeup and everything will be fine." He said Trump called him while she was in his office and said, "Wow, she's really good looking."

Trump could be assured that most of his nominees, including most federal judges, would be approved by McConnell's Senate majority, which would only need a simple majority vote. "In one of the great ironies of modern politics, the Democrats are going to die by the sword that they created when they broke the rules of the Senate to change the rules of the Senate," McConnell said in late 2016. He was referring to the moment in 2013 when Harry Reid moved to approve nominations other than the Supreme Court with a simple majority. The parliamentarian ruled that move out of order. Reid then appealed that ruling. It was overturned with fifty-two votes, all from Democrats, changing the rule.

"We were all mad as hell about it," McConnell said of Republicans. At the same time, he saw the potential now to use his power in the same way when his party was in the majority. "So even though I didn't like the way they did it by breaking the rules of the Senate, I wasn't all that unhappy with what they did." He was able to persuade Republicans that they should not change the rule back for the sake of the institution. Needing only a simple majority to seat the cabinet, Republicans could confirm controversial Trump nominees like Betsy DeVos to be education secretary, and Tillerson, an oil company executive, on party line votes.

Senator Michael Bennet conceded that Democrats abolishing the rules gave McConnell a runway. "I think both parties have blood on their hands when it comes to our constitutional obligations to advise.

And the Senate and the American people are worse off as a result of what we've done."

Once the cabinet officials had been confirmed, McConnell's focus was rarely far from the courts. He controlled the Senate calendar and could set a fast timeline for confirmation votes. He told Republican members after they elected him as leader that "the 114th Congress will be known more than anything as the Senate that saved the Supreme Court." He was mindful that his blocking of Merrick Garland had been an animating, and possibly decisive force, in Trump's victory by energizing white social conservatives. Now, dealing with the court vacancy he had blocked under Barack Obama, he needed to deliver.

For that, he counseled Trump that his nominee had to have unassailable credentials, to give McConnell and Republicans the rationale they would need to end the filibuster for Supreme Court nominees. Trump could expect more than one vacancy given the rumors that Justice Anthony Kennedy could also retire soon, giving Trump a chance to remake the court.

Trump took McConnell's advice and selected Gorsuch. Then McConnell methodically went to his members and convinced them that if Democrats were to block Gorsuch, then no Republican conservative justice could be confirmed without extending the simple majority rule to the high court. From the start, he instructed his staff and other senators to talk only about the qualities of the nominee in public comments, not about the process to get him on the court. When McConnell was asked about the process by reporters, he consistently answered by simply saying that Gorsuch "would be confirmed." For once, McConnell had no plan B.

In the first vote, Democrats filibustered the Gorsuch nomination as expected. That gave McConnell the predicate he needed to persuade Republicans that their only recourse was to change the rules. In doing so, he further eroded public confidence in the idea that the nation's highest court was guided by law, not politics. The narrowly divided vote to confirm Gorsuch stood in marked contrast to that of the justice he was replacing, Antonin Scalia, who had been approved 98–0.

On judges, McConnell and Trump were largely aligned. On most everything else, McConnell was in crisis management mode dealing with a president who governed by whim. Trump would frequently call McConnell without warning, or after watching a segment on *Fox and Friends*.

Since Trump thrived on chaos and McConnell on control, they were an awkward fit from the start.

One of Trump's purported priorities, a major infrastructure bill, became a long running Washington joke because his administration never produced one. "Infrastructure Week" morphed into "Infrastructure Month" on an issue that could have easily gained bipartisan support. (After Biden became president, McConnell delivered enough Republican votes to finally pass one.)

McConnell sized Trump up early as someone he and House Speaker Paul Ryan could probably win over on most policy matters, in no small part because Trump had no legislative agenda of consequence. They had to endure Trump telling them that they had made a lot of bad deals, and that he could make better ones. McConnell didn't engage. Instead, he just encouraged the president to get legislation he wanted to the Senate, where McConnell could ensure it would get a vote.

In practice, things didn't turn out to be so easy. Because Trump was so mercurial, it was difficult to know how he would react day to day. "He notices every slight," McConnell said. During the fall campaign, McConnell had dealt with "the Trump factor" by keeping quiet to avoid causing issues for Republican candidates in Senate races.

His calculated caution was evident again when he criticized Trump over the *Access Hollywood* tape, but did not withdraw his support. At the time, he considered that posture politically wise, particularly compared with Ryan, who was far more critical of Trump after his remarks about assaulting women. "I was so close to pulling my support and I talked to Mitch an hour before doing a conference call, and he basically said don't unendorse, it will fracture us," Ryan recalled McConnell saying. "He's going to lose, but don't take down all of us in Congress."

Once Trump was in office, the two men spoke almost daily comparing notes about their new leader. "We saw things the same way, and we frankly took turns talking to Trump," Ryan told me. "We both felt an institutional obligation just to keep the country going in the right direction. We had an obligation for the nation's sake to make this thing work."

One time Ryan asked McConnell to come to the House and "take some bullets" for him by talking to recalcitrant members. McConnell, accustomed to doing the same for Senate colleagues, defused more arguments than he fomented. Ryan, a novice in House leadership, said he learned from McConnell. "His method and sense of principles were extremely instructive to me and turned me into a radical institutionalist." Ryan would be more emotional in arguments with members, McConnell more modulated. "He has this different type of temperament," Ryan said. "He's a less-is-more guy when it comes to speaking," and has "indefatigable" patience. "His best weapon among all is that he doesn't care what people think about him."

In 2017, they put together a two-year legislative plan, with little input from Trump, who would throw things off track with what Ryan called "aberrant Tweets." Ryan and McConnell kept working toward forward progress on legislation. "That was an absolute tandem effort by Mitch and myself. . . . Mitch and I erected Jersey barriers on the highway."

As time went on, Ryan and McConnell both came to view Trump essentially the same way. "He's just a narcissist, an amoral narcissist who is looking for satiating his needs and wants and desires on a daily basis with zero regard for institution and the Constitution," Ryan said.

"We believed we needed, for the long game, to keep the trains of government going in the right direction and keep people busy, not just fighting."

They kept Trump busy by passing bills the president could take credit for. The legislation Ryan was most interested in was a tax bill. As a lawmaker who enjoyed a reputation as a master of policy details, this was friendly terrain for Ryan. McConnell had far less experience on granular tax issues, other than the typical conservative orthodoxy favoring lower taxes.

It was not difficult to sell Trump on the idea of a bill that could be called the Trump Tax Cut, so it was really a matter of Ryan fashioning the legislation and McConnell steering it through the Senate. When Trump signed the legislation in late December 2018, he complained that his administration was not getting enough credit.

"We were just more surprised every day, every week, every month just how loopy he was, how erratic he was, how strange he was," Ryan said. "He would shoot the messengers, and Mitch and I were always the messengers. We would always have to explain to him the practical limitations of government. He never liked hearing that."

Then the right wing of the party would echo Trump's criticisms, leaving Ryan and McConnell feeling like "punching bags." Ryan referred to the hard right as the "entertainment wing" of the party, more interested in being on Fox News or getting a social media following than getting any kind of legislative result.

This is not to say that Trump was never preoccupied with legislative matters. He was, for instance, livid when Congress had failed to repeal the Affordable Care Act, with McCain dramatically providing the decisive vote to preserve it. He directed his anger specifically at McConnell, via his favorite medium, Twitter. He called for the Senate to end the filibuster, saying that Republicans "look like fools." "Mitch M. go to 51 votes NOW and WIN. IT'S TIME." He attacked McConnell for not repealing the Affordable Care Act, "Mitch, get back to work and put Repeal & Replace, Tax Reform & Cuts and a great infrastructure Bill on my desk for signing." It was his third tweet in two days calling out McConnell. Trump even went so far as to suggest McConnell should resign if he did not repeal the health care law. "I'm very disappointed in Mitch," Trump said. The *New York Times* wrote: "Like many of his actions over the past few weeks, the president's fusillade against Mr. McConnell seems aimed at reassuring his core supporters and shifting the blame for a lack of accomplishments from the White House to Congress—even at the expense of his fellow Republicans."

McConnell responded a week later in a speech in Louisville by praising Trump.

That was not sufficient to stop Trump's criticism. McConnell and the president had a heated argument on the phone. "I was pretty assertive, and he was, too," McConnell said. "I was angry enough to raise my voice back." Weeks went by without the two men talking. Then Trump, perhaps realizing he needed to be in touch with the Senate's leader, invited McConnell to the White House. They had a good talk, McConnell said, then Trump decided in the moment to call a joint press conference.

Though unprepared, McConnell said the event went fine. "My view is it's not hard to look more knowledgeable than Donald Trump at a press conference."

With Trump, though, if things go poorly, "it's always somebody else's fault," McConnell said.

Things went well with the tax bill. Ryan and McConnell engineered its passage by using a procedure called reconciliation, which requires only a simple majority vote, the same move Democrats used to pass the health-care law. "The passage of the tax bill was hailed as a great success," McConnell said. "All of a sudden, I'm Trump's new best friend."

The calm waters did not last long. They never did. Up next was a special Senate election in Alabama, a deep red state where Republican primary voters had chosen the ethically dubious Roy Moore over

Senator Luther Strange, who had been appointed to the position to replace Jeff Sessions, Trump's first attorney general. "I recommended Trump stay out of it," McConnell said. Instead, "Trump got right in the middle of it and tried to get Moore elected, and, amazingly enough, Alabama elected a Democrat to the Senate." Said McConnell: "I'm glad the Democrat won."

Moore would have drawn ethics investigations almost from the start, McConnell thought, following a *Washington Post* series of articles that documented Moore pursuing young women, including teenagers.

Despite that embarrassment, McConnell reflected in an oral history interview that 2017 was the best year for conservatism in his three decades in the Senate. He drove through fifteen repeals of regulations, which delighted the business community, including his donors.

On substance, he thought Trump had done fine policy-wise in his first year, essentially adopting what he and Ryan recommended to him. "But his behavior is so off-putting that he is mired in a mid- to high-thirties approval rating, which is basically his core supporters. Every once in a while, he does something that makes him look good to independents."

McConnell praised Trump's State of the Union speech and noted that a significant number of independents reacted positively to it. "But within twenty-four hours, he was tweeting again." Trump was particularly obsessed with the special counsel investigation into Russian election interference and Trump's possible involvement.

"There's no question the Russians were messing around in our election," McConnell said in an oral history interview that covered 2017. "They do that all over the world. They do it in Europe. It's a challenge. Nobody thinks the Russians had any real impact on the outcome of our election, so the issue that remains is, was there actual collusion between the Russians and the Trump campaign? I doubt it, but we don't really know yet."

Though Trump, during the 2016 campaign, preemptively made

allegations that the election he would end up winning would be stolen from him, McConnell did not think outside forces were significant enough to affect the outcome. On September 6, 2016, John Brennan, the director of the Central Intelligence Agency, had told McConnell that intelligence reports indicated that Russia was trying to influence the election in ways that would be detrimental to Hillary Clinton. Brennan said McConnell accused him of "making claims to prevent Donald Trump from being president." McConnell didn't recall saying those precise words, but acknowledged that indeed was what he thought. "I took great umbrage at that and told him this was something of critical importance," Brennan told me, adding that he thought McConnell had put politics above national security. McConnell said Brennan was the only partisan CIA director he had encountered in his four decades in the Senate. "I think Brennan wanted to hurt me," McConnell said.

McConnell, who had been a Russia hawk his entire career, said in both an oral history and in an interview that he did believe the intelligence reports that the Russians were trying to interfere, but not with the alarm that Brennan presented, and not in a way that swayed the election. A later report from the Senate Intelligence Committee confirmed that the Russians had been trying to meddle.

In anger over the investigation, Trump in May 2017 fired James Comey, the FBI director, which McConnell saw as a major blunder. "His own actions have put him in jeopardy, and I'm sure his lawyers are probably going nuts, because he won't shut up about it. He's completely uncontrollable."

He tried to convince Trump that attacking fellow Republicans simply made things harder. "His behavior hangs over everything in a counterproductive way, and he's got a good chance of being overall viewed as a failure," McConnell said at the end of 2017. Trump's achievements were things Ryan and McConnell wanted to do anyway. "What's different about him is him."

McConnell was looking ahead to the 2018 midterm elections,

which typically result in heavy losses for the president's party. As usual, he was most concerned about preserving the Republican majority.

He saw a potential political "tsunami" forming. "You can sort of see it building and heading our way, and it doesn't have anything to do with major policy mistakes. It's just a visceral negative reaction to [Trump's] behavior, which he seems unable to control or at least to control for very long. It's like a caged animal; he jumps out again."

He counseled candidates to talk about the tax bill and a strong economy, and to "hope that they can convince people to vote on something other than a referendum on Trump."

That kind of thinking had little purchase with Trump supporters, including a lot of Republicans in Congress. Their fervor and anger were directed in particular at Ryan, and by April 2018, the man who had been anointed to save House Republicans from themselves had decided abruptly that he would step down, adding to the chaos of the moment and further dimming Republican prospects for November.

But at the end of June 2018, Justice Anthony Kennedy announced he was retiring from the Supreme Court, just as McConnell had suggested he would. McConnell would again be asked to push through Trump's nominee. McConnell saw a glimmer of light in an otherwise dark political forecast for Republicans: it was possible that the right nominee might actually help Republican fortunes, at least in Senate races.

McConnell again pushed for Amul Thapar, but Trump nominated federal appeals court Judge Brett Kavanaugh. McConnell also liked Kavanaugh, though he was concerned that his long time in government service and on the federal bench had produced a lot of paper, which could complicate and certainly delay the confirmation process.

Even so, it seemed at first that Kavanaugh's elevation would be relatively easy. Then the *Washington Post* published an explosive allegation from a woman who claimed Kavanaugh had sexually assaulted her at a party when they were in high school. McConnell thought it might be a redux of the Clarence Thomas hearings from more than three decades ago, an ugly national spectacle involving a Republican nominee. When the woman, Christine Blasey Ford, testified about her allegations, McConnell found her to be a sympathetic and credible witness. At least as important, so did Trump, who called McConnell to ask if he thought he should pull the nomination. McConnell told Trump "it's only halftime" and said they should see how Kavanaugh responded in his own defense that afternoon. Senator Lindsey Graham of South Carolina, whose face went beet red, railed against what he said was the unfairness, cementing the partisan divide.

Kavanaugh forcefully defended himself and denied the allegations. Trump and McConnell talked afterward, and McConnell said he thought Kavanaugh deserved an up or down vote. In public, McConnell argued that Kavanaugh was entitled to the presumption of innocence and said his support for him was "as strong as mule piss." A perfunctory one-week investigation ensued to explore new allegations, but nothing broke through the Republican firewall for the nominee. When Kavanaugh was confirmed a month before the 2018 midterms, McConnell and a small number of staff gathered in his office to celebrate. The drink of choice? A "Mule Piss Cocktail," a concoction of several types of alcohol that they thought tasted as bad as it sounded. McConnell enjoyed a brief burst of popularity among Republicans, saying he had seen a poll that showed his approval rating with Republican voters had almost doubled, to sixty-two.

When things had looked grim for the Kavanaugh nomination Trump scolded McConnell in an "expletive-filled tirade" over the phone for how he handled it. But a short time later, Trump bathed in the victory of Kavanaugh's confirmation and said McConnell was the "greatest leader in history" during a rally in Kentucky.

Among Republicans, the controversy over Kavanaugh was an animating issue in several key Senate races. In Indiana, for one, the race between Republican Mike Braun and incumbent Democratic senator Joe Donnelly had been close, but after the Kavanaugh confirmation, Braun surged into a lead and went on to defeat Donnelly. Republicans had just enough other victories to keep control of the Senate, in no small part thanks to the $191 million raised by the Senate Leadership Fund. The new class of senators included Mitt Romney of Utah and Josh Hawley of Missouri, who McConnell predicted would be a star. In the House, Democrats crushed Republicans and retook the majority. But among Senate Republicans, McConnell had never felt in a stronger position.

Kavanaugh was another critical part of his plan to reshape the federal judiciary from the Supreme Court down to the lower courts. Getting Kavanaugh confirmed ensured that Republicans had locked down the swing vote on the court, with a 5–4 majority that McConnell had orchestrated.

But there was no orchestrating Trump. "The big problem is the occupant of the White House, who has every characteristic you would not want a president to have," McConnell said. "Not very smart, irascible, nasty, just about every quality you would not want somebody to have." It was thanks to Trump, he thought, that House Democrats had reclaimed the majority, ensuring at least two years of divided government. Though he was relieved his judge project could continue apace, McConnell knew that passing major legislation was unlikely with Democrats in control of the House.

He also thought, at the outset of 2019, that his party was heading into "the danger zone" because of Trump's views on foreign policy and defense. Most Republican senators, he said, had no appetite for going to war with Trump but did want him to change. "So trying to figure out how to influence him to take a different path is going to be quite challenging," McConnell said. "I'm thinking of ways to try to, without having a complete fracture with him, trying to figure out how to get him into a better place."

As always, McConnell was also looking ahead, and the 2018 midterm election results did not send a promising signal for Republicans in 2020. They had lost substantially among suburban women and college educated voters, an acceleration of a shift in which the parties were in many ways trading places. McConnell put it starkly: "There's just not enough white men that didn't finish college to win." He added that he would be "shocked" if Trump didn't get crushed when he ran for reelection.

Trump did not help things by starting the year with a government shutdown over a spending dispute involving his desire to build a wall at the southern border. McConnell called it a "ridiculous two-month government shutdown because Trump wouldn't take any advice from us." It produced no tangible benefit for Republicans. Trump eventually "capitulated, as I told him he almost certainly would," McConnell said.

McConnell was looking forward to the Senate's August recess, when he could spend time in Kentucky doing political events around the state. But the first weekend of August, as he was going down steps near the patio of his townhouse, he said, his Nike shoes split, and he fell onto the concrete, breaking his left shoulder. "Hurt like hell," McConnell said. He had to have surgery, which involved securing the shoulder with a titanium plate and twelve screws. He spent the recess at home, rehabilitating. Some members of his staff told me privately they thought his left leg prompted the fall.

It was not a quiet August in Washington. An anonymous CIA official submitted a whistleblower complaint that Trump, in a half-hour phone call in July, had tried to get Volodymyr Zelenskyy, the new Ukrainian president, to announce investigations into former vice president Biden and other Democrats just as Trump was holding back $400 million in military assistance for Ukraine. If proven, it would be a clear violation of his oath of office.

Democrats, who had been vowing to investigate Trump from the day he took office, now had a serious foundation for doing so. House Democrats did an extensive investigation, and Republicans stood almost in lockstep behind Trump. By December, the House voted to impeach Trump, marking the third presidential impeachment in the nation's history.

McConnell was cautious in his initial assessment of the impeachment case—he continued to try to maintain some kind of rapport with the president, particularly when it was in his interest—saying, "Trump has done a number of things that one could argue, depending upon your point of view, are impeachable, but they finally seized on a couple of things that, frankly, are pretty weak."

He then began using his power—in ways that Trump might not have understood—to undermine the Democrats' case. For one, he strongly pushed to not have witnesses testify, a move designed to shorten the proceedings and put impeachment in the public's rearview mirror as quickly as possible. McConnell believed Democrats were fully aware of this, too, and that they were also approaching the matter with a political motivation rather than a serious inquiry into misconduct and he made no pretense about being impartial. "This is not a time for impartiality," McConnell said. "This is a purely political process."

"We all know that Trump is not going to get removed from office, so what this is all about is making four or five of my vulnerable senators vote on calling witnesses," McConnell said in an oral history. "I don't want them to have to cast those votes. [Schumer] does want them to cast them. So that's really all this is about." Nearly alone, Republican Senator Lisa Murkowski criticized McConnell saying he was coordinating with the White House.

McConnell accurately predicted Trump's acquittal in February 2020. Only Romney crossed party lines and voted to convict. Voters would have the chance to render their own verdict on Trump in November.

McConnell was far less focused on Trump's reelection effort in 2020 than on his own and that of his fellow Republican senators. He had known for months that his likely Democratic opponent would be Amy McGrath, a candidate whose résumé was the stuff of political consultants' dreams. After graduating from the Naval Academy, she became the first woman to serve as a Marine combat aviator. She flew on extremely dangerous bombing missions over Iraq and Afghanistan and had duty, honor, and country written all over her. And there was more. When she was just a young girl growing up in northern Kentucky, she decided she wanted to attend the Naval Academy and fly fighter jets. When she learned that women were not allowed to fly in combat, she wrote to elected officials in Washington, including McConnell, to ask why. He never replied. And she never forgot.

McGrath had become famous almost overnight when she ran for a House seat in 2018, with an announcement video that went viral and seeded her campaign with more than $1 million. She continued to be an extraordinary fundraiser, and up until election night, it looked like she would defeat the incumbent Republican, Andy Barr. She ended up losing narrowly and thought about taking a break from politics. Schumer pitched her hard on running for the Senate to take on McConnell, and she finally agreed. She saw McConnell as emblematic of everything that was wrong with Washington and public service.

Her campaign was a magnet for contributions from outside the state, and McConnell quickly realized that even with his prodigious fundraising operation, he would be badly outspent by his opponent.

McConnell started planning for his campaign for a seventh term earlier than ever before. He had watched McGrath during her House race, and knew he had to build his own campaign structure sooner. In her House race, McGrath honored a pledge to not run negative advertising against her opponent. She made no such vow this time. And McConnell's formula for victory, unremitting attacks on his opponent, had been vital to his unparalleled winning streak in his state.

Shortly after Trump's acquittal, which McConnell had helped to ensure, both men were confronted with a crisis that the country had not seen in more than a century, a coronavirus pandemic killing people indiscriminately around the globe. Americans were panicked, and Trump was the kind of president better at creating a crisis than managing one.

The virus was so lethal that it forced the U.S. economy to shut down. Members of Congress stopped coming to the office. People learned to work from home, wipe down their groceries with Lysol, and watch for what seemed like ever changing, ever worsening developments. The economy was near collapse, and serious people were using words like "Depression."

Congress responded by passing the CARES Act, which pumped nearly $3 trillion into the economy almost immediately to try to slow the fall. McConnell worked with Treasury Secretary Steven Mnuchin and Speaker Nancy Pelosi to get it passed, delivering direct financial assistance to small businesses and individual families, and expediting vaccines for health-care workers, among other provisions.

Pelosi proposed an additional $3 trillion in aid, which McConnell rejected, and though he thought an additional $1 trillion might be in order, his own members would only approve $350 million more.

By August, McConnell thought that the safeguards Trump's White House put in place to limit infection were too cavalier, and he stopped going there. His own experience from childhood with viral infection led him in many ways to do the opposite of Trump. He would later use his own political funds to place ads in Kentucky encouraging people to get vaccinated. And McConnell, like other members of Congress, the Supreme Court, and other top officials, was among the first group to be vaccinated.

McConnell even confined his fundraising meetings to Zoom. At the few public events he held, safety protocols like masks and social distancing were in place. Speakers had separate microphones.

McGrath was running the kind of campaign that McConnell could appreciate on some level, arguing that Kentucky should fire McConnell, that he had been in the job too long, and it was time for change. But she also had to navigate how to handle her criticisms of Trump, who had exceptional approval ratings in Kentucky; he was much more popular in the state than McConnell.

McConnell said Trump offered to come to Kentucky and have a rally for him, even with all of their differences. But he saw no upside to that. "I told him, I'm okay in Kentucky, you're okay in Kentucky. Why don't you do it elsewhere?"

McConnell had something far more meaningful to deliver for Trump and Republicans. After the death of Supreme Court Justice Ruth Bader Ginsburg on September 18, 2020, he immediately went to work on pushing the Senate to confirm her replacement before the election less than two months away. It was a head-snapping turn from his insistence that Obama should not be able to fill the Scalia vacancy, which had occurred in February of 2016. McConnell's rationale was thin; he claimed that because the Senate and the White House were controlled by the same party, the proximity to the election was irrelevant. The audacity of the move enraged Democrats, and even some Senate Republicans criticized it. None of that mattered. Trump nominated Amy Coney Barrett, a federal appeals court judge in Chicago with decidedly conservative leanings, and McConnell jammed through her confirmation to the Supreme Court, ensuring a conservative supermajority that in rapid succession would undo decades-old precedents on some of the era's most polarizing issues. It was McConnell's rawest flex of power since blocking Garland, and a move he hoped would energize Republicans.

It turned out that Democrats were motivated and outraged, in ways that proved detrimental to Trump. As for his own fortunes, McConnell's victory in 2020 was never in serious doubt.

The pandemic foreclosed the possibility of much in-person campaigning, so McGrath could not benefit from drawing the contrast between a younger, athletic mother of three with a valorous military record and the aged, intrepid political insider who had dispatched far more experienced opponents. They were in the same room only once, for a debate. The only other time they spoke was when McGrath called to concede on election night. McConnell had been right about being outspent. McGrath's campaign raised about $100 million compared with $60 million for McConnell. This time, money lost.

McConnell won, 58–38, with almost 420,000 more votes. "These elections are a choice," McConnell told me. "It's not Mitch McConnell against a perfect candidate. It's Mitch McConnell against somebody. Everybody's got a record."

His campaign emphasized comments McGrath made at a fundraiser in Massachusetts when she said she was to the left of most voters in Kentucky and made negative comments about Trump. It was just about all McConnell needed in such a conservative state.

McConnell's victories extended beyond Kentucky, in no small part because of the financial muscle of the Senate Leadership Fund, which raised $464 million in 2020, almost $300 million more than it had in its first year. McConnell could not be directly involved in its activity, but he kept in close touch with Law, and the two were so close it is unlikely there would be much of a difference in strategy.

On election night, November 3, 2020, McConnell celebrated his own victory, cheered when he got good news about a Republican Senate candidate, and watched closely as it seemed increasingly likely that Donald Trump would not win reelection. Both Republicans and Democrats know there are no perfect elections. There are modest instances of fraud, on both sides, and only in the rarest circumstances does it affect the outcome. This was not one of those times. Most signs pointed to a Biden victory, but McConnell did not say anything that night. Two Georgia senator races appeared headed for a runoff, and Senate control was in the balance.

Trump tried to claim victory, citing his lead early in the night. But both sides knew to expect that lead because his supporters were more likely to vote on Election Day than were Biden supporters in this most unusual pandemic year. As more of the advance votes were counted through the night, Biden overtook Trump's lead and added to his margin.

Trump had enough of a grip on his party that it was clear few Republicans—including McConnell—were willing to risk calling him out for his baseless claims of election fraud in the early days after the election, as counting in key states continued, but Biden looked to be on the path to victory. Four days after the election, at 11:26 a.m. on November 7, the Associated Press declared him the winner.

McConnell chose to wait to say anything until the Electoral College had met on December 14, an event that typically is seen as a ceremonial ratification of the voters' will. On that day, he congratulated Biden on his victory and broke off his relationship with Trump, who had berated him in an angry phone call, reinforced by more angry posts on Twitter. Trump went on to falsely claim that he was somehow responsible for McConnell winning reelection by twenty percentage points.

Even with the disruption that Trump was creating with his false allegations of fraud, the government still needed to function. McConnell and Republicans resumed negotiations with Pelosi, Schumer, and Democrats over an additional aid package to deal with the coronavirus. They had agreed to an additional $900 billion, then Trump balked at signing it, saying Congress needed to send out relief checks for more than the $600 lawmakers had agreed to. Moreover, Trump wanted his signature on the checks.

"His behavior since losing the election has been beyond erratic," McConnell said. "It's included allegations of voter fraud, none of which has been proven." He noted that Trump was tweeting almost daily about how he thought the election was stolen from him. "Unfortunately, about half the Republicans in the country believe whatever he says."

McConnell was not finished unloading on the defeated president in these comments to his oral historian in late December 2020. "This despicable human being," he said, "is sitting on this package of relief that the American people desperately need."

McConnell also was also concerned that Trump's actions would cost Republicans one or both Senate seats in Georgia. "He is not only—well, he's stupid as well as being ill-tempered and can't even figure out where his own best interests lie, and that's certainly been on full display."

Trump's behavior, he said, "only underscores the good judgment

of the American people. They've just had enough of the misrepresen-
tations, the outright lies almost on a daily basis, and they fired him.
And for a narcissist like him, that's been really hard to take, and so
his behavior since the election has been even worse, by far, than it
was before, because he has no filter now at all." McConnell continued
steaming over Trump's bogus election claims and his stalling on the
COVID relief bill, "which he's doing right now down in Mar-a-Lago,
simply because he's having a tantrum.

"I think I'm pretty safe in saying it's not just the Democrats who
are counting the days until he leaves on January 20, but the Republicans as well."

Trump finally signed the COVID bill on December 27. His election grievances, on the other hand, were not going anywhere.

In December 2020, McConnell did not think Trump would disap-
pear once out of office. "He's still going to probably have an enemies
list. He can't stand being out of the limelight, so I think he's going to
be an ongoing challenge for us in future elections as he decides to play
in primaries. So I don't think we're totally rid of him, but I think the
country is, and even though there were some good things that happened during these four years, particularly the judges and the 2017
tax bill and some other things that were clearly worth doing, he made
every one of those harder, but it did happen while he was president."

Meanwhile, Trump continued to train his ire on McConnell, calling him a "dour, sullen, and unsmiling political hack." He said the Republican Party could never be strong or respected if it relied on leaders
like McConnell. A relationship that at the best of times was fraught, if
fitfully productive, had now become poisonous.

TWENTY-TWO

"THE McCONNELL
COURT"

Justice Ruth Bader Ginsburg, the revered liberal jurist, was hospital-
ized on July 14, 2020, for a possible infection likely related to her pancreatic cancer. She had been diagnosed with the disease in 2009 and
had undergone extensive treatment. At eighty-seven, it was now obvious her health issues were more acute.

McConnell's mind quickly went back to Scalia's abrupt death, and
he and his staff decided they needed to discretely have a plan in place
should Ginsburg die or be unable to continue to serve on the Supreme
Court. He was both mindful of the lessons of the past and unafraid to
make a controversial decision.

Staff lawyers put together a structure for how they would deal
with the prospect of Ginsburg's passing. They worked on a statement
for McConnell, which would start with gracious praise of Ginsburg, a
pathbreaking lawyer and giant on the court, then pivot to his explanation of why he would fill a vacancy so close to the election when that
was the precise reason he had blocked Merrick Garland's nomination
in 2016. McConnell stuck to the core argument that the situations

were different. Garland was nominated during an election year, with a divided government. This time, Republicans controlled the White House and the Senate, so the nomination should be put forward. No more talk about "letting the voters decide." Once again, it did not matter that there was no rule in place; McConnell was positioning himself as though one existed.

One of Ginsburg's final wishes was that her vacancy not be filled before the election. But McConnell was determined to do so if he could. "That was not, obviously, what I had in mind because I was afraid we would not be able to fill the vacancy if it was not dealt with until after the election, because Trump might lose and we might not be in the majority, neither of which was known at the time."

First, he had to talk to other Republican senators, focusing on those who might disagree or at least be wavering in their support. He started to have those conversations in August, while the Senate was in recess. Just as he had after Scalia died, also during a recess, McConnell was trying to avoid having senators express widely disparate views. He did not need to talk to those who would back him, or to those who he knew would oppose him, but there was a significant number McConnell needed to persuade, including one senator in particular, Mitt Romney.

For his part, McConnell was already on record saying he would fill a vacancy should it arise. His counsel to his members was that if they did not favor going forward with a nomination so close to the presidential election, they should initially say nothing. "Don't take a position you might regret," he said. He encouraged them to get through the August recess to give themselves time, should something happen to Ginsburg. He wanted to freeze them in place.

There was another fundamental issue: Who should the nominee be if a vacancy arose? McConnell instructed his chief of staff, Sharon Soderstrom, to call the White House counsel, Pat Cipollone, to say that McConnell wanted to be involved in making whatever list of candidates Trump would consider. She said Cipollone agreed.

McConnell wanted his home state favorite, appeals court judge Amul Thapar, to be on the list, though he realized he would almost certainly not be the choice. The candidate McConnell really wanted was the federal appeals court judge whom he often referred to as "the professor from Indiana," Amy Coney Barrett, who had taught law at Notre Dame. "I don't really care who else is on there," McConnell told the White House. He used his influence to advocate for Barrett to Trump directly and to Cipollone and White House Chief of Staff Mark Meadows. He went so far as to essentially demand that if Trump decided on someone else, he at least wanted the opportunity to talk him out of it. For the other Supreme Court nominees, Gorsuch and Kavanaugh, McConnell was the mastermind of creating the opportunity. For Barrett, he was also forcefully involved in pushing a specific nominee.

So well before there was an actual opening to contemplate, McConnell had a fully formed plan in place, unseemly as it might have been. "You don't out-prepare Mitch McConnell," a top staff member said.

On September 18, Ginsburg died, just six weeks before the election. A member of McConnell's staff had a source at the court who tipped him off an hour before the news became public, and he quickly relayed the information to McConnell, whose first reaction was "Oh, my God," followed by "We've got to fill that seat." He wanted the statement out quickly.

Now McConnell had a race against the calendar, and also against the coronavirus, which could slow down the process if any of those involved became infected. Trump, for once, showed restraint and made kind remarks about Ginsburg, not mentioning replacing her. McConnell's team thought that was the right move: let Trump appear presidential and leave the rest to McConnell. Restrictions were still in place in Washington, except apparently at the White House. Trump announced that he was nominating Barrett on September 26, then introduced her at an event at the White House the next night, which turned into a super-spreader event and underscored how the virus could derail McConnell's plan.

Even with the speed of the statement, McConnell's team knew that one of the principal arguments against going forward was that the nomination was moving far too fast, at odds with Senate precedent. So they started doing research, reaching back into the 1800s to look at how quickly justices had been confirmed. In the earlier days of the country, it was sometimes a matter of a few days, but that smaller number when put into an average made it look like Barrett was on a reasonable timetable, at least according to their definition of prec- edent. There also had been quick confirmations, including Ginsburg, Sandra Day O'Connor, and John Paul Stevens, three examples that were quickly distributed to the press.

In reality, the Supreme Court confirmation process often takes several months. McConnell was trying to push Barrett's through in a matter of weeks and still honor the convention of having her meet with senators. The Judiciary Committee had to figure out how to meet its attendance rules if members were down with the virus. Then there was the matter of actually voting on the Senate floor in an environ- ment that could be medically dangerous, particularly for the many el- derly members of the Senate, including McConnell. He thought the White House had been lax and careless about COVID protocols, and even skipped the event when Trump introduced Barrett at the White House for fear of contracting the virus. The fact that McConnell skipped it showed how seriously he took the virus. He was on the bal- lot for reelection in Kentucky, where Trump's popularity far exceeded his own, and bathing in the light of Trump and Barrett would no doubt have helped him.

McConnell was insistent on moving forward, telling staff mem- bers "I don't care" if a senator has tested positive for the virus, "figure out a safe way to have all my members able to vote." The situation seemed so dire that McConnell said if it takes "space suits" to be able to vote safely, then get space suits. McConnell instructed his staff to call Meadows to ask for the right protective gear. They had conver- sations with the nation's best-known infectious disease specialist,

Dr. Anthony Fauci, about whether NASA might have the right protective wear. They even created what in effect would have been a mov-
able plexiglass tunnel so a senator could have "two feet on the floor"
to make a vote official in the eyes of the Parliamentarian, something
one staff member referred to as "just enough thin ice to stand on."

They also tried to keep all these extraordinary contingency plans
quiet, knowing that if they became public, it could easily thwart a
vote. "Mitch McConnell has trained us to leave it all on the tracks,
and if you go down, you go down in a blaze of glory," one staff member
said. The tunnel was never used.

The White House team at the time had little experience in han-
dling a Supreme Court nomination. Mark Meadows tried to assert
himself but McConnell convinced him that he had larger issues, like
Trump's reelection, and he should leave the court to McConnell.

McConnell had internal work to do as well. He knew he was unlikely to persuade Susan Collins. She disagreed with his decision on
Garland and said there was a clear inconsistency with his decision to
move ahead with Barrett. "It caused me to vote against Amy Coney
Barrett, not based on the merits, but I thought we've established this
precedent and this one really too close to the election," Collins said.

McConnell's real audience was Senators Lisa Murkowski and Mitt
Romney, whose votes were needed to prevent a situation where Vice
President Mike Pence would have to break a tie, a move that would
have seriously undercut the credibility of the Senate.

Romney and McConnell began to exchange emails. Romney initially said he did not see how the Senate could go forward given what
McConnell had done in 2016. He was not certain, but told McConnell
he would not "play Hamlet" much longer. McConnell asked Romney,
a former management consultant driven by numbers, to take one more
look at data, and his staff sent additional documents to Romney's. The
next morning, he and Romney talked, and Romney had been convinced.

Trump talked to McConnell about possibly holding the vote until after the election, to help generate support among the president's conservative base. McConnell was less concerned about Trump and more about his own legacy, which he thought would be cemented by Barrett's confirmation.

Barrett ended up being confirmed 52–48, the same vote as Clarence Thomas.

Reflecting on the process near the end of the year, McConnell said: "Of course, she was a spectacular nominee, and there was really no real argument against her, other than that McConnell was a hypocrite because he filled this vacancy during a presidential election year when he didn't fill the other one. Of course, the answer I consistently gave to that was it depends on who controls the Senate. I said that in 2016. I said it again in 2018. The stars were aligned in 2018. There was a Republican president, a Republican Senate, and enough time to fill the vacancy, and we did."

Barrett's elevation to the nation's highest court fundamentally shifted its ideological balance to the right, giving the conservatives on the court a 6–3 supermajority that they would use to overturn precedents—some of them a half-century old—on cultural flashpoint issues like abortion and affirmative action. McConnell was willing to take all the criticism for how he used his power to change the court, and the country.

On September 12, 2021, Barrett traveled to Louisville at McConnell's invitation to be a featured speaker at the McConnell Center. The event had to be moved off campus to a downtown hotel because of security concerns. In her remarks, Barrett criticized the media for coverage that she said made the court look like it acted with political motivations.

————

Justice Samuel Alito walked stiff-legged to the door of his spacious office on the second floor of the Supreme Court building to greet me. The decor reflected a mix of his passions: several baseball bats and other souvenirs, a street sign with his name on it, and shelves filled with books. He has an oversize desk, spacious seating, and area rugs. It's as though everything is set at perfect right angles.

Alito is one who admires what McConnell has accomplished in populating the Supreme Court and the rest of the federal judiciary with like-minded conservatives. Other public officials, he said, including presidents, made their choices because they might enhance their election prospects. He cited President Eisenhower's selection of Justice William Brennan, a Catholic from New Jersey, in part as an effort to win the Catholic vote.

"The difference between Merrick Garland and Neil Gorsuch is night and day," Alito said. "Senator McConnell has taken a long view. He has an idea about how a judge should perform the role, how should the judge interpret the Constitution. Should the judge follow the text of the Constitution? The original public understanding of the constitution? Is it appropriate for the judge to make provisions of the Constitution mean what a lot of people would like them to mean? To interpret the Constitution to get public approval, immediate public approval? He's been against all that and he's helped shape this court and the federal judicial system to reflect his view of what judges should do, which is critically important.

"What does it mean for American life?" Alito continued. "I hope we are moving back to the traditional role of a judge. We're supposed to be judges. We're supposed to be interpreting the statutes, not imposing our own policy views on the country. That's what I think we should be doing and that is absolutely what all of President Trump's appointments to this court have said, and I have now seen in operation."

Alito acknowledged that critics of the court think that's precisely what they have done, that they have imposed their views on the country. "But we're not doing that," Alito said.

McConnell, he said, has had a very positive effect because he's done an enormous amount to move the federal courts back to the role that they should be playing. "He's a good litigator in the public square."

His role in shaping the justices who sit alongside Alito and pass judgment on the most fundamental questions on American life has been so profound that Alito now calls it "The McConnell Court."

———

When he was a senior at Saint Xavier High School in Kentucky, Justin Walker, a gifted student, was working on an analysis of historic Republican election victories in 1994. It was sophisticated research, certainly beyond most of his age. He had shared it with his grandfather Norton Cohen, a business owner in Louisville, who was impressed by the writing and thought it could benefit from an authoritative source. So he asked McConnell if he would do an interview with his grandson, whose parents named him for Justin Hayward, the guitarist in the rock group the Moody Blues. Cohen had been a longtime McConnell supporter and modest contributor to his campaigns, beginning in his race for county judge, when Cohen stepped forward at a fundraiser and said he would double the amount that was being solicited. It was the kind of gesture McConnell would not forget.

McConnell obliged, and a nervous Walker put on a suit and went to meet the senator early in 2000, shortly after John McCain had won the New Hampshire primary. After Walker sent him his final paper, McConnell thought it read like a "Master's thesis." He had convinced Walker that Newt Gingrich and his "Contract with America" were not decisive in delivering Republican victories that led them to take control of the House for the first time since the Eisenhower era. McConnell said the real reason for the victory was that President Bill Clinton had overreached in his first two years, on both health care and economic policy, and 1994 represented a dramatic course correction from voters. McConnell asked Walker to send him the paper, and stay in touch, which Walker took as merely a courtesy. It was not long, though, before he got a letter from McConnell praising his work.

Walker had grown up in a Democratic household, and another grandfather was a multimillionaire and Democratic power broker who had served as Kentucky's transportation secretary. Walker did not inherit that political fealty. At age thirteen, Justin had written a letter to the editor of the *Courier-Journal* defending the Christian Coalition. McConnell's eye for talent was again on display, and what he liked most was that he had identified a young, smart conservative who largely shared his worldview.

Walker went off to Duke, then Harvard Law School, and McConnell loosely followed his path. In the summer of 2002, while an undergraduate, Walker was an intern in McConnell's office. After law school, Walker was selected for prestigious clerkships, first by then–appeals court Judge Brett Kavanaugh, followed by Supreme Court Justice Anthony Kennedy. Walker taught at the University of Louisville Brandeis School of Law for a while and hoped to one day serve as a federal judge. In June 2018, he and McConnell had lunch at one of the senator's favorite eateries in Louisville, Cunningham's Restaurant, where most of the fare is fried and beer can be served by the five-bottle bucket.

McConnell told him he was considering putting Walker's name forth to fill Kavanaugh's prospective vacancy after his elevation to the Supreme Court. No promises were made, and to Walker, it felt more like a conversation than a job interview.

In July, Trump nominated Kavanaugh to fill the Supreme Court vacancy created by Justice Kennedy's retirement. Kavanaugh was a man Walker knew well and admired deeply. Kavanaugh's confirmation was controversial for a number of reasons, among them his participation in political matters during the Bush administration. He was also defending himself against an allegation of sexual assault that arose shortly before his confirmation hearing.

Walker made more than 115 appearances on television and radio, gave speeches and wrote articles in support of Kavanaugh, praising his intellect and vouching for his integrity. Walker was an effective advocate. He was on Fox, CNN, and MSNBC, part of a public relations campaign to counter Kavanaugh's critics and get him confirmed. Trump had seen some of them. Walker continued to espouse his conservative views, criticizing the special counsel investigation of Trump's firing

of FBI director James Comey. In one speech, he said, "In Brett Kavanaugh's America, we will not surrender while you wage war on our
work, or our cause, or our hope, or our dream."

By September, McConnell told Walker he could expect to hear
from the White House to be interviewed for the position to replace
Kavanaugh on the appeals court. Walker went to Washington to meet
Justice Department and White House officials, including Don Mc-
Gahn, Trump's White House counsel. About ten people were in the
room and this session felt very much like a job interview. Walker did
not feel much pressure because he thought he had nothing to lose. He
was young and ambitious, and if he was not selected this time, there
would probably be other opportunities. After the interview, a friend
told him it was unclear what would happen, which Walker took to
mean he would not get the job. He was right about that.

In March 2019, Walker was teaching his legal writing class at the
University of Louisville when his phone buzzed with a call from Mc-
Connell. Walker stepped out of class and McConnell told him he would
recommend that the White House nominate him for a federal district
court judgeship, a rung below the appeals court. Walker was extremely
grateful. McConnell was all business during the call. The White House
approved McConnell's recommendation, and Walker was confirmed
on a party line vote. At age thirty-seven, with no trial experience as a
lawyer, which resulted in a rare negative rating from the American Bar
Association, Walker was now on the bench.

McConnell wasn't finished being Walker's champion. Later in
2019, McConnell called Walker and said he thought they should make
a run at getting Walker into a new opening on the DC Court of Appeals, often a springboard to the Supreme Court. Walker's rise was meteoric, but he also had the right person pushing his ascent. Walker did
not think McConnell could pull it off and persuade Trump to nominate him. McConnell told him he would write a letter to Trump and
thought he could at least get Walker an interview.

He was able to do that on January 8, 2020, when Walker found himself with McConnell in the Oval Office talking to Trump. McConnell had counseled Walker to let Trump do most of the talking, and they had an iPad loaded with Walker's media appearances supporting Kavanaugh, thinking Trump would be far more interested in that than any legal opinions Walker had written.

McConnell was right. Trump dominated the conversation, saying he was disappointed in Chief Justice John Roberts, and he questioned Kavanaugh's firmness. McConnell offered some back and forth, Walker said very little. McConnell said at one point Trump looked at him and asked, "Mitch, is this important to you?"

"Yes sir, it is," McConnell replied.

Trump made some more small talk, then looked at Walker and said, "You're going to be very happy." As McConnell and Walker started to leave the office, Trump said, "The guy looks like Cary Grant."

There were others vying for the coveted position, and other Republican senators pushing them. McConnell had to decide whether to spend his political capital with Trump on Walker getting the position. What was the point of having leverage if he wasn't going to use it? McConnell wondered. And use it he did. He told Walker, "I don't mind a good fight."

On April 2, Walker received the call from the White House that he would be nominated. McConnell was not finished. One of the powers of the Senate majority leader is to set the agenda on the Senate floor, including when confirmation votes would happen. In May 2020, much of Washington had shut down because of the COVID pandemic. And Democrats were in no rush to have votes on Trump-nominated judicial appointments.

McConnell pushed Walker to the front of the line. Only Walker and the senators would be in the hearing. Asked to drive instead of fly because of COVID issues, Walker hit the road for the ten-hour drive from Louisville to Washington in his Subaru Outback.

A short time later, the Senate again confirmed Walker, this time to one of the most important courts in the country.

Now Walker has a spacious wood-paneled office not far from the Capitol. The office has a sleek, modern look. The walls are lined with photos of family and friends. There is a white stand-up desk. Walker spends much of his time reading in a nearby lounge chair. An oval table seats four for conferences. The trappings underscore the rarefied perch.

One wall behind his desk has a single photo of a smiling Walker and a jovial McConnell, commemorating Walker's nomination to the federal district court in Kentucky. McConnell signed it with the words: "Justin, this is what you were born to do. I know you will excel. Mitch McConnell, MAJORITY LEADER USS."

McConnell was thinking about Walker's future. "He's got Supreme Court written all over him someday."

During Trump's presidency, McConnell used his power as Senate majority leader to set the schedule and make confirming judges like Walker a priority. In those four years, the Senate confirmed fifty-four judges to appeals courts, which are among the nation's most influential. Those courts hear thousands of cases a year, impacting the lives of millions on some of the most contentious issues in American life, among them abortion, immigration, gun laws, and environmental protection. Many cases stop at the appellate level since the Supreme Court only hears about eighty cases a year. The reason Trump had so many opportunities to appoint appeals court judges was that McConnell had prevented Obama's nominees from going forward. Sean Hannity of Fox News asked McConnell why Obama had left so many judgeships unfilled. McConnell replied, "I'll tell you why. I was in charge of what we did in the last two years of the Obama administration."

McConnell had presaged this outcome in 2013 when Reid broke norms by eliminating the filibuster for federal judges. "You'll regret this," McConnell said, "and you may regret this a lot sooner than you think."

The Congressional Research Service found that during the last two years of Obama's presidency, only 28.6 percent of judicial nominees

were confirmed, and added that was the lowest percentage of confirmations from 1977 to 2022. After Trump came into office, thirty of
his appeals court nominees were quickly confirmed, "the largest number of appeals court nominees confirmed in the first two years of any
presidency since" the Congressional Research Service began tracking
those numbers. Indeed, Trump in his one term seated almost as many
appeals court judges as Obama did in two terms, the Pew Research
Center found.

By the time Trump left office, McConnell had engineered the confirmation of 228 federal judges, not including the three seated on the
Supreme Court. Most of them were young, white, and male. The appointments are for a lifetime, and their imprint will last for genera-
tions.

McConnell gives Trump little credit. "Of course, President Trump
didn't know much of anything about any of this," he said, steering
praise to McGahn instead for the White House end of things. And Mc-
Connell had vowed to "leave no vacancy behind," filling the void.

Of his work on shaping the courts, he said, "I think the whole effort with regard to the courts is the single most consequential thing
I've been involved in in my time in public life, with the longest impact, and I think it's the hallmark of my period." He took particular
pride in the fact that some of his Democratic opponents had said, "Mc-
Connell's the best Majority Leader since LBJ."

"When the people on the other side say that, that's the highest
compliment," McConnell said.

TWENTY-THREE

JANUARY 6

Senator Mitch McConnell arrived in the U.S. Capitol at 8 a.m. on January 6, 2021, looking noticeably out of uniform. In place of his usual suit and tie, he was wearing blue jeans and an open collar shirt. He had come early to get his second COVID-19 vaccine.

After he and two of his aides received their shots, McConnell went home to dress for the day's main event, a ministerial ceremony of certifying the election of Joe Biden as president by the formal counting of the Electoral College vote, a proceeding overseen by the vice president and required by the Constitution. There had been rumors of potential disruptions, possibly from Iran, but far more likely from those attending a rally that President Donald Trump had scheduled for later that morning.

Within the Senate, McConnell was trying to forestall a challenge to the legitimacy of the vote by a new Republican senator, Josh Hawley of Missouri, and the chronically obstreperous Ted Cruz. But at that point, McConnell had no serious concerns. He thought Trump's rally was both destructive to the country and futile in its aim to somehow reverse the election. Hawley's and Cruz's moves, he thought, were more likely to be publicity stunts by two men with presidential ambitions than a serious impediment to the process.

The Capitol was mostly empty when he returned before noon, with much of the congressional staff working remotely because of the pandemic. His own staff had been pared down as well. He reviewed the speech he would give in the Senate a few hours later, remarks that he had meticulously prepared. He wanted each word to convey his precise sentiment about the folly and danger of Trump's baseless protest. He also was briefed on the procedural mechanics of Hawley's and Cruz's objections. One of his main goals was to have as few Republicans as possible join them.

McConnell had believed since Election Day that Biden was the winner, an outcome ratified by the Electoral College vote in December. The Senate majority leader saw "reputational damage" to Republicans as the only possible outcome of Trump's "fantasy" and those colleagues who continued to nurture it. "We had two grandstanders in the Senate, Josh Hawley from Missouri and Ted Cruz from Texas, competing with each other over who could take the lead on this totally irresponsible effort to set aside the results of the Electoral College."

The Electoral College met on December 14, 2020, in all fifty states to cast votes for president and vice president. Representative Liz Cheney, a member of the House Republican leadership, had been concerned about Trump for some time. She issued a statement that day affirming the Electoral College vote and texted McConnell to ask him if he was going to do the same. McConnell said he would address the issue from the floor of the Senate the next day, December 15, in a move designed to capture more attention than a simple written statement.

The bulk of McConnell's remarks consisted of praise for Trump's accomplishments, then turned to the meat of what he wanted to say. "As of this morning, our country officially has a president-elect and a vice president–elect. . . . The Electoral College has spoken." As usual, he spoke with a clear political calculation. He knew there were two runoff Senate elections coming up in Georgia on January 5, and he did not want Trump supporters to sit them out. He also wanted independent-leaning voters to know he was not buying into Trump's desperate efforts to cling to power.

In the days that followed, Cheney became increasingly concerned about the security of the Capitol on January 6. On December 22, she spoke to McConnell around 8 p.m., and she said he, too, expressed concern about potential violence. They weren't alone. Mitt Romney texted McConnell on January 2.

He had heard from Maine senator Angus King that Pentagon officials were tracking alarming social media posts about January 6. "There are calls to burn down your home, Mitch," Romney wrote. He questioned whether there were adequate security protections. Romney said McConnell did not respond.

Cheney's worries grew more dire. She called McConnell on January 4, trusting a man she had known for decades over House Minority Leader Kevin McCarthy. She told him about a Trump plan to have Vice President Mike Pence consider an alternate slate of electors. McConnell agreed the Senate needed to have a plan to counter that effort.

The next day, the Senate runoff elections in Georgia would determine the balance of power in the chamber. McConnell had tried without success to persuade Trump to stop talking about nonexistent election fraud, suspecting it would likely depress Republican turnout. Trump ignored the advice, and his false insistence that the election had been "stolen" probably ended up costing the Republicans both of those seats, and with them, the Senate majority and McConnell's position as majority leader. So when McConnell was preparing for the ceremonial counting of the vote on the sixth, he had additional reasons to loathe Donald Trump.

Sharon Soderstrom, McConnell's chief of staff, and Stefanie Muchow, his deputy chief of staff for operations, went over the schedule for the January 6 certification with him hour by hour in his stately suite of offices, the entryway of which once served as the Library of Congress. The office walls are wood paneling, the furniture is heavy, and some of it is more than one hundred years old. The portraits he chose reflect his politics; in one room, Theodore Roosevelt, Ronald Reagan, and both presidents Bush. In another, former Republican Senate majority leaders. In his main office hung a framed picture of John Marshall Harlan, the justice from Kentucky who dissented in *Plessy v. Ferguson*, the Supreme Court decision that sanctioned slavery; his idol, Senator John Sherman Cooper; and Democrat Alben Barkley, another Senate leader from Kentucky who also served as vice president. The location, thirty some paces to the Senate chamber, radiated power and authority.

McConnell, always meticulous in his preparation, did not leave details to chance. The women were more concerned than their boss at that moment because all the Trump supporters converging in Washington was not a "recipe for a normal peaceful day," as Soderstrom put it.

McConnell's aides had met on January 3 with the sergeants at arms in Congress, the officials responsible for security of the Capitol. They asked if they needed to be concerned about the safety of staff during the certification vote and where they should park on January 6. They asked if the security perimeter at the Capitol should be extended. The sergeants at arms assured them they had seen "no flashing warning signs" and things were "under control."

On January 5, as Muchow was leaving the Capitol, several Trump supporters walked slowly around her car, peering into the windows. It gave her a strange, disquieting feeling, and she called Soderstrom and asked her to stay on the line until she was on the road home. Still, neither thought the incident portended serious violence.

The next morning, McConnell went home to change after his vaccination, returning in a dark suit, crisp shirt, and tie. He ate an early lunch at 11:30 a.m. and readied himself to go to the floor of the Senate at 1 p.m. for opening remarks as the Senate went into session. He told members of his conference that this vote to certify the election would be his most important in thirty-six years in the Senate, and that this was no conventional political matter. "This is about whether we're going to break this democracy," McConnell said. "I said to them, 'You are never going to cast a more important vote than this.'" He was prepared to walk in with Pence in a ceremonial procession in which Senate staff carried mahogany boxes "bound with leather straps that held the electoral votes."

Pence, with his Secret Service detail and members of his family, including his brother, Greg, a congressman from Indiana, also arrived to preside over the ritual designed to showcase the United States of America's commitment to the peaceful transfer of power.

Soon McConnell rose to speak from his Senate desk, a spot from which he had delivered hundreds of speeches, often rote partisan attack messages of the day. But these words, he said, he chose more carefully than any before.

"We'll either hasten down a poisonous path where only the winners of elections actually accept the results, or show we can still muster the patriotic courage that our forebears showed not only in victory, but in defeat," McConnell said. "The framers built the Senate to stop short-term passions from boiling over and melting the foundations of our republic. So I believe protecting our constitutional order requires respecting the limits of our own power.

"It would be unfair and wrong to disenfranchise American voters and overrule the courts and the states on this extraordinarily thin basis. And I will not pretend such a vote would be a harmless protest gesture while relying on others to do the right thing. I will vote to respect the people's decision and defend our system of government as we know it."

He had watched only a few moments of Trump's rally an hour or so before, during which the president exhorted his supporters to march to the Capitol with a vow that he would not honor, namely to be right there marching with them. McConnell's aides were more attuned and went so far as to ask Senate parliamentary officials whether the president could be barred from the chamber. They were told he could not be, but that he could be required to stand in the rear.

At about 1:15 p.m., Soderstrom looked at her phone and saw a call from the deputy sergeant at arms, who said that the West Lawn of the Capitol had been breached. That alone was not unusual, and McConnell stayed focused on his speech. "We knew it was a high moment," she said. "But we internalized it and moved on."

McConnell had long ago made up his mind on Trump. He and Trump had not spoken since Trump yelled at him when McConnell acknowledged the obvious, that Joe Biden had been fairly elected after the Electoral College vote. McConnell blamed Trump for costing Republicans the Senate majority, at first by refusing to sign a major aid package that McConnell had put together with administration officials, and then by becoming a negative force in the special elections in Georgia. When Trump made a belated campaign appearance in Georgia, he only made things worse, and, unsurprisingly, talked mainly about himself. Both parties had spent hundreds of millions of dollars, the stakes were that high, and the Republicans lost. "The principal reason for it was the president himself, who, in his own perverse way, probably really didn't want them to win, because he didn't do anything to unify the party or make it look more likely they would be victorious," McConnell said.

McConnell's hope that only Hawley and Cruz would object to the certification was also dashed. Cheney had texted him at 4:10 on January 6, asking if senators could be persuaded to withdraw their objections to the count. McConnell responded, "That's exactly the plan." But that plan did not work. Senator James Lankford, an Oklahoma Republican and former minister with a deep voice and a manner that rarely showed sharp partisan edges, was among five others joining the objection, no doubt trying to forestall primary challenges from the Trumpist right. But in the middle of his remarks, Lankford stopped abruptly. "I looked to my left and there was a guy with an assault rifle standing beside me," McConnell said. His security detail had rushed onto the Senate floor.

Soderstrom and Muchow joined McConnell. Then Robert Karem,

McConnell's national security adviser, came into the Senate cloak-room. He said there was an emergency meeting with the sergeants at arms in another part of the Capitol. Soderstrom and Muchow rushed over. Through the windows they could see the enormous size of the crowd outside. They took a back stairway, then saw police who had been hit with chemical sprays by the rioters dousing their eyes. They saw other rioters on the platform that had been built for Biden's inau-guration, including a man standing on top with a Trump flag. We are in big trouble, Soderstrom thought.

The sergeant at arms briefed them, then asked if he had permis-sion to call in the National Guard. "I said, 'Call in the Guard. Call in the Guard!'" Soderstrom recalled. She checked to make sure the doors to the Senate, and to McConnell's office, were locked.

Then they heard the sound of rioters bashing in windows. They knew they had to get back to McConnell in the Senate. They raced to a small elevator when a security officer yelled, "Get upstairs, get up-stairs." "Then I hear this kind of horrid yell," Soderstrom said. "They were breaching that door right at the sergeant of arms."

Back in the Senate, the two women told staffers in McConnell's of-fice to lock their doors. Soderstrom and Muchow got inside the cham-ber just before the doors were locked and rushed to find McConnell. Secret Service agents came and pulled Pence out. A Capitol Police of-ficer took the Senate gavel and told the members, "We are in a state of emergency. Please stand away from the Senate doors."

The consequences of years of Trump's serial lying and self absorp-tion, which McConnell at times had effectively sanctioned, were fi-nally crashing down on the Senate. Men and women who thought of themselves as members of "the world's most exclusive club" were now being led out of the chamber by armed guards.

"I wasn't thinking we were going to get killed or something," Mc-Connell recalled. "But I was absolutely appalled when I think that for the first time since the War of 1812 you had uninvited military person-nel in the Capitol. There were military personnel here during the Civil

War, but they were there to protect the place. Then you are getting whisked away. It's like a movie in a sense, but it was very real, and one would think that the leaders in a normal situation would have wanted to engage directly with the president to convey what was going on. But I guess the collective view was that would not help."

Instead, as he had so often, Trump adopted the role of a bystander, watching on television as his supporters laid siege to the building that is one of the most enduring symbols of American democracy, leaving his vice president and members of Congress who had largely bent to his will for four years to find their own way out of the chaos.

"You know with the Capitol under direct attack, with its top leaders under direct threat, the president of the United States isn't doing anything," McConnell said.

"I was appalled by not only the lack of respect for our core system, which is to honor the results of the Electoral College, but then to encourage people to come here," he said of Trump's beckoning. "And I don't know whether you can make a conclusive argument that he's directly responsible for them storming the Capitol, but I think it's not in dispute that those folks would not have been here in the first place if he had not asked them to come and to disrupt the actual acceptance of the outcome of the election."

As the rioters headed to the Senate chamber, Capitol Police crafted a safe escape route for the senators, many of whom were elderly, and some of whom had trouble walking, including McConnell. They hurried down a back stairwell into one of the Capitol's tunnels and headed for a secure location in the adjacent Hart Senate Office Building. Senators were asked to not divulge their locations. By that time, rioters were in the Senate, looking over the documents left on desks and pretending to serve as presiding officers. Mere minutes had elapsed between the chamber's evacuation and the breach of the Senate doors.

After doing a headcount of the senators, McConnell and other Senate leaders were then quickly ushered into waiting vans to head to another secure location at Fort McNair, about three miles away.

Soderstrom and Muchow were jammed into the back of a van when a security officer with a submachine gun joined them. Another security guard sat next to McConnell. A small motorcade soon headed the wrong way down C Street for a frantic exit, and within minutes, they were deposited at the military installation.

Republican officials were in one room, Democrats, including House Speaker Nancy Pelosi, were in another. McConnell instructed his aides to deliver a message to the Democrats. "We're going back in session at eight o'clock, in prime time, and reassure the American people that the siege has failed and that their government is going to function."

"That's good Mitch feels that way," Senator Dick Durbin of Illinois, the number two Democrat in the Senate, said to McConnell's aide. Soderstrom checked with David Popp, the communications director, who was barricaded in McConnell's office with other staffers. He replied by text message. "Can't talk," he said. "They are right outside our door."

"I glanced up and on this little television there was commotion on the floor," Popp recalled of the moments before the breach. "I opened the door and chief counsel said, 'Get the fuck back in the office.' He runs into our office. We barricade it with an armchair and a heavy couch. It was second nature to us because everyone goes through security training. . . . You barricade yourself. Then it was like, all right, now what?"

They unplugged landlines, silenced cell phones, and started using hand signals.

At one point there was a bang on the door, accompanied by men shouting, "Capitol Police!" But McConnell's staff was in contact with security officers who told them it was the insurrectionists, not the police, so they did not open the door.

Popp was among more than a dozen members of McConnell's staff who were trapped. They had pushed desks and a refrigerator to block the door and could hear the protesters screaming and the beating on the other side. Some texted their parents, others their spouses. Among them was a twenty-five-year-old woman on her first job after graduating from the University of Kentucky. Most of them were terrified.

One member of McConnell's staff dialed Bill Barr, who had been Trump's attorney general until he, too, refused to parrot Trump's fraud claims. McConnell had talked to Barr about Trump's irrational claims of a stolen election and asked him to deliver the reality to the president. Barr was unsuccessful and resigned. On January 6, he was sitting at his home in his study watching the violence unfold when his phone rang. In hushed tones, McConnell's staffer told him they could not get through to the federal law enforcement officials and asked for help. Barr agreed and made contact with officials at the Justice Department and FBI and asked them to go help free McConnell's staff.

At Fort McNair, McConnell was also working the phones. He talked to Pence four times and asked him to push for more police at the Capitol. Mark Meadows, Trump's White House chief of staff, called McConnell twice. McConnell told him, "Get it back under control, ASAP." McConnell delivered the same message to the acting defense secretary, the chairman of the Joint Chiefs of Staff, and the acting attorney general. "My recollection of that was there was a lot of caution about getting military personnel up there," McConnell said.

McConnell was furious but did not show emotion. One person he did not talk to: Trump. The two had not spoken since December 15, after McConnell announced that he would accept the results of the Electoral College. "His post-election behavior was increasingly detached from reality," McConnell told me, "and it seems to me he made up this alternate universe of how things happened." Trump, he said, had engaged in a "fantasy" that he had somehow won, and had been listening to "clowns" who served as his private lawyers, like Rudy Giuliani, Sidney Powell, and Lin Wood.

After the riot was finally contained, the congressional leaders headed back to the Hart Building, with a long walk ahead to the Capitol. McConnell looked at Soderstrom and asked, "Can I ride the subway? My leg is tired." It was a rare concession. He was in pain, a persistent residual effect of polio.

He huddled with his staff in the Hart Building. Speechwriters had been frantically crafting a draft of remarks for him to say when the Senate reconvened.

They returned to the Capitol to find the marble floors coated in tear gas. McConnell could not enter the front door of his office; the furniture still blocked it. The staff who pushed it in front of the door had been fueled by adrenaline. Afterward, they found they could not summon the strength to move it back.

Back in the Senate, McConnell still had to navigate the process of certifying the election. His hope was that the riot would deter senators like Hawley from going through with their fruitless objections. His wish was half granted. Cruz had come around, and he even tried to talk Hawley out of it.

"Believe it or not, Ted Cruz, who sort of made a career out of being wherever I'm not on issues, called me up last night to get my advice on how to deal with it all," McConnell said later. "That was almost an out of body experience." He reminded Cruz of an old saying by Lyndon Johnson for situations like this: "Hunker down like a jackrabbit in a windstorm and wait for it to blow over."

But Hawley would not relent. The vote, even with its predetermined outcome, would go forward.

One by one, the Senate voted down Hawley's objections, and Biden's election received its final, formal sanction. McConnell spoke from the Senate floor in unambiguous terms. The Senate, he said, would do its duty, "by the book" and not be deterred by the violent mob's attempt at intimidation. McConnell said he felt "an overwhelming sense of relief that our basic underpinning had been threatened but we had come through it. The idea was to break it, and it didn't break." The Senate affirmed Biden's election, but the American catechism of a peaceful transfer of power had been sullied.

Reflecting on that day, he said, "It's hard to imagine this happening in this country, such a stable democracy we've had for so long, to have not only the system attacked but the building itself attacked," he said later. "It was very disturbing." He was sickened by the damage done to the Capitol itself. "They broke windows," McConnell said. "They were narcissistic, just like Donald Trump, sitting in the vice president's chair taking pictures of themselves." He called it a "shocking occurrence and further evidence of Donald Trump's complete unfitness for office."

After his Senate remarks, McConnell walked the short distance from the Senate floor to his office to address his staff. He told them how brave they were and how much he appreciated them at this tragic, historic moment. McConnell, a man often characterized as almost soulless and possessing no emotion, started to sob softly, along with many on his staff.

"You are my staff, and you are my responsibility," McConnell told them. "You are my family, and I hate the fact that you had to go through this." He was shaken. As one aide put it, "For a man who doesn't wear his heart on his sleeve ever, you could see it there."

After composing himself, he turned to Soderstrom and said, "We have to figure out how this doesn't happen on Inauguration Day." Recalling that conversation, Soderstrom said: "The reputation of the Republican Party was looking bad in the moment. He was looking ahead."

It was approaching 2 a.m. on January 7 when Popp, carrying McConnell's shoulder bag, walked his boss, then seventy-eight, out of the building, through a door near the law library, with his SUV and security detail waiting for him. "He was physically just beat," Popp said. "He was shaking and nervous. He just kept thanking his detail." He was stooped, and his blue shirt was wrinkled, his left leg was aching. He gingerly stepped into the SUV driven by his security detail and headed home, just a couple of blocks away.

When he arrived, Chao was there to meet him. She had made the decision to resign from Trump's cabinet, blaming him for inciting the

riot, but her husband was so tired that she waited until the next morning to tell him. She said he slept until at least nine.

One of the invaders had used a flag pole to bash the window of
McConnell's office. The fortified window shattered internally, but did
not break. Months after the attack, it had still not been repaired, but
served as a daily reminder of the violence and how narrowly he and his
staff had escaped.

Calls quickly came to investigate the cause of the riot. Polls
showed that a majority of Americans supported an inquiry. The House
passed bipartisan legislation to create a commission modeled after the
one that examined the September 11, 2001, terrorist attacks, a body
that would have an equal number of Democrats and Republicans.
Thirty-five Republicans in the House joined Democrats to support the
measure.

Then the legislation went to the Senate, and McConnell pivoted.
Congressional committees, he said, were capable of conducting the
investigation, and the commission was largely a Democratic ploy to
"relitigate" that day and Trump's role in it. So on May 28, fewer than
six months after his own life had been jeopardized during the riot, he
blocked perhaps the nation's best chance at getting a full accounting
of what happened.

McConnell was well aware that he would be criticized, and, as at
so many other times during his tenure in the Senate, he did not let that
deter him from his larger goal. He had said a few weeks earlier that his
focus was to thwart Biden's agenda "100 percent." McConnell's best
shot at making good on that threat would be to regain just one seat in
the Senate, retaking the majority for Republicans and restoring him to
the position he had coveted.

Abandoning the commission could readily be seen as a craven
concession to his party's right flank, but McConnell has a decidedly
unsentimental view of tactics and strategies that do not lead to victories and majorities. McConnell blocked the inquiry by deploying the
filibuster and requesting the support of some Republicans, like Senator

Rob Portman of Ohio, as a rare "personal favor" to him. McConnell was worried Trump would encourage more fringe candidates, the kind who had doomed Republican hopes in previous elections. If Trump were not a unifying force in the midterm elections, when the president's party typically suffers heavy losses, then Democrats were in a position to defy history and keep power in Congress. So McConnell ignored the insults and chose what he saw as the surest path back to the majority.

There was still another potential remedy to deal with Trump: a second impeachment.

A week after the insurrection at the Capitol, McConnell noted in an oral history interview that the House was likely to impeach Trump very soon. "Someone listening to this years from now might wonder what's the point; he's leaving office anyway on January 20," he said. "But apparently you can impeach somebody after they leave office, and if that happens, there's a second vote in the Senate, which only has to pass by a simple majority, that prevents that person from seeking office again. So he could not only be impeached, but also eliminated from the possibility of a comeback for this office. So it is significant." While not showing his hand, he was signaling an inclination.

McConnell said it would be difficult to vote in the Senate until after Trump had left office. He talked to Biden about the challenge of getting his cabinet in place if the Senate was caught up in an impeachment trial. The Senate also had time off scheduled. Still, it was at least theoretically possible to have them back in session to deal with impeachment.

"I'm not at all conflicted about whether what the president did is an impeachable offense. I think it is. Urging an insurrection and people attacking the Capitol as a direct result . . . is about as close to an impeachable offense as you can imagine, with the possible exception of maybe being an agent for another country." Even so, he was also persuaded by other legal opinions that the Senate could not impeach someone after they had left office. He was not yet certain how he would vote.

Democrats pushed to impeach Trump, and the House moved quickly to do so. Up until the day of the Senate vote, it was unclear which way McConnell would go. "I wish he would have voted to convict Donald Trump, and I think he was convinced that he was entirely guilty," Senator Mitt Romney told me, while adding that McConnell thought convicting someone no longer in office was a bad precedent. Romney said he viewed McConnell's political calculation being "that Donald Trump was no longer going to be on the political stage. . . . That Donald Trump was finished politically."

George Will, the owlish, intellectual columnist who has been artfully arguing the conservative cause for half a century, has long been a friend and admirer of McConnell. They share a love of history, baseball, and the refracted glories of the eras of Ronald Reagan and Margaret Thatcher. On February 21, 2021, Will sent an advance version of his column for the *Washington Post* to a select group of conservatives, a little-known practice of his. One avid reader and recipient was Senator Bill Cassidy, Republican of Louisiana, who read this column with particular interest. Will made the case that Republicans like Cassidy, McConnell, and others should override the will of the "Lout Caucus," naming Lindsey Graham, Ted Cruz, Josh Hawley, Marco Rubio, Ron Johnson, among them. "As this is written on Friday [Saturday], only the size of the see-no-evil Republican majority is in doubt." Will harbored no doubt. He abhorred Trump. He had hoped others would vote to convict, including his friend. The last sentence of his early release was bracketed by parentheses: "(Perhaps, however, a revival began on Saturday when the uncommon Mitch McConnell voted 'Aye.')" Will either had been given an indication of McConnell's vote or had made a surmise based on their long association.

Cassidy thought that meant McConnell had clued Will in on his vote, so he called Will on Saturday. Will told him the column was premature, and he was filing a substitute.

Will talked to McConnell less than an hour before the actual vote. His new column highlighted McConnell's decision to vote not guilty, saying the time was "not quite ripe" for the party to try to rid itself of Trump. "No one's detestation of Trump matches the breadth and depth of McConnell," Will wrote. Nevertheless, "McConnell knows . . . that the heavy lifting involved in shrinking Trump's influence must be done by politics." McConnell's eyes were on the 2022 midterm elections.

Will told me he did not recall writing the earlier version.

On the morning of the Senate vote on impeachment, there was still some thought among both Republicans and Democrats that McConnell might vote to convict Trump. The opening of his remarks certainly suggested as much.

"January 6th was a disgrace," McConnell began. "American citizens attacked their own government. They use terrorism to try to stop a specific piece of domestic business they did not like. Fellow Americans beat and bloodied our own police. They stormed the center floor. They tried to hunt down the Speaker of the House. They built a gallows and chatted about murdering the vice president.

"They did this because they'd been fed wild falsehoods by the most powerful man on Earth because he was angry. He lost an election. Former President Trump's actions preceded the riot in a disgraceful dereliction of duty. . . . There's no question, none, that President Trump is practically and morally responsible for provoking the events of the day. No question about it."

Cheney knew McConnell had, at one point, been firm in his view that Trump should be impeached, but she had grown concerned about his "resolve." When Senator Rand Paul of Kentucky made a motion that the trial was unconstitutional because Trump was no longer president, McConnell voted for it, a sign to Cheney that his position was shifting.

But rather than serving as a moment of moral clarity for McConnell, it was merely a prelude to the kind of contradiction that has marked his time as one of the nation's most powerful leaders; he held a strong belief that Trump had committed an impeachable offense but made a political decision that overrode it.

McConnell thought that Cheney, who lost her primary election because she was willing to so clearly confront Trump, had made a mistake. "Where I differed with Liz is I didn't see how blowing yourself up and taking yourself off the playing field was helpful to getting the party back to where she and I probably both think it ought to be," McConnell told me, later adding, "I think her sort of self-sacrificial act maybe sells books but it isn't going to have an impact changing the party. That's where we differed."

Cheney thought that it was McConnell who had abdicated his duty and responsibility to do more to rid the GOP of Trump. In a post on X, she said, "Mitch McConnell knows Trump provoked the violent attack on our Capitol. . . . he knows Trump refused for hours to tell his mob to leave. . . . he knows Trump committed a 'disgraceful dereliction of duty.' . . . Trump and his collaborators will be defeated and history will remember the shame of people like @LeaderMcConnell who enabled them."

McConnell, in part to preserve his position with the Republican members and mindful of what had happened to senators like Mitt Romney, who had become an outcast to many in his party for simply standing firm on principle, decided against voting to convict. He argued the Constitution did not provide for such a penalty once a president had left office. There is ample debate about that point, but for McConnell, as usual, the political rationale was sufficient. "I can understand the rationale—not agree with it—understand the rationale to say, 'If I don't do this, I may be gone,'" Biden told me.

His goal was to preserve a Senate majority. He wanted the energy of Trump's voters in Senate races, without the baggage of Trump. He gambled on his belief that Trump would fade from the political stage in the wake of the insurrection. Instead, Trump reemerged every bit as strong among core supporters. It was likely the worst political miscalculation of McConnell's career.

TWENTY-FOUR

THE FALL

The evening of March 8, 2023, McConnell walked into Washington's Waldorf Astoria hotel on a familiar mission: seeking money for the Senate Leadership Fund, a political Super PAC aligned with him that had become one of the most powerful forces in American elections.

The Super PAC was holding a reception in the hotel's grand ballroom, and McConnell's first order of business was to mingle with potential donors. That was followed by a private dinner with Stephen Ubl, president and chief executive officer of the Pharmaceutical Research and Manufacturers of America (PhRMA), a political power center of its own, and one that has helped provide millions of dollars to SLF.

He left the larger reception and the two met in a private dining room in the hotel, which until 2022 had been the Trump International Hotel in Washington. McConnell excused himself to use the private restroom located nearby. Typically, whenever McConnell entered a public restroom, his security detail accompanied him, both to check for potential attackers and to assist McConnell if need be. The detail members had clear operational guidance to "stay on the shoulder" just in case McConnell were to stumble, which had happened several times over the years due to weakness in his left leg, which some on his staff referred to as his "polio leg."

Shortly after McConnell had entered the restroom, another dinner companion, David Gershanik, who worked as a fundraiser for the Super PAC, heard a loud thud. The eighty-one-year-old senator, the longest serving party leader in history, had taken a violent, concussive fall. He hit so hard that he lost both of his hearing aids and was bleeding at the back of his head. For a time, he also lost consciousness. His security detail rushed in and quickly called for help.

McConnell was put in an ambulance and whisked to nearby George Washington University Hospital. A member of the detail put out a call to Stefanie Muchow, one of McConnell's top aides, and she raced to the hospital to meet him. So did Terry Carmack, who ran McConnell's Kentucky Senate office and had by far the longest tenure with him. Gershanik came as well. Soderstrom, his top leadership aide, arrived a few hours later. Steven Law, who had been close to McConnell for more than thirty years, and was with him at the event, immediately called Josh Holmes, another former chief of staff and one of the senator's most trusted political advisers. Law said they had a very serious problem.

Holmes called Kyle Simmons, yet another former chief of staff, at his home in North Carolina, and Simmons, who saw McConnell as a father figure, was in Washington before eight the next morning. Muchow spent the night at the hospital. She did not want to leave McConnell's side. He had given her a chance to work in politics when she was still a student at Northern Kentucky University. She had made it to Washington and over nearly two decades became one of the most important people on the staff. Carmack stayed at the hospital, too.

McConnell's staff provided only the sparest detail to the public. "This evening, Leader McConnell tripped at a local hotel during a private dinner. He has been admitted to the hospital where he is receiving treatment," Popp said in a statement.

Those close to McConnell suspected immediately what had caused the fall: weakness in the left leg. He had two other serious falls since 2017 that were made public—and had others that were not. For more than thirty years, McConnell had been careful to avoid showing any physical weakness. He would refuse help and grit through discomfort, always wanting to appear normal.

But that night at the hospital, there were troubling signs. Though McConnell had regained consciousness and was communicative, he was not particularly verbal. A neurological team went into action to check for signs of bleeding or swelling in the brain and other possible trauma. They quickly concluded that at minimum the Senator had suffered a serious concussion. His aides conferred. They were somewhat relieved that McConnell did not seem to be in mortal danger, but they had no idea what the morning would bring. A traumatic brain injury can have profound consequences. They were terrified.

The morning after the fall, things were looking a little better. McConnell spoke with doctors and his aides. Holmes had also joined them. Elaine Chao, who had been out of town the previous night, had arrived as well. McConnell wanted to engage with people who sent him messages and well-wishes.

In the hospital, McConnell underwent both occupational and physical therapy. Doctors quickly diagnosed that he had suffered a cracked rib in addition to the concussion. They instructed him to not use his phone, read, or do anything remotely mentally or physically taxing, as that could worsen what in effect was a badly bruised brain. His prognosis remained uncertain.

McConnell, in a rare turn of events, was not in control, depriving him of a source of strength and conviction that had long been a central part of his identity. This was a man whose staff either called him "Leader" or "Boss." He was the man who had the answers. He was known to refuse any assistance or to be aided even in the privacy of his home, though he did have a chair lift installed in his townhouse in Washington so he did not have to deal with the stairs. He balked at the idea of an extended hospital stay followed by physical therapy, but eventually yielded. He spent two weeks under evaluation in the hospital, after which his doctors said that his neurological examination showed he was healing and likely to make a full cognitive recovery.

Naturally, questions were immediately raised by officials and the media about whether McConnell could continue to serve in such a demanding job. But doctors said he needed to stay at the hospital's in-patient rehabilitation facility to undergo intensive physical therapy. Initially, he took a few steps at a time in the hospital rooms with staff close by his side. Doctors continued to insist that he not look at a screen of any kind. Muchow read him messages, and McConnell would dictate his responses, even as he tried to reach for his phone.

The physical therapy was challenging, with lots of pulling and working on his left leg to try to make it as functional as possible. Sometimes, it lasted three hours a day. Nearly eighty years after he had been diagnosed with polio, McConnell was undergoing extensive physical therapy triggered by the same affliction that had robbed him of two years of his childhood.

He was far from ready to be in public again, even after the hospitalization and in-patient physical therapy. By an accident of the calendar, he got more time out of the limelight when the end of the therapy coincided with a congressional recess. He continued to work through physical issues at home in Washington, but he kept an unusually low profile, with almost no public statements. Carmack was with him for almost thirty straight days to help.

On Monday, April 17, six weeks after the fall, McConnell returned to work. He decided to make remarks on the Senate floor rather than do a news conference. As he stood by his desk Muchow was next to him, speaking into his ear. Her face was unusually serious, as though she was giving him very precise instructions, mindful of his still fragile state. He decided to jump right into an issue of the day—whether Congress would raise the debt limit—criticizing President Biden for not being more proactive in the fight that was emerging on Capitol Hill. But he also tried to defuse the moment with humor. "I'm very happy to be back," McConnell said. "Suffice it to say, this isn't the first time that being hard-headed has served me very well." Mainly, it was a moment to try to get through without incident, a chance to prove that there was a road to recovery.

The debt ceiling fight offered an immediate opportunity to offer further proof. McConnell had been a critical player in a similar struggle during the Obama administration, and he had personally negotiated with Biden to reach a deal, which many in hindsight thought was a better bargain for McConnell.

But this time, McConnell made a strategic decision to largely sit out the fight. He said it was up to Biden to strike a deal with House Speaker Kevin McCarthy because the hard-right conservatives in the House would be unlikely to accept any agreement brokered between Biden and the Senate. Initially, there were members and staff in the meetings. McConnell gave Biden private advice to make it a one-on-one negotiation: "Shrink the room," he told the president. McConnell knew that sometimes it's important to know when not to use power.

His confident public prediction that the nation would not have a first-ever default proved correct. But it was also a rare time during his leadership that he was not central to negotiations.

After the concussion, McConnell became noticeably more frail, and his speech sometimes seemed garbled and labored. But he insisted that while his physical recovery was slow, he had never lost any cognitive ability, and he continued to maintain an aggressive schedule. What was actually happening is that McConnell was recovering in public, and despite his insistence to the contrary, the public could easily see that he was not yet fully well. That led to more stories about his health and speculation that his condition was worse than he was letting on.

Among the many rituals in Congress are the weekly lunches that each party holds. These internal discussions are largely private as McConnell takes a measure of the room and also gives him a sense of where he wants to take the conference. By custom, after the lunches

McConnell and his leadership team would walk to a cluster of reporters to take questions. McConnell would give members of his team an
assigned speaking part, deliver remarks, and take questions.

The lunch on July 26 was no different. McConnell stepped up to
the microphones and said there was progress to report on a major defense bill. "We've had good bipartisan cooperation and a string of —"

Then he froze. For about twenty-five seconds, his eyes fixed in a
motionless stare, his mouth sometimes seeming to quiver. Legend-
ary Capitol Hill journalist Scottie Applewhite of the Associated Press
captured a photograph of the moment in which McConnell seems to
be gripped by fear. Gamely, Senator John Barrasso of Wyoming, part of
the leadership team and a physician, leaned in and asked McConnell,
"Do you want to say anything else to [the] press?" McConnell made a
guttural sound, then walked haltingly away.

It was a highly disconcerting moment. Some who were there said
they wondered if McConnell might die at that moment. His aides were
again stricken, unsure what to do about what they had just witnessed.
Video of the moment rocketed around social media, and just as quickly
there were questions about whether this might be the end of McConnell's long run.

After reaching his office, McConnell sat down briefly as his aides
tried to look after him. Some in his circle were angry that there might
be a more profound medical problem that somehow wasn't picked
up when he suffered the concussion. But McConnell wasn't thinking
about his health.

McConnell was thinking about the moment that had just been
captured and how damaging it might be to him politically. So instead
of seeking an evaluation by a doctor, he insisted on going back out
to face the media and even take more questions than usual. He did
exactly that, but the damage was done. His reappearance did little to
defuse the alarm set off by those seconds when he was unable to speak.

That night, he was scheduled to give remarks at a gathering of Major
League Baseball owners in Washington. He kept the appointment, and

the speech went off as planned. Then, as he was riding back to the Senate for votes that evening, he called me on the phone. "I'm fine," he said.

He didn't see a doctor until the next day, and then he underwent a battery of tests. One of McConnell's advisers said it included a brain scan, but McConnell would not confirm that.

There is a denialism, and a sense of indispensability, that comes with power. McConnell ignored the advice of some friends who suggested he take it easy during the coming August recess. They said he owed it to himself and to his staff not to put himself in a difficult position. Instead he did seventeen events all over Kentucky. There was no time for leisure. "It's his life," one McConnell confidant said. And as with so many polio survivors, appearing "normal" was paramount.

In an interview with me on August 24, in the McConnell Center at the University of Louisville, the senator tried to downplay the episode. The freeze, he said, was simply a matter of being dehydrated. "I was thinking what a huge mistake I had made because I was pretty sure it was dehydration, and how much of a problem it was going to be afterwards, and how do I demonstrate that I'm fine. Of all the dumb mistakes I've made in my life, that's a really bad one. . . . My problem was dealing with the public relations associated with it." During the interview, he showed no cognitive problems, though his hearing impairment was evident. A bottle of water on the desk next to him remained unopened.

Just two days earlier, he and Chao had flown to Utah to accept an award from the Hatch Foundation. He returned to Louisville at 2 a.m. On the morning of August 24, he had addressed the Farm Bureau Ham Breakfast, a staple of Kentucky politics, and later boasted that he had received a standing ovation before and after he spoke while the incumbent governor, Andy Beshear, had not.

The previous week, Jonathan Martin of *Politico* had published a lengthy article that looked both at McConnell's efforts to maintain a traditional Republican position on Ukraine in the face of resistance from Trump and the far-right members of Congress, and at how the July freeze episode had set off talk about who might succeed him. Reflecting on that piece, McConnell told me, "At my age I am not offended by people wanting to come next. They tried taking me on directly [in the leadership election in 2022], and it didn't work out too well for them."

When I asked if he was considering not running for the position again, he said he had not yet decided. "Look, I've been in this a long time. A lot longer than anybody else in history. I am near the end zone, but I haven't made a final decision yet."

But in saying that, it seemed to signal that he had in fact made one. Having seen other colleagues decline in the sunset of their careers, he did not want to be one who was not at—or at least near—the top of his game.

Less than a week after that interview, with Congress still in recess, McConnell continued to travel his state, arriving in Covington for the Northern Kentucky Chamber of Commerce luncheon, a mainstay on his political calendar. He gave remarks and took questions from the audience. Then, as was his custom, he held a press conference afterward.

A reporter asked an obvious question: Would he seek another term? McConnell offered a slight chuckle, then looked to his right, and again, his face froze, for about the same amount of time as the first episode. His hands continued to grip the lectern. His state director, Robbin Taylor, calmly told reporters that they "needed a minute," and she called for a member of McConnell's security detail. They talked briefly.

McConnell knew he had the same public relations problem as before, but it was compounded by the repetition. Citing dehydration would no longer persuade anyone, if indeed it ever had. He acknowledged to me that he was still dealing with the lingering effects of the concussion. He said such freezes had not happened in private. "I didn't black out," he said. "I felt lightheaded."

He knew that kind of simple explanation would not be accepted, either by his colleagues or the media. So he consulted the Senate physician, Dr. Brian Monahan, who the next day issued a brief statement on his letterhead.

"After evaluating yesterday's incident, I have informed Leader McConnell that he is medically clear to continue with his schedule as planned," the letter said.

The letter did little to defuse the situation. If anything, it seemed to invite more questions. The incidents came as other politicians, notably Biden, were dealing with the questions of age and capacity to serve. So Monahan issued another letter, this time with more detail. He wrote, "there is no evidence that you have a seizure disorder or that you experienced a stroke, TIA [transient ischemic attack, brief symptoms similar to those of a stroke but less serious], or movement disorder such as Parkinson's disease." He noted that neurologists had conducted a "comprehensive neurological assessment." He recommended no changes in McConnell's treatment for recovery from his concussion.

Publicly, the letter lowered the temperature of the discussion of McConnell's fate. At the policy lunch that week, an overwhelming majority of his members accepted his explanation, at least for the time. His persistent critics, Senator Rand Paul, a fellow Kentuckian, and Josh Hawley of Missouri, were outliers in not offering support, with Paul, a retired ophthalmologist, going so far as to challenge the credibility of Monahan's assessment.

"I've always been a little unsteady well before the concussion," McConnell told me. "These two events happened, and unfortunately they happened right in front of reporters and left people with the impression there was something seriously wrong, which is difficult to confront. So I ended up realizing that I needed to confront it in a more open way than I typically talk about these things."

McConnell was confident leaving the lunch, as he again walked to face reporters in the Capitol. He said he thought the letter was a full explanation and he had little to add. McConnell had spent years carefully cultivating certain reporters who cover Congress, and as a result he had a far less hostile relationship with the media than many of his colleagues. So he was knocked back when several reporters aggressively asked if he was providing the full story.

"I would describe it as the toughest experience I've had since polio," McConnell said several days later. "I got nailed by three different reporters with a question about what did not happen. Not what did happen."

McConnell also complained that he was being lumped in with Senator Dianne Feinstein of California, who, at ninety, had suffered serious cognitive issues before she died in September 2023, and Senator John Fetterman of Pennsylvania, who suffered a stroke and depression, in addition to questions about Biden's capacity due to age. "I am thrown into the mix with them?" McConnell asked, incredulous. "Really? There's no evidence of that."

"It was an extremely unpleasant experience," McConnell said. "I've been in a lot of tough spots but never in a spot like this where I couldn't convince people I was okay. Part of my anger was I felt like I was addressing the issue and getting no credit for it."

His sensitivity to criticism was again in play. So was his underlying fear of failure.

TWENTY-FIVE

POWER

Over the course of his career, a narrative about McConnell has congealed: that he only wanted power for the sake of power, that it was both his means and his end. Early in his life that was certainly true, when he sought low-stakes elective office in high school and college, and even in his first races for county judge executive and the U.S. Senate. But as he accrued power in the Senate, he wielded it mightily and at times ruthlessly, and in the process brought far-reaching and at times deleterious change not only to the institution he cherished but also to the country. If measured by how America is now different, particularly in its federal judiciary—most prominently and impactfully the Supreme Court—it is clear that McConnell used his power to achieve a political outcome, even if it is one for which at least half of the country has vilified him. There is a ledger of his use of power and it contains entries on both sides.

"Do I want to have power? Absolutely," McConnell said when I asked about this. "What's the point of being here if you are not trying to have an outcome? I gather my critics view this as some kind of craven desire to be dominant. First of all, I don't have that kind of power, and second, it's not the point of power." The point, he said, is to make policy in the mold of your political view, and in the Senate, that happens when your party is in the majority. Senator Bill Cassidy neatly summed up this approach, and it's potential downside, saying, "I am not sure that he was ever quite as interested in being bold on policy if he thought being bold on policy would cost him a seat."

He took a great risk when he decided unilaterally that he would block Merrick Garland from getting so much as a Senate Judiciary Committee hearing. That decision went against every Senate convention, but he did it anyway, largely because he could. In a country that was becoming increasingly polarized, it served to further divide people along ideological lines and accelerate a belief among Americans that the courts had become instruments of politics.

McConnell's self-interest was clearly at work as well. By putting the court at the center of the presidential campaign in 2016, he was inoculating himself against more attacks from the increasingly hostile populist wing of his party and ingratiating himself with the business interests who knew what a tilt in the court could mean for them.

It was also an unusually risky move by a politician known for cold and objective calculation. Had Hillary Clinton won the presidency, she almost certainly would have nominated a justice more liberal than Garland. And since Ruth Bader Ginsburg had made it known that she wanted Clinton to name her replacement, the court would have ended up with a liberal majority. It turned out to be a risk that paid off far more consequentially than McConnell could have envisioned, ultimately both for his most important donors but also for the GOP's social conservatives. At the same time, it hurt his party politically. He acknowledged that the court's decision on abortion in particular, overturning the half-century precedent of *Roe v. Wade*, angered and energized Democrats, leading to victories in elections and ballot referendums across the country, even in red states like Kansas and Ohio.

No Democrat defended what McConnell did, but several tried to explain it. Biden was vice president when McConnell asserted that power, and he was highly critical of McConnell's action. Still, the two men were of the same generation, with a common experience of long Senate tenure, and a relationship that passed for a professional friend-ship, at least by McConnell's distant standards. Each had seen his share of blunt-force power moves.

On a December afternoon in 2023, I sat with President Biden in the light-filled Oval Office and asked him about his relationship with McConnell and the senator's use of power. There was a bust of Robert F. Kennedy on a side table and a framed photo of Benjamin Franklin on one wall. Biden was dressed in a royal blue suit with a subtle chalk pin-stripe, crisp white shirt, and blue tie. He and McConnell had fought, to be sure, he said, but they had also worked together, and he had seen the full spectrum of McConnell's use of his authority.

On Garland, "I thought he—it was going beyond what was within his power to do," Biden said. "That's as close as I've ever seen him come to going beyond the institutional limits by not even allowing a debate to be brought up. We had a strong disagreement. We never were attacking each other, and we never were personalizing it."

Biden balances that decision of McConnell's against others, like working with him to make sure that the country did not default on its debt, or by passing bipartisan legislation that has become central to Biden's legacy like the infrastructure bill and the CHIPS Act to strengthen domestic semiconductor manufacturing, design, and re-search. When negotiating, he said, McConnell has never misled him, nor has he ever miscounted how much support he had for his posi-tion. They have talked about specific issues, and the threat to democ-racy posed by matters like Trump falsely claiming the 2020 election was stolen. "He understands that democracy has to be constantly de-fended," Biden said. "Now, I'm not saying he's going out pouring his heart out to me. He's not. But he's always been straight with me." It is overly simplistic, the president said, to say that McConnell wanted power only for power's sake. And on most policy matters, McConnell is an acid-tongued Biden critic.

Biden also acknowledged McConnell's grace in attending Beau Biden's funeral. When the Senate passed the Cures Act to spur biomedical research, Biden as vice president was presiding over the chamber. McConnell asked that the legislation be renamed in Beau Biden's honor. At that point, McConnell had nothing to gain from doing so, and Biden considered it an act of personal decency.

Other Democrats view McConnell the same way, damning him for his action on Garland, acknowledging their fundamental disagreements with him, but allowing that they admire his strategic skills. "I think that there are ways that he has shamelessly used the Senate that were inimical to the public interest," said Senator Angus King of Maine, an independent who votes with Democrats and started his public career as a Senate aide when Mansfield was majority leader. The Garland nomination "offended my sense of fundamental process and fairness and it just wasn't right."

More often, he said, McConnell understands that most Senate work is rooted in comity and cooperation. He recalled having McConnell to his home for a dinner of ribs and how much McConnell said he enjoyed meeting Senator Tammy Baldwin of Wisconsin that evening for the first time. "The idea that we don't like each other is not true," King said. "I think Mitch to some extent gets a bad rap because his obstructions are notorious and obvious and his cooperation is not usually visible."

Rahm Emanuel, U.S. Ambassador to Japan, Obama's first chief of staff, and an astute power player himself, said that McConnell "has used his power to pursue his policy objectives. He doesn't just harbor his power. He has deployed it. From a technical standpoint, I give him a high grade."

McConnell's power was built on fealty to two constituencies, the voters of Kentucky and Republicans in the Senate, and not always in that order. Rob Portman, a former senator from Ohio who was close to McConnell, said McConnell "always had his finger on the pulse of his constituents," and by that he meant his Republican Senate colleagues. "Sometimes he takes a risk as he did with Garland and gets out front but he only does so for the most part knowing that the parade will follow him." McConnell has skillfully cultivated the "great middle" of the conference, members who are quite conservative "but not crazy, and he knows that's where he is. So I think that's a key to his success." Portman disagreed with McConnell and thought Garland was entitled to confirmation hearings, though he voted to confirm Gorsuch.

In Kentucky, he used his power to build the state's Republican Party and its majorities in the legislature, which he then prodded to change the state law so that a Democratic governor could not name the replacement of a senator of the opposite party, the political equivalent of an insurance policy that if McConnell left office early, another Republican would follow him.

He also has delivered what his staff estimates at $60 billion in federal aid, everything from major environmental cleanup to erosion projects and infrastructure. In addition, he took care of his alma mater at the University of Louisville, and the University of Kentucky, securing more than $840 million over his career to help improve higher education in the state.

Even with all he has done for the state and the Republican Party, there are signs his power is ebbing there as well. A far-right faction known as the Liberty Republicans has grown into a political force. One of the things that binds them, the *Lexington Herald-Leader* recently reported, is "disdain" for McConnell. Twenty county Republican parties in Kentucky have "censured McConnell for being" too "moderate."

McConnell likes to say that he does not hold grudges. That's not quite true. He believed that Joe Fishman, one of his fraternity brothers, cost him an election in college that he lost by one vote. When Fishman, who became a doctor, was in line for a federal contract and McConnell was working in Washington, he made sure Fishman didn't get it. "Who do you want?" McConnell recalled being asked. "Anybody but that son of a bitch" was his reply. He never mentioned it to Fishman. He just enjoyed the silent revenge.

In the Senate, he cultivated personal relationships by finding out

as much as he could about his colleagues' needs, political and personal, while never revealing much about himself. He focused on their
success, and they rewarded him with their loyalty. They also appreciated his directness and his honesty. As Portman put it, McConnell was
"very low key, but no bullshit." When McConnell pressures another
senator for a vote, he never does it publicly. One day McConnell approached Senator James Lankford on the Senate floor and said, "You
think I am close to the vest, huh?" "Tell me I'm wrong," Lankford
replied. McConnell responded, "Everything I ever say to anyone anywhere goes public, so yes, I'm very guarded."

He believed in Congress as a coequal branch of government and
was not cowed by presidents of either party. "He was not there to be
a patsy for anybody, even the president of the United States," Portman said. "He and George Bush got along fine, but it was not a warm
relationship." His relationship with Obama was frosty from the start,
so he dealt with Biden. Obama, David Axelrod said, chose to view Mc-
Connell as a "fact of life," so "he didn't go on tirades about him." Axelrod and others knew that a Senate majority was McConnell's priority
and "he wasn't going to sacrifice that for some larger policy points."

He even managed to vex Trump. Josh Holmes recalled meetings
in the Oval Office when Trump would try to flatter McConnell, cajole
him, do almost anything to get a human reaction, and McConnell did
not so much as arch an eyebrow. He was a sphinx.

It should be noted, however, that not everyone was taken in by
McConnell's steely poker face. Senator Cassidy, who is also a physician, said that McConnell is not nearly as emotionless as many seem
to believe, noting that "sometimes . . . there's a stressful situation and
his face will flush. And it's interesting because he'll still be dispassion-
ate, but you can tell that literally his blood is up and that there's a boiling passion there. It's just that he has become so well trained that . . .
you got to be really looking for it."

Maintaining leadership of the party in Congress does not require
overwhelming popularity. It merely requires a majority of one's own

party. When McConnell was first elected the Republican leader, that was easily achieved. Over time, the party he knew began to look more like the party of Trump, but never with enough hard-right Republican senators to dislodge him. "He's tried to keep the party together, the mainstream party, and he holds the outliers close to create critical mass," said former Alabama senator Richard Shelby. "He's good at that. He probably has no peer."

For the most part, he avoided payback, and he is fond of saying that the most important vote is the next vote. He treated the moderates in his party, like Lisa Murkowski and Susan Collins, with respect and did not punish them when they broke from the party line. That also earned their loyalty and fortified his numbers against the Trumpist wing. His fixation on winning the Senate majority took on many dimensions, including trying to recruit Democrats like Kyrsten Sinema of Arizona, who has since become an independent, and Joe Manchin of West Virginia, who did not seek reelection in 2024. "He certainly has sway over his conference members, but it's not a fear-based sway, it is persuasive," Sinema said. "I think he's very calculating. He's very careful in what he does, very thoughtful and largely effective."

The day after the horrific school shooting in Uvalde, Texas, on May 24, 2022, Sinema walked up to McConnell and said, "'I want to do something on Uvalde. Who should I work with?' And he said to me, Thom Tillis and John Cornyn. He wouldn't have told me who to work with in the conference if he didn't want something to happen." It was difficult to get anything passed, but Sinema said McConnell gave her strategic counsel that worked. "While he is a partisan, he is willing to allow a bipartisan process to work when he thinks that is something good for the country or good for his state." Part of what McConnell did was help to frame the legislation not as gun control, but rather as a bill focused on gun safety and mental health.

He has also used his power subtly, for causes that matter to him personally. To generate more federal money for polio research, he worked closely with Bill Gates, the founder of Microsoft, who is now one of the world's leading philanthropists. Gates has frequently come to talk to McConnell about getting money in the foreign aid budget for polio research.

"In one of those visits people told me in advance that the senator had polio but you may not want to be the one to bring that up," Gates told me. "The first few meetings he didn't bring it up. As he and I got to know each other, the next several times, he brought it up, including how tough it was for him and how it really shaped him and that he didn't talk about it a lot but he was very hopeful we would succeed. Mitch normally is a very serious person. But when he talked about polio, he was way more vulnerable and personal than his normal business demeanor."

Most times, McConnell is all business, especially when it involves politics, and one of his prime skills is the ability to scout talent. McConnell's party has gone through a political transformation not seen since southern Democrats left for the GOP during the 1960s, with the base of the party and a growing number of Senators marching to Trump's blaring siren of grievance and defiance. The GOP has become whiter, more rural, less educated, and angrier. McConnell had limited room to maneuver in his party, according to Donald Ritchie, the Senate's historian emeritus. "The leader really does have to be a reflection of the party. FDR said it is a very dangerous thing to be a leader and look over your shoulder and realize nobody was following."

This volatility in the party that started in 2010 led it to nominate a series of unelectable candidates, judged too extreme by voters, costing Republicans and McConnell a chance to be in the majority. After 2010, McConnell started to scout more aggressively for talent to find quality candidates and elevate them before a more bombastic, unelectable alternative emerged.

In 2012, he saw an ideal candidate in Tom Cotton, a Harvard-educated veteran who had served in combat in Iraq and Afghanistan. Tall, lean, and decidedly conservative, Cotton had written derisively about the "sacred cows" of affirmative action in the editorial pages of the *Harvard Crimson*. He had little patience for liberals, and he was a strong communicator—precisely the kind of candidate McConnell wanted in the Senate. To have a long game, McConnell knew he also needed a short game.

The problem was that in 2012, Cotton was simply running for a House seat. He won his race easily. When he came to Washington for orientation and to get his committee assignments, he received a call from Arkansas Senator John Boozman. "Tom, Senator McConnell is try-ing to reach you," Cotton recalled Boozman saying. "He'd really like to meet with you. I think right now. He's sitting in his office waiting for you." So before he'd even been sworn in, Cotton went to McConnell's office, where McConnell started recruiting him to run for the Senate in 2014 against the incumbent Democrat, Mark Pryor. McConnell coun-seled him to not answer any reporter's question about running for the Senate so he would not have to look like he had changed his mind on the off chance his plans changed. "Or, to put it differently," Cotton said, di-vining what McConnell really meant, "I don't want you to say anything now that will set back my efforts to win the Senate majority."

They met regularly over the next year, often out of view, so as not to send a signal that Cotton was running for the Senate. McConnell's pursuit of Cotton followed a distinct political pattern of consistently thinking of the next election and how to build a majority. Even to his enemies, Cotton said, "I don't see how you cannot respect his skill and talent and accomplishment as a legislative leader." Cotton won his race easily in 2014 and has remained one of McConnell's allies in the Senate, and one of very few younger Republicans in his corner who is also a vocal supporter of Trump.

By the next cycle, 2016, McConnell's Super PAC was up and run-ning, and his candidate recruitment efforts accelerated as well. In the Senate, he could rely on the loyalty of members he had helped elect, then helped reelect. For McConnell, this was a virtuous circle. He had a vested interest in candidates from the start, grounded himself in their political needs, and fed them continuously. Within limits, McConnell has also told his members to criticize him if it helps them politically, a dispensation Cruz seemed to habitually abuse. McConnell is willing to take public hits for his colleagues if it gives them the cover they need. "The truth is he is sacrificial on behalf of the ultimate goal," Tim Scott said. "And the ultimate goal is winning." He built a quiet but sturdy loyalty structure that helped keep Republicans united and empowered—with the added benefit of keeping his party leadership position secure.

Similarly, Senator Cassidy pointed to McConnell's ability to disassociate himself from the personal attacks and to maintain an even keel as a defining characteristic responsible for his success and influence as a leader, which he used "always with an eye to electing the maximal number of Republicans."

The Senate, as Cotton quickly found out, was a much different place from the House. As Tim Scott put it, the House is like a football team: joint effort is required to make a play work; the Senate is more like a track team, where individualism is the order of the day. McConnell knows well the Senate ego, where 90 percent of his colleagues look in the mirror in the morning and see the next president, and he nurtures it accordingly.

His fellow Republicans' election burdens were his election burdens. If they needed a moment to shine, McConnell yielded the floor. McConnell is also consciously economical with what he says, recalling House Speaker Sam Rayburn's well-worn line: "No one has a finer command of language than the person who keeps his mouth shut." McConnell has adapted this advice for his colleagues by telling them, "Just because there's a microphone does not mean you have to speak."

"His unwavering focus on managing his members has come at the expense of seeing his name attached to many major policy achievements, or taking many policy risks," Todd Young said. "Self-preservation and perpetuation of our majority status is his first, second, and third priority. If you are not in power, he would argue, you can't make policy." Young added that McConnell's quiet manner belies his fiercely competitive nature.

Among Senate Republicans, McConnell often leads by listening. Before he became leader, he craved attention, wanted to be on television news programs, and did whatever else he could to stand out among colleagues. In turn, as leader, he proved his commitment by helping his members elevate their own profiles. When he chose Tim Scott to respond to the State of the Union address, Scott said it changed his life. McConnell, sitting in his office, cried after Scott had finished his speech. McConnell routinely took new, often younger senators on foreign trips to try to impress upon them the gravity of America's role in the world. Two such members were Katie Britt and Markwayne Mullin, both of whom later backed McConnell on urgent international matters like supporting Ukraine.

"He doesn't just tell you the good side, he tells you both sides," Scott said of McConnell's political advice. "And that's usually rare. When thinking about political decisions, he is probably the most objective person I know."

McConnell listened to the more moderate voices like Murkowski, Collins, Portman, Roy Blunt, and Lamar Alexander. Murkowski and Collins disagreed with McConnell on how he handled the Supreme Court nominees, the issue he considers the most important work of his career. He also considers them to be among his better friends in the Senate. "Mitch has always been very fair," Murkowski said, "just very decent with me when I break ranks. And it's not to suggest that he doesn't try to encourage me in subtle ways, and he is very subtle. We have a little joke. Every now and again he'll give a call and he'll say, 'Your spiritual adviser would like to have a few moments with you if you would agree.'"

McConnell is an astute reader of his colleagues' priorities. He knows when he can push Murkowski or Collins and when to retreat. "I think he realized with me very early on that political influence, or pressure, was going to get him nowhere with me," Murkowski said. "And then if it was really, really important, he would say, 'This would be important to me.' That's always the worst."

The Senate is rarely far from his mind. McConnell is effective because he is dogged and largely one-dimensional, obsessed with politics and an occasional dabble in watching sports. His is a hermetic existence, as he travels three blocks between his townhouse and the Capitol in a large SUV driven by his security detail. He does political events at night and on the weekends. When he travels to Kentucky, he does more politics.

"He thinks about power all the time, the accumulation of power, using his power to prevent crises, to manage crises, political crises," Young said. "He's usually a step or two ahead of others. His mind is very active. I think he's masterful in the accretion, preservation, and enhancement of power. McConnell has figured out how to centralize a lot of what occurs here and manage risk through the centralization of it, and that takes a lot of skill. And he does it in a really pleasant way."

The Trump era, though, was not one for pleasantries. It was one for animus and vengeance. Almost without exception, the more moderate members who left the Senate were replaced by those who were more harshly conservative, abrasive, and performative in their approach, and increasingly likely to paint McConnell as old and out of touch.

McConnell liked to keep most disputes among Republicans private, but in March 2022, Senator Rick Scott of Florida left him little choice but to go public. Scott, who was chairman of the National Republican Senatorial Committee, revealed an eleven-point agenda for Republican Senate candidates that included a proposal to require all Americans to pay at least some income tax, which would have amounted to a tax increase for a large swath of voters. The plan also called for sunsetting all legislation after five years. McConnell noted that could be seen as an attack on cherished programs like Medicare and Social Security.

Whatever the merits of offering an agenda for voters to consider, McConnell looked at the politics, and he thought Scott's platform was laughably bad. It was a midterm election, and McConnell thought Republicans needed to make it a referendum on an unpopular President Biden. So, soon after Rick Scott revealed his plan, McConnell took the highly unusual step of repudiating it during a news conference with Republican leaders. Scott had left the news conference just moments before he started speaking.

"Let me tell you what will not be a part of our agenda: We will not have as part of our agenda a bill that raises taxes on half the American people and sunsets Social Security and Medicare after five years," McConnell said. At that same news conference, McConnell also made clear that he planned to continue as Republican leader.

McConnell, who had known Scott since the 1990s when Scott was a rising executive at a health care company in Louisville, tried to make sure Scott's plan died a fast death, but Democrats were quick to ridicule it for the same reasons that McConnell laid out.

The dissonance was unusual for McConnell. Since he had established the Senate Leadership Fund, he had been able to work almost synchronously with the Senate campaign committee. Scott going off script with his plan was a clear challenge to McConnell's authority and his political judgment. It also signaled that a growing segment of the Senate Republicans wanted new leadership.

That was just one part of McConnell's problem. The other was that Trump was trying to weigh in on the selection of Senate candidates. McConnell and his team had been active in trying to recruit Republicans who could win general elections in competitive states. Their research was painstakingly thorough, but Trump operated more on whim than data. McConnell was worried that Trump would back Eric Greitens in Missouri and Herschel Walker in Georgia. And there were other Trump acolytes to contend with, like Blake Masters in Arizona and JD Vance in Ohio. Trump was free with his endorsement, but tight with his money, providing essentially no financial support to the candidates he anointed.

McConnell also knew that Trump's view of the world was reinforced almost nightly by the Fox News opinion shows, and he wanted to do something about it. Paul Ryan, the former speaker and friend of McConnell, served on the board of Fox Corp. In June 2022, he arranged a dinner at his suburban home with McConnell, Fox founder Rupert Murdoch, and Murdoch's son Lachlan. McConnell laid out the case against Trump, and he thought the Murdochs agreed. "I don't think Murdoch has been in love with Trump for a long time," McConnell said.

"Mitch got to air his feelings and reflect mine as well," Ryan said. "And they [the Murdochs] found it very valuable. They definitely understand Mitch's political acumen and respect it." There is little evidence, though, that the Fox opinion shows became any less slavish in their support for Trump.

Frustrated by the state of several campaigns in critical states, McConnell issued a warning to Republicans in August 2022. He said they had a problem with "candidate quality," and he was obviously referring to those who had Trump's strongest backing.

"I did mean it," McConnell told me. "I didn't say anybody, but that was the message. Basically the two guys, JD Vance and Blake Masters, got nominated in May, and didn't do squat for three months, nothing." He was referring to their anemic fundraising. That meant those candidates were going to have to rely on outside sources, like Super PACs, which had to pay a much higher advertising rate than a candidate's campaign account would. "I said it on purpose, and I thought it would probably kick up a bit of a storm, but the message needed to be sent."

What's more, Scott had spent millions of dollars raised for the Senate campaign committee on consultants, so the committee was cash-strapped going into the fall, with few prospects for refilling its coffers quickly. Scott, McConnell said, had conveyed an unrealistic view of the Republicans' chances that put donors and candidates "to sleep."

Thus, it fell to the Senate Leadership Fund to try to rescue flailing campaigns. McConnell sardonically noted that Trump was spending almost no money from his own Super PAC, which he was using to help pay for his mounting legal bills. "It'll be interesting to see if he's willing to part with his own money, to do anything beyond having a self-serving rally in their state."

McConnell-aligned operatives worked hard to doom the Trump-backed Greitens campaign in Missouri, and in Alabama, to make sure that "that idiot" Mo Brooks would lose the Republican primary to McConnell's candidate, Katie Britt. They succeeded on both fronts.

Part of the Republicans' problem going into the 2022 election was at least indirectly of McConnell's making. Democrats were enraged by the Supreme Court's overturning of *Roe v. Wade* on June 24, 2022, a decision that was set in motion when McConnell blocked Merrick Garland's confirmation and rammed Brett Kavanaugh's and Amy Coney Barrett's through. Barrett was the bookend to McConnell's unparalleled move to block Garland, justified by a contorted logic that a new justice could be confirmed at any point before an election if the president and the Senate majority were of the same party, a case of first impression in which McConnell presided as both judge and jury, likely cementing a conservative supermajority on the Supreme Court for years to come. "There is a lot of contradiction in the man," Ritchie told me. "He considers himself an institutionalist, but a lot of his actions and certainly on Merrick Garland were a great case of not being an institutionalist. It was something none of his predecessors would have dared to do."

McConnell conceded that the *Dobbs* decision had hurt his party politically. But he also thought that Republicans' fortunes dimmed because Trump inserted himself into the election, allowing Democrats to frame each Senate race as a choice essentially between Trump and Biden, rather than a referendum on Biden. He was also concerned about the revelations that Justice Clarence Thomas has accepted free trips from a wealthy Republican donor. "I do think Justice Thomas exercised pretty questionable judgment," McConnell said. "But then again, I'm not sure what the rules are."

McConnell told me several times that the people he dealt with to shape the Supreme Court from the Federalist Society cared little about social issues, and that the donors to the Senate Leadership Fund almost never mentioned abortion. The high court delivered precisely the outcome they wanted in June 2024, when they overturned the forty-year precedent of the *Chevron* case, which had held that experts in government could interpret statutes when Congress had left laws ambiguous. In ruling for the business interests, the court almost assured a weakened regulatory structure on everything from the quality of air and water to food and drug safety, a change that could be a financial windfall for corporate interests. It was precisely the outcome McConnell wanted, too. On criminal charges against Trump, the Supreme Court ruled that the former president had broad immunity for his official actions and in the process scaled back the federal government's case against Trump. The court made that ruling on the final day of its term, ensuring a delay in the trial. Another federal judge in Florida, Aileen Cannon, appointed by Trump and pushed through the Senate by McConnell, dismissed charges against Trump, citing the Supreme Court's immunity ruling.

Despite McConnell's influence within the Senate, Trump's sway with the Republican base far exceeded McConnell's. He was even navigating Trump at home in Kentucky. McConnell skipped the Kentucky Derby, an event he was never especially fond of, in 2022 because he knew Trump would be in attendance and holding a fundraiser. In Ohio, McConnell and Portman worked behind the scenes to try to ensure that Vance would not win the primary. They offered strategic counsel indirectly to other campaigns and outside groups on how to undermine him. In May 2022, Portman called McConnell to update him on the race and said Vance seemed to be surging. McConnell responded that the only way to defeat Vance would be to hit him with repeated negative attacks in the final weeks before voting. Vance had taken too many contradictory positions, McConnell thought, making him more vulnerable. It didn't work. Trump swooped in with an endorsement late in the race, and Vance won the primary.

At that point, McConnell, ever the rational actor, swallowed his opposition and backed Vance, essentially saving his campaign. The Senate Leadership Fund spent more than $32 million in Ohio to help Vance narrowly defeat his Democratic opponent, Tim Ryan. Trump went on to choose Vance as his running mate in 2024.

The Super PAC also worked to reelect McConnell critic Ron Johnson in Wisconsin, and another Trump-aligned candidate in North Carolina, Ted Budd. McConnell even tried mightily to help Herschel Walker—whose campaign was dogged by personal and financial scandal—who had won his nomination thanks to Trump's backing. Gaining a majority mattered more for retaining power than lockstep allegiance, even if it meant supporting problematic candidates.

Still, there were challenges to McConnell's authority. Trump had publicly questioned his leadership and even delivered racist attacks on McConnell's wife, Elaine Chao, calling her Coco Chow and suggesting her family's shipping business had untoward ties to China. A relationship that had been deeply split was now irretrievably fractured.

"I can't think of anybody I'd rather be criticized by than this sleazeball," McConnell told me. "So every time he takes a shot at me, I think it's good for my reputation." He could take Trump's wrath, but his wife, he said, was "not used to taking a punch" and was deeply disturbed by Trump's comments. In an interview, Chao declined to say whether she would support Trump in 2024.

Meanwhile, Scott was increasingly coming under fire from fellow Republicans, and he tried to rationalize his spending decisions. "I don't think Rick makes a very good victim," McConnell said. "I think he did a poor job of running the [Senate campaign] committee. His plan was used by the Democrats against our candidates as late as the last weekend [before the election]. He promoted the fiction that we were in the middle of a big sweep when there was no tangible evidence of it. And I think his campaign against me was some kind of ill-fated effort to turn the attention away from him and onto somebody else."

With respect to individual races, McConnell spent heavily to elect some candidates who said they would oppose him as their Senate leader. "He looks at these things extremely antiseptically," Holmes said. McConnell was furious with Scott. "He's angry about it because since he's been leader he's always had command and control of the conversation during a midterm and this changed that," Holmes said.

After the 2022 midterm elections, which left Democrats in control of the Senate, Republicans gathered in late November to select their leader for the coming term. As he had done twice before, Tom Cotton nominated McConnell. Rick Scott, unchastened by his poor performance leading the Senate campaign committee, decided to challenge his party's longest serving leader.

In the party meeting, some senators were openly critical of McConnell. Others were harsh about Scott, who Cotton said was "the most emotional" and felt unfairly attacked. Cotton reminded Scott and the others how McConnell had built the Senate Leadership Fund while others "washed their hands of grubby politics." Many of McConnell's critics, he noted, were beneficiaries of his funding. Others complained the party needed a younger, better communicator. Cotton argued that legislative bodies were different, and people with inside prowess were best suited to the role.

McConnell won another term, with Scott receiving only ten votes. McConnell relished the win like his childhood pummeling of Dicky Mc-Grew. His competitive fire could sometimes flare hotter when he was confronting Republicans who opposed him than when he was tangling with Democrats. He had secured another two years of power, but given the direction his party was moving and the strength of Trump's continued influence, the longer term trajectory for his leadership was not positive.

When I asked him how he felt about his party's populist, nationalistic drift, he responded dryly, "not good."

"I have a pretty high disapproval rating among Republicans just by occasionally being a critic [of Trump]. What I'm trying to do is preserve at least in part the Republican Party, the one I identified with early on." That meant a platform of strong national defense, international trade agreements, lower tax rates, and economic assistance abroad to maintain alliances. "Trump to some degree or another has called into question all of those things."

McConnell's longtime colleague and friend, Susan Collins, agreed with his assessment of the changes in the party, saying that the Trump faction in the Senate "is both larger and louder and far more aggressive." It used to be rare for a freshman senator to challenge the party leader. "Now there is a segment of the caucus that constantly challenges the leader," she said.

Senator Michael Bennet, Democrat of Colorado, worked with McConnell closely on legislation to provide aid to Ukraine. Elected in 2010, he has only seen a Senate with McConnell as Republican leader, and in that time he has seen the party "careen" away from him. "There's nothing left of that party," Bennet said of the GOP McConnell hopes to preserve. Bennet said he found McConnell to often be "a ruthless power politics player, very conscious of his own survival," but also one who at times stood on principle.

"If you measure it by someone's ability to direct the caucus, he'll go down as one of the best, not only in terms of longevity, but just in terms of batting average," Senator Tim Kaine said.

McConnell kept his power for so long, in part, because he was able to get his party to reach a consensus, rarely distracted by simply pressing his own views. McConnell likes to say that his leadership style is to use "all carrots and no sticks." When I mentioned this to Senator Cotton, he rolled his eyes. There was a notable exception after the leadership election. The leader has final say over some committee assignments. "This is a rare occasion," McConnell said. When four people vied for two slots on the Commerce Committee, McConnell used a stick. He chose the two who had supported him, Shelley Moore Capito and Cynthia Lummis, rejecting the two who had opposed him, Mike Lee and Rick Scott. "I rest my case," McConnell said.

McConnell's victory over Scott also meant he could achieve another goal that had seemed unachievable when he first stepped onto the Senate floor: to be the longest serving party leader in Senate history. He was within months of breaking the record set by Mike Mansfield, a Democrat of Montana, who served as majority leader from 1961 until his retirement in 1977.

He broke Mansfield's record on January 3, 2023. As he ate his fruit at breakfast, he "burst into tears" while reading a congratulatory email from Josh Holmes. Then he met with staff in his office that morning and again wept openly. Mansfield used to give away ashtrays with his signature on it as mementos. McConnell's staff bought one for their boss to mark the occasion. They lit up cigarettes, then crushed them in the ashtray, telling him that he had crushed the Mansfield record. McConnell detested smoking his entire life, but there in front of him was an ashtray full of cigarettes, and he was smiling.

In the Senate chamber, new members were sworn in. Some veteran members came to watch. Mark Kelly came with his granddaughter. Lisa Murkowski with her father, Frank, who had been a senator. Former senator Barbara Mikulski came with Senator Chris Van Hollen. Senator Chuck Schumer, the majority leader, made a pro forma speech, gave a brief nod to McConnell, then quickly noted he had set his own record that day, as New York's longest serving senator.

Then McConnell rose to speak. On the surface, his speech was an ode to Mansfield, but he was clearly projecting his belief that the two shared many traits: not dominating their members, but serving them, not being the loudest voice, and not being concerned about having their name attached to legislation. It was an homage to a Senate of another era, one more civil and less riven by partisanship.

About a dozen Republican senators were in the chamber, and some of them walked out before he was finished. Amy Klobuchar sat alone on the Democratic side, while Sinema was presiding. Neither Chao nor any of McConnell's children were there.

But it was significant to McConnell. Sitting with me in his office about three hours later, his eyes again welled with tears as he reflected on the moment. "It's been kind of an emotional day, which is unusual for me," McConnell said. "I spent a lot of time thinking about all the people who were there at critical moments along the way that made this last this long. I had a lot of help from a lot of really smart people at every step of the way.

"Honestly the odds of me making it this far were pretty daunting, and even though this was my goal for a long time, I didn't have any realistic thoughts that I would actually get there. I wasn't sure I was good enough. And frankly, as long as it took me, was I going to last that long? And one other guy who's lasted a long time is Joe Biden. And he gave me a call yesterday about this just to say he thought it was a really big deal and congratulations."

He conceded that by focusing on Mansfield's many good traits he hoped people would ascribe some of those to him as well. "I think he thought his job was to try to help everybody succeed. That's the way I view this job."

As powerful as the role is, it can also be lonely. "I've from time to time taken a lot of crap from some of my members, and I'm still there for them," McConnell said. But the condemnation he received from Republican senators was tepid compared with Trump's unsparing ridicule, whose approach became a playbook for a lot of aspiring Republican candidates. McConnell thought Trump cynically but skillfully cultivated voters. "Trump is appealing to people who haven't been as successful as other people and providing an excuse for that, that these more successful people have somehow cheated, and you don't deserve to think of yourself as less successful because things haven't been fair. . . . He's done a lot of damage to our party's image and our ability to compete."

Even in early 2023 McConnell was focused on retaking the Senate majority in 2024, and to him, the road started in West Virginia. McConnell made an early trip there to try to recruit the governor, Jim Justice, to run. Justice was seen as a very strong candidate, and more important, one who could defeat the incumbent Democrat, Joe Manchin. Justice agreed to run, and Manchin decided to not seek reelection. This meant that Republicans had an extremely favorable path to regaining the Senate majority because they would only have to win one more seat.

In other states, McConnell again found himself on a collision course with Trump, who had announced in November 2022 that he was seeking the presidency in 2024. McConnell hoped that his party would turn the page by selecting another presidential contender, and he particularly liked the candidacy of Tim Scott, whom McConnell saw as an heir to the legacy of Reagan Republicans. Scott proved to be an ineffective candidate, then he pivoted quickly to being an unapologetic cheerleader for Trump.

After recovering from his fall in March 2023, McConnell focused on recruiting strong candidates in the other two states where Republicans felt they had the best chance of picking up Senate seats, Ohio and Montana. In this effort, McConnell and the Senate campaign committee, now chaired by Steve Daines of Montana, were well aligned. Even that unity did not mean they got their preferred candidate. In the Ohio primary, the Trump-backed candidate Bernie Moreno beat back a challenge from a more moderate Republican in the mold of Portman.

Shortly after Trump announced his 2024 presidential campaign, Merrick Garland, whom Biden had named attorney general, announced that he had appointed a special counsel to investigate Trump's actions connected to the 2020 election and the January 6 insurrection. McConnell said with a faint laugh that surely would have angered his critics that Garland was now in the right position. From the start, McConnell thought the charges brought by federal prosecutors against Trump had merit.

"I think it was the single most—in a category by itself—of how wrong all of it was and there's no doubt who inspired it, and I just hope that he'll have to pay a price for it," McConnell said. Less than a month after special counsel Jack Smith brought the charges, McConnell said of Trump in an interview with me, "If he hasn't committed indictable offenses, I don't know what one is."

None of those charges seemed to carry political consequences for Trump among Republicans. And he continued to try to direct Republican action in Congress. Trump's outside agitation on issues like opposition to raising the debt ceiling or forcing a government shutdown put McConnell in the position of being, as he put it, "the adult in the room," a posture that endeared him to the major establishment figures and donors, but not to Trump's seemingly immovable base. "I may not have a huge following, but I have a following among educated, close watchers of what's going on. So I know I can't influence the broad

Republican Party, but I have influence here, and I'm going to use it because I think this is important to the country, and I think the MAGA movement is completely wrong.

"I think Trump was the biggest factor in changing the Republican Party from what Ronald Reagan viewed and he wouldn't recognize today," McConnell said. "I think his approach of attacking people every day kind of caught on and produced a lot of candidates who thought that was the way to succeed. Reagan was exactly the opposite. The Eleventh Commandment: Be hopeful and optimistic. It's hard to know what came first, whether it was Trump creating a whole new mindset or the mindset already being there and he just capitalized on it." In either case, the outcome was clear. The era of the Reagan Republican was rapidly fading away.

For much of his career, despite the physical effects of polio, McConnell projected vigor. In his early eighties, though, he knew he was somewhat physically diminished. His voice on the Senate floor, its deep timbre and hint of the South, was strong, but his gait was slow and sometimes uneven. After his fall, he lost considerable weight, and his face looked gaunt and drawn. For a time, as he recovered, he walked along furniture to steady himself. The focus on Biden's age in the media and among voters didn't help.

In late 2023, he suggested that he might not seek another term as leader but said he had not made a definitive decision. He knew where he stood. "The Democrats hate me because of the Supreme Court, and half the Republicans hate me because of Trump. So I've achieved a unique level of unpopularity here, and frankly I've just gotten used to it."

By midday on February 28, 2024, there was no more ambiguity. He had turned eighty-two the previous week. His sister-in-law, Angela Chao, a highly accomplished business executive, had died in a mysterious car accident. Trump was the all-but-certain Republican nominee for president. It was time. Holmes, McConnell's longtime political consigliere, had been working on remarks. Other former aides were alerted and beckoned to Washington. McConnell's office sent out a notice to senators in the late morning, telling them that he would be speaking but not why. Somehow, word of what he was about to say had not leaked.

His staff and former aides lined the back of the chamber and several rows in the second story gallery. No family seemed to be present.

He walked slowly down the center aisle of the Senate chamber to the desk he had coveted on the day he had first arrived in 1985. Only a small group of senators, including Collins, knew he was about to say that he would step down as party leader after his term ended in November.

"One of life's most underappreciated talents is to know when it's time to move on to life's next chapter," he said. "So I stand before you today . . . to say that this will be my last term as Republican leader of the Senate." He told the gathering, "I always imagined a moment when I had total clarity and peace about the sunset of my work. A moment when I am certain I have helped preserve the ideals I so strongly believe. It arrived today."

He acknowledged the shift in his party, the rise of politicians in the burn-it-all-down Trump mold, and he vowed to be a counter voice. "Believe me, I know the politics within my party at this particular moment in time. I have many faults. Misunderstanding politics is not one of them. That said, I believe more strongly than ever that America's global leadership is essential to preserving the shining city on a hill that Ronald Reagan discussed. For as long as I am drawing breath on this earth, I will defend American exceptionalism."

"I love the Senate," he said. "It has been my life. There may be more distinguished members of this body throughout our history, but I doubt there are any with more admiration for it." He continued, "Father Time remains undefeated. I am no longer the young man sitting in the back, hoping colleagues would remember my name. It is time for the next generation of leadership."

It was a triumphal moment, much like his February 13 speech about the January 6 attacks, in which he excoriated Trump, saying that while he would not vote to convict him in his impeachment trial, Trump would be subject to criminal prosecution and civil action. But he could have gone further. He could have pressed for Trump's conviction in the impeachment. He said he could not have persuaded enough Republicans to get the sixty-seven votes needed. He chose not to try, and that choice meant that Trump could again become his party's dominant and domineering force.

The week following his announcement about stepping down, he issued a tepid statement saying he would support Trump for president in 2024. He said he was merely reaffirming the statement he had made three years ago: he would support his party's nominee. His real motives were to help Republicans win back a Senate majority and the desire to stay in his job through November. He could not remain the leader of his team if he did not support the top of the ticket. Other Republicans, including Young of Indiana, Cassidy of Louisiana, Murkowski of Alaska, and Collins of Maine, went against the party base and said they would not endorse Trump. Both Cassidy and Young are from deep red states, and their posture might invite primary challenges from the right. It was a risk they were willing to take.

Even with his obvious contempt for Trump, and his belief that he was not fit for the presidency, if Mitch McConnell were to continue as his party leader, if he were to play a role in shaping the makeup of the next Senate and the nation's agenda, he had no choice but to support the nominee. Trump came to the Senate to try to fashion a show of unity. McConnell attended the meeting, exchanged a few words with the former president, and awkwardly shook his hand. He declined to say who he would vote for in 2024.

It was the price he paid for power.

EPILOGUE: "THE LAST THING YOU DO"

Lamar Alexander, who has known McConnell since 1969, gave his friend some counsel as he was retiring from the Senate after the 2020 election: "You'll always be remembered for the last thing you do." Both men were steeped in American history and held a generational reverence for established political order. In the winter of their careers, Alexander was advising his friend to carefully consider how he wrote his last chapter.

For McConnell, that "last thing" actually had its start after a long plane flight on July 7, 1993. The itinerary called for McConnell and other members of a congressional delegation to land in Kyiv, Ukraine, at 8:30 a.m., six months after the United States had officially opened its embassy there, and two years after the country had declared independence from the Soviet Union. McConnell was given a detailed briefing about the political, economic, and social conditions of the country. After decades under Soviet domination, Ukraine was still sorting out its own fledgling democracy and how its political system would operate, including drafting a constitution and establishing relations with other countries like the United States. McConnell had seen the collapse of the Soviet Union as the final triumph of the Cold War and a validation of the Reagan Republican vision of "peace through strength."

The Americans met with a variety of Ukrainian officials and business leaders, and made connections with U.S.-based interests in the country like Pepsi and Johnson Wax. Two months after the visit, Ukraine's president, Leonid Kravchuk, wrote to McConnell. "I can see that your sincere desire to help Ukraine to meet the challenges it is facing, is now being embodied in a concrete and very important matter. I have been informed that you have taken the lead in ensuring that Ukraine receives an adequate share of the assistance which the United States will be providing to the nations of the former Soviet Union."

Kravchuk had a particular interest in McConnell because he was on the Senate Appropriations Committee, meaning he had clout when it came to distributing foreign aid. In a subsequent letter sent to other senators, Kravchuk adopted a more urgent tone. He complained that the United States was not providing the needed financial assistance to Ukraine, noting that only Azerbaijan and Uzbekistan had received less money per capita. Ukraine could only become a stabilizing force in the region if it could develop a strong economy, he contended. "I am informed that Senator Mitch McConnell is proposing an amendment to the Foreign Assistance Appropriation Bill which would direct some of the NIS assistance [aid for newly independent states] specifically to Ukraine. We are grateful to him, welcome this initiative and urge you to support it. . . . Ukraine is eager to become a full member of the nations. We are committed to peace, stability, human rights."

That would be a long pull for a country like Ukraine, beset by infighting, corruption, high inflation, and a stagnant economy, none of which was surprising for a newly independent nation trying to get back on its feet. Congress earmarked $300 million for Ukraine aid, and in subsequent years pushed for additional targeted assistance. McConnell had been concerned that Ukraine would not get adequate funding because of a larger focus on Russia, which received $2.5 billion.

McConnell traveled to Ukraine again for a ten-day trip in August 1997, accompanied by his wife, Elaine Chao, and Robin Cleveland, a top foreign policy adviser. In May of that year, Russian President

Boris Yeltsin had signed a treaty of "friendship and cooperation" with Ukraine, but that did little to lift the nation's economic situation, which, according to a State Department memo sent to McConnell and others, had become dire. There were also concerns about widespread instability in the government. (Even with those more global concerns on his agenda, McConnell also made time to discuss the prospect of a coal slurry facility in Ukraine, an idea that had been promoted to him by a Kentucky businessman.)

Ukraine would become the epicenter of a controversy that resulted in Trump's first impeachment. For McConnell, it was a country with which he had more than passing familiarity, unlike many members of Congress. The United States had not yet come through with a major military assistance package for the country. Trump made a phone call trying to pressure Zelenskyy to investigate Biden. Zelenskyy's election had given McConnell and others some hope that Ukraine could emerge from its years of failed leadership to become a strong democracy that shared a border with Russia, a country with which it had been fighting a low grade war since 2014, when Russia illegally annexed Crimea.

After weeks of lesser provocation, Russia dramatically escalated the conflict when it invaded Ukraine on February 24, 2022, instigating the most significant war in Europe since World War II. Russian aggression, the very threat that McConnell's father, Mac, had been concerned about since returning from the battlefront in World War II, was now on full display. Russian officials had boasted that it would wrest control of Ukraine in a matter of days. To McConnell, there was no ambiguity about what the United States should do. It should give Ukraine whatever was needed to fight back. McConnell's allegiance to the Republican Party began with President Dwight Eisenhower, who led Allies to victory in World War II and then repelled Ohioan Robert Taft and his isolationist views to win his party's nomination for president. It was carried forward by Reagan's commitment to national defense, spreading democratic values around the world, and maintaining strong international alliances. With that framework, McConnell could only view the current Russian invasion in one way: an assault on democratic ideals that had to be stopped. McConnell was clear-eyed about Russian President Vladimir Putin's desire to restore the old Soviet Union, and he strongly believed Putin would not stop at Ukraine.

It quickly became apparent, though, that massive financial support for Ukraine would be no easy sell among Republican senators, notably because of Trump's isolationist views, which were reinforced and amplified night after night on Fox News opinion shows.

On May 1, House Speaker Nancy Pelosi made a dramatic, clandestine visit to Ukraine to meet with Zelenskyy and express support on behalf of the United States. McConnell would make his own trip two weeks later. Before he left, he met with President Biden, telling him, "I've got internal issues here with the former president and others trying to undermine this. I've got skeptical Europeans who wonder if this is the way all Republicans are . . . I think this would be beneficial to you to help me make this [message] more broadly bipartisan." Biden signed off on the trip, which was necessary for security reasons.

McConnell, along with Republican senators Susan Collins, John Cornyn of Texas, and John Barrasso of Wyoming, flew to Poland then boarded a train for a tense, eleven-hour journey to Ukraine, in an effort to show Zelenskyy and the world that the U.S. was united in its support for Ukraine. McConnell popped an Ambien on the train to help him sleep. They were accompanied by "a couple of guys with the biggest arms I've ever seen," with "very large and intimidating weapons," McConnell told me. McConnell had a private berth on the train with a bathroom; his other senate colleagues shared their space. "The truth is none of us took a bath for about two days. And it was a long train ride and I had a lot of time to think about a lot of things."

When they arrived in Kyiv, Zelenskyy greeted them dressed in his signature green military fatigues. McConnell wore a blue blazer, blue shirt, and khakis. He gripped the Ukrainian president's hand as firmly as he could. They held a two-hour meeting around a large rectangular table, McConnell in the center across from Zelenskyy. The atmosphere was serious, but the conversation was cordial, with McConnell trying to convey that backing for Ukraine had support from both U.S. political parties. "I tried to reassure them that I, at least for myself, I thought the goal was the same as theirs, to win. And that my view was that the definition of victory depends upon what they think, not us."

He returned from the trip even more resolved to try to get the Ukrainians the help they needed, and he was convinced that the NATO alliance would be a crucial bulwark in sustaining their defense. McConnell also came away impressed with the Ukraine president, thinking that he, like Reagan, might have been underestimated because they both came from the world of acting. "I think there are going to be statues all over the country to this guy. . . . I expect he even surprised himself with his courage and his ability to communicate."

Armed with firsthand knowledge of the situation and the chance to take a personal measure of Zelenskyy, McConnell found an opportunity to finally counter Trump's bluster. "I had spent a lot of time when I didn't have all that big a megaphone during the Trump years, trying to reassure Europeans that we still thought NATO was important, because Trump was frequently publicly questioning that," he said. He wanted to "push back against the isolationists of my own party." McConnell knew Trump had a vastly larger audience, but he was hoping that his own was the one that would ultimately matter.

McConnell was able to deliver all but eleven Republican members for a $40 billion aid package. "I wanted to restore the notion that America ought not to try to exist in splendid isolation from the rest of the world," he added. For once, Trump's opposition did not win the day.

McConnell thought the trip had a "really significant impact on unifying my party behind something I thought was right for the country." Trump had damaged the idea that support for an ally abroad was a natural American instinct. "And I was trying to repair the damage and get my party and at least 50 percent of the American people who identify with us into a different place, than the voices of isolation."

"He may have a bigger following than I do, but I have some

following and I have a lot more following than he does in the Senate," McConnell said at the time. "And that's where the action was."

McConnell worked to fill a void in the Republican Party. He wanted to make sure that European allies realized that while Trump was a powerful voice, he was out of office. "I thought there wasn't anybody else who could do that any better than me and that I ought to get over there and try to solve both those problems at once, both how the Europeans felt about Republicans in America. And at the same time, I thought it would be helpful in diminishing the number of votes against the Ukraine package and set us up for a big bipartisan vote on NATO admission for Finland and Sweden."

McConnell also maintained a strong relationship with Ukraine's ambassador to the United States, Oksana Markarova. After their very first meeting, she already felt her nation had an ally. "You see right away that the person has a really deep knowledge of many things and yet is not a very talkative person," she said. "But he listens for a long time and when he says it, he speaks in very concise phrases. You sense he not only understood everything discussed but he knows so much about it." "I didn't have to explain to him when I said it was a 1939 moment. . . . He said, 'exactly.'"

"Very early on, he started educating the people of the Senate in his party about the implications of this [Ukraine aid]. He never missed an opportunity to speak about it," she said in 2023. McConnell invited her to speak at one of the Republican Party lunches so members could hear directly from someone affected by the war.

As the war dragged into its second year, with the Ukrainians making fitful progress, Trump's opposition to the U.S. sending billions of dollars in aid to Ukraine grew louder. He repeated his absurd conviction that he could bring the conflict to a close in twenty-four hours if he were president, and Republican senators, especially those in vulnerable elections or fearing a primary challenge from the right in 2024, either embraced his views or were muted in their criticisms. Echoing Trump, most Republicans made the case in speeches and on Fox News that the United States needed to put its own problems, like the war in Ukraine and the migrant crisis at the border, ahead of those in other countries.

That was the outside game. McConnell was playing the inside game.

Mitch McConnell is almost always on time. When I arrived to interview him on October 6, 2023, I was asked to wait. "The reason I was fifteen minutes late is I was talking to Biden," McConnell said when he entered his office. McConnell had called the president with a plan that he thought was good politics and good policy for both men. He knew Biden was enduring sharp criticism for his border policy and its effect on cities around the country. He knew that Republicans, including himself, were demanding a crackdown. And he knew that because Hamas had initiated a deadly attack on Israel, aiding the most important U.S. ally in the Middle East would have broad support of both parties. The trick was to try to wrap all three issues together, and thus deliver the much needed aid to Ukraine as well.

"I said this needs to be a really big package," McConnell recalled. "The Israelis probably would prefer it just be them and you may get pressure from them and some of the Jewish community in this country to take care of Israel. We are all in favor of taking care of Israel. That isn't going to be controversial. But I think you need a large package, and Ukraine needs to ride on the package. And in my opinion, we can only pull this off once on Ukraine, and it ought to be big enough to get through the '24 election." For good measure, McConnell suggested also providing aid to Taiwan, another initiative both parties could embrace.

McConnell came away thinking that Biden agreed with his approach. "I think we're in the same place. I like Joe, and I have a good relationship with him. But he's up next year, and he will be under a lot of pressure to not get Israel tied up in these other things."

His plan was to develop the proposal in the Senate, under his guidance, and "hope for the best in the House," where support for Trump was stronger and support for Ukraine was far weaker. "To me, support for Ukraine is a no brainer. This is a Trump-inspired bunch of nonsense. We're losing no one. They're killing Russians and we are spending money in the United States. This is a manufactured controversy among Republicans, Trump-driven, which has no rational basis in my view."

McConnell asked Senator James Lankford of Oklahoma, who had strong conservative support, including from Trump, but also had worked closely with Democrats, to come up with the border portion of the package. Lankford worked for weeks to put it together, and when he was finished, the border portion of the legislation called for the toughest restrictions on immigration and migrant traffic in decades: a $20 billion package that included hiring thousands of new Border Patrol agents and asylum officers, investing in technology to combat drug smuggling, and increasing the space to hold the migrants. That was pieced together with aid for Ukraine and aid for Israel. McConnell thought this would be widely accepted because it was the only way Republicans could achieve a tougher border plan, something they desperately wanted. If Republicans held the White House and Congress, Senate Democrats would filibuster a border bill they could not abide. The same would be true if Democrats controlled each branch. In this case, a divided government actually offered a rare chance for both parties to get something they wanted in exchange for reasonable-seeming concessions.

But House Republicans did not want to take yes for an answer. Trump came out opposed to Lankford's proposal, saying it was not tough enough, and that was like a bullhorn call to action for House Republicans. "Opposition to Ukraine is about as much nonsense as [saying] Biden wasn't legitimately elected," McConnell said. "It makes no sense. Which is very frustrating, but the former president has a lot of followers outside, and that leads to followers inside."

The aid package, at least in its initial form, was doomed. A month later, little progress had been made. Even as Gaza was engulfed in violence, McConnell was convinced the war waged by Ukraine against Russia was "the most important thing going on in the world right now."

"Ronald Reagan would turn over in his grave if he saw we were missing an opportunity to impact the Russian army and not lose a single American, to support a democratic country against an invasion by the Russians, and to spend most of the money in the United States, in thirty-eight different states, to rebuild our industrial base," McConnell said. "The argument against helping Ukraine is nonsense. I think it's an example of Donald Trump's influence over the modern Republican Party. He's got a lot bigger megaphone than I have but I am doing the best I can to argue the facts."

McConnell, as he had from the beginning, framed the legislation as serving American interests rather than international ones. His staff did research that showed how many states, and how many congressional districts, would benefit by the additional weapons production the aid would require, and how the U.S. stockpiles would be replaced with the most modern equipment. He noted that Russia was expending extraordinary resources to fight its battle, and that it was Ukrainian soldiers, not American ones who were dying for the cause.

But for a lot of Republicans in the House, and probably more than a dozen in the Senate, emotion carried more weight than evidence. To further complicate matters, the House had deposed Kevin McCarthy as speaker and elected Mike Johnson, a little-known member from Louisiana whose most prominent career highlights were writing legal briefs in support of Trump's specious claims of election fraud. Johnson hardly seemed like someone who would be open to arguments from someone like McConnell, let alone Biden and Democrats.

The House indeed rejected the Senate proposal, claiming it was too weak on the border. Senators like JD Vance argued that supporting Ukraine was a lost cause and that the money should be spent at home. The Trumpist wing of the Senate seemed content to settle for no deal rather than one they considered perfect.

McConnell's strategy called for trying to at least persuade Trump to be neutral, given the extraordinary stakes. If the United States did not come through with more aid, what signal would that send to Europe, including vital NATO allies? McConnell was certain they would view it as an isolationist retreat. So McConnell sent Trump-friendly emissaries to ask authoritarian leaders in other countries who had influence with the former president to try to persuade him to at least be silent. Some made trips to Mar-a-Lago. He also included senators in meetings with foreign officials who came to see him, so they could feel more part of the process. McConnell wanted to show his own members that foreign leaders saw that helping Ukraine was in their collective security interest.

Meanwhile, McConnell, Schumer, Representative Hakeem Jeffries, the Democratic leader in the House, and Biden all tried to talk the issue through with Johnson. In one meeting in February, McConnell was the first to speak, an effort to convey to Johnson that there was broad-based agreement on the plan. Paralysis, McConnell noted, was in effect a decision, and delay was having real time consequences on the battlefield. McConnell also met multiple times with Johnson one-on-one, asking staff to leave the room.

There were additional meetings, and Johnson had his own constituencies to manage, notable among them the former president. Johnson, too, had traveled to Mar-a-Lago, and Trump sent out social media posts praising his leadership, providing cover for action.

Publicly and privately, from every angle he could manage, McConnell was urging Johnson to have a vote. The Senate had passed a package that would provide $60 billion to Ukraine and billions in aid to Israel and Taiwan. Johnson and House Republicans made some modest amendments to the package, then finally passed it.

That's when McConnell went to work to whip the vote among his own members. He again laid out the facts as he saw them. This package was of vital national interest for the United States. It would stimulate economic development and replenish the American arsenal. No American troops were at risk, and Russia was spending billions it could not afford. He and his staff did not stop trying to persuade Republicans until the final vote was cast, and the extra effort resulted in ten more Republicans backing the House bill than had backed the one passed by the Senate.

It was a rare victory of the Reagan Republican wing of the party over the Trumpist wing. But even with that win, McConnell knew that his party was drifting rightward. He said he thought his views represented about 40 percent of the Republican Party in 2024. There was a general rightward shift at work, with a substantial number of Republicans trying to position themselves as the natural inheritors of Trump's populist appeal to the white working-class voters who were Democrats when McConnell started out in politics. That is clearly where the base of the Republican Party is in the Trump era, and the trends that drove that change, a feeling of being left out and being treated unfairly in a multicultural, global economy, were in play in 2024. Republicans were developing their own kind of identity politics.

Once the bill had passed, McConnell and aides gathered in his office for a toast. There was a bottle of Ukrainian vodka, a bottle of Taiwanese whiskey, and a bottle of Old Crow, the Kentucky bourbon that doubled as Trump's nickname for McConnell, which he readily embraced. At one of McConnell's fundraisers, each donor was presented with a bottle of Old Crow with McConnell's picture on the label.

"It's been, from a personal point of view, it's been an out of body experience for somebody who spends most of his time getting beat up," McConnell told me.

McConnell agreed to do two Sunday news programs, a rarity in the latter part of his career, appearing on *Meet the Press* and *Face the Nation* to both revel in his victory and to stake out his position against the isolationist forces in his party.

Zelenksyy wrote McConnell to thank him. "As Ukraine continues to courageously fight Russian aggression, I would like to personally and on behalf of the entire Ukrainian people thank you for your steadfast position and unwavering support for our country and our common human values," Zelenskyy wrote. He invited McConnell to return to Ukraine for a ceremony honoring its constitution and a national day of prayer.

In one of our final interviews, McConnell said he plans to serve out his senate term, which does not end until 2026. He said he will feel liberated, no longer having to serve as the heat shield for his members, or to listen to their complaints and concerns large and small. He will no longer have his magnificent suite of offices, or large staff, or full security detail. Few others in his position have ever voluntarily ceded their power, so the question of how much authority he will retain remains open. He will, he insisted, still have his voice, and he plans to use it to argue that the United States should not turn inward, but rather should play an activist role in the international order, maintain strong alliances, with a muscular national defense.

"I'm going to make John McCain sound like a dove," McConnell said. He said he would spend his remaining time in the Senate pushing for strong alliances and robust defense spending. "I'm not ready to have the last thing."

McConnell was reaching for a storybook ending, just as he did when telling the story of receiving his first pair of shoes after recovering from polio. At the Republican National Convention in late July of 2024, he got a preview of how difficult that would be to achieve. When he stood to announce the Kentucky delegation's support for Trump—who had selected JD Vance, a persistent McConnell critic who opposed continued aid to Ukraine, as his running mate—he was roundly booed.

ACKNOWLEDGMENTS

The most energizing part of a project like this is going into it with one set of expectations and ideas and coming out of it with a completely different set of both. Many people only see Senator McConnell in monochrome. The real portrait has many hues.

I would like to thank my agent, David Black, who in many ways was the inspiration for this project, and stayed with it every step of the way. He's also a gifted editor and thinker, and that is reflected in the book.

At Simon & Schuster, Priscilla Painton instantly saw the potential in this book, and was its champion throughout the process, from deft word editing to broad-brush framing that gave invaluable perspective. Ian Straus, my editor, was a writer's dream: tireless, insightful, supportive, and gifted at the keyboard.

My colleague at the Associated Press, Cal Woodward, was indispensable to bringing this book to life and ensuring a rigorous check of facts. He is the epitome of a professional. I would also like to thank Julie Pace, AP's executive editor, and Anna Johnson, the Washington bureau chief, for their exceptional support and understanding, and Nancy Benac for her wonderful feedback.

My friend Jim Warren, as ever, spent countless hours, at all hours, helping me shape the narrative. Add to that list Al Hunt, Michael Duffy, Christi Parsons, Luke Albee, Paul Kane, Al Cross, and Ki Miller.

This book would not have happened without the help of so many people and for that I am grateful.

The Price of Power was greatly enriched by unparalleled access to Senator McConnell's vast archive at the University of Louisville. One person there in particular, Nan Mosher, was vital in making sense of it all, and with good cheer responded to my every request, sometimes on off days and at off-hours. Others on the senator's staff were also quite helpful, including David Popp, his communications director, who served his client well and also understood my objectives. Stefanie Muchow, Terry Carmack, and Sharon Soderstrom provided great background and context. Josh Holmes and Billy Piper made themselves available numerous times and added to my knowledge with each meeting.

Of course, I also owe thanks to Senator McConnell for agreeing to cooperate with this project, and for not shying from hard questions. He sat for more than fifty hours of interviews and granted access to sensitive oral histories well before he had initially planned to do so, and certainly not to his political benefit.

My family also stood with me over the more than three years of researching and writing. Our daughter, Kate, an organizational whiz, helped to bring order to the wide body of information and interviews I collected. Our son, Lee, was a faithful reader along the way and asked astute questions that made the book better. My wife, Julie Carey, pushed me for more and better answers for McConnell's actions, and never complained about the lost nights and weekends.

NOTES

In the course of researching this book, the author conducted dozens of private interviews, well over fifty hours, with Senator Mitch McConnell between March 2021 and June 2024. Senator McConnell also granted the author access to his extensive oral history project, which he started in 1995. That project includes annual interviews with the senator, conducted primarily by members of his staff and occasionally by outside historians and biographers. The author had access to transcripts of those interviews.

FOREWORD
vii *He talked about the many stories*: "Senate Chambers Desks," U.S. Senate Historical Office, https://www.senate.gov/art-artifacts/decorative-art/furniture/senate-chamber-desks/traditions.htm.

viii *When he was stricken by polio*: Letters and doctors' reports in the McConnell family papers.

ONE: POLIO
1 *Mitchie stood at eight and half months*: McConnell family papers.

2 *Dr. Phillips's diagnosis*: Correspondence from doctors in the McConnell family papers.

3 *The day Mitchie first complained*: Associated Press, "Eight New Polio Cases Reported In Alabama," *Birmingham News*, July 21, 1944.

3 *In his memoir*: Bentz Plagemann, *My Place to Stand* (New York: Farrar, Straus, 1949), 136.

4 *"Actually, it's not"*: Ibid., 94.

4 *He made his first trip*: "Franklin D. Roosevelt and the Spirit of Warm Springs," National WWII Museum, posted online April 12, 2021, https://www.nationalww2museum.org/war/articles/franklin-d-roosevelt-little-white-house-warm-springs.

5   *"Patient was extremely uncooperative"*: Photocopies in McConnell family papers of Warm Springs doctor and staff reports.

6   *At one point*: Copy of Dean's letter to the rationing board, in McConnell family papers.

6   *His back and abdomen*: Warm Springs doctors' report #4353 in McConnell family papers.

6   *"They said"*: Oral History Interview, 1995.

7   *In one photo*: Original letters between Dean and Mac in McConnell family collection.

7   *"I will never forget this"*: McConnell interview with author.

8   *He would go on*: Author review of estate property records.

8   *His appointment that July*: Warm Springs correspondence to McConnell family.

9   *On VE Day*: Mac's letter to his wife in the McConnell family papers.

10 *"There's not a doubt"*: Oral History Interview, 1995.

10 *Instead, he later recalled*: Ibid.

11 *"The cultural expectations"*: Daniel J. Wilson, "Psychological Trauma and Its Treatment in the Polio Epidemics," *Bulletin of the History of Medicine* 82, No. 4, (Baltimore: Johns Hopkins University Press, 2008), 848–77.

12 *"Candidly, I think"*: McConnell Oral History Interview, 1995.

12 *When polio survivors*: Richard L. Bruno, *The Polio Paradox: Understanding and Treating "Post-Polio Syndrome" and Chronic Fatigue* (New York: Grand Central, 2002), 99.

13 *For most polio survivors*: Ibid., 101.

13 *Bruno wrote in his book*: Ibid., xvii.

13 *"Several thousand victims"*: Victor Cohn, "Recurrent Polio Strikes Victims of Epidemics," *Washington Post*, May 26, 1984.

14 *In a 1995 interview*: Oral History Interview, 1995.

TWO: DEAN AND MAC

16 *At age ten*: Childhood diary in McConnell family papers.

16 *She was also an excellent student*: Essays in McConnell family papers.

17 *She enrolled in Massey Business College*: Correspondence in McConnell family papers.

17 *His grandfather was a "circuit riding Calvinist preacher"*: Mitch McConnell, *The Long Game: A Memoir* (New York: Sentinel, 2016), 9.

18 *At Wake Forest*: Family letters in McConnell papers.

18 *They exchanged a series of letters*: Preserved in the McConnell family files.

19 *Still, he lamented*: Ibid.

19 *Then he received a letter*: Ibid.

21 *In the days that followed*: Ibid.

22 *Dean wore a "costume suit"*: Ibid.

THREE: A CHANGED MAN

25 *"I won't accept a deferment under any conditions"*: Letter to Dean.

25 *In June 1944*: Letters and military correspondence in McConnell family papers.

25 *"It was, of course, too short"*: Dean letters to Mac's parents, in the McConnell family papers.

26 *Four months after D-Day*: "Story of the 2nd Division," *Stars and Stripes* booklet, 1944, Maneuver Center of Excellence Libraries, Donovan Research Library, Fort Benning, Georgia, https://mcoecbamcoepwprd01.blob.core .usgovcloudapi.net/library/Documents/Hardcopy/paper/D808.3_2nd_A21 _no.2.pdf.

27 *Another account, the official one by the Army*: U.S. Army, "The Thirty Eighth United States Infantry," paper files in McConnell collection.

27 *Mac's regiment had bored through Germany*: Ibid.

27 *Under relentless fire, Mac's company moved on four successive nights*: Ibid.

27 *In a letter from Germany*: Letters in McConnell family papers.

28 Stars and Stripes *said the welcome*: "The Story of the 2nd Division," *Stars and Stripes* booklet, 40.

29 *"The question in most of the doughboys' minds"*: Ibid.

31 *"It's a hell of a mess now"*: Letter from Mac in McConnell family papers.

FOUR: JIM CROW SOUTH

33 *"As a young boy that's just the way it was"*: Oral History Interview, 1995.

34 *"Archie would come over"*: Ibid.

34 *Decades later, McConnell sought her out*: McConnell interview with author.

34 *They went through a fundamentalist period*: Oral History Interview, 1995.

35 *One of them is Dicky McGrew*: Oral History Interview, 1995.

35 *So Mitch went across the street*: Oral History Interview, 1995.

35 *The family didn't have a car or a television*: Oral History Interview, 1995.

36 *She wrote to Mac's parents*: Letters in the McConnell family papers.

36 *"You couldn't get a single kid of a native to be a Yankee"*: Oral History Interview, 1995.

37 *"Dear Mamie and Rube, I love you"*: Letters in the McConnell family papers.

39 *One memory that stuck with McConnell*: Oral History Interview, 1995.

39 *"Obviously the southern society did not respond to that quickly"*: Ibid.

40 *"My mother never got over it"*: Oral History Interview, 1995.

FIVE: BECOMING YANKEEFIED

41 *"Here is the only American city"*: William Manchester, "Louisville Cashes in on Culture," *Harper's*, August 1955.

41 *Louisville's hospitals and schools were segregated*: Tracy E. K'Meyer, "The Gateway to the South: Regional Identity and the Louisville Civil Rights Movement," *Ohio Valley History* 4, no. 1 (Spring 2004): 43–60.

43 *Nevertheless, white Louisvillians maintained*: Ibid.

44 *"I was lost"*: Oral History Interview, 1995.

44 *"I remember him as being a bit aloof"*: Billy Reed, "I first met Mitch when we were the hapless Giants of the Pony League; what happened to him?," *Northern Kentucky Tribune*, April 18, 2020. https://nkytribune.com/2020 /04/billy-reed-i-first-met-mitch-when-we-were-the-hapless-giants-of-the -pony-league-what-happened-to-him/.

44 *"Baseball was sort of the way I measured my worth"*: Oral History Interview, 1995.

45 *"The days and weeks"*: Ibid.

46 *In an essay titled "New Beginnings"*: McConnell family papers.

46 *"It's a lot easier in forming your party affiliation"*: Oral History Interview, 1995.

47 *Then, knowing he was not particularly popular*: Ibid.

47 *McCoy didn't take the race as seriously*: McCoy went on to Dartmouth College and Duke Law School and became a prominent attorney in Louisville. He died in 2023.

48 *In September*: McConnell family papers.

48 *In another essay*: Ibid.

49 *McConnell did not give anyone credit*: Bessie Anderson Stanley, "Success," All Poetry, https://allpoetry.com/poem/8601717-Success-by-Bessie-Anderson-Stanley.

50 *"Man, it's hot in Texas"*: Road trip letters in McConnell family papers.

51 *He kept the ticket stub*: It cost him $2.50.

51 *"They lined up a couple"*: Letters in McConnell family papers.

SIX: THE EXERCISE OF POWER

53 *In his freshman year*: Oral History Interview, 1995.

54 *"It was really quite a learning experience"*: Oral History Interview, 1995.

54 *"As soon as I figured out"*: Oral History Interview, 1995.

54 *"He was treated like an unpleasant relative"*: McConnell interview with author.

55 *"I thought to myself"*: Oral History Interview, 1995.

56 *McConnell secured a print*: Oral History Interview, 1995.

57 *In his first week*: Letter in McConnell papers.

60 *"This was the period"*: Oral History Interview, 1995.

60 *He became increasingly "irritated"*: Ibid.

60 *"Within thirty minutes"*: Ibid. Kennedy was pronounced dead at 1 p.m., about a half hour after being shot.

61 *In a 1964 essay*: Essay in McConnell personal files.

62 *"I thought we ought to have a little balance"*: Oral History Interview, 1995.

62 *"It is easy to smear"*: John David Dyche, draft of *Republican Leader*, located in the McConnell Chao Archives at the McConnell Center, University of Louisville.

63 *"You sort of had the feeling"*: Oral History Interview, 1995.

64 *On July 5, 1964*: Letter from Mac in McConnell family papers. He ended the letter on a wistful note: "I still get soupy about Independence Day and all that."

65 *"It appeared to me pretty clear"*: Oral History Interview, 1995.

66 *"That made a lasting impression"*: Ibid.

SEVEN: "ANTSY AS HELL"

68 *He soon told his military superiors*: McConnell's personal papers contain military personnel records, doctors' reports, and letters concerning his case for health-related discharge from the Army Reserves.

69   *His father contacted a member of Senator Cooper's staff*: Letter in McConnell files.

69   *So McConnell said*: McConnell interview with author.

69   *"Mitchell anxious to clear post"*: Letter in McConnell files.

69   *The director of the graduate division*: Letter in McConnell files.

69   *His handwritten notes to her*: Notes in McConnell files.

70   *He said that he never sent the application*: McConnell interview with author.

70   *As one measure of how inconsequential his legal work was*: Receipt in McConnell files.

71   *On September 21, Sherrill wrote a long, gracious letter*: Letter in McConnell personal files.

71   *"We traveled the state"*: McConnell interview with author.

72   *"I had a ball working in the campaign"*: Ibid.

73   *When his parents were traveling*: McConnell family papers.

73   *"I couldn't think of anything I didn't love"*: McConnell interview with author.

73   *Alexander was impressed with McConnell*: Ibid.

73   *Additional evidence came in a six-page memo*: McConnell files.

75   *"We think this issue"*: Ward Sinclair, "Rights-for-Women Fight Dies Quietly in Congress," *Courier-Journal*, November 20, 1970.

77   *"Even if he were mediocre"*: William R. Honan, "Roman L. Hruska Dies at 94," *New York Times*, April 27, 1999.

78   *McConnell argued that Haynsworth's rejection*: A. Mitchell McConnell Jr., "Haynsworth and Carswell: A New Senate Standard of Excellence," *Kentucky Law Journal* 59 (1970): 7–34. https://www.govinfo.gov/content/pkg/GPO-CHRG-REHNQUIST/pdf/GPO-CHRG-REHNQUIST-4-23-1.pdf.

80   *Reflecting later on such sentiments*: McConnell interview with author.

80   *They attended dinners*: Redmon letter to McConnell's parents, May 5, 1969.

81   *But she was suspicious*: Letter in McConnell files.

EIGHT: THE "LOST DECADE"

83   *McConnell believes this was because*: McConnell interview with author.

83   *In a letter to the editor*: *Courier-Journal*, July 7, 1970.

83   *"How can Quimsey"*: June 15, 1972, letter in McConnell files.

86   *"I sat around"*: McConnell interview with author.

87   *McConnell later told biographer*: John David Dyche, *Republican Leader: Political Biography of Senator Mitch McConnell* (Washington, DC: ISI Books, 2009).

87   *"Some of his cronies"*: McConnell interview with author.

87   *"It would have been absurd"*: Ibid.

87   *"So there I am"*: Ibid.

89   *"Levi was very tolerant"*: Ibid.

89   *"I finally just made a decision"*: Ibid.

90   *"What I had chosen"*: Ibid.

91   *"It was natural"*: Oral History Interview, 2002

91   *"We came up the hard way"*: Dyche, *Republican Leader*, 33.

91 *He listed his assets*: Oral History Interview, 1997.

92 *"I really felt like I was rolling the dice"*: McConnell interview with author.

92 *"It took a helluva lot"*: Ibid.

92 *He compiled a list*: Ed Ryan, "Stansbury wins mayoral primary; Hollenbach, McConnell look to fall," *Courier-Journal*, May 25, 1977.

93 *"I know that he was"*: McConnell interview with author.

93 *"It was one of the few things"*: Oral History Interview, 1997.

93 *He also tried to exploit the fact*: Ed Ryan, "Hollenbach faces big bout against McConnell in fall,"*Courier-Journal*, May 25, 1977.

93 *"The reality is"*: Oral History Interview, 1997.

94 *The newspaper's endorsement*: Editorial, "Why McConnell should be elected," *Courier-Journal*, October 30, 1977.

95 *"Most people don't risk everything"*: Oral History Interview, 1997.

95 *McConnell later told Dyche*: Republican Leader, 36.

NINE: "ROLE PLAYING"

96 *"I see my role in this effort"*: Mitch McConnell, "Prepared text of Judge McConnell's inaugural address," *Courier-Journal*, January 3, 1978.

97 *"I see a rising star"*: Jim Adams, "Subdued Celebration," *Courier-Journal*, January 3, 1978.

97 *Sweets, for one*: McConnell interview with author.

97 *"There were plenty of ways"*: Ibid.

97 *To overcome the Democratic blockade*: Ibid.

98 *So he took away their responsibilities*: Ibid.

98 *"He looked at me"*: Ibid.

99 *"I guess I began to figure out"*: Ibid.

99 *"I looked at the record"*: Ibid.

99 *"If you are surrounded by a bunch of liberals"*: Oral History Interview, 1997.

100 *Brown eventually was placed*: Joseph Gerth, "Once a Promising Louisville Politician, Carl Brown Died Alone, Fighting His Demons," *Courier-Journal*, updated April 20, 2018, https://www.courier-journal.com/story/news/local/joseph-gerth/2018/04/20/louisville-republican-carl-brown-died-mental-illness-bi-polar/532511002/.

100 *"It's the only experience"*: McConnell interview with author.

100 *McConnell realized that Brown*: Oral History Interview, 1997.

100 *His roommate was another young man*: Oral History Interview, 1997.

101 *"He was the best elected official"*: McConnell interview with author.

101 *He knew that shortly after*: Oral History Interview, 1997.

102 *"With regret, we jointly announce"*: Ibid.

102 *After divorcing his first wife*: J.Y. Smith, "Lorraine Cooper, 79, Leader in Washington Society, Dies," *Washington Post*, February 5, 1985.

102 *Reagan, McConnell said*: McConnell interview with author.

103 *"He was a really reasonable guy"*: Ibid.

103 *He did things to cultivate his reputation*: F.W. Woolsey, "A Mellowed Fellow?" *Courier-Journal*, August 15, 1982. https://www.newspapers.com/newspage/110881065/.

104 *"We finally figured out"*: McConnell interview with author.
105 *"It was the worst race ever"*: Oral History Interview, 1997.
106 *"I never start late"*: Ibid.
106 *McConnell readily admits*: Ibid.
107 *"If I were going to pick 10 senators"*: Quoted in Senator Wendell Ford letter, February 21, 1983, distributed by the Committee to Re-elect Senator Huddleston.
107 *"Our problem is"*: McConnell letter to Baker, March 12, 1984.

TEN: "WIN OR DIE TRYING"
109 *She had spurned the advances of Packwood*: Mullins interview with author.
110 *Carmack's response*: McConnell interview with author.
111 *At events, Carmack recalled*: Ibid.
112 *McConnell's rejoinder*: "Cook's action 'disappoints' McConnell," *Courier-Journal*, March 1, 1984.
112 *Huddleston anticipated a harshly negative campaign*: *Lexington Herald-Leader*, January 23, 1984.
112 *He was able to persuade*: Bob Johnson, "McConnell gets boost from major GOP donors," *Courier-Journal*, April 18, 1984.
113 *He took that idea to Roger Ailes*: McConnell, *The Long Game*, 61.
115 *"It was really late at night"*: McConnell interview with author.
115 *"Enclosed please find information"*: University of Kentucky Archive collection of *Courier-Journal* files.
116 *Reagan had performed poorly*: McConnell, *The Long Game*, 64.
117 *When he went inside*: Ibid., 57.
117 *"It was just a sort of metaphor"*: Oral History Interview, 1998.
118 *She told him his margin had shrunk*: McConnell, *The Long Game*, 67.
118 *"Jefferson County Judge Mitch McConnell"*: Bob Johnson, "McConnell claims win in tight race," *Courier-Journal*, November 7, 1984.
119 *A dejected Huddleston*: Ibid.
119 *"We'd lost seats in the Senate"*: Oral History Interview, 1998.

ELEVEN: LAND OF GIANTS
121 *He was not sure how to do his job*: Oral History Interview, 1998.
123 *He knew his place*: Associated Press, "McConnell's first year is quiet," *Kentucky Post*, February 3, 1986.
123 *The Almanac of American Politics*: Michael Barone and Grant Ujifusa, *The Almanac of American Politics 1986* (Washington, DC: National Journal, 1986), 521–22.
123 *Sure enough*: Dyche, *Republican Leader*, 62–63.
123 *"It was a thrill"*: Oral History Interview, 1998.
124 *In the process, he learned to loathe town meetings*: Oral History Interview, 1998.
124 *He found working to pass*: Ibid.
124 *He also noted that African Americans*: Ibid.
125 *"I felt we needed to do everything we could"*: McConnell, *The Long Game*, 72.

125   *"The person who knows the most"*: Oral History Interview, 1998.
126   *"I had to appear"*: Ibid.
126   *"It was a pretty tough article"*: Ibid.
127   *He found one way*: Oral History Interview, 1998.
127   *"It was a stupid mistake"*: Ibid.
127   *Janet Mullins, for one*: McConnell interview with author.
127   *McConnell entered the Senate*: Oral History Interview, 1998.
127   *The lethal effectiveness*: Ibid.
128   *McConnell spoke out against the bill*: Ibid.
128   *At the time*: Oral History Interview, 1998.
129   *His contrarian position*: Ibid.
130   *He came to find*: Oral History Interview, 1998.
131   *"I wanted to make it difficult"*: Ibid.
131   *He told Heyburn*: Ibid.
131   *As McConnell put it*: Ibid.
132   *The tension led to a debate*: Ibid.
133   *"It seems to me"*: Congressional Record, S11275, August 5, 1987.
133   *Still, he said*: Ibid.
134   *He said that 1987*: Oral History Interview, 1998.
135   *After McConnell finished briefing him*: Ibid.
135   *"It was clear to me"*: Ibid.
135   *"Every time Harvey"*: Ibid.

TWELVE: RESEARCH AND DESTROY
136   *He started by making an appeal*: Oral History Interview, 1998.
137   *Still, the president reinforced McConnell's message*: Dyche, *Republican Leader*, 76.
137   *"I was very interested in the paycheck"*: Law interview with author.
138   *"And, truth of the matter"*: Oral History Interview, 1998
149   *"I never will forget the night"*: Ibid.
142   *Later, Sloane acknowledged*: Sloane interview with author.
142   *"I don't own a gun"*: Oral History Interview, 1998
143   *In a letter dated July 10, 1990*: Copy in McConnell files.
144   *"McConnell is indeed lackluster"*: Kentucky Post, August 22, 1990.
144   *He did not mention that mere months prior*: Clarence Matthews, "Sloane is criticized for making 'flip flop' on the abortion issue," *Courier-Journal*, January 23, 1990.
144   *"Upon serious reflection"*: Congressional Record, S16409, November 20, 1989.
145   *Law, with a straight face*: Charles Wolfe, "Sloane seeks U.S. probe of postcard, fake memo from unknown source," *Associated Press story in the Courier-Journal*, April 25, 1990.
145   *Law conceded*: McConnell interview with author.
146   *Looking back with grudging admiration*: Frank Greer interview with author.
147   *Law wrote a remarkably detailed after-action report*: Memo in McConnell files, November 28, 1990.

THIRTEEN: MASTERY OF PROCESS

150 *"Gramm treats all NRSC resources"*: McConnell files.

151 *"It was very close"*: Oral History Interview, 1999.

152 *"We always denied it publicly"*: Ibid.

152 *McConnell noted with some pleasure*: Ibid.

152 *As the* Courier-Journal's *longtime political writer*: Oral History Interview, 1999.

152 *In 1992, Law wrote a twenty-three-page homage*: McConnell files.

153 *"She's a good lawyer"*: Oral History Interview, 1999.

154 *"It was a time for me to really refine"*: Oral History Interview, 1999.

154 *He said that he had checked the Senate rules*: Oral History Interview, 1998.

156 *Finally, he did*: Chao interview with author.

157 *McConnell said Boxer thought*: McConnell, *The Long Game*, 100.

158 *"I asked the doctor and nurses"*: Ibid., 87–88.

159 *When the panel tried to subpoena the diary*: Ibid., 99–101.

159 *McConnell had weighed the politics*: Ibid., 101.

159 *After Packwood resigned*: Michael Wines, "THE PACKWOOD CASE: Man in the News; Kentucky Blend of Understatement and Ambition—Addison Mitchell McConnell," *New York Times*, September 7, 1995.

160 *There was criticism from some Republicans*: Dyche, *Republican Leader*, 106.

FOURTEEN: "FIRST-CLASS ASS-KICKING"

163 *McConnell thought Gingrich received far too much credit*: McConnell interview with author.

163 *Babbage had it right*: Oral History Interview, 1998.

163 *In an editorial*: Editorial, "The great escape," *Courier-Journal*, January 21, 1996.

164 *McConnell said later*: Oral History Interview, 1998.

164 *McConnell hewed to his strategy*: Ibid.

165 *On this front*: *Courier-Journal*, November 6, 1996.

165 *The new role led to more media coverage*: George Lardner Jr., "The Man Who Makes Money Talk," *Washington Post*, September 7, 1997.

166 *"I don't think it's a scandal at all"*: Francis X. Clines, "A Free-Speech Senator Fights Limits on Donations," *New York Times*, August 21, 1997.

166 *McConnell had support in unlikely places*: ACLU letter, March 6, 1997.

167 *"McConnell went nuts"*: Feingold interview with author.

168 *Fred Wertheimer*: McConnell interview with author.

168 *As he walked away*: Oral History Interview, 2000.

169 *As his national profile grew*: Dyches, *Republican Leader*, 123.

169 *"It's a very competitive situation"*: *Republican Leader*, 126.

170 *His view on foreign aid*: Oral History Interview, 2000.

170 *But things got off to a rocky start*: Ibid.

171 *"Well, fundraising letters are outrageous"*: Oral History Interview, 2000.

171 *McConnell told Neumann*: Oral History Interview, 1998.

172 *McConnell bathed in the attention*: Oral History Interview, 1999.

173 *McCain had called the campaign finance system corrupt*: Ibid.

173 *She called McConnell the hard-boiled madam*: Maureen Dowd, "Liberties; Capitol Hill Bordello," *New York Times*, October 17, 1999.

174 *"The Appropriations Committee"*: Oral History Interview, 1999.

FIFTEEN: "NO SUBSTITUTE FOR WINNING"

175 *The reservations he had about McCain*: Oral History Interview, 2002.

176 *For thirty-six days*: Ibid.

178 *"Do we really want"*: Mitch McConnell, "In Defense of Soft Money," *New York Times*, April 1, 2001.

178 *He implored Democrats*: Dyche, *Republican Leader*, 153.

179 *One of Weinberg's prime attacks*: Oral History Interview, 2003.

179 *"It's amazing what winning big does for your image"*: Ibid.

180 *Still, things had not gone according to plan*: Ibid.

181 *"Would I like to be majority leader? You bet"*: Ibid.

181 *In public, when asked*: *Courier-Journal*, December 14, 2002.

181 *Through the holiday season*: Oral History Interview, 2003.

182 *The heart catheterization revealed*: Ibid.

182 *Feingold wrote him a note*: McConnell interview with author.

183 *"We don't really know any of this yet"*: Oral History Interview, 2003.

184 *Otherwise, he wasn't so charitable*: Ibid.

184 *Carl Hulse wrote in the* New York Times: Carl Hulse, "Losing Crusade May Still Pay Dividends for a Senator," *New York Times*, December 27, 2003.

185 *"The sad thing for the Senate"*: Oral History Interview, 2003.

185 *Bush recalled his frustration*: Bush interview with author.

186 *Things got worse after the first debate*: Oral History Interview, 2004.

186 *He began to feel increasingly confident*: Ibid.

187 *He was getting positive national notice*: Dyche, *Republican Leader*, 185.

SIXTEEN: DREAM DEFERRED, ACHIEVED

190 *Nothing in the Senate rules*: Oral History Interview, 2005.

191 *He couldn't do so*: Ibid.

193 *Otherwise, McConnell said*: Dyche, *Republican Leader*, 189.

194 *"I sort of stuck with Lott"*: Oral History Interview, 2005.

195 *"Mitch has a sharp political nose, and he smelled trouble"*: George W. Bush, *Decision Points* (New York: Crown, 2010), 355.

196 *McConnell has a distinctly different recollection of that conversation*: Oral History Interview, 2010.

196 *Democrats crushed Republicans*: Oral History Interview, 2006.

196 *He was in the minority, but he was finally on top*: Ibid.

197 *"Yet the challenges ahead"*: Congressional Record, vol. 153, no. 1 (January 4, 2007): S11–S13, https://www.govinfo.gov/content/pkg/CREC-2007-01-04 /html/CREC-2007-01-04-pt1-PgS11-2.htm.

198 *He soon met with Reid*: Oral History Interview, 2006.

199 *McConnell was somewhat indifferent*: Ibid.

SEVENTEEN: THE POWER OF NO

202   *Unlike McCain, McConnell had a clear theory*: Oral History Interview, 2008.

202   *"It's no accident"*: Ibid.

202   *McConnell ran his race like he was running for governor*: Ibid.

203   *"Let me say it one more time"*: McConnell, *The Long Game*, 170.

203   *"Everyone in the room was spellbound"*: Ibid., 173.

203   *The following morning*: Ibid., 174.

204   *"I know we're looking at a potential loss tonight"*: Ibid., 181.

206   *Though diminished with his smaller minority*: Ibid., 184.

206   *He thought the government*: Oral History Interview, 2008.

207   *When asked what Obama was really like*: McConnell, *The Long Game*, 184.

207   *David Axelrod, Obama's senior adviser, recalled*: Axelrod interview with author.

207   *"Joe's a good guy"*: Oral History Interview, 2008.

207   *Emanuel instantly smelled a trap*: Emanuel interview with author.

208   *In public, McConnell said the administration*: Jeff Zeleny, "Initial Steps by Obama Suggest a Bipartisan Flair," *New York Times*, November 23, 2008.

209   *Yet he worried that the honeymoon*: Oral History Interview, 2010.

209   *"Republicans are monolithically against the health care legislation"*: *New York Times*, March 6, 2010.

210   *More than a decade later he conceded*: McConnell interview with author.

211   *McConnell was dismissive*: Oral History Interview, 2010.

212   *"Almost without exception"*: McConnell, *The Long Game*, 206.

212   *McConnell badly misread that race*: Oral History Interview, 2010.

213   *"People always assumed bad blood"*: Salter interview with author.

214   *"No, it was calculated"*: Oral History Interview, 2010.

215   *McConnell was not persuaded*: *New York Times*, David M. Herszenhorn, "House Set to Follow Senate in Approving Tax Deal," *New York Times*, December 15, 2010.

215   *"This gives McConnell immense clout"*: Jennifer Steinhauer, "McConnell Eases Talk of a Thaw," *New York Times*, November 4, 2010.

EIGHTEEN: "ANYBODY . . . KNOW HOW TO MAKE A DEAL?"

216   *Though he could be windy*: Oral History Interview, 2011.

217   *"The crisis seemed to demand"*: Paul Kane, "Debt deadline may provide another Mitch McConnell moment," *Washington Post*, July 30, 2011.

218   *"Pivotal to the final deal-making"*: Jackie Calmes and Jennifer Steinhauer, "Deal Was Forged Over Choices and Chinese Food," *New York Times*, August 1, 2011.

219   *McConnell held his opinions*: Boehner interview with author.

220   *As troubling as the inertia was*: Oral History Interview, 2011.

220   *But he said the record shows*: Zamore interview with author.

223   *He thought Mitt Romney was the only credible candidate*: Oral History Interview, 2011.

223   *McConnell called the selection of candidates like them*: Oral History Interview, 2013.

225   *If no deal was reached*: Oral History Interview, 2012.
225   *The Senate voted for the deal*: David A. Fahrenthold, Paul Kane, and Lori Montgomery, "How McConnell and Biden pulled Congress away from the fiscal cliff," *Washington Post*
226   *"I think the so-called establishment forces"*: Oral History Interview, 2013.
227   *"What gets you respect"*: Oral History Interview, 2015.
227   *In November, though, Obama*: "Transcript: President Obama's Nov. 5 News Conference on Midterm Election Results," *Washington Post*, November 5, 2014, https://www.washingtonpost.com/politics/transcript-president-obamas-remarks-on-midterm-election-results/2014/11/05/491a02b2-6524-11e4-9fdc-d43b053ecb4d_story.html.
227   *McConnell's first speech*: Congressional Record, vol. 1, no. 2 (January 7, 2015): https://www.congress.gov/114/crec/2015/01/07/CREC-2015-01-07-pt1-PgS27.pdf.
229   *He was aligning himself*: McConnell interview with author.
230   *"Most of the time he's brutal"*: Boxer interview with author.
230   *"What we just saw today"*: Mike DeBonis, "Ted Cruz calls Mitch McConnell a liar on the Senate floor," *Washington Post*, July 24, 2015.
232   *"Imagine that in 2016"*: Oral History Interview, 2013.

NINETEEN: "SCALIA'S SEAT"
234   *When I first asked him*: McConnell interview with author.
235   *"It's the exercise of power"*: Gold interview with author.
237   *McConnell defiantly told the president*: Carl Hulse, *Confirmation Bias* (New York: Harper, 2019), 46.
238   *McConnell, as he had done*: McConnell interview with author.
238   *One thing both sides agreed on*: New York Times, February 18, 2016.
239   *Abegg, who was visiting his parents*: Abegg interview with author.
239   *He consulted with Leonard Leo*: Hulse, *Confirmation Bias*, 15.
241   *"I hope they're fair"*: White House transcript, March 16, 2016. https://obamawhitehouse.archives.gov/the-press-office/2016/03/16/remarks-president-announcing-judge-merrick-garland-his-nominee-supreme.
241   *"We had this most unusual nominee"*: Oral History Interview, 2017.
242   *Trump took the advice*: Ibid.
242   *McConnell urged Trump*: Ruth Marcus, *Supreme Ambition* (New York: Simon & Schuster, 2019).
242   *"What I tried to do"*: Oral History Interview, 2016.
244   *"This guy's a central casting perfect"*: Oral History Interview, 2017.
245   *Gorsuch would go on to hear a case*: Hulse, *Confirmation Bias*, 6.
245   *"Just looking at the politics"*: Oral History Interview, 2017.
245   *Murkowski, for one*: Murkowski interview with author.
246   *In many ways, Kaine likes McConnell*: Kaine interview with author.
247   *Senator Angus King*: King interview with author.
247   *Other Republicans, like Susan Collins, and later Mitt Romney*: Collins and Romney interviews with author.
247   *To Keith Runyon*: Runyon interview with author.

248 *"The vast majority of cases"*: Karlan interview with author.

248 *Karlan noted that*: Ibid.

TWENTY: POWER BASE

251 *"If you open the door a crack"*: Holmes interview with author.

252 *Fred Wertheimer*: Wertheimer interview with author.

252 *In multiple interviews*: McConnell interviews with author.

253 *Instead, he was blunt*: Holmes interview with author.

253 *"Basically American Crossroads"*: Oral History Interview, 2016.

254 *"He didn't leave a backbench member of Congress behind"*: Young interview with author.

254 *"I'm not one to allow things to be ambiguous"*: Ibid.

256 *Brian Slodysko of the Associated Press*: Brian Slodysko, "Bayh Didn't Stay Overnight in Indiana Condo Once in 2010," Associated Press, October 21, 2016, https://apnews.com/united-states-government-united-states-congress -senate-elections-united-states-senate-51a716548ddb41efad6e2dd06ae3366b.

TWENTY-ONE: "NOT VERY SMART, IRASCIBLE . . . DESPICABLE . . . BEYOND ERRATIC"

261 *"We were all mad as hell about it"*: Oral History Interview, 2016.

262 *Senator Michael Bennet conceded*: Bennet interview with author, May 21, 2024.

264 *"I was so close to pulling my support"*: Ryan interview with author.

266 *"Like many of his actions"*: Carl Hulse, "Trump's Twitter Fury at McConnell Risks Alienating a Key Ally," *New York Times*, August 10, 2017.

266 *McConnell and the president had a heated argument*: McConnell interview with author.

268 *"I took great umbrage"*: Brennan interview with author.

268 *"I think Brennan wanted to hurt me"*: McConnell interview with author.

269 *"You can sort of see it building"*: Oral History Interview, 2018.

270 *When things had looked grim*: *Newsweek*, October 1, 2018.

270 *But a short time later*: Oral History Interview, 2018.

271 *But there was no orchestrating Trump*: Oral History Interview, 2018.

272 *McConnell put it starkly*: Oral History Interview, 2018.

276 *"I told him, I'm okay in Kentucky"*: McConnell interview with author.

277 *Four days after the election*: Brian Slodysko, "EXPLAINER: Why AP Called the 2020 Election for Joe Biden," Associated Press, November 7, 2020, https://apnews.com/article/why-did-ap-call-election-for-biden-fe79276cd9175fffc 7cf4fb58045fcf9.

278 *"His behavior since losing the election"*: Oral History Interview, 2022.

TWENTY-TWO: "THE McCONNELL COURT"

281 *That was not*: Oral History Interview, 2020.

283 *There also had been quick confirmations*: Background interview.

284 *They even created*: Author interview with Senate staff on background.

284 *"Mitch McConnell has trained us"*: Ibid.

284 *"It caused me to vote"*: Collins interview with author.
284 *The next morning*: Author interview with Senate staff on background.
285 *Reflecting on the process*: Oral History Interview, 2020.
287 *When he was a senior*: Background interview.
287 *So he asked McConnell*: Elizabeth Williamson and Rebecca R. Ruiz, "McConnell Protégé Takes Center Stage in Fight to Remake Judiciary," *New York Times*, May 5, 2020.
287 *It was not long, though*: McConnell interview with author.
288 *No promises were made*: Senate Judiciary Committee questionnaire for the nomination of Justin Walker to the United States Court of Appeals for the DC Circuit, May 13, 2020, https://www.judiciary.senate.gov/imo/media/doc/Walker%20Responses%20to%20QFRs1.pdf.
289 *In one speech*: Elizabeth Williamson and Rebecca R. Ruiz, "McConnell Protégé Takes Center Stage in Fight to Remake Judiciary,"
289 *He was able to do that*: Background interview.
290 *Trump dominated the conversation*: McConnell interview with author.
290 *"Yes sir, it is"*: Ibid.
290 *Trump said, "The guy looks like Cary Grant"*: Ibid.
291 *"He's got Supreme Court"*: Oral History Interview, 2020.
291 *The Congressional Research Service found*: Judicial Nomination Statistics and Analysis: U.S. Circuit and District Courts, 1977–2022, https://sgp.fas.org/crs/misc/R45622.pdf.
292 *Indeed, Trump in his one term*: Pew Research Center, January 12, 2021, https://www.pewresearch.org/short-reads/2021/01/13/how-trump-compares-with-other-recent-presidents-in-appointing-federal-judges/ft_21-01-07_trumpjudges_2-png/.
292 *McConnell gives Trump little credit*: Oral History Interview, 2020.

TWENTY-THREE: JANUARY 6
294 *"We had two grandstanders in the Senate"*: Oral History Interview, 2024.
294 *The bulk of McConnell's remarks*: Liz Cheney, *Oath and Honor* (New York: Little, Brown, 2023), 39–40.
295 *Mitt Romney texted McConnell on January 2*: McKay Coppins, *Romney: A Reckoning* (New York: Scribner, 2023), 274.
296 *The women were more concerned than their boss*: McConnell interviews with author.
296 *"This is about whether we're going to break this democracy"*: 2021.
297 *He was prepared to walk in with Pence*: Cheney, *Oath and Honor*, 88.
297 *"We'll either hasten down a poisonous path"*: Congressional Record, vol. 167, no. 4 (January 6, 2021): https://www.congress.gov/117/crec/2021/01/06/CREC-2021-01-06.pdf.
298 *At about 1:15 p.m., Soderstrom*: Soderstrom interview with author.
298 *"The principal reason for it was the president himself"*: Oral History Interview, 2021.
298 *McConnell responded, "That's exactly the plan"*: Cheney, *Oath and Honor*, 103.

298 *"I looked to my left"*: McConnell interview with author.

298 *Soderstrom and Muchow*: Soderstrom and Muchow interviews with author.

299 *"I wasn't thinking"*: McConnell interview with author.

300 *"You know with the Capitol under direct attack"*: Ibid.

301 *"I glanced up and on this little television"*: Popp interview with author.

302 *One member of McConnell's staff dialed Bill Barr*: Barr interview with author.

303 *"Believe it or not, Ted Cruz"*: McConnell interview with author.

303 *Reflecting on that day, he said, "It's hard to imagine this happening"*: McConnell interview with author.

304 *Recalling that conversation*: Soderstrom interview with author.

304 *"He was physically just beat"*: Popp interview with author.

306 *"I'm not at all conflicted"*: Oral History Interview, 2021.

307 *Cassidy thought that meant*: Cassidy interview with author.

308 *"January 6th was a disgrace"*: Congressional Record, vol. 167, no. 28, (February 13, 2021): S735–S736, https://www.govinfo.gov/content/pkg/CREC-2021-02-13/html/CREC-2021-02-13-pt1-PgS735-2.htm.

309 *"I can understand the rationale"*: Biden interview with author.

309 *"Where I differed with Liz"*: McConnell interview with author.

309 *"Mitch McConnell knows"*: Liz Cheney post on X, June 13, 2024, https://x.com/Liz_Cheney/status/1801357007707898160.

TWENTY-FOUR: THE FALL

311 *McConnell was put in an ambulance*: Author interviews with McConnell's closest aides.

312 *In the hospital*: Accounts by McConnell and his aides in interviews with author.

313 *But he also tried to defuse the moment with humor*: Congressional Record, vol. 169, no. 63 (April 17, 2023): https://www.congress.gov/118/crec/2023/04/17/169/63/CREC-2023-04-17-senate.pdf.

314 *"Shrink the room"*: McConnell interview with author.

316 *The previous week*: Jonathan Martin, "McConnell in Winter: Inside the GOP Leader's Attempt to Thwart Trump," *Politico*, August 14, 2023, https://www.politico.com/news/magazine/2023/08/14/mitch-mcconnell-trump-00110969.

TWENTY-FIVE: POWER

322 *On Garland, "I thought he"*: Biden interview with author, December 2023.

323 *Rahm Emanuel, an astute power player*: Emanuel interview with author.

323 *Rob Portman, a former senator from Ohio*: Portman interview with author.

324 *Twenty county Republican parties*: Austin Horn, "Who Are the 'Liberty' Republicans in Kentucky Politics? What Do They Want?," *Lexington Herald-Leader*, May 20, 2024, https://www.kentucky.com/news/politics-government/article288555164.html.

325 *Obama, his senior adviser said*: Axelrod interview with author.

325 *Josh Holmes recalled meetings*: Holmes interview with author.

326 *"He's tried to keep the party together"*: Shelby interview with author.

326 *"He certainly has sway"*: Sinema interview with author.

327 *Gates has frequently come*: Gates interview with author.

327 *McConnell had imited room to maneuver*: Ritchie interview with author.

328 *When he came to Washington*: Cotton interview with author.

329 *"The truth is he is sacrificial"*: Scott interview with author.

329 *"His unwavering focus"*: Young interview with author.

330 *He also considers them to be among his better friends*: Murkowski interview with author.

332 *"Let me tell you what will not be a part of our agenda"*: Amy B. Wang, Josh Dawsey, and Mariana Alfaro, "McConnell Rejects GOP Sen. Rick Scott's Tax Plan and Agenda, Insists He Will Remain Republican Leader," *Washington Post*, March 1, 2022.

333 *McConnell laid out the case*: McConnell interview with author.

333 *"Mitch got to air his feelings"*: Ryan interview with author.

334 *"There is a lot of contradiction in the man"*: Ritchie interview with author.

335 *In Ohio, McConnell and Portman*: McConnell and Portman interviews with author.

336 *"I don't think Rick makes a very good victim"*: McConnell interview with author.

337 *McConnell's longtime colleague and friend*: Collins interview with author.

338 *"There's nothing left of that party"*: Bennet interview with author.

338 *"If you measure it"*: Kaine interview with author.

342 *"The Democrats hate me"*: McConnell interview with author.

343 *"One of life's most underappreciated talents"*: "McConnell Remarks on Last Term as Republican Leader," Republican Leader, U.S. Senate, February 28, 2024, https://www.republicanleader.senate.gov/newsroom/remarks/mcconnell-remarks-on-last-term-as-republican-leader.

EPILOGUE: "THE LAST THING YOU DO"

346 *Two months after the visit*: McConnell Center archives, University of Louisville.

348 *Before he left, he met with President Biden, telling him, "I've got internal issues here"*: Oral History Interview, 2022.

348 *"The truth is none of us took a bath for about two days"*: McConnell interview with author.

349 *The atmosphere was serious*: Ibid.

349 *He wanted to "push back"*: McConnell interview with author.

350 *After their very first meeting*: Markarova interview with author.

355 *"It's been, from a personal point of view"*: McConnell interview with author.

BIBLIOGRAPHY

Bade, Rachel, and Karoun Demirjian. *Unchecked: The Untold Story behind Congress's Botched Impeachments of Donald Trump.* New York: William Morrow, 2022.

Baker, Peter, and Susan Glasser. *The Divider: Trump In The White House, 2017–2021.* New York: Doubleday, 2022.

Barone, Michael, and Grant Ujifusa. *The Almanac of American Politics 1986.* Washington, DC: National Journal, 1986.

Boehner, John. *On the House: A Washington Memoir.* New York: St. Martin's Press, 2021.

Boxer, Barbara. *The Art of the Tough: Fearlessly Facing Politics and Life.* New York: Hachette, 2016.

Bruno, Richard L. *The Polio Paradox: Understanding and Treating 'Post-Polio Syndrome' and Chronic Fatigue.* New York: Grand Central, 2002.

Calmes, Jackie. *Dissent: The Radicalization of the Republican Party and Its Capture of the Court.* New York: Twelve, 2021.

Cheney, Liz. *Oath and Honor: A Memoir and a Warning.* New York: Little Brown, 2023.

Coppins, McKay. *Romney: A Reckoning.* New York: Scribner, 2023.

Dyche, John David. *Republican Leader: Political Biography of Senator Mitch McConnell.* Washington, DC: ISI Books, 2009.

Greene, Robert. *The 48 Laws of Power.* New York: Penguin Books, 1998.

Haberman, Maggie. *Confidence Man: The Making of Donald Trump and the Breaking of America.* New York: Penguin Press, 2022.

Halstead, Lauro. *An Unexpected Journey: A Physician's Life in the Shadow of Polio.* Scotts Valley, CA: CreateSpace, 2016.

Hulse, Carl. *Confirmation Bias: Inside Washington's War over the Supreme Court, from Scalia's Death to Justice Kavanaugh.* New York: Harper, 2019.

Jentleson, Adam. *Kill Switch: The Rise of the Modern Senate and the Crippling of American Democracy.* New York: Liveright, 2021.

Lemire, Jonathan. *The Big Lie: Election Chaos, Political Opportunism, and the State of American Politics after 2020*. New York: Flatiron Books, 2022.

MacGillis, Alec. *The Cynic: The Political Education of Mitch McConnell*. New York: Simon & Schuster, 2014.

McConnell, Mitch. *The Long Game: A Memoir*. New York: Sentinel, 2016.

Obama, Barack. *A Promised Land*. New York: Crown, 2020.

Oshinksy, David. *Polio: An American Story*. New York: Oxford University Press, 2006.

Paulson, Henry M., Jr. *On the Brink: Inside the Race to Stop the Collapse of the Global Financial System*. New York: Business Plus, 2010.

Plagemann, Bentz. *My Place to Stand*. New York: Farrar, Straus, 1949.

Reid, Harry. *The Good Fight: Hard Lessons from Searchlight to Washington*. New York: Putnam, 2008.

Rucker, Philip, and Carol Leonnig. *A Very Stable Genius: Donald J. Trump's Testing of America*. New York: Penguin Press, 2020.

———. *I Alone Can Fix It: Donald J. Trump's Catastrophic Final Year*. New York: Penguin Press. 2021.

Shapiro, Ira. *The Betrayal: How Mitch McConnell and the Senate Republicans Abandoned America*. Lanham, MD: Roman & Littlefield, 2022.

Strauss, Elaine M. *In My Heart I'm Still Dancing*. New York: Strauss, 1979.

Tobin, James. *The Man He Became: How FDR Defied Polio to Win the Presidency*. New York: Simon & Schuster, 2013.

Woodward, Bob. *Rage*. New York: Simon & Schuster, 2020.

INDEX

Abegg, John, 239, 240, 243
abortion, x
  Harry Blackmun's majority opinion on, 77–78
  James Bopp's work on, 168
  and filling of Scalia's Supreme Court seat, 238, 246
  impact of appeals court rulings on, 291
  McConnell's block of Fiscal Court legislation on, 100–101
  McConnell's early position on, 92, 101
  McConnell's legislative record on, 143, 144
  Mark Neumann's opposition to, 171
  overturning constitutional right to, 242, 285, 321
  Senate Leadership Fund donors on, 334
  see also Roe v. Wade
Abrams, Floyd, 184
Abramson, Jerry, 83, 92, 151–52, 162–63, 187
Access Hollywood (TV series), 242, 243, 263
Achille Lauro, seizure of, 123
ACLU (American Civil Liberties Union), 167
Adelson, Miriam, 252
Adelson, Sheldon, 252
affirmative action, x, 285, 327
Affordable Care Act (Obamacare), 206, 208–11, 227–28, 265–66
Afghanistan, War in, 183, 327
"Against the Tide" (Law), 152–53
Aiken, George, 197
Ailes, Roger, 113–16, 139, 141, 148
Akin, Todd, 223–24

Alabama, 2017 special election, 266–67
Alda, Alan, 13
Alexander, Lamar, 73, 127, 330, 345
Alfalfa Club dinner, 181, 228
Ali, Muhammad, 43
Alito, Samuel, 192–93, 221, 285–87
Almanac of American Politics, The, 123
Al Saud, Bandar bin Sultan, 156
American Bar Association, 289
American Civil Liberties Union (ACLU), 167
American Council of Young Political Leaders, 100
American Crossroads, 226, 251–53
America's Most Wanted (TV series), 106
Angle, Sharron, 214
Applewhite, Scottie, 315
Archie (McConnell house employee), 33, 34
Ashbrook, John, 256
Ashcroft, John, 100
Ashland Oil Company, 160
Associated Press, 3, 123, 226, 256, 278, 315
Athens, Ala., 17–18, 23, 24, 31, 33–36
Auburn University, 18
Augusta, Ga., 36–40
Augusta Tigers, 39
Aung San Suu Kyi, 170, 222
Axelrod, David, 207, 325

Babbage, Bob, 163
Baker, Howard, 73, 107
Baker, Rose, 178–79
Baldwin, Tammy, 323
Barkley, Alben, 202, 296

Barnett, Barney, 84, 89
Barnett, Ross, 56
Barnett & McConnell (law firm), 84
Barr, Andy, 274
Barr, Bill, 302
Barrasso, John, 315, 348
Barrett, Amy Coney, 248, 276, 282–85, 334
Bayh, Birch, 65, 78, 255
Bayh, Evan, 255–57
Baytown, Tex., 18–19
Beechmont Pony League, 44
Bellarmine University, 155
Bennet, Michael, 261, 338
Berea College, 34
Bernanke, Ben, 203, 224
Beshear, Andy, 165, 316
Beshear, Steve, 162–63, 165
Bevin, Matt, 226
Biden, Beau, 229
Biden, Joe, and administration, 232, 259, 299, 313, 348
    in 2020 presidential election, 277–78, 293, 294, 298, 303
    and 2022 midterm election, 331, 334
    capacity to serve questions about, 318, 319, 342
    death of son, 229, 323
    on election-year Supreme Court nominees, 234, 237, 238
    foreign aid and border bill, 351, 353, 354
    Merrick Garland's appointment by, 341
    infrastructure bill, 263
    McConnell's debate with, 132–34
    McConnell's Obama-era deals with, 214–19, 225, 314, 325
    McConnell's relationship with, 323, 339–40
    on McConnell's Supreme Court power play, 321–22
    McConnell's views of, 207
    oppositional politics targeting, 305
    presidential aspirations of, 122
    requests for Ukrainian investigation of, 272, 347
    and second Trump impeachment, 306, 309
    Supreme Court nominee of, 239
Bingham, Barry, Jr., 94
bin Laden, Osama, 222
Birmingham, Ala, 17, 18

Black Americans
    appeal of South African sanctions to, 124–25
    Jefferson County discrimination lawsuit, 99
    Jim Crow South for, 33–34, 39
    racial inequality in Louisville, 42
    racism targeting, 33, 57, 59, 77, 180, 181, 336
    Republican senators representing, 225–26
    and Clarence Thomas's Supreme Court nomination, 151
    see also racial segregation
Blackmun, Harry, 77–79
Bloch, Julia Chang, 155
block and blame strategy, 198, 214–15
    see also oppositional politics
Blunt, Roy, 222, 330
Boehner, John, 217–19, 224, 231, 232
Bonenburg, Germany, 27–28
Bono, 170
Boozman, John, 328
border crisis, 351–56
Boren, David, 128
Bork, Robert, 89, 132–34, 150, 240
Boxer, Barbara, 157–58, 171, 230
Boyd, Janet, 47
Boy Scouts of America, 35
Bradlee, Ben, 13
Bradley, Bill, 122, 151
Brandeis School of Law, 288
Braun, Mike, 270–71
Brennan, John, 268
Brennan, William, 286
Britt, Katie, 330, 333
Bronze Star, 30
Brooke, Edward, 74–75
Brooklyn Dodgers, 39
Brooks, Mo, 333
Brown, Carl, 99–100
Brown, John Y., 107
Brown, Mike, 99, 115, 126–27
Brown, Scott, 211
Brownback, Sam, 183
Brown-Foreman distillery, 91
Brown v. Board of Education, 39, 56
Bruno, Richard, 9, 11–13
Buchanan, Pat, 151
Buck, Ken, 214
Buckley v. Valeo, 166
Budd, Ted, 335

budget reconciliation, 126
Bunning, Jim, 107, 186, 187
Burger-Phillips department store, 21
Burma (Myanmar), 170, 222
Burr, Richard, 257
Bush, George H. W., and administration, 139,
    156, 206, 296
  in 1980 Republican primary, 102
  in 1987 Republican primary, 129
  1992 presidential campaign of, 151
  campaigning for McConnell by, 116–17,
    136, 137
  declining popularity of, 141, 146, 147, 150
  McConnell's Kennebunkport visit with,
    134–35
  at McConnell's swearing-in ceremony, 121
  Supreme Court nominees of, 150–51
  tax policy of, 141
Bush, George W., and administration, 199, 201
  in 2000 presidential election, 175–77
  2004 presidential campaign for, 183–84,
    186, 187
  2006 midterm as referendum on, 194–96
  Cabinet recommendations to, 176
  entitlement reform efforts of, 207
  filibustering of judicial nominees of, 178,
    185, 189–90, 222
  judicial recommendations to, 153
  Brett Kavanaugh and, 288
  McConnell on confirming nominees of,
    198, 234
  McConnell's relationship with, 325
  McConnell's work for agenda of, 181–83,
    193, 210
  in subprime housing crisis, 203, 204
  Supreme Court nominees of, 191–92
  tax cuts under, 215, 217, 224, 296
  on Trump's inaugural address, 259
  on working with McConnell, 185–86, 204
Bush, Prescott, 185
Bush v. Gore, 176, 184
Butler, Mike, 50–52
Button (dog), 35, 37, 44
Byrd, Robert, Jr., 121, 126, 129, 180

campaign finance legislation
  1973 op-ed by McConnell on, 85–86
  1986 Senate debate on, 128–30
  and Citizens United v. FEC, 251, 252
  Clinton-era Democratic violations of,
    169–70

McCain–Feingold Act, 166–68, 177–78,
    184, 193
  McConnell–McCain debate on, 173–74
  McConnell's failed attempt at, 138
  opposition by McConnell to, 153–54,
    160–61, 166–68, 177–78, 182, 212–13
Campbell, Bill Nighthorse, 183
Camp Gordon, 36
Camp Swift, 30–31
candidate quality, 171, 195, 333
Cannon, Aileen, 335
cap-and-trade energy policy, 211–12
Capital Gang (TV series), 173
Capito, Shelley Moore, 338
Capitol Police, 115, 299–301
CARES Act, 275, 278, 279
Carlson, Margaret, 173
Carmack, Terry, 110–14, 152, 311, 313
Caro, Robert, 187
Carswell, Harrold, 76–77, 79
Cassidy, Bill, 307, 325, 329, 344
Central Intelligence Agency (CIA), 268, 272
Chao, Angela, 342
Chao, Elaine, 181, 233, 312, 316, 339, 346
  in George W. Bush's 2000 presidential
    campaign, 175
  cabinet appointments for, 176, 261
  in McConnell's 1994 campaign, 164
  McConnell's first date with, 155–56
  resignation of, from Donald Trump's
    cabinet, 304–5
  Donald Trump's attacks on, 336
Chavez, Linda, 176
Cheney, Dick, 176, 193
Cheney, Liz, 294, 295, 298, 308, 309
Chevron, 252
Chevron decision, overturning, 245, 334–35
CHIPS Act, 322
Christian Coalition, 288
CIA (Central Intelligence Agency), 268, 272
Cipollone, Pat, 281, 282
CIT finance company, 17, 18
Citizens United v. FEC, 238, 251, 252, 257
civil rights
  John Sherman Cooper's views on, 62–63
  Barry Goldwater's views of, 56
  legislation on, 63–66
  Dean and Mac McConnell's support for,
    63–64
  Mitch McConnell's views on, 60–63
Civil Rights Act (1964), 63, 64, 125, 153, 197

civil rights movement, 42, 59–62, 193–94
Civil War
  Democratic Party in, 39, 40, 86
  Jim Crow South's commemoration of, 33, 36
  Kentucky's allegiance in, 42
  military personnel in U.S. Capitol during, 299–300
  slave trade in Louisville before, 42
Clark, George Rogers, 41
Clark, Joe, 64
Clay, Cassius, Jr., 43
Clay, Henry, vii, viii, 161, 187
Cleveland, Robin, 124, 346
Clinton, Bill, and administration, 175, 184, 213
  1992 presidential campaign, 151, 201
  1996 presidential campaign, 163
  campaign finance reform efforts of, 160, 177
  health care plan of, 167, 287
  impeachment of, 172
  scandal involving Monica Lewinsky and, 171, 172
  soft money scandal during, 169–70
Clinton, Hillary, 246
  2008 Democratic primary campaign, 199, 201
  2016 presidential campaign, 232, 235
  2016 presidential election for, 250, 260, 268
  potential Supreme Court nominees of, 241, 321
  support of Iraq War by, 212
Club for Growth, 226, 254–55
CNN, 288
Coats, Dan, 254
Cohen, Norton, 287
Cohn, Victor, 13–14
collective bargaining, 93
Collins, Martha Layne, 127
Collins, Susan, 343
  on Amy Coney Barrett's nomination, 284
  and blocking of Merrick Garland's confirmation, 240, 247, 284
  on changes in Republican Party, 337
  failure of, to endorse Donald Trump, 344
  McConnell's treatment of, 326, 330
  support for Ukraine from, 348
Columbia Law School, 137
Comer, James, 223

Comey, James, 268, 289
Common Cause, 252
compromise, 216–17, 229, 237, 352
Congress: The Sapless Branch (Clark), 64
Congressional Quarterly, 128
Congressional Research Service, 291–92
Connally, John, 86–87
Connally, Nellie, 87
Constitutional Coalition, 167
"Contract with America" bills, 163, 287
Cook, Marlow
  1974 Senate campaign of, 80, 87
  Dee Huddleston and, 107, 112
  as Jefferson County judge executive, 88, 92
  McConnell's falling out with, 80, 82, 112
  McConnell's work for, 70–80, 83
  John Yarmuth's work for, 104
Cook, Nancy, 81
Cookie (dog), 35, 37, 44
Coolidge, Calvin, 104
Cooper, John Sherman, 67, 179, 191, 211
  ambassadorship for, 82
  death of, 153
  endorsement of McConnell by, 92
  and McConnell's discharge from Army Reserves, 69, 70
  McConnell's internship for, 58, 62–65, 296
  as McConnell's role model, 46, 102, 123, 159
  at McConnell's swearing-in ceremony, 121
  policies of McConnell vs., 123–24
  support of civil rights bill by, 66, 125, 153
Cornyn, John, 326, 348
coronavirus pandemic, 274–79, 282–83, 290–91, 294
Cotton, Tom, 327–28, 336–38
Courier-Journal, 70, 82, 95, 112, 147, 247–48
  on 1984 Senate election, 119
  Jerry Abramson's support of McConnell in, 83, 152
  on campaign finance reform, 130
  civil rights issues in, 42
  editorial on McConnell's campaign strategy in, 163–64
  endorsement of McConnell by, 93–94, 139, 140
  on McConnell as county judge executive, 99
  McConnell on women's equality in, 75
  on McConnell's campaigning, 146
  McConnell's criticism of, 98–99

on McConnell's early political positions, 92

on McConnell's efforts for missing and exploited children, 106

McConnell's first year in the Senate, 126–27

on McConnell's image, 103–4, 111

on McConnell's internship for Gene Snyder, 57

McConnell's op-ed on campaign finance in, 85–87

on McConnell's record-setting number of terms, 165, 205

opposition research leaked to, 115, 145

photo of McConnell and Barry Goldwater in, 55–56

on William Rehnquist's confirmation hearing, 81

on South African sanctions, 125

Justin Walker's defense of Christian Coalition in, 288

Craig, Larry, 180

Crimson Record, 49

Cross, Al, 152, 205

Cruz, Ted

and certification of 2020 presidential election, 293, 294, 298, 303

criticism of McConnell by, 230–31, 329

on filling Scalia's Supreme Court seat, 236

in Lout Caucus, 307

McConnell's Alfalfa Club remarks on, 228

Cunningham's Restaurant, 288

Cures Act, 323

Czechoslovakia, 27–30

Daines, Steve, 341

D'Amato, Alfonse, 137

Daniels, Mitch, 110

Darlington School, 18

Daschle, Tom, 157

Davidson, Philip, 56

Davis, Jefferson, vii, 33

Day, Maxine, 36

Dean, Howard, 184, 186

debt limit crises, 216–19, 313–14, 322, 341

Decision Points (Bush), 196

DeMint, Jim, 214, 225

Democratic Senatorial Campaign Committee, 205

Democrats and Democratic Party

in 1980s, 122

backlash to overturning *Roe v. Wade* from, 321, 334

on blocking of Merrick Garland's confirmation, 322–24

campaign finance violations by, 169–70

changes to judicial nominee approval process by, 261–62, 291

Civil War–era, 39, 40, 86

filibustering of judicial nominees by, 178, 185, 189–90, 222, 244, 262

McConnell family support for, 39, 40

McConnell's work with, 97–99, 140, 160, 183, 193, 198, 213–14, 219, 224–25, 338

oppositional politics by, 229

view of McConnell by, 202, 205, 227, 292, 321–23

see also specific individuals

DeVos, Betsy, 168, 261

Dionne, E. J., 237

Dirksen, Everett, 153

Distinguished Service Medal, 30

District of Columbia Circuit Court of Appeals, 220, 240, 243, 288–91

Dobbs decision, 334

Dodd, Christopher, 125

Dole, Bob

McConnell on position of, 75

presidential runs for, 101, 129, 156

as Senate Republican leader, 121–23, 154

support for McConnell from, 95, 117, 150

Dole, Elizabeth, 117

Donnelly, Joe, 270–71

Douglas, William O., 13

Dowd, Maureen, 173–74

Dred Scott case, 78, 184

Dudgeon, Pete, 47

Duke University, 288

DuPont Company, 37, 39–40, 43–44

duPont Manual High School, 42–50

Durbin, Dick, 301

Durenburg, Germany, 26

Dyche, John David, 55, 86, 95, 169, 179

Edsall, Thomas, 130

Eighth Circuit Court of Appeals, 248

Eisenhower, Dwight D., and administration, 49, 134

John Sherman Cooper's work for, 63

McConnell family's support for, 37, 39, 347

Eisenhower, Dwight D. (cont.)
  Republican majority during, 161, 287
  Supreme Court nominees of, 286
Eisenhower, Susan, 134
Electoral College
  2020 meeting of, 278, 294, 302
  formal counting of the vote of, 293, 294,
    298
  McConnell on Donald Trump's respect
    for, 300
  Ross Perot's performance in, 151
Eleventh Circuit Court of Appeals, 248
Emanuel, Rahm, 207–8, 323
Emberton, Tom, 83–84
Emerson, Ralph Waldo, 49
environmentalism, 96, 99, 117, 291
Equal Rights Amendment (ERA), 75
Estrada, Miguel, 185
European–African–Middle Eastern Campaign
    Medal, 30
Exxon, 139

Face the Nation (TV series), 172, 355
family and medical leave, 145
Fancy Farm event, 113–14, 135, 143, 179
Farm Bureau, 124, 255, 316
Farrow, Mia, 13
Fauci, Anthony, 284
Federal Bureau of Investigation (FBI), 302
Federal Election Commission, 130
  see also Citizens United v. FEC;
    McConnell v. the Federal Election
    Commission
Federalist Society, 234, 242, 243, 246, 334
Federal Maritime Commission, 156
Feingold, Russ, 166–68, 171, 182, 258
  see also McCain–Feingold Act
Feinstein, Dianne, 319
Fetterman, John, 319
Fifth Circuit Court of Appeals, 248
filibuster
  to block January 6th commission,
    305–6
  budget reconciliation and, 126
  of Bush-era judicial nominees, 178, 185,
    189–90, 222
  of conference committee appointees, 154,
    160–61
  elimination of, for federal judges, 291
  of judicial nominees, by Democrats, 178,
    185, 189–90, 222, 244, 262

McConnell on compromise in light of,
    197, 229
and McConnell's failed campaign finance
    bill, 138
McConnell's use of, 154, 160–61, 220–22,
    305–6
  of Obama-era judicial nominees, 220–22
  of Supreme Court nominees, 150, 193,
    221, 234–36, 244, 262
  as threat to border bill, 352
  as threat to Obama-era legislation, 210
  Donald Trump's call for McConnell to
    end, 265
Filibustered! (Zamore and Merkley), 220
Fillmore, Millard, 237
Fineman, Howard, 187
First Amendment, 167
  see also free speech
Fishman, Joe, 324
Fitzgerald, Peter, 171
Five Points, Ala., 1–2, 7, 8, 158
Flack, Roberta, 156
flag burning, 164, 179, 194
Fleming Bulls, 38
Fong, Matt, 171
Ford, Christine Blasey, 270
Ford, Gerald, and administration, 88, 89, 97
Ford, Wendell, 80, 105, 114, 124, 126, 150
foreign aid and border bill (2024), 351–56
Foreign Assistance Appropriation Bill, 346
foreign policy, 31, 124–25, 170, 351–56
  see also Ukraine
Forrester, Chase, 98
Fort Bliss, 1, 25
Fort Campbell, 124
Fort Knox, 67–70, 124, 174
Fort McNair, 300–302
Fort Meade, 32
Fox, Ann, 34
Fox and Friends (TV series), 263
Fox News, 228, 291
  on aid for Ukraine, 348, 350–51
  Jim Bunning on, 187
  Paul Ryan on Republican interest in, 265
  Donald Trump and, 332–33, 348
  Justin Walker on, 288
Fox News Sunday (TV series), 172
Franklin, Benjamin, 322
Fraternal Order of Police, 140
Freedom Caucus, xi, 254
"Freedom Now" rally, 61–62

free speech, 164, 166–69, 193
Frist, Bill, 180–82, 184, 190–92, 194
fundraising
for George W. Bush's presidential campaign, 175
in horse-trading for legislative support, 183, 210
for Kentucky Republican Party, by McConnell, 187, 195
for McConnell, by George H. W. Bush, 136–37
for McConnell Center, 148, 154–55
by McConnell for his own campaigns, 89–91, 104, 110–12, 117, 128, 135, 146, 147, 165, 275, 287
by McConnell's opponents, 132, 149, 162, 226, 274, 276, 277
for NRSC, 149, 168–71
for Republican Senate candidates in Kentucky, 186
by Super PACs, 226, 251, 253, 254, 277, 310
by Donald Trump, 241, 335
for Trump-backed Republican candidates, 333
Donald Trump's campaign donation to McConnell, 143
Fred Wertheimer on McConnell's, 168
see also campaign finance legislation
Furman University, 18

Gaddafi, Muammar, 222
Galbraith, John Kenneth, 57
Galveston, Tex., 22
Garland, Merrick
2022 election and blocking confirmation of, 334
blocking hearings to confirm, xii, 234–36, 240–41, 244–47, 262, 276, 280–81, 284
Democrats' view of blocking, 322–24
effects of blocked confirmation, for Republicans, 321
January 6th insurrection investigation by, 341
McConnell's personal feelings about, 243
nomination of Amy Coney Barrett vs., 280–81, 284
Barack Obama's nomination of, 240
view of judiciary of Neil Gorsuch vs., 286

Garrett, Robert T., 146
Gates, Bill, 326
gay marriage, 187
Georgia, 2020 runoff elections, 277, 278, 294, 295, 298
Gershanick, David, 253, 311
Gillespie, Ed, 251
Gingrich, Newt, xi, 163, 287
Ginsburg, Ruth Bader, 276, 280–85, 321
Giuliani, Rudy, 302
Glenn, John, 122
global financial crisis, 203, 208, 216
Gold, Martin, 235–36
Goldwater, Barry, 58
Grant Hicks's support for, 54
McConnell's view of, 54–56, 60, 64, 122
opposition to civil rights legislation by, 60, 63, 125
University of Louisville speech, 55–56
Gorbachev, Mikhail, 123
Gore, Al, 127, 175–77
Gorsuch, Neil, 244–46, 262–63, 282, 286, 324
government shutdown, 272, 341
Graham, Bob, 182
Graham, Lindsey, 236, 270, 307
Gramm, Phil, 149–50, 162
Grassley, Chuck, 236
Grayson, Trey, 212, 214
Great Depression, 15, 18
Greater Louisville Central Labor Council, 93
"Great Expectations" (speech), 45
Greer, Frank, 141, 145–48
Gregg, Judd, 203
Gregory, Cleburne, 4–5
Greitens, Eric, 332, 333
Grimes, Alison Lundergan, 226–27
Grover (Dean's fiancé), 18–20
Gulf War, 150
gun rights, 106, 142–43, 238, 291, 326

Hamas, 351
Hannity, Sean, 292
Harlan, John Marshall, 296
Harriman, Averell, 57
Hart Senate Office Building, 300, 302–3
Harvard Crimson, 327
Harvard University and Law School, 57, 58, 179, 288, 327
Hatch Act, 88
Hatch Foundation, 316

Hawley, Josh
  2018 midterm election of, 271
  and certification of 2020 election, 293,
    294, 298, 303
  criticism of McConnell by, 318
  in Lout Caucus, 307
Hayek, Friedrich, 55
Haynie, Hugh, 106
Haynsworth, Clement, 76–79
Hayward, Justin, 287
health care, 140, 287
  see also Affordable Care Act (Obamacare)
Helms, Jesse, 123, 129
Heyburn, John, 91, 104–5, 131, 132, 206
Hicks, Grant, 54, 55
Hill, Anita, 150
Hill, Baron, 255
Hillbilly Elegy (Vance), 260
Hoffa, Jimmy, 57
Holch, Niels, 139
Hollenbach, Todd, 90–95
Holmes, Josh, 311, 312
  on fundraising by One Nation, 251
  on McConnell and Rick Scott, 336
  and McConnell's record as majority leader,
    338
  and McConnell's stepping down as Senate
    leader, 342
  opposition research by, 256, 257
  on Donald Trump and McConnell, 325
Holmes, Oliver Wendell, 234
Houston, Tex., 21–23
Hruska, Roman, 77
Huber, Dave, 74, 90, 98
Huddleston, Walter "Dee," 84, 105, 107,
    112–19, 124, 126
Hulse, Carl, 184–85, 209, 226
Humana, 155
Humble Oil Company, 18
Hunt, Al, 173
Hunt, Nelson Bunker, 112
Hurricane Katrina, 195

"I Have a Dream" (speech), 59–60
immigration, 151, 291, 351–56
  see also border crisis
impeachment, 172, 272–73, 306–9, 344, 347
"In Defense of Soft Money" (McConnell),
    177–78
Indiana, Senate races, 254–58, 270–71
Indianapolis Star, 256

infrastructure bills, 263, 266, 322
Inglis, Bob, 172
Inside Edition (TV series), 172
institutionalism, 245, 264, 334
Iraq War, 183, 193, 195–96, 212, 327
isolationism, xi, 347–49, 354, 355
Israel, 351–56

Jackson, Jesse, Jr., 193
Jackson, Ketanji Brown, 239
Jackson, Stonewall, 33
James Madison Center for Free Speech,
    168–69
January 6th insurrection, 293–309, 341,
    343–44
Japan, 29, 30
Jean Lafitte Hotel, 22
Jefferson County, Ky., 88–94, 96–107, 117,
    131, 287
Jeffries, Hakeem, 354
Jennings, Scott, ix
Jim Crow South, 33–40
Johnson, Lyndon B., 92, 303
Johnson, Lyndon B., and administration
  George W. Bush on meeting, 185–86
  civil rights legislation of, 65
  McConnell's support of, 63
  persuasiveness of, ix, 229
  as Senate leader, x, 186–87, 230, 292
  Supreme Court nominees, 237
  work ethic of, 141, 202
Johnson, Mike, 353, 354
Johnson, Ron, 222, 258, 307, 335
Johnson Wax, 346
Jones, David, 155
Joyce, Michael, 168
judicial nominations
  appeals court, 220, 248, 288–91, 291, 292
  federal, 126, 261, 286, 289, 291, 292, 320
  federal appeals court, 178, 185, 189–91,
    222, 242–44, 248
  McConnell on Senate confirmation of,
    78–80, 132–34, 198
  and McConnell's influence on the courts,
    280–92
  see also U.S. Supreme Court; specific
    appeals courts
Justice, Jim, 340

Kagan, Elena, 221
Kaine, Tim, 246–47, 338

Kane, Paul, 217
Karem, Robert, 298–99
Karlan, Pamela, 248
Kavanaugh, Brett, 269–71, 282, 288, 289,
    290, 334
Keating, Kenneth, 58
Kefauver, Estes, 59
Kelly, John, 260–61
Kelly, Mark, 339
Kennedy, Anthony, 238, 245, 262, 269, 288
Kennedy, Edward "Ted," 157
    in 1964 plane crash, 65
    Chappaquiddick incident involving, 81
    McConnell Center speech by, 190–91
    on nutrition committee, 72
    as role model for McConnell, 74, 122, 182
    South African sanctions drafted by, 125
    special election to fill seat of, 210–11
Kennedy, Joan, 81
Kennedy, John F., and administration
    1960 presidential campaign of, 52, 201
    civil rights efforts of, 57, 59, 61
    John Sherman Cooper and, 63, 191
    Edward Kennedy and, 122
    McConnell's criticism of, 60, 61
    Mullins family's reverence for, 108
    Gene Snyder's mail criticizing, 57
Kennedy, Robert F., 322
Kentucky
    federal spending in, 165, 174, 202, 324
    McConnell's influence on politics in, 195,
        222–23, 250, 323, 324
    McConnell's premature entry in legislative
        race in, 84
    Republican support in, 85–86, 111, 174,
        179, 187, 195, 222, 250, 324
    Donald Trump's fundraiser in, 335
Kentucky Bar Association, 126
Kentucky Commerce Cabinet, 109
Kentucky Derby, 102, 335
Kentucky Hospital Association, 140
Kentucky Law Journal, 77
Kentucky Right to Life, 144
Kentucky Task Force of Missing and
    Exploited Children, 106
Kerry, John, 186, 212
Kilpatrick, James K., 134
King, Angus, 247, 323
King, Martin Luther, Jr., 59–60
Klobuchar, Amy, 339
Koch brothers, 252, 253

Kopechne, Mary Jo, 81
Kravchuk, Leonid, 346
Krieble, Helen Elizabeth, 168
Ku Klux Klan, 180

Langone, Ken, 252
Lankford, James, 298, 325, 352
Lardner, George, Jr., 165
Las Vegas, Nev., 50–51
"Late Effects of Polio, The" (Newsweek),
    13
Law, Steven, 311
    "Against the Tide" narrative by, 152–53
    campaign finance research by, 137–38
    as Elaine Chao's chief of staff, 176
    in McConnell's campaign against Harvey
        Sloane, 138–41, 145, 147
    on negative advertising, 145
    Karl Rove and, 226
    Super PAC work by, 251, 253, 277
    "What's So Bad about Money in Politics?"
        book proposal by, 166
Leahy, Patrick, 236–37
Lee, Mike, 338
Lee, Robert E., 33
Le Havre, France, 26
Leipzig, Germany, 26
Leo, Leonard, 239, 246
Levi, Edward, 88–89
Lewinsky, Monica, 171, 172
Lexington Herald-Leader, 112, 147, 324
Liberty Republicans, 324
Life magazine, 102
Limbaugh, Rush, 169, 231
Limestone County, Ala., 17
Lincoln-Douglas-style debates, 141–42
Liverpool, England, 26
Long Game, The (McConnell), 112–13, 249,
    260
Longworth, Alice Roosevelt, 104
Lott, Trent, 176, 180, 181, 194–95
Louisville, Ky., 40–50
    see also University of Louisville
Louisville Courier-Journal, see Courier-
    Journal
Louisville Times, 85
Lout Caucus, 307
Loving, Jessica, 100–101
Lugar, Richard, 110, 117, 122
Lummis, Cynthia, 338
Lunsford, Bruce, 201–2, 205

MAGA movement, 241, 342
Major League Baseball, 315–16
Malone, Jim "Pop," 105
Manchester, William, 41
Manchin, Joe, 326, 340
Mansfield, Michael "Mike"
  bipartisan efforts of, 197, 198, 229
  Angus King and, 323
  as role model for McConnell, 229, 230
  Senate leadership record of, viii, 338, 339
March of Dimes, 3
March on Washington, 59–60
Markarova, Oksana, 350
Marr, Bobby, 47
Marshall, John, 234
Marshall, Thurgood, 238
Martin, Jonathan, 316–17
Massey Business College, 17, 21
Master of the Senate (Caro), 187
Masters, Blake, 332, 333
Mathias, Charles "Mac," 74
Mattis, James, 261
McCain, John, 171, 356
  2000 presidential primary for, 175, 287
  2008 presidential campaign of, 199–203
  and Affordable Care Act, 265
  campaign finance legislation by, 166–68,
    177–78, 184, 193
  disavowal of Donald Trump by, 242
  McConnell's relationship with, 184,
    212–13
  McConnell's Senate debate with, 173–74
  media savviness of, 172
  speech on POW experience by, 198–99
  Jim Warner and, 164
McCain–Feingold Act, 166–68, 177–78, 184,
  193
McCarthy, Joe, 63
McCarthy, Kevin, 295, 314, 353
McConnell, Addison Mitchell, III "Mitch,"
  25
  1984 campaign and first Senate term,
    105–35
  1990 campaign and second Senate term,
    124, 136–61
  1996 campaign and third Senate term,
    162–74
  2002 campaign and fourth Senate term,
    178–79, 181–88
  2008 campaign and fifth Senate term,
    201–5

  2014 campaign and sixth Senate term,
    226–27
  2020 campaign and seventh Senate term,
    273–77, 356
  2024 foreign aid and border bill for, 345–56
  in Army Reserves, 67–70
  Joe Biden and, 339–40
  campaigning style of, 71, 90–92, 95, 111,
    113, 114, 147
  career interests of, 47–48, 65–67
  challenges to authority of, 230–31, 336–37
  changes in Republican Party over career of,
    xi, 231, 327, 337–38, 342, 343, 355
  childhood in Jim Crow South, 33–40
  childhood interests of, 35–38, 44–45
  college years for, 53–57, 60–62
  on Marlow Cook's staff, 70–80
  dating and romantic relationships of, 51,
    55, 58, 70, 102, 127, 134, 153, 155–56
    (*see also* Chao, Elaine; Redmon, Sherrill)
  in debt limit crisis, 216–19
  decision to step down from Senate
    leadership for, 342–44
  Democrats' view of, 202, 205, 227, 321–23
  early political career of, 81, 87–89
  falls by, 272, 310–19
  father's relationship with, 28, 31–32, 35,
    39, 46, 50–52, 72
  filibuster of judicial nominees, 220–22
  and filling Scalia's seat on Supreme Court,
    233–49
  "Great Expectations" speech, 45
  heart surgery for, 181–83
  high school years, 41–50
  hiring of women by, 98, 104, 109, 124, 153
  "In Defense of Soft Money" op-ed, 177–78
  influence of, in 2016 Senate elections,
    250–58
  influence of, in Kentucky politics, 195,
    222–23, 250, 323, 324
  internship with John Sherman Cooper for,
    62–65
  internship with Gene Snyder for, 56–60
  and January 6th insurrection, 293–305,
    305–6, 309
  as Jefferson County judge executive,
    88–94, 96–107, 287
  judicial influence of, 280–92
  lasting impact of, on Supreme Court, 276,
    281–82, 285–87, 320–24, 330, 334, 342
  law school for, 57, 58, 65–66

leadership style of, 338
legacy of, 147, 148, 152, 161, 165, 245, 285
legal career of, 70, 84, 85, 87–89
as longest-serving Senate party leader, 338–40
The Long Game memoir, 112–13, 249, 260
Lost Decade for, 82–95
media and, xii–xiii, 169, 172–74, 187, 319, 329–30
as moderate Republican, 89, 94, 97, 123, 163, 324
mother's bond with, 15, 45, 46, 50–53, 66, 72, 158–59
national Republican Party support for, 107, 110, 116
"New Beginnings" essay, 45–46
"Now I Am a Senior" essay, 48
Obama-era use of filibuster by, 220–22
oppositional politics used by, 206–12, 214–15, 305–6
physical and psychological effects of polio for, 11–14, 68, 98, 302–3, 310–13, 316, 327
polio diagnosis and treatment for, 1–11, 25–26, 32, 158–59
post-graduation road trip of, 50–52
power as driver of positions/policies for, 220, 238, 308–9, 321, 323
power of, over Republican Party, 235–36, 240
pursuit of power by, viii–xi, 54, 73–74, 125, 147, 149, 320–44
as Republican whip, 179–80, 187–89, 191
Paul Ryan and, 231–32, 263–68
on second Trump impeachment, 306–8
Senate aspirations of, 96, 100, 101, 103
on Senate confirmations of justices, 78–80, 132–34, 198
as Senate historian, vii–viii
Senate leadership aspirations of, 121, 162, 165, 177, 179–81, 186, 194
Senate Leadership Fund, One Nation, and, 250–58
as Senate majority leader, 227–31, 235, 250–51, 261, 262, 269, 290, 292, 295, 326
as Senate minority leader, 196–97, 202, 205–6, 220, 222, 224, 336–37
sequestration deal for, 224–25
and Tea Party in 2010 midterm elections, 212–14

and Donald Trump, xi–xii, 242–43, 259, 263–68, 271, 273, 275–79, 298, 302, 335, 336, 340, 344
Justin Walker and, 287–91
What's So Bad about Money in Politics? book proposal by, 166
working relationship of, with Democrats, 97–99, 140, 160, 183, 193, 198, 213–14, 219, 224–25, 338
"You and Time" essay, 48–49
McConnell, A.M. "Mac" (father), 7, 11, 12, 58, 69, 347
Dean's relationship with, 18–24, 31, 32
declining health and death of, 134, 146–47, 158
early life, 17–18
in Jim Crow South, 34–37, 39–40
in Louisville, 43, 44
Mitch's relationship with, 28, 31–32, 35, 39, 46, 50, 51, 72
political leanings of, 39, 64
Sherrill Redmon's relationship with, 70, 71, 80, 81
support for Mitch from, 47, 83, 90, 119, 121
in World War II, 1, 2, 9–10, 25–31
McConnell, Claire (daughter), 90, 102, 121, 155
McConnell, "Dad" (grandfather)
Dean's letters to, 23, 36
financial support for McConnell family from, 6
Mac's childhood with, 17–18
Mac's relationship with, 31
Mitch and his parent's life with, 24–26, 34–35
Mitch's letters to, 37, 40, 42
on Mitch's move to Kentucky, 40, 42
Texie and Archie's employment by, 33–34
McConnell, Eleanor Hayes (daughter)
birth of, 84
and Mitch and Sherrill's divorce, 102
Mitch's early efforts to support, 84, 85
at Mitch's first campaign announcement, 90
and Mitch's first job in Washington D.C., 88
and Mitch's image, 103–4
at Senate swearing-in ceremony, 121
at Smith College, 144, 155
McConnell, Ethel "Dick," 18, 27–32, 37, 40

McConnell, Julia Odene (née Shockley)
  "Dean" (mother), viii, 58
  on Civil Rights Bill, 63–64
  declining health and death of, 158–59
  early life of, 15–17
  in Jim Crow South, 34, 36, 37, 39
  in Louisville, 40, 43–44
  Mac's relationship with, 18–24, 31, 32
  Mitch's bond with, 15, 45, 46, 50–53, 66,
     72, 158–59
  Mitch's polio rehabilitation by, 1–3, 5–12,
     25–26, 109, 158–59
  Sherrill Redmon's relationship with, 70,
     71, 80, 81
  support for Mitch from, 83, 90, 121
McConnell, Mamie, 1
McConnell, Mamie (grandmother)
  Dean's letters to, 23, 36
  financial support for McConnell family
     from, 6
  Mac's childhood with, 17–18
  Mac's relationship with, 31
  Mitch and his parent's life with, 24–26,
     34–35
  Mitch's letters to, 37
  Texie and Archie's employment by, 33–34
McConnell, Porter (daughter), 121, 144, 155
McConnell, Robert, 18, 22, 30
McConnell Center, 148, 154–55, 191, 285,
  316
McConnell Funeral Home, 18, 24
McConnell v. the Federal Election
  Commission, 184
McCoy, Terry, 45–47
McGahn, Don, 241–43, 246, 289, 292
McGovern, George, 72
McGrath, Amy, 273–77
McGrew, Dicky, 35, 72, 337
McNamara, Robert, 57
Meadows, Mark, 282, 283, 284, 302
Medicare, 206
  Affordable Care Act and, 206
  George W. Bush's attempts to reform, 183,
     207
  compromises on, 216–17
  McConnell's early view of, 58
  effects of Rick Scott's agenda on, 331, 332
  Barry Goldwater's view of, 56
  McConnell on Obama-era reforms to,
     207–8
Meet the Press (TV series), 169, 172, 214, 355

Merkley, Jeff, 220
Meyer, Bonnie, 61
Miers, Harriet, 191–92
Mikulski, Barbara, 339
Mineta, Norm, 176
missing and exploited children, 106
Mississippi: The Closed Society (Silver), 64
Mitchell, George, 161
Mnuchin, Steven, 275
Monahan, Brian, 318–19
Mondale, Walter, 116
Mongiardo, Daniel, 187
Moody Blues, 287
Moore, Roy, 266–67
Moreno, Bernie, 341
Morton, Thruston, 70, 95
Moseley Braun, Carol, 171
Mourdock, Richard, 223–24
Moynihan, Daniel Patrick, 122
MSNBC, 288
Muchow, Stefanie
  after McConnell's fall, 311, 313
  January 6th insurrection for, 295, 296, 298,
     299, 301
Mullin, Markwayne, 330
Mullins, Janet, 108–10, 114–16, 118–20, 127,
  128
Mullins, Shannon, 110
Mulroney, Brian, 127
Murdoch, Lachlan, 332, 333
Murdoch, Rupert, 332, 333
Murkowski, Lisa
  and blocking of Merrick Garland's
     confirmation, 236, 240, 245–46, 284
  failure of, to endorse Donald Trump, 344
  at McConnell's Senate leadership record-
     breaking session, 339
  McConnell's treatment of, 326, 330
Murray State University, 110
Myanmar (Burma), 170, 222
My Place to Stand (Plagemann), 3–4

Nagourney, Adam, 209
National Aeronautics and Space
  Administration (NASA), 284
National Association of Broadcasters, 167
National Education Association, 167
National Guard, 299
nationalism, xi, 337
National Journal, 169, 213
National Labor Relations Board, 221

National Republican Senatorial Committee
  (NRSC), 176
  2000 election results for, 177
  2002 election results for, 180
  2016 election results for, 250
  Steve Daines's leadership of, 341
  McConnell's challenge of Phil Gramm for
    leadership of, 149–50, 162
  McConnell's fundraising efforts for,
    170–71
  McConnell's successful campaign to lead,
    165
  Rick Scott's leadership of, 331–33, 336
National Rifle Association, 142–43, 167
NATO, 243, 349, 350, 354
Neumann, Mark, 171
"New Beginnings" (McConnell), 45–46
Newsweek, 13, 187
New York Times, 42, 43, 138, 159–60, 169,
    173–74, 177, 184, 209, 215, 218, 226, 266
New York University (NYU), 69–70
Nixon, Richard M., 86
Nixon, Richard M., and administration
  McConnell's job offer from, 81
  McConnell's support for, 52, 60, 85
  Sherrill Redmon's support for, 72
  Supreme Court nominees, 76–78, 81
  Watergate scandal and resignation, 81,
    85, 88
Nordhausen, Germany, 26
Northern Kentucky Chamber of Commerce,
    317
Northern Kentucky University, 311
Notre Dame University, 282
Novak, Bob, 173
"Now I Am a Senior" (McConnell), 48
NRSC, see National Republican Senatorial
  Committee
nuclear energy, 140–41
Nunn, Louie, 83, 84
NYU (New York University), 69–70

Obama, Barack, and administration
  2004 Senate election for, 188
  2008 presidential campaign of, 201–5
  debt limit crisis for, 216–18, 314
  Rahm Emanuel and, 207, 323
  and filling of Scalia's Supreme Court seat,
    234, 237–41, 276
  judicial confirmations for, 220, 221, 243,
    291–92

McConnell's opposition to agenda of,
    206–10, 212–15, 221, 224
  McConnell's relationship with, 206–7,
    212, 219, 227, 228, 325
  Harry Reid's encouragement of, 199
  sequestration for, 224–25
  Supreme Court nominees, xii, 237–41, 262
Obamacare, see Affordable Care Act
O'Connor, Sandra Day, 184, 191, 193, 283
O'Donnell, Christine, 214
Old Crow, 355
Olson, Ted, 184
One Nation, 251–53
oppositional politics, 206–12, 214–15, 305–6
opposition research, 138–39, 145, 148, 150,
    178–79, 256
Oswald, Lee Harvey, 61

Packwood, Bob
  budget reconciliation use by, 125–26
  McConnell on, 75
  McConnell's failed campaign finance bill
    with, 130
  as moderate Republican, xi
  Janet Mullins work for, 108, 109
  sexual harassment and assault scandal,
    109, 156–60, 230
PACs (political action committees), 128–30
  see also Super PACs
Paducah, Ky., 174
Parks, Rosa, 194, 229
partisanship
  in Central Intelligence Agency, 268
  in confirmation of judicial nominees,
    133–34, 244, 246–47
  at fundraising events, 113
  increase in, over McConnell's tenure, 339
  McConnell on, 96, 197
  McConnell's record of, x, 79, 197–99, 297,
    326
  by Senate leadership, 153, 189, 227, 228
  in Supreme Court, 177, 244, 246–47
  see also oppositional politics
Parvin, C. Landon, 228
Patriot Act, 212
Paul, Rand, vii–viii, 212, 308, 318
Paulson, Henry M. "Hank," 203, 204
Peace Corps, 164
Pearl Harbor, attack on, 24
Pelosi, Nancy, 203, 210, 275, 301, 348
Pence, Greg, 297

Pence, Mike
  and Amy Coney Barrett's confirmation
    vote, 284
  January 6th insurrection for, 295, 297, 299,
    300, 302, 304, 308
Pendennis Club, 90
Pepsi Cola, 346
Percy, Charles, 72, 74
Perot, Ross, 151
Pew Research Center, 292
Pharmaceutical Research and Manufacturers
  of America (PhRMA), 310
Phi Kappa Tau fraternity, 53–54, 60–62
Phillips, W. Park, 2
Pilsen, Czechoslovakia, 28–29
Piper, Billy, 182, 204, 205
Plagemann, Bentz, 3–4
Plastridge, Alice Lou, 4
Plessy v. Ferguson, 296
polio
  Bill Gates's support for research on,
    326–27
  McConnell's diagnosis and treatment,
    1–11, 25–26, 32, 109, 158–59
  personality traits of survivors of, 12–13
  physical and psychological effects of,
    11–14, 68, 98, 302–3, 310–13, 316, 327
  recurrent polio and post polio syndrome,
    13–14
Polio Paradox, The (Bruno), 13
political action committees (PACs), 128–30
  see also Super PACs
political advertising
  in 1984 Senate campaign, 110, 112–13,
    115–16, 118, 119, 128
  in 1990 Senate campaign, 141, 145–47
  in 1996 Senate campaign, 164
  in 2002 Senate campaign, 179
  in 2020 Senate campaign, 274
  Roger Ailes on positive, 112–13
  in Jim Bunning's campaign, 187
  in Jefferson County judge executive
    campaign, 91, 92, 94–95
  McConnell's use of negative, 91, 92,
    94–95, 110, 112–13, 115–16, 128, 141,
    145–47
  in Mark Neumann's campaign, 171
  One Nation's funding of, 252
  in Todd P'Pool's campaign, 223
  in Todd Young's campaign, 256–57
Popp, David, 301, 304, 311

populism, xi, 151, 231, 321, 337, 355
Pornography Victims Compensation Act,
  155
Portman, Rob, 306, 323, 325, 330, 335
Powell, Sidney, 302
P'Pool, Todd, 222–23
prescription drug benefit, Medicare, 183
presidential elections
  2000, 175–77
  2004, 184–87
  2012, 223–24
  2016, 232, 259–60, 267–68
  2020, 277–78, 293–300, 303
  certification vote for 2020, 293–300, 303
  "rule" on Supreme Court nominations
    before, 234–38, 247, 280–81, 284, 285
  Russian interference in, 267–68
Prince Foundation, 168
Prunty, Bert, 69
Pryor, Mark, 328
Putin, Vladimir, 348

Quayle, Dan, 135

racial segregation
  Harrold Carswell's support for, 76–77
  and civil rights vs. property rights, 61
  Barry Goldwater's support of, 56
  in Jim Crow South, 33, 34, 39
  in Louisville, 41–43
  during Mac and Dean's childhoods, 16, 63
  Strom Thurmond's support for, 180
racism
  in constituent letters to Gene Snyder, 57
  in Jim Crow South, 33
  Trent Lott's condemnation for racist
    remarks, 180, 181
  McConnell on, 59
  Donald Trump's racist attacks on Elaine
    Chao, 336
  see also white supremacy
Rakestraw, Vince, 88
Rayburn, Sam, 329
Reagan, Nancy, 116
Reagan, Ronald, and administration, 156,
  296, 307
  and aid for Ukraine, 345, 347, 349,
    353
  campaigning for McConnell by, 144
  changes in Republican Party since, xi,
    342, 343

and Make America Great Again slogan, 241
McConnell's appointees in, 134
McConnell's independence from, 125, 129
McConnell's support for presidential candidacy of, 87, 89, 97, 102
McConnell's view of conservatism of, 104, 123
McConnell's win on "coattails" of, 116–19, 124, 153
and Republican support for McConnell's first Senate campaign, 107, 110, 116
Supreme Court nominees of, 128, 238
Reagan Republicans, 212, 340, 355
reconciliation process, 266
Redmon, Lee Ann, 72
Redmon, Sherrill, 74, 95
household income of McConnell, 91
letters to Dean and Mac from, 71, 80, 81, 83
McConnell's children with, 83–85, 88, 90
McConnell's dating of/engagement to, 55, 58, 64, 65, 71
McConnell's divorce from, 101–3, 114
on McConnell's efforts to pass ERA, 75
and McConnell's late NYU application, 69–70
McConnell's marriage to, 72, 80
support for McConnell's career from, 62, 72, 87, 90
Redstone Arsenal, 25, 36
Reed, Billy, 44
Rehnquist, William, 76, 81, 128, 191
Reid, Harry, 203, 236
advancement of Barack Obama's agenda by, 210
on Affordable Care Act, 209, 210
Sharron Angle's campaign against, 214
bipartisan efforts of, 198–99
blocking of George W. Bush's judicial nominees by, 189–90
change to judicial approval rules by, 243–44, 261, 291
effect of McConnell's oppositional politics on, 215
McConnell's relationship with, 198, 205, 229
sequestration deal for, 225
Reno, Janet, 170
Republican Governor's Association, 251
Republican National Committee, 156
Republican National Convention, 356
Republican Party, 34, 40, 46
in 1980s, 122
1996 Republican Revolution, 163–64
2016 core voters for, 260
2018 midterm voters for, 271–72
Black senators in, 225–26
Black voters in, 42
changes in, over McConnell's career, xi, 231, 327, 337–38, 342, 343, 355
European allies' feelings about, 350
in Kentucky, 85–86, 111, 174, 179, 187, 195, 222, 250, 324
Liberty Republicans, 324
MAGA movement, 241, 342
McConnell as moderate in, 89, 94, 97, 123, 163, 324
McConnell family's switch to supporting, 39
McConnell's power over, 235–36, 240
publicized disputes within, 241–42, 245–47, 330–32, 340
Reagan Republicans, 212, 340, 355
Paul Ryan on Fox News and, 265
support for McConnell's first Senate campaign from, 107, 110, 116
support for Donald Trump in, 277–78, 309, 356
Donald Trump's attacks on members of, 265–66, 268
Donald Trump's impact on, xi, 294, 295, 298, 306, 326–28, 331, 337, 340–43, 350–51, 353, 355
Donald Trump's presidential nomination in, 241–42
see also Senate Republicans
Rice University, 18
Richmond, Ky., 174
Ritchie, Donald, 327, 334
Road to Serfdom, The (Hayek), 55
Roberts, John, 191, 192, 290
Robertson, General, 29
Rockefeller, Jay, 122, 151
Rockefeller, Nelson, 72
Rocky (cat), 72
Roe v. Wade
Harry Blackmun's majority opinion in, 77–78
Democratic backlash to overturning, 321, 334

Roe v. Wade (cont.)
  McConnell's anti-abortion address on
    anniversary of, 144
  restrictions on access to abortion after,
    100, 101
  Donald Trump's Supreme Court nominees
    and overturning of, 242
  see also abortion
Romney, Mitt
  2008 presidential primary for, 200
  2012 presidential campaign of, 223, 224,
    232
  2018 Senate election of, 271
  in Amy Coney Barrett's confirmation,
    281, 284
  on blocking of Merrick Garland's
    confirmation, 247
  and January 6th insurrection, 295, 307,
    309
  vote to impeach Donald Trump by, 273,
    309
Roosevelt, Franklin Delano, 3–5, 10, 327
Roosevelt, Theodore, 296
Roth, Philip, 246
Rove, Karl, 181, 183, 187, 251, 252
Rubio, Marco, 232, 257–58, 307
Ruby, Jack, 61
Rudolph, Wilma, 13
Runyon, Keith, 92, 94, 102, 247
Russell, Richard, 186
Russia, 31, 267–68, 347–48, 352, 353,
    355–56
Ryan, Paul, 231–32, 263–69, 332, 333
Ryan, Tim, 335

St. Vith, Belgium, 26–27
Saint Xavier High School, 287
Salter, Mark, 213
Sasser, Jim, 127
Saturday Night Live (TV series), 227
Saxbe, William, 75, 88
Scalia, Antonin
  confirmation of Neil Gorsuch vs.,
    263
  filling Supreme Court seat of, 233–49,
    262, 276
  filling Supreme Court seat of Ginsburg vs.,
    280, 281
  on Edward Levi's staff, 89
  Ronald Reagan's nomination of, 128
Scalia, Maureen, 243

Schiff, Joe
  drafting of, 73
  in McConnell's 1984 Senate campaign,
    108–10, 118
  in McConnell's Jefferson County
    campaign, 90, 95
  and McConnell's relationship with Sherrill
    Redmon, 83
  on McConnell's staff in Jefferson County,
    98
  in Reagan administration, 134
Schultz, Pam, 127, 130
Schumer, Chuck
  and coronavirus relief bill, 278
  filibuster for Bush-era judicial nominees
    by, 190, 222
  on filibustering Supreme Court nominees,
    234, 238
  and first impeachment of Donald Trump,
    273
  and Amy McGrath's Senate campaign, 274
  Senate service record for, 339
  Donald Trump's fundraiser for, 241
  and Ukraine aid package, 354
Schweiker, Richard, 75
Scott, Rick, 331–33, 336–38
Scott, Tim, 225–26, 329, 330, 340–41
Scranton, William, 60, 63, 64
Second Infantry Division, 26–32
Segal, Isenberg, Sales, and Stewart, 70
Senate Agriculture Committee, 124, 142
Senate Appropriations Committee, 174, 346
Senate Commerce Committee, 338
Senate Conservatives Fund, 214, 226
Senate Ethics Committee, 156–59
Senate Foreign Relations Committee, 129
Senate Intelligence Committee, 268
Senate Judiciary Committee, 221
  Amy Coney Barrett's hearing, 283
  Joe Biden on election-year hearings by, 234
  blocking of Merrick Garland's hearing
    before, 236–37, 241, 247, 321
  Marlow Cook's seat on, 72, 76
  Neil Gorsuch's hearing, 244
  McConnell's seat on, 128, 137, 233
  Antonin Scalia's hearing, 233
Senate Leadership Fund
  and 2018 midterm election results, 271
  fundraising and fundraisers for, 253, 277,
    310, 311
  interests of donors to, 334

McConnell's creation of, 251–53
One Nation and, 253
and Rick Scott's leadership of NRSC, 332, 333, 337
JD Vance's support by, 335
Todd Young's support by, 256–57
Senate Republicans
attacks on McConnell by, 328–29
change to Supreme Court nominee approval process by, 262–63
Bob Dole's leadership of, 121–23, 154
Eisenhower-era, 161, 287
McConnell as majority leader of, 227–31, 235, 250–51, 261, 269, 295, 326
McConnell as minority leader of, 196–97, 202, 205–6, 220, 222, 224, 336–37
McConnell as whip for, 179–80, 187–89, 191
McConnell's aspirations of leading, 121, 162, 165, 177, 179–81, 186, 194
McConnell's assistance in campaigns of, 254–58
McConnell's decision to step down from leadership of, 342–44
McConnell's efforts to protect, 235, 240, 273, 329
McConnell's leadership style with, 325–26
McConnell's power over, 235–36, 240, 281
McConnell's scouting/recruitment of, ix–x, 226, 327–28
support for McConnell from, x, 281, 323–24
tenure of leaders of, vii, x
see also National Republican Senatorial Committee (NRSC); specific individuals
Senate Rules Committee, 172, 176
seniority, in U.S. Senate, 129, 149
sequestration, 224–25
Sessions, Jeff, 221, 267
Seventh Circuit Court of Appeals, 276, 282
sexual harassment and assault, 150, 156–60, 230, 263–64, 269–70, 288
Sharrard, W. J. W., 9
Shelby, Richard, 326
Shevlin, Lorraine Rowan, 102
Shields, Mark, 173
Shockley, Arnold, 7
Shockley, "Babe," 15–16
Shockley, Lala Viola, 15, 16
Shockley, Nell, 7
Shoulders, Isaac, 97

Shrader, Edward C., 68
Silberman, Jan, 88
Silberman, Laurence, 88, 89
Silbersher, Marvin, 118
Silver, James, 64
Simmons, Kyle, 203, 311
Simpson, Alan, 157
Simpson, Chuck, 101
Sinclair, Ward, 75
Sinema, Kyrsten, 326, 339
Singer, Paul, 252
Sixth Circuit Court of Appeals, 248
Skaggs, Jerry and Colleen, 70
Sloane, Harvey, 102–3, 105, 108, 131–32, 135, 139–48
Slodysko, Brian, 256–57
Smartt, Edrie Mae "Sister," 16, 22
Dean's relationship with, 8, 15, 19–20, 25
financial support for McConnell family from, 6
Mitch's polio diagnosis while living with, 1–2
Smartt, Julius, 1, 8
Smith, Jack, 341
Smith College, 144
Snowe, Olympia, 209, 210
Snyder, Gene, 56–60, 62–65
Social Security, 207–8, 331, 332
Soderstrom, Sharon
after McConnell's fall, 311
and blocking of Merrick Garland's confirmation, 238–41
and filling of Ginsburg's Supreme Court seat, 281
January 6th insurrection for, 295–99, 301, 302, 304
soft money, 169–70, 177–78
South Africa, 124–25
Southampton, England, 26
Southern Baptist church, 34–35
Soviet Union, 31, 122–23, 346, 347
Specter, Arlen, 211
Squire Patton Boggs, 218
Standard Gravure shooting, 142
Stanley, Bessie Anderson, 49
Starr, Claudia, 104
Starr, Kenneth, 184
Stars and Stripes, 27–29
Stennis, John, 122
Stephens, Warren, 252
Stern, Doug, 139

Stevens, John Paul, 283
Stevenson, Adlai, 59
Stewart, Don, 239
Stone, W. Clement, 112
Strange, Luther, 267
Student Bar Association, 65–66
Stutzman, Marlin, 254–55
subprime housing crisis, 203, 208, 216
Sunstein, Cass, 189
Super Committee on deficit reduction,
    219–20
Super PACs, 250–58, 310, 311, 328, 333, 335
    see also specific organizations
Sweets, Meme, 91, 97–99, 102, 104

Taft, Robert, 347
Taiwan, 351–56
Taney, Roger, 78
TARP, see Troubled Asset Relief Program
taxes
    George W. Bush's tax cuts, 199, 215, 217,
        224, 296
    George H. W. Bush's tax policy, 141
    in McConnell's Jefferson County executive
        campaign, 94
    in Rick Scott's Republican agenda, 331
    and sequestration deal, 224–25
    Donald Trump's tax cut, 265, 266, 269, 279
Taylor, Robbin, 317
Tea Party movement, xi, 212–14, 218,
    222–24, 226
Teeter, Robert, 139, 152
Texie (McConnell house employee), 33–34
Thapar, Amul, 244, 269, 282
Thatcher, Margaret, 307
This Week (TV series), 172
Thomas, Clarence, 80
    confirmation hearings of, 150–51
    confirmation vote for, 150, 190, 285
    gifts from Republican donors to, 334
    ideological changes to Supreme Court
        since confirmation of, 238
    McConnell on politics of appointing, 237
    sexual harassment claims against, 150,
        270
Thomas, Norman, 62
Thune, John, 239
Thurmond, Strom, 180
Tillerson, Rex, 260, 261
Tillis, Thom, 326
Time magazine, 76, 124–25, 173

tobacco program and industry, 72, 113–14,
    124–26, 174, 202
Toyota, 127
Tribe, Laurence, 189–90
Troubled Asset Relief Program (TARP),
    203–4, 208, 217
Truman, Harry, 3, 30, 202, 210
Trump, Donald, and administration, 259–79,
    317
    2016 presidential election for, 250, 258–61
    in 2020 presidential election, 276–79,
        284–85, 322
    and aid for Ukraine, 348–52, 354
    attacks on fellow Republicans by, 265–66,
        268
    Cabinet appointees of, 260–62
    confirmations of judicial nominees of,
        291, 292
    in coronavirus pandemic, 274–75, 282, 283
    and filling of Scalia's seat on Supreme
        Court, 235, 236
    flattering of McConnell by, 325
    Fox News's support for, 332–33
    impact of, on Republican Party, xi, 294,
        295, 298, 306, 326–28, 331, 337, 340–43,
        350–51, 353, 355
    impeachment for, 272–74, 306–9
    inaugural address of, 259–60
    and January 6th insurrection, 293–300,
        302, 304, 306, 343–44
    legislation passed by McConnell and Ryan
        during, 263–68
    McConnell campaign donation from, 143
    McConnell's relationship with, 259, 340
    presidential nomination for, 235, 241–42
    relationship of McConnell and, xi–xii,
        242–43, 263–68, 271, 273, 275–79, 298,
        302, 335, 336, 344
    Republican support for, 277–78, 309, 356
    selection of Senate candidates by, 332–34
    Supreme Court nominees of, 241–42,
        244, 249, 262–63, 269–71, 276, 281–82,
        284–86, 288
    Supreme Court ruling on presidential
        immunity for, 335
    and Ukrainian investigation of Joe Biden's
        family, 272, 347
    Justin Walker's appellate court nomination
        by, 289–90
    Todd Young and popularity of, 257
Trump Tax Cut, 265, 266, 269, 279

TWA Flight 847 hijacking, 123
Twitter, 265, 278
  see also X
Tyree, J. D., 18

Ubl, Stephen, 310
Ukraine, 170, 272, 316–17, 330, 338, 345–56
United Association of Constitutional
  Conservatives, 54–55
United Way, 164
University of Chicago, 88, 234
University of Kentucky, Lexington, 65–66,
  69, 72, 82, 302, 324
University of Louisville, 50, 74, 94, 98
  McConnell Center at, 148, 154–55, 191,
    285, 316
  McConnell's archives at, 213
  McConnell's education at, 52–57, 60–62
  McConnell's efforts to secure funding for,
    174, 324
  McConnell's paid lectures at, 103
  McConnell's run for alumni trustee at,
    82–83
  Justin Walker's work at, 288, 289
University of Louisville Hospital, 100
University of Mississippi, 56
University of Virginia, 57
U.S. Agriculture Department, 134
U.S. Army, 25–32
U.S. Army Reserves, 67–70
U.S. Constitution, 286, 309
U.S. Department of Homeland Security, 261
U.S. House of Representatives
  2018 midterm election, 271
  2024 foreign aid and border bill in, 351–54
  cooperation in Senate vs., 329
  on January 6th commission, 305
  Republican leadership in, x, xi
  second Trump impeachment vote in,
    307
  Trump-era legislation in, 263–68
  see also specific members by name
U.S. Justice Department, 76, 233, 289, 302
U.S. Navy, 25
U.S. Senate
  in 1980s, 122, 128, 199
  1984 campaign and first term for
    McConnell, 105–35
  1990 campaign and second term for
    McConnell, 124, 136–61
  in 1990s, 162

1996 campaign and third term for
  McConnell, 162–74
2002 campaign and fourth term for
  McConnell, 178–79, 181–88
2006 midterm election, 195–96
2008 campaign and fifth term for
  McConnell, 201–5
2010 midterm election, 212–14, 327
2014 campaign and sixth term for
  McConnell, 226–27
2016 election, 250–58
2017 special election in Alabama, 266–67
2018 midterm election, 268–72
2020 campaign and seventh term for
  McConnell, 273–77, 356
2022 midterm election, 335–36
2024 election for, 340–41
2024 foreign aid and border bill in, 354–55
affirmation of 2020 election by, 293, 294,
  298, 303
confirmation of judicial nominees by,
  76–80, 132–34, 150–51, 190–93, 198,
  221, 222, 238, 243–44, 248, 280–81, 283,
  290–92
confirmation of Donald Trump's Cabinet
  appointees by, 261–63
consequences of rules changes in, 261–63,
  291
cooperation in House of Representatives
  vs., 329
COVID protocols for, 283–84
debates on campaign finance legislation,
  128–30, 173–74
Mike Mansfield's leadership record in, viii,
  338, 339
McConnell's cultivation of personal
  relationships in, 324–25
McConnell's strategic use of rules of, 138,
  154, 160–61
norms of, 220–21, 230, 231, 245
partisanship by leaders of, 153, 189, 227,
  228
respecting limits of power of, 297
"rule" on Supreme Court nominations
  before elections in, 234–38, 247, 280–81,
  284, 285
Chuck Schumer's service record in, 339
seniority in, 129, 149
Trump-era legislation in, 263–68
Donald Trump's second impeachment vote
  in, 307–8

U.S. Senate (*cont.*)
see also Senate Republicans; specific
committees by name; specific members
by name
U.S. Supreme Court, x, xii, 39, 56, 57, 128
Joe Biden's nominee to, 239
blocking Merrick Garland's confirmation
to, xii, 234–36, 240–41, 244–47, 262,
276, 280–81, 284, 321–24, 334
Brown v. Board of Education, 39, 56
Buckley v. Valeo, 166
George H. W. Bush's nominees to, 150–51
George W. Bush's nominees to, 191–92
Bush v. Gore, 176, 184
on campaign spending, 166
caseload of, 291
Citizens United v. FEC, 238, 251, 252, 257
Hillary Clinton's list of potential
nominees to, 241, 321
decisions leading to desegregation, 43
Dobbs decision, 334
Dred Scott case, 78, 184
Dwight D. Eisenhower's nominees to, 286
filibustering nominations to, 150, 193,
221, 234–36, 244, 262
filling Ruth Bader Ginsburg's seat on,
280–85
filling Antonin Scalia's seat on, 233–49,
262, 276, 280, 281
Lyndon B.Johnson's nominees to, 237
Brett Kavanaugh's confirmation to, 269–71
McConnell's lasting impact on, 276, 281–
82, 285–87, 320–24, 330, 334, 342
McConnell v. the Federal Election
Commission, 184
Richard M. Nixon's nominees to, 76–78,
81
Barack Obama's nominees to, xii, 237–41,
262
overturning of Chevron decision, 245,
334–35
in Packwood case, 158
partisanship in, 177, 244, 246–47
Plessy v. Ferguson, 296
Ronald Reagan's nominees to, 128, 238
Republican shaping of, 260
Roe v. Wade, 77–78, 100, 101, 144, 242,
321, 334
"rule" on election-year nominations to,
234–38, 247, 280–81, 284, 285
ruling on presidential immunity from, 335

Senate confirmation of justices to, 76–80,
132–34, 150–51, 190–93, 221, 222, 238,
243–44, 248, 280–81
Donald Trump's nominees and list of
potential nominees to, 241–42, 244, 249,
262–63, 269–71, 276, 281–82, 288
see also specific justices by name
USS *Monticello*, 26
Uvalde school shooting, 326

Valero, 252
Vance, JD, 260, 332, 333, 335, 353, 356
Vanderbilt Law School, 99
Van Hollen, Chris, 339
VE Europe Day, 28, 29
Vietnam War, 63, 67
Voting Rights Act (1965), 248

Wadley, Ala., 15–17
Wadley High School, 16–17
Wake Forest University, 18
Walker, Herschel, 332, 335–36
Walker, Justin, 287–91
Wall Street Journal, 128, 169, 173
Walsh, Adam, 106
Walsh, John, 106
Ward, Bernie, 38
War in Afghanistan, 183, 327
Warm Springs, Ga., 3–8, 10, 26, 109
Warner, Jim, 164
War of 1812, 299
Warren Commission, 63
Washington Post, 241
on allegations against Brett Kavanaugh,
269–70
Joe Biden on election-year Supreme Court
nominees in, 237
on Clinton–Lewinsky scandal, 171
on debt limit crisis, 217
on McConnell's campaign finance bill, 130
on McConnell's fundraising, 165
on Roy Moore's behavior, 267
on Bob Packwood's scandal, 156
on politicians taking honoraria, 130
on "recurrent polio," 13–14
on second impeachment of Donald Trump,
307–8
on sequestration, 225
on Donald Trump's *Access Hollywood*
comments, 242
Watergate scandal, 81, 85, 86

Watson, Sylvia, 99
Waxman, Seth, 184
Weicker, Lowell, xi, 122
Weinberg, Lois, 178–79
Weissmuller, Johnny, 13
Wertheimer, Fred, 168, 252
West, Paul, 169
What's So Bad about Money in Politics?
    (Law and McConnell), 166
Wheeler, Aaron, 1
White, Daniel, 72
white supremacy, 63, 77
Wicker, Roger, vii
Wilkinson, Wallace, 131–32
Will, George, 307–8
Wilson, Daniel J., 11
Wines, Michael, 160
women, McConnell's hiring of, 98, 104, 109,
    124, 153

women's rights, 75
Wood, Lin, 302
Woodward, W. E., 80
Woolsey, Bill, 56
World War II, 1, 2, 9–10, 24–32, 347

X social media platform, 309
    see also Twitter

Yale University, 57, 58, 139, 142
Yarmuth, John, 71, 104–5
Yeltsin, Boris, 347
"You and Time" (McConnell), 48–49
Young, Todd, 254–58, 329, 344

Zamore, Mike, 220, 221
Zelenskyy, Volodymyr, 272, 347–49,
    355–56
Zelizer, Julian, 215

ABOUT THE AUTHOR

MICHAEL TACKETT is an award-winning journalist with more than three decades of experience covering national politics, including nine presidential elections. He is currently the Deputy Washington Bureau Chief for the Associated Press. Before that, he was an editor and reporter for the *New York Times*, Washington Bureau Chief for both Bloomberg News and the *Chicago Tribune*, and National Editor for *U.S. News & World Report*. He is a recipient of the White House Correspondents' Association's Edgar A. Poe Award for National Reporting. His first book, *The Baseball Whisperer*, tells the story of a summer league baseball team in Clarinda, Iowa, that helped shape dozens of major league players. He lives in Alexandria, Virginia.